This book makes a major contribution to the ongoing debate about the synoptic problem, especially concerning the question of which gospel was written first. The scholarly consensus, developed over two hundred years of discussion, has favoured Markan priority and the dependence of both Matthew and Luke upon Mark. In an ongoing contemporary revival of the Griesbach hypothesis, some scholars have advocated the view that Mark used, conflated and abbreviated Matthew and Luke. Dr Head explores the role played by arguments connected with christological development in support of both these views. Deploying a new comparative redaction-critical approach to the problem, Dr Head argues that the critical basis of the standard christological argument for Markan priority is insecure and based on anachronistic scholarly concerns. Nevertheless, in a thoroughgoing comparative reappraisal of the christological outlooks of Matthew and Mark, the author finds decisive support for the hypothesis of Markan priority, arguing that Matthew was a developer rather than a corrector of Mark.

SOCIETY FOR NEW TESTAMENT STUDIES

MONOGRAPH SERIES

General editor: Richard Bauckham

94

CHRISTOLOGY AND THE SYNOPTIC PROBLEM

Christology and the synoptic problem

An argument for Markan priority

PETER M. HEAD

Oak Hill College, London

CAMBRIDGE
UNIVERSITY PRESS

Published by the Press Syndicate of the University of Cambridge
The Pitt Building, Trumpington Street, Cambridge CB2 1RP,
United Kingdom

Cambridge University Press
The Edinburgh Building, Cambridge CB2 2RU, United Kingdom
40 West 20th Street, New York, NY 10011–4211, USA
10 Stamford Road, Oakleigh, Melbourne 3166, Australia

First published 1997

Printed in the United Kingdom at the University Press, Cambridge

Typeset in 10/12 Times

A catalogue record for this book is available from the British Library

Library of Congress cataloguing in publication data
Head, Peter M.
Christology and the synoptic problem : an argument for Markan
priority / Peter M. Head
    p.   cm. – (Society for New Testament Studies monograph series: 94)
Revision of author's thesis (doctoral) – Univ. of Cambridge, 1994.
Includes bibliographical references and index.
ISBN 0 521 58488 4 (hardback)
1. Synoptic problem.
2. Bible. N.T. Mark – Criticism, interpretation, etc.
3. Bible. N.T. Matthew – Criticism, interpretation, etc.
4. Griesbach hypothesis (Synoptics criticism).
5. Jesus Christ – History of doctrines – Early church, ca. 30–600.
I. Title.
II. Series: Monograph series (Society for New Testament Studies) : 94.
BS2555.2.H33   1997
226'.066–dc20   96–43921   CIP

ISBN 0 521 58488 4 hardback

CE

**To Fiona
with love**

οὐ πᾶν τραῦμα τῇ αὐτῇ ἐμπλάστρῳ θεραπεύεται
(Ignatius, *Epistle to Polycarp* II.1)

CONTENTS

x   *Contents*

PREFACE

This book is a revision of a doctoral dissertation submitted to the University of Cambridge in 1994. I am particularly grateful to my supervisor, Professor Morna D. Hooker, for the guidance and help, encouragement and incisive criticism which she provided. Dr E. Bammel offered useful guidance on the history of synoptic research and NT textual criticism. I was helped in the process of revision by comments from the two examiners, Professor D. R. Catchpole and Professor C. M. Tuckett, and subsequently by comments received from the Revd Dr David Wenham and an unknown reader appointed by the publisher.

Although I have been well served by a number of libraries in Cambridge and London, particular thanks must be given to Bruce Winter and the staff at Tyndale House in Cambridge and to Wendy Bell of the Rocke Library (Oak Hill College). The final revision took place during a sabbatical leave as 'Visiting Scholar' at Ridley College, University of Melbourne. For financial help I am deeply indebted to my parents, Keith and Allison Head, who have generously supported my research, Indiginata Theological Consultancy Inc., the Tyndale House Council, and the Principal and Council of Oak Hill College. Friends and students who have helped or encouraged in tangible and less tangible ways are too numerous to mention here.

For her love, patience, faith and support, and in part-exchange for the holidays I have ruined, I thank my beloved wife, Fiona, to whom the book is dedicated.

ABBREVIATIONS

Abbreviations for biblical books, Qumran literature, Old Testament Pseudepigrapha, Rabbinic literature and other ancient literature follow standard forms and are generally cited according to their own conventions, which should be clear (see 'Instructions for Contributors' *JBL* 107 (1988) 579–596). NT quotations are from UBS4 = NA27, or RSV (unless otherwise specified). Text-critical abbreviations follow UBS4 conventions (see the introduction to UBS4, pp. 1*–52*).

We have used the form (8 − 7 − 6 + 5 − 4) to display the number of occurrences of a word in Matthew–Mark–Luke + Acts–John (although more often data for Acts and John is not provided).

Secondary sources are cited by author and title (with a shorter form of the title used after the first occurrence for commonly cited books). Dates of publications are included only when relevant to the discussion. Standard reference works are normally cited by abbreviation and page number.

AB	Anchor Bible
ABRL	Anchor Bible Reference Library
AGJU	Arbeiten zur Geschichte des antiken Judentums und des Urchristentums
AnBib	Analecta biblica
ANRW	*Aufstieg und Niedergang der römischen Welt*
ASNU	Acta seminarii neotestamentici upsaliensis
ASTI	*Annual of the Swedish Theological Institute*
ATANT	Abhandlungen zur Theologie des Alten und Neuen Testaments
ATLA	American Theological Library Association
ATR	*Anglican Theological Review*
AUS	American University Studies

AUSS	*Andrews University Seminary Studies*
BAGD	Bauer, Arndt, Gingrich and Danker, *A Greek–English Lexicon*
BARev	*Biblical Archaeology Review*
BDF	Blass, Debrunner and Funk, *A Greek Grammar of the New Testament*
BETL	Bibliotheca ephemeridum theologicarum lovaniensium
BEvT	Beiträge zur evangelischen Theologie
BHT	Beiträge zur historischen Theologie
BJRL	*Bulletin of the John Rylands Library, University of Manchester*
BNTC	Black's New Testament Commentaries
BR	*Biblical Research*
BSOAS	*Bulletin of the School of Oriental and African Studies*
BTB	*Biblical Theology Bulletin*
BU	Biblische Untersuchungen
BWANT	Beiträge zur Wissenschaft vom Alten und Neuen Testament
BZ	*Biblische Zeitschrift*
BZAW	Beihefte zur Zeitschrift für die alttestamentliche Wissenschaft
BZNW	Beihefte zur Zeitschrift für die neutestamentliche Wissenschaft
CBC	Cambridge Biblical Commentary
ConBNT	Coniectanea biblica, New Testament
CBQ	*Catholic Biblical Quarterly*
CBQMS	Catholic Biblical Quarterly Monograph Series
CGTC	Cambridge Greek Testament Commentaries
CurTM	*Currents in Theology and Mission*
DBSup	*Dictionnaire de la Bible, Supplément*
DJD	*Discoveries in the Judean Desert*
EKK	Evangelisch-katholischer Kommentar
EncJud	*Encyclopedia Judaica*
ETL	*Ephemerides theologicae lovaniensis*
EvQ	*Evangelical Quarterly*
EvT	*Evangelische Theologie*
ExpT	*Expository Times*
FB	Forschung zur Bibel
FRLANT	Forschungen zur Religion und Literatur des Alten und Neuen Testaments
GCS	Griechischen christlichen Schriftsteller

GTA	Göttingen theologische Arbeiten
HKNT	Hand-Kommentar zum Neuen Testament
HTK	Herders theologischer Kommentar
HTR	*Harvard Theological Review*
IBS	*Irish Biblical Studies*
ICC	International Critical Commentary
IEJ	*Israel Exploration Journal*
IGNTP	International Greek New Testament Project
Int	*Interpretation*
IRT	Issues in Religion and Theology
JBL	*Journal of Biblical Literature*
JBR	*Journal of Bible and Religion*
JETS	*Journal of the Evangelical Theological Society*
JJS	*Journal of Jewish Studies*
JSJ	*Journal for the Study of Judaism*
JSNT	*Journal for the Study of the New Testament*
JSNTSS	Journal for the Study of the New Testament Supplement Series
JSOTSS	Journal for the Study of the Old Testament Supplement Series
JTSA	*Journal of Theology for Southern Africa*
KD	*Kerygma und Dogma*
KEK	Kritisch-exegetischer Kommentar
LCC	Library of Christian Classics
LCL	Loeb Classical Library
LEC	Library of Early Christianity
LN	Louw and Nida, *Greek–English Lexicon*
LQ	*Lutheran Quarterly*
LSJ	Liddell, Scott and Jones, *A Greek–English Lexicon*
MM	Moulton and Milligan, *The Vocabulary of the Greek Testament*
NA27	Aland (and Nestle), *Novum Testamentum Graece* (1993[27])
NASB	New American Standard Bible
NCB	New Century Bible
NEB	Neue Echter Bibel
NewDocs	Horsley, *New Documents Illustrating Early Christianity*
NGS	New Gospel Studies
NIGTC	New International Greek Testament Commentary
NJBC	*New Jerome Biblical Commentary*

NovT	*Novum Testamentum*
NovTSS	Novum Testamentum Supplement Series
NRT	*La nouvelle revue théologique*
NTA	Hennecke and Schneemelcher, *New Testament Apocrypha*
NTS	*New Testament Studies*
OED	*Oxford English Dictionary*
OTP	Charlesworth, *The Old Testament Pseudepigrapha*
OTS	*Oudtestamentische Studiën*
OxyPap	Grenfell and Hunt, *The Oxyrhynchus Papyri*
PGL	Lampe, *A Patristic Greek Lexicon*
PSTJ	*Perkins School of Theology Journal*
QD	Quaestiones disputatae
RB	*Revue biblique*
RevQ	*Revue de Qumran*
RGG	*Religion in Geschichte und Gegenwart*
RSR	*Recherches de science religieuse*
SBEC	Studies in the Bible and Early Christianity
SBLDS	Society of Biblical Literature Dissertation Series
SBLEJL	Society of Biblical Literature Early Judaism and its Literature
SBLSP	*Society of Biblical Literature Seminar Papers*
SBS	Stuttgarter Bibelstudien
SBT	Studies in Biblical Theology
SD	Studies and Documents
SJLA	Studies in Judaism in Late Antiquity
SJT	*Scottish Journal of Theology*
SNTSMS	Society for New Testament Studies Monograph Series
SNTW	Studies of the New Testament and its World
StIGC	Studies zur interkulturellen Geschichte des Christentums
Str–B	Strack and Billerbeck, *Kommentar zum Neuen Testament aus Talmud und Midrasch*
SUNT	Studien zur Umwelt des Neuen Testaments
SVTP	Studia in Veteris Testamenti pseudepigrapha
TCL	Translations of Christian Literature
TDNT	Kittel and Friedrich, *Theological Dictionary of the New Testament*
TF	Theologische Forschung
THKNT	Theologischer Handkommentar zum Neuen Testament

TICP	Travaux de l'Institut Catholique de Paris
TS	*Theological Studies*
TSAJ	Texte und Studien zum antiken Judentum
TSK	Theologische Studien und Kritiken
TU	Texte und Untersuchungen
TynBul	*Tyndale Bulletin*
TZ	*Theologische Zeitschrift*
UBS4	Aland *et al.*, *The Greek New Testament. Fourth Revised Edition* (1993)
USQR	*Union Seminary Quarterly Review*
VC	*Vigiliae Christianae*
VT	*Vetus Testamentum*
WBC	World Biblical Commentary
WMANT	Wissenschaftliche Monographien zum Alten und Neuen Testament
WUNT	Wissenschaftliche Untersuchungen zum Neuen Testament
ZAW	*Zeitschrift für alttestamentliche Wissenschaft*
ZNW	*Zeitschrift für neutestamentliche Wissenschaft*
ZTK	*Zeitschrift für Theologie und Kirche*

1

INTRODUCTION AND A HISTORY OF RESEARCH

1. Introduction

Forty years ago the two-source hypothesis was accepted by the vast majority of New Testament scholars as *the* fundamental solution to the synoptic problem. This hypothesis was developed in the middle of the nineteenth century in Germany by C. H. Weisse (*Die evangelische Geschichte*, 1838), C. G. Wilke (*Der Urevangelist*, 1838) and H. J. Holtzmann (*Die synoptischen Evangelien*, 1863); and had been consolidated under the influence of scholars such as B. Weiss ('Zur Entstehungsgeschichte der drei synoptische Evangelien', 1861, and *Die Quellen der synoptischen Überlieferung*, 1908), P. Wernle (*Die synoptische Frage*, 1899) and B. H. Streeter (*The Four Gospels*, 1924) – to name only a few of its more prominent advocates. These scholars argued, with some differences on matters of detail, for the priority of Mark in relation to Matthew and Luke and for their independent utilisation of both Mark and an additional sayings source (Q) – hence its designation as a two-source hypothesis.

Throughout the nineteenth century the two-source hypothesis had vied for scholarly ascendancy with the initially more popular Griesbach hypothesis. This hypothesis took its name from its most prominent early advocate and proposed that Mark had been written after, and in dependence upon, both Matthew and Luke – hence its other designation as the two-gospel hypothesis. The earliest proponent of this view was H. Owen, whose *Observations on the Four Gospels* (1764) preceded the more influential work of Griesbach by twenty-five years. The theory was established in the scholarly community by J. J. Griesbach (*Commentatio*, 1789–90) and his student W. M. L. de Wette (*Lehrbuch der historisch-kritischer Einleitung in die kanonischen Bücher des Neuen Testaments*, 1826, 1848[5], 1860[6]). Other scholars to advocate this position during the nineteenth century included H. E. G. Paulus (*Philolo-gisch-kritischer und historischer Commentar über das neue Testa-ment*, 1804–5), H. Saunier (*Ueber die Quellen des Evangeliums des Marcus*, 1825), F. Sieffert (*Ueber den Ursprung des ersten kano-nischen Evangeliums*, 1832), K. R. Köstlin (*Der Ursprung und die Komposition der synoptischen Evangelien*, 1853) and F. Bleek, *Einleitung in das Neuen Testament* and *Synoptische Erklärung der drei ersten Evangelien* (both 1862). The Tübingen scholars F. C. Baur and A. Schwegler as well as the famous D. F. Strauss, whose work shall be discussed later in this chapter, also advocated the Griesbach hypothesis.

In the scholarly contest between the wide range of synoptic theories proposed during this period these two hypotheses emerged as the front-runners, and by the end of the nineteenth century the two-source hypothesis had drawn ahead and laid claim to the crown of victory.[1] Indeed, for many scholars the two-source hypothesis lost its 'hypothetical' status and became an 'assured result of research', taking upon itself the role of a Himalayan base camp from which further advances could be made, even to the extent of serving quite different routes. Consider, for example, A. Schweitzer's appraisal, published in 1906, of Holtzmann's early work: 'the Marcan hypothesis . . . is carried by Holtzmann to such a degree of demonstration that it can no longer be called a mere hypothesis'.[2] Such a conclusion was strongly held in the middle of the twentieth century when A. M. Hunter asserted that 'the Synoptic problem has been solved' and V. Taylor introduced his learned commentary with the statement, 'in a modern commentary, it is no longer necessary to prove the priority of Mark'.[3] It is certainly no exaggeration to say that the two-source hypothesis became the foundation for practically the whole edifice of

---

[1] The history of this contest can be traced in a number of works including Kümmel, *Das neue Testament: Geschichte der Erforschung seiner Probleme*; Neill, *The Interpretation of the New Testament*; Farmer, *The Synoptic Problem*; Schmithals, *Einleitung in die drei ersten Evangelien*; Stoldt, *Geschichte und Kritik der Markus-hypothese*; Kealy, *Mark's Gospel: A History of its Interpretation*; Baird, *History of New Testament Research*.

[2] Schweitzer, *Geschichte der Leben-Jesu-Forschung*, p. 202 (cited from ET, p. 202); for a similar sentiment see Holtzmann, *Die Synoptiker* (1889), p. 3.

[3] Hunter, *Interpreting the New Testament*, p. 140; cf. pp. 40–6; Taylor, *Mark*, p. 11. For similarly representative statements see Foakes-Jackson and Lake, *The Begin-nings of Christianity*, vol. I, p. vii; Dibelius, 'The Contribution of Germany to New Testament Science', p. 537; Kümmel, 'New Testament Research and Teaching in Present-Day Germany', p. 231.

twentieth-century gospel studies, and specifically for the development of both form and redaction criticism.

Among the early form critics note Dibelius, *Die Formgeschichte des Evangeliums* (1919) (cf. 1959[3], p. 8; ET, p. 9); Schmidt, *Der Rahmen der Geschichte Jesu* (1919), pp. 15–17; Bultmann, *Die Geschichte der synoptischen Tradition* (1921) (cf. 1961[5], p. 7; ET, pp. 6–7) (although both Schmidt and Bultmann are prepared to speak of an Urmarkus). For the early redaction critics note Bornkamm, 'Die Sturmstillung im Matthäusevangelium' (1948), 'Evangelien, Synoptische' (1958), p. 754; Held, 'Matthäus als Interpret der Wundergeschichten' (1960), pp. 155–6 (cf. ET, pp. 165–6); Marxsen, *Der Evangelist Markus* (1956), pp. 9–10 (cf. ET, p. 19); Conzelmann, *Die Mitte der Zeit* (1954) (cf. 1960[3], p. 4; ET, p. 12); cf. also Rohde, *Die redaktionsgeschichtliche Methode* (1966), pp. 7–10 (cf. ET, esp. p. 2).

In recent decades, however, this scholarly consensus has come under close scrutiny and even suspicion amidst a revival of interest in other explanations of synoptic relations, especially the Griesbach hypothesis. Much of this renewed interest can be traced to the work of W. R. Farmer, the most prominent modern advocate of the Griesbach hypothesis, whose history of synoptic scholarship, *The Synoptic Problem: A Critical Analysis* (1964), incorporated a range of telling criticisms of the two-source hypothesis. Farmer offered a new interpretation of the course of the nineteenth-century debates, contending that the rejection of the Griesbach hypothesis in the mid nineteenth century had more to do with external political and religious factors than with the internal strengths or weaknesses of the theory itself.[4] In addition, Farmer argued, and modern defenders of the two-source hypothesis have partially conceded, that many of the standard arguments for Markan priority, particularly those summarised by Streeter concerning agreement in content, wording and order, are inconclusive at best, and that the material could be explained at least as well on the Griesbach hypothesis.

See Streeter, *The Four Gospels*, pp. 159–68 for a representative and influential summary of arguments for Markan priority. Streeter was guilty of the so-called Lachmann fallacy, see Butler, *The Originality of St Matthew*, pp. 62–71; Palmer, 'Lachmann's Argument'; Farmer, 'The Lachmann Fallacy'; also Lowe, 'The Demise of Arguments from Order for Markan Priority'. The inconclusive nature of this argument is admitted by Tuckett, *The Revival of the Griesbach Hypothesis*, pp. 6–7, 'Arguments from Order'; Styler, 'The Priority of Mark', pp. 289–90. Cf.

---

[4] Farmer, 'State *Interesse* and Marcan Primacy 1870–1914'; also Reicke, 'From Strauss to Holtzmann and Meijboom: Synoptic Theories Advanced During the Consolidation of Germany, 1830–1870'; for criticism of this point see Tuckett, 'The Griesbach Hypothesis in the 19th Century'.

also Black's criticism of arguments based on the supposed grammatical primitivity of Mark ('Some Dissenting Notes on R. Stein's *The Synoptic Problem* and Markan «Errors»'; cf. Stein, *The Synoptic Problem*, pp. 52–4; Streeter, *The Four Gospels*, p. 164).

Although the arguments of *The Synoptic Problem* were largely negative Farmer has continued to explore, clarify and energetically defend a modern version of the Griesbach hypothesis in numerous writings.[5] His influence has also been mediated and extended both through the work of his students and followers (including E. P. Sanders, D. B. Peabody, O. L. Cope, D. L. Dungan, T. R. W. Longstaff),[6] and through a series of conferences organised, at least in part, on his initiative; the published proceedings of which include numerous important statements in support of the Griesbach hypothesis.[7] Eight major conferences have occurred since 1970:

1. Pittsburgh: Festival of the Gospels, April 1970 (Proceedings: Miller (ed.), *Jesus and Man's Hope*);
2. Münster: Griesbach Bicentenary Colloquium, July 1976 (Proceedings: Orchard and Longstaff (eds.), *J. J. Griesbach: Synoptic and Text-Critical Studies, 1776–1976*);
3. San Antonio (Texas), May 1977 (Proceedings: Walker (ed.), *The Relationships Among the Gospels*);
4. Cambridge: Owen–Griesbach Conference, August 1979 (Proceedings: Farmer (ed.), *New Synoptic Studies*);
5. Fort Worth (Texas), November 1980 (Proceedings: Corley (ed.), *Colloquy on New Testament Studies*);
6. Ampleforth: Gospel Conferences, 1982 and 1983 (Proceedings: Tuckett (ed.), *Synoptic Studies*);

---

[5] See the bibliography in E. P. Sanders (ed.), *Jesus, the Gospels, and the Church*, pp. xxxi–xxxviii.

[6] Especially Sanders, *The Tendencies of the Synoptic Tradition*; 'The Argument from Order and the Relationship between Matthew and Luke'; 'The Overlaps of Mark and Q and the Synoptic Problem'; Peabody, 'A Pre-Markan Prophetic Sayings Tradition and the Synoptic Problem'; 'The Late Secondary Redaction of Mark's Gospel and the Griesbach Hypothesis'; *Mark as Composer*; 'Chapters in the History of the Linguistic Argument for Solving the Synoptic Problem'; Cope, *Matthew: A Scribe Trained for the Kingdom of Heaven*; 'The Argument Revolves'; Dungan, 'Mark – The Abridgement of Matthew and Luke'; 'Reactionary Trends in the Gospel Producing Activity of the Early Church'; 'The Purpose and Provenance of the Gospel of Mark according to the "Two-Gospel" (Owen-Griesbach) Hypothesis'; 'A Griesbachian Perspective on the Argument from Order'; Longstaff, *Evidence of Conflation in Mark?*; 'Crisis and Christology: The Theology of Mark'.

[7] Note also the continuing work of the SBL working group on 'Redaction Criticism and the Two-Gospel Hypothesis' (chaired by D. B. Peabody).

7. Jerusalem: Symposium de interrelatione evangeliorum, April 1984 (Proceedings: Dungan (ed.), *The Interrelations of the Gospels*);
8. Göttingen: Minor Agreements, July 1991 (Proceedings: Strecker (ed.), *Minor Agreements Symposium Göttingen 1991*).

There is little doubt that Farmer and other neo-Griesbachians have played an important role in provoking a current loss of (over-)confidence in the two-source hypothesis and a consequent contemporary openness regarding synoptic source criticism.[8] According to Farmer, 'It may be said that today there is no New Testament scholar who any longer maintains that the Two Document Hypothesis is, as an earlier generation of students was led to believe, "an assured result of nineteenth century criticism". '[9] Neo-Griesbachian hyperbole has, however, been occasionally excessive in announcing the demise of the two-source hypothesis: in 1965 A. Isaksson referred to 'the Babylonian captivity of the Two Document Hypothesis'; in 1966 Farmer described the two-source hypothesis as 'little more than a vestigial remain from a bygone day' and as a 'far from harmless relic of the past'; a comment followed up by Cope in a public lecture entitled 'Requiem for a Relic' (delivered in 1975).[10]

Such hyperbole is, however, both excessive and unjustified in the current scholarly climate. The two-source hypothesis remains the majority position within contemporary gospel scholarship, as can be seen in the fact that mainstream commentaries on all three synoptic gospels continue to maintain Markan priority, albeit with some variations concerning the form and nature of the Q material.[11] Nevertheless, dissatisfaction with standard proofs of

---

[8] See, for one example, Goulder's comments in *Luke: A New Paradigm*, p. 181 n. 36.

[9] Farmer, 'Source Criticism: Some Comments on the Present Situation', p. 51; similarly Longstaff, 'At the Colloquium's Conclusion', pp. 172–4; Walker, *The Relationships Among the Gospels*, p. 3; Powers, 'The Shaking of the Synoptics', pp. 38–9; Tuckett, *Synoptic Studies*, p. viii.

[10] Farmer, 'The Two-Document Hypothesis as a Methodological Criterion in Synoptic Research', p. 396; Cope's lecture referred to in Farmer, 'The Present State of the Synoptic Problem', p. 3; Isaksson, *Marriage and Ministry in the New Temple*, p. 103; cf. p. 70.

[11] See, for example, the following: Gundry, *Matthew*; Luz, *Matthäus*; Gnilka, *Matthäusevangelium*; Davies and Allison, *Matthew*; Hagner, *Matthew*; Pesch, *Markusevangelium*; Gnilka, *Markus*; Guelich, *Mark*; Hooker, *Mark*; Gundry,

Markan priority combine with a large variety of alternative hypotheses currently on offer to suggest that, in many circles, there is a willingness to explore new possibilities. Many of these alternative hypotheses have noteworthy antecedents within eighteenth- and nineteenth-century scholarship, and include: primarily or totally oral tradition theories,[12] various types of written Urgospel theories,[13] multiple-source theories,[14] and even Lukan priority.[15] Even among those who accept Markan priority, 'Q' remains problematic: although many continue to affirm the existence of Q as a separate, identifiable source-document,[16] others are less sure;[17] and while some have argued that Matthew utilised Luke,[18] a rather more significant case has been made for Luke's use of Matthew.[19]

Although it cannot be argued fully at this point, purely oral

Mark; Marshall, *Luke*; Fitzmyer, *Luke*; Nolland, *Luke*; Bovon, *Lukas*; C. F. Evans, *Luke*.

[12] J. A. T. Robinson, *Redating the New Testament*, pp. 93–4; Rist, *On the Independence of Matthew and Mark*; Reicke, *The Roots of the Synoptic Gospels*; France, *Matthew: Evangelist and Teacher*, pp. 41–6; Chilton, *Profiles of a Rabbi*; Wenham, *Redating Matthew, Mark and Luke*; cf. Gieseler, *Historisch-kritischer Versuch über die Entstehung und die frühesten Schicksale der schriftlichen Evangelien* (1818), pp. 53–111; Westcott, *An Introduction to the Study of the Gospels* (1860). Discussed briefly below.

[13] Often associated by Catholic scholars with an Aramaic form of Matthew, held as a source for Mark: Vaganay, *Le problème synoptique*; Cerfaux, 'Le problème synoptique'; Léon-Dufour, 'Autour de la question synoptique'; earlier Chapman, *Matthew, Mark, and Luke*, pp. 181–99. For earlier studies cf. Eichhorn, 'Über die drei ersten Evangelien' (1794): forty-two passages in a Semitic source; Herder, 'Vom Erlöser der Menschen. Nach unsern drei ersten Evangelien' (1796) and *Eine Regel der Zusammenstimmung unserer Evangelien aus ihrer Entstehung und Ordnung* (1797): Mark was closest to a shorter original composition; Marsh, *A Dissertation on the Origin and Composition of our Three First Canonical Gospels* (1801), pp. 194–211. The 'Jerusalem School of Gospel Studies' advocates an original Hebrew gospel source.

[14] Particularly associated with Boismard, *Synopse*; 'The Two Source Theory at an Impasse'; 'Théorie des niveaux multiples'.

[15] Lindsey, 'A Modified Two-Document Theory'; *A Hebrew Translation of the Gospel of Mark*; Stegner, 'Lucan Priority in the Feeding of the Five Thousand'; 'The Priority of Luke'; cf. Büsching, *Die vier Evangelisten* (1766); Evanson, *The Dissonance of the four generally received Evangelists* (1792), pp. 117–18.

[16] For example Kloppenborg, *The Formation of Q*; Jacobson, *The First Gospel: An Introduction to Q*; Catchpole, *The Quest for Q*; NB also the SBL Q seminar.

[17] See the surveys by Bigg, 'The Q Debate since 1955' and 'The Present State of the Q Hypothesis'; Piper, 'In Quest of Q: The Direction of Q Studies'; Tuckett, 'The Existence of Q'.

[18] Huggins, 'Matthean Posteriority'; cf. Wilke, *Der Urevangelist*, p. 685; B. Bauer, *Kritik der evangelischen Geschichte der Synoptiker*, vol. I, pp. xii–xiii.

[19] Gundry, *Matthew*, p. 608 and *passim*; Goulder, *Luke*. Discussed briefly below.

theories do not adequately explain the synoptic phenomena.[20] No doubt oral traditions and historical reminiscences continued to influence and inform transmission of the Jesus tradition throughout the period in which the gospels were written – purely literary approaches to the synoptic problem often anachronistically picture the evangelists as scholars collecting information or correcting proofs. But the evidence of common wording in Greek, extending even to 'redactional links', as well as the common order and selection of material in the synoptic gospels, militates against purely non-literary approaches. F. G. Downing's discussion shows that Josephus, even when clearly and explicitly dependent upon written sources, deliberately varied his presentation.[21] In this regard, the resolution agreed by delegates to the 1984 Jerusalem symposium that synoptic relationships are 'primarily literary' is a landmark.[22]

At the heart of the disagreement among literary approaches to the synoptic problem, especially but not exclusively between the two-source hypothesis and the Griesbach hypothesis, is the question of Markan priority – was Mark written before or after Matthew? The answer to this question divides synoptic scholars into two clear groups, especially now that defenders of various forms of Matthean priority have apparently united under the banner of the Griesbach hypothesis.[23] On the other hand, numerous variants from the two-source hypothesis continue to maintain Markan priority. The most significant of these is probably the Farrer–Goulder hypothesis.[24] This hypothesis accepts the priority of Mark but dispenses with Q by advocating Luke's use of Matthew in addition to Mark.[25] Inasmuch as the Farrer–Goulder

---

[20] Cf. Llewelyn, 'A Stylometric Analysis of Parallel Sections of the Synoptic Gospels', pp. 119–20. For criticisms of three recent attempts to advocate oral or independence theories see Head, 'Review of Wenham, *Redating Matthew, Mark, and Luke*'; 'Review of Linnemann, *Is There a Synoptic Problem?*' and 'Review of Kim, *The Sources of the Synoptic Gospels*'.

[21] Downing, 'Redaction Criticism: Josephus' Antiquities and the Synoptic Gospels'.

[22] Dungan, *The Interrelations of the Gospels*, p. 609. The importance of this conclusion is obviated somewhat by the fact that this was a criterion in the selection of delegates (p. xvii and n. 14).

[23] According to Green the heirs of the Benedictine tradition of Matthean priority (understood with Butler in an Augustinian manner), have now opted (like Orchard) for the Griesbach hypothesis (H. B. Green, 'The Credibility of Luke's Transformation of Matthew', p. 131).

[24] For this designation see Boring, 'The Synoptic Problem, "Minor Agreements", and the Beelzebul Pericope', p. 588 n. 4; Kloppenborg, 'The Theological Stakes in the Synoptic Problem', p. 93.

[25] Farrer, *St Matthew and St Mark*, p. vii and 'On Dispensing with Q'; Drury,

hypothesis accepts Markan priority it stands with the two-source hypothesis over against the Griesbach hypothesis in the most crucial aspect of synoptic relations which is of primary concern in the following chapters.[26]

Since it is the Griesbach hypothesis which has emerged as the major single alternative to Markan priority (normally associated with Q in the two-source hypothesis) in the scholarly arena, with a substantial history of scholarly work and with specific interests in the christological aspects of the problem, this work shall take these two hypotheses as sparring partners in a prolonged duel. This book attempts to address the current situation, and specifically the relative strengths of the Griesbach hypothesis and the two-source hypothesis, by means of an investigation into what can be termed *the christological argument for Markan priority*. This argument has played a relatively minor role in scholarly discussions of the last two centuries but provides an interesting and important point of departure. We shall begin by tracing the history of this argument, especially in relation to source criticism and the question of gospel priority.

2.   Christological development and gospel priority

2.1   Introduction

From an early date readers were no doubt aware of distinctive christological features of the four canonical gospels. Late in the second century Irenaeus compared the evangelists with the four creatures of Revelation 4.7 (*Adversus haereses* III.11.8): John emphasised Jesus' royal power and generation from the Father (cf. the lion) and Luke his priestly character (cf. the calf), while Matthew was 'the gospel of his humanity' (cf. the man) and Mark pointed to his prophetic character (cf. the eagle). Later, the distinc-

---

Tradition and Design in Luke's Gospel, pp. 120–73; Goulder, *Luke*; earlier advocates include Ropes, *The Synoptic Gospels*, pp. 66–8; Enslin, *Christian Beginnings*, pp. 426–36.

[26] It is also possible to maintain a combination of Markan priority, the existence of Q and Luke's use of Matthew, so even the later Holtzmann, *Lehrbuch der historisch-kritischen Einleitung in das Neue Testament*, (1892[3]) p. 350 (on the basis of Simons, *Hat der dritte Evangelist den kanonischen Matthäus benutzt?* (1880)); Morganthaler, *Statistische Synopse*, pp. 301–3; Gundry, 'Matthean Foreign Bodies in Agreements of Luke with Matthew against Mark Evidence that Luke used Matthew' (n. 7 on p. 1468 provides further references to his *Matthew*).

tiveness of John's presentation was more clearly recognised: Clement, for example, described John as 'the spiritual gospel' (Eusebius, *Historia ecclesiastica* VI.14.7).

Augustine in particular distinguished the synoptic presentation of the humanity of Jesus, from the Johannine presentation of his deity (*De consensu evangelistarum* I.5–7). He also rearranged the four creatures: the lion points to Matthew (who emphasises the kingly, messianic character of the lion of Judah), the man points to Mark (who 'handles the things which the man Jesus did'), the calf points to Luke (who emphasises Jesus as priest), and the eagle points to John (whose presentation 'soars like an eagle above the clouds of human infirmity' and emphasises the deity of Christ; *De consensu evangelistarum* I.9). In no case, however, did any Patristic writer relate these differences to historical and critical questions. For such discussions we must concentrate on the modern era.

2.2 Christological development and Markan priority

J. B. **Koppe** (1782) was the first scholar to suggest a relationship between christology and literary priority. His argument against Augustine's view that Mark was the epitomiser of Matthew played an important role in the demise of the traditional view of Matthean priority.[27] In the course of that argument Koppe argued that if Augustine was right and Mark had been following or epitomising Matthew, it would mean that Mark had omitted a number of sayings and incidents which would have been very useful to underline the power, wisdom and majesty of Jesus (he specified the following: Matt. 3.14f; 4.1–11, 13–17; 9.13, 37f; 13.16f; 10.5f; 15.23f; 7.24–30; 15.12–14; 16.2–4; 21.28–32; 17.20; 24.11f; 25.31–46; 26.25, 50, 63; 27.19, 24f; 27.52f).[28] Koppe obviously regarded such a procedure as implausible.

Although it is not made explicit, Koppe presupposes an argument from christological development: a later writer using earlier traditions is unlikely to diminish the majesty of Jesus in his representation of the gospel traditions, rather he will at least maintain the 'level' of reverence, if not actually heighten it. This line of argument, although similar to the text-critical argument that

---

[27] Koppe's general arguments were anticipated by Jones, *A Vindication of the Former Part of St Matthew's Gospel* (1719), pp. 43–100.
[28] Koppe, *Marcus non epitomator Matthaei*, pp. 49–52.

doctrinally developed variants were likely to be secondary readings (defended by both R. Simon in 1689 and J. J. Wettstein in 1730 and 1751), does not appear to have been taken up by other gospel scholars.[29] A different kind of argument, focussing on the general primitivity of Mark, proved more popular.

J. G. **Herder** (1797) argued not only that Mark reflected the primitive gospel outline of Acts 1.21f more closely than Matthew,[30] but also that of the two Palestinian gospels we had: 'Ein kürzeres, früheres, gelinderes, den Markus; Ein vollständigeres, späteres, härteres, den Matthäus.' One gospel is shorter, earlier, milder – that of Mark; one gospel is more complete, later, harsher – that of Matthew.[31] Nevertheless, the mildness and harshness of which he speaks are not christological, but related to Mark's lenience towards Israel.

This type of argument was supported by H. **Ewald** (1849), who emphasised the originality or *Ursprünglichkeit* of Mark compared to both Matthew and Luke. He understood this in terms of Mark's *narrative* originality and primitivity, rather than *christological* primitivity. He argued that

> Mark's presentation has a fresh liveliness and a picturesque fullness and despite its over-flowing abundance also a taut conciseness, proportion and a higher peace . . . everything which one finds present in the related gospels, both Matthew and in Luke but bearing no more the same lustre of the fresh bloom, the full pure life of the material.[32]

C. H. **Weisse** (*Die evangelische Geschichte kritisch und philosophisch bearbeitet*, 1838), often regarded as 'the principal founder of

---

[29] Simon, *A Critical History of the Text of the New Testament*, part 2, p. 123; Wettstein, *Novum Testamentum Graecum*, vol. II, p. 864 (see Head, 'Christology and Textual Transmission', pp. 108–9 for brief discussion).

[30] Herder, *Eine Regel der Zusammenstimmung unserer Evangelien aus ihrer Entstehung und Ordnung*, p. 394.

[31] Herder, *Eine Regel*, p. 408.

[32] 'Die darstellung [of Mark] hat eine frische lebendigkeit und malerische ausführlichkeit, und troz ihrer überströmenden fülle wieder eine straffe gedrängtheit gleichmäßigkeit und höhere ruhe, . . . alles was sich im jezigen Matthäos – und im Lukas – evangelium verwandtes findet, trägt nichtmehr diesen schmelz der frischen blume, dieses volle reine leben der stoff.' (Ewald, 'Ursprung und Wesen der Evangelien', part II, p. 204 (his spelling!)). Ewald argued for Markan priority in relation to Matthew and Luke within the context of a complex nine-source theory (pp. 190–224). On the 'proof from originality' see Stoldt, *Geschichte und Kritik der Markus-hypothese*, pp. 147–56 (ET, pp. 159–68).

the Marcan hypothesis',[33] was impressed with 'die Originalität und Priorität des Marcusevangeliums vor den übrigen' – the originality and priority of Mark's gospel over against the others (p. V; cf. pp. 29–45). Within the context of his general historical purpose – to distinguish the genuine historical picture of Christ ('die Herstellung des geschichtlichen Christusbildes', p. III) from the traditions and dogmas with which it had been obscured – he advanced various arguments for Markan priority: the vividness of its narrative (pp. 55, 66), the clumsiness of its style (pp. 66–7), the agreement in order between Matthew and Luke (pp. 72–3) and the likelihood that Markan details were omitted by later writers rather than added to them by Mark (pp. 64–6).

According to Weisse Mark's presentation is distinguished clearly from the other gospels by 'das Gepräge einer frischen Natürlichkeit und anspruchslosen Lebendigkeit' – the stamp of a fresh naturalness and unassuming liveliness (p. 67). In addition Matthew's redaction of Mark consisted of softening Mark's hardness and expunging Mark's idiomatic expressions (p. 68). Weisse even refers to Matthew's omission of 'good teacher' (Matt. 19.16f cf. Mark 10.17f) as a dogmatic stumbling-block (pp. 564–5: 'einen dogmatischen Anstoss').[34] It is apparent, however, that Weisse did not depend upon a christological argument to prove Markan priority; rather, having already asserted it on other grounds, he is able to observe the christological nature of Matthew's redactional activity.

Like Weisse, H. J. **Holtzmann** (1863) also sought a firm historical basis for the Jesus tradition (*Die synoptischen Evangelien: Ihr Ursprung und geschichtlicher Charakter*, p. 1). This firm foundation was to be found in Markan priority and the two-source hypothesis, which with Holtzmann's work was well on the way to becoming fully established in the scholarly world.[35] Holtzmann argued in general that Mark's gospel is more primitive in style and diction, and in particular that in Mark's gospel the human Jesus stands out more clearly than in the other gospels (p. 475), and that Mark

---

[33] Stoldt, *Geschichte und Kritik der Markus-hypothese*, p. 47 (ET, p. 47); cf. Holtzmann, *Die synoptischen Evangelien*, p. 29; Schweitzer, *Geschichte der Leben-Jesu-Forschung*, pp. 124–8 (ET, pp. 121–4).

[34] Wilke, by comparison, rejected this text of Matthew as a false reading (*Der Urevangelist*, p. 225).

[35] Kümmel, *Das neue Testament: Geschichte der Erforschung seiner Probleme*, p. 185 (ET, p. 151); cf. Schweitzer's comment cited earlier (p. 2).

provided the original versions of the baptism (p. 476) and passion (p. 486).[36]

The idea of christological redaction emerged more clearly in P. **Wernle**'s discussion (1899) of Matthew 19.17f. He regarded Matthew as a redactor who heightens the christological presentation of Mark (*Die synoptische Frage*, p. 142). As with Weisse, however, this is not part of Wernle's argument for Markan priority; rather it belongs to his assessment of the freedom of Matthean redaction of Mark, having already established priority on other grounds, especially an argument from order (p. 80). He also cites examples of Matthew's ethical alterations to Mark (19.9, 21 etc., p. 143).

2.3   Christological development and the Griesbach hypothesis

Most nineteenth-century Griesbachians made use of the concept of christological development in their discussions of the Griesbach hypothesis. J. J. **Griesbach** himself (1796) accepted the principle of theological and christological development as an important element in evaluating variant readings ('where there are more readings than one at any place, that reading which favours orthodoxy is an object of suspicion'), but does not appear to have applied this to the synoptic problem.[37] His student, W. M. L. **de Wette** (1826 and 1860), in arguing for Markan posteriority was concerned to refute the suggestion that the lack in Mark of a report of Jesus' supernatural birth implied Mark's originality.[38] He argued that Mark 6.3, in not referring to Jesus' father, showed awareness of this belief, and that Mark in any case, attests throughout the idea of the deity (*Gottheit*) of Christ (Mark 1.1; 3.11; 5.7; 15.39). He even suggested, albeit somewhat hesitantly, that Mark moves towards a docetic christology. Mark's later standpoint in relation to Matthew and Luke is betrayed by his modest interest in the sayings of Jesus, and his use of the term 'gospel' (Mark 1.1, 15; 8.35; 10.29). This discussion at the least indicates that christological factors were seen as bearing some relation to the problem of synoptic relationships.

---

[36] It is notable, however, that it is only in his later work that Holtzmann abandoned Urmarkus, his A source (*Lehrbuch der historisch-kritischen Einleitung in das Neue Testament*, (1892[3]) p. 350; *Die Synoptiker* (1901[3]), p. v).

[37] Griesbach, *Novum Testamentum Graece* (1796[2]), vol. I, p. LXII (cited from Head, 'Christology and Textual Transmission', p. 109).

[38] De Wette, *Lehrbuch der historisch-kritischen Einleitung in die kanonischen Bücher des Neuen Testaments*, p. 184 (ET, p. 163).

F. C. **Baur**'s *Tendenzkritik* (1847) provided both a new method for approaching the gospels and the theoretical foundations for a developmental view of NT christology (*Kritische Untersuchungen über die kanonischen Evangelien, ihr Verhältnis zu einander, ihren Charakter und Ursprung*, pp. 71–6).[39] He described the gospels as *Tendenzschriften*, products of a certain time, directed towards and revealing the situation of the church at the time of their composition.[40] Baur argued that Mark omitted the Jewishness of Matthew and the Paulinism of Luke, resulting in a neutral *Tendenz* without any historical value (pp. 560–7). He suggested that Mark's redaction of Matthew and Luke produced miracle stories closer to those of the apocryphal gospels; and that he altered Matthew 16.28 in view of the delay of the *parousia* (p. 562). Baur also suggested that Mark has traces of both Ebionite and docetic christologies and thus requires a late date (pp. 563–4).

Baur later articulated clearly the idea of christological development within the context of the early history of Christianity (*Das Christenthum und die christliche Kirche der drei ersten Jahrhunderte*, 1853).

> It is in the doctrine of the person or the divine dignity of Christ that the whole development of dogma, in its first period, is concentrated . . . Each age, each party, invests the person of Christ with all the determining notions which, in its opinion, it is necessary to presuppose in order to make him capable of being, in the determinate sense in which he requires to be, the Redeemer.
>
> (p. 307; cited from ET, vol. II, pp. 64–5)

Applied to the NT this meant that the christology of the synoptic gospels was the most primitive. To Baur the synoptics imply a human Messiah without pre-existence, distinguished from humanity in general by the influence of the Holy Spirit, a Messiah who was exalted through his death and resurrection and ascension: 'In this Christology, the general point of view is the elevation of the human to the divine' ('die Erhebung des Menschlichen zum Göttlichen'). Baur contrasts John, for whom the humanity of Jesus is

---

[39] First applied in Baur, 'Der Ursprung und Charakter des Lukasevangelium', (1846) pp. 596–615.

[40] In 1764 Owen had formulated a similar method, as the full title suggests: *Observations on the Four Gospels; Tending chiefly to ascertain the Times of their Publication; and to illustrate the Form and Manner of their composition.*

secondary, whose Logos-christology is 'from above' ('von oben nach unten') and who conceives of Jesus' essence as divine in itself ('das an sich Göttliche seines Wesens'). In between these two stands Paul, whose christology 'gives us the key of the transition from the one to the other' (p. 309; ET, vol. II, p. 66).

Thus, for Baur, NT christologies can be placed on a kind of ascending scale, with the synoptics at the bottom, Paul occupying the key middle point, and the Apocalypse and Hebrews between Paul and John (pp. 313–20; ET, vol. II, pp. 70–7). Baur did not, however, use the idea of christological development as an argument for Markan posteriority; like many since he dealt with the synoptic gospels as representing a fairly unified stratum of NT theology. Nevertheless, his influence greatly affected later discussions.

In his first attempt at a life of Jesus (*Das Leben Jesu kritisch bearbeitet*, 1835) D. F. **Strauss** accepted the Griesbach hypothesis without argument (citing Griesbach and Saunier in a brief footnote to vol. I, p. 69, n. 14 (ET, p. 71)). This prompted Baur's comment that he had offered a criticism of the gospel history without a criticism of the gospels themselves ('eine Kritik der evangelischen Geschichte ohne eine Kritik der Evangelien'), a fault that Strauss was to rectify in his later work.[41] Nevertheless, even in this earlier work he utilised an argument based on the principle of christological development in assessing the historical worth of various narratives. For example, discussing Jesus' relation to John the Baptist, Strauss appealed to

> the universal canon of interpretation, that where, in narratives having a tendency to aggrandise a person or a fact (a tendency which the Gospels evince at every step), two contradictory statements are found, that which best corresponds to this aim is the least historical; because if, in accordance with it, the original fact had been so dazzling, it is inconceivable that the other less brilliant representation should afterwards arise.
>
> (vol. I, p. 401 (cited from ET, p. 229))

This 'universal canon' presupposes a pattern of christological development of wide relevance. Strauss invoked the same principle in connection with the record of Jesus' last hours in Gethsemane, discounting the historical value of all the accounts because they

---

[41] Baur, *Kritische Untersuchungen über die kanonischen Evangelien*, p. 42.

comprise three different levels of pious modification in order to depict Jesus as foreknowing (and foretasting, and even fore-triumphing over) his sufferings. They are 'devotional, but unhistorical embellishments' (vol. II, p. 472 (ET, p. 649)).

The general principle, that gospel traditions were affected by christological beliefs and that this material was adapted to the prevailing beliefs of the age in which it was transmitted, was restated by Strauss, along with a fuller defence of the Griesbach hypothesis, in *Das Leben Jesu für das deutsche Volk bearbeitet*, published in 1864. He quoted approvingly from A. Schwegler in support of the view that obsolete and offensive material tended to be omitted and later theological watchwords introduced into the gospel texts (pp. 117–18 (ET, p. 155)).[42]

Strauss discussed two specific examples of this type of correction, arguing firstly that the trinitarian baptismal formula of Matthew 28.19, which 'savours of the late ecclesiastical ritual' (when compared to Acts 2.38 etc.), had been added by a late corrector (p. 118 (ET, p. 155–6)). Secondly he pointed to the alterations to Matthew 19.16f, which occurred at a time when the more elevated conception of Christ which appeared to be contradicted by the disclaimer of 'good' was in vogue: this reflects a Gnostic abuse of the prevailing text which affected Matthew alone, because of its prominence in the early church. In this respect Strauss, unlike Schwegler, gives no specific indication that this process influenced the composition of the gospels, as opposed to their later transmission. So while Strauss held to the principle that christological factors affected the redaction of gospel texts, this was not applied directly to source-critical questions, indeed his acceptance of the Griesbach hypothesis resulted in attributing such alterations to later scribes.

Strauss followed Baur in arguing that Mark sought to unite Matthew's Jewish teaching with Luke's Gentile emphasis (p. 132 (ET, p. 176)). He also drew support for Markan posteriority from what he took to be consistent tendencies in the redaction of gospel traditions towards a concentration on narratives and a growing emphasis on the miraculous (p. 134 (ET, pp. 178–9)).

H. U. **Meijboom** (*Geschiedenis en critiek der Marcushypothese*, 1866, cited from ET: *A History and Critique of the Origin of the*

---

[42] Schwegler, *Das nachapostolische Zeitalter*, pp. 258–9: for Schwegler, if not unambiguously for Strauss, this process also influenced the composition of the gospels.

Marcan Hypothesis) did apply the principle of christological development to the question of literary priority, arguing that defenders of Markan priority had not made a sufficiently serious comparison between the christologies of Matthew and Mark (pp. 131–48, this comment on p. 147). For Meijboom, Mark's more advanced christology was 'decisive in the argument regarding priority' (p. 131). Indeed, he turned to christology as his first positive argument after criticising the main arguments for Markan priority: 'brevity' (pp. 97–104) and 'literary imagery' (pp. 104–15).

Meijboom argued that Mark's gospel has a single christological focus, in which possession of God's Spirit marked out Jesus as the 'Son of God' (pp. 133–5), a divine, superhuman figure whose miracles are divine acts (pp. 135–9), whose authoritative teaching had divine character (pp. 139–42), and whose authority over demons and angels attested his divine status (pp. 145–7). Such a uniform christological interest is more likely to derive from Matthew's variety of christological images than vice versa: Matthew's christology reflects 'seminal beginnings', 'a fruit still rooted in its soil of origin', but with Mark 'the fruit has been picked and . . . detached from its historical context' (pp. 138–9). Furthermore, in terms of content Mark's christology represents a later point of development than Matthew's (p. 147).

At around the same time, but apparently independent of Meijboom's work, T. **Keim** also applied the christological principle directly to the synoptic problem in support of the Griesbach hypothesis (*Geschichte Jesu von Nazara in ihrer Verkettung mit dem Gesammtleben seines Volkes frei untersucht und ausführlich erzählt*, 1867). In general Keim argued that Mark was designed to unite the excessively Jewish theology of Matthew with the excessively Pauline thought of Luke (vol. I, pp. 92–3 (ET, vol. I, p. 128–9)), although for Keim (with Griesbach and others) Mark is closer to Matthew, and had Luke as his second source. He argued that Mark's redaction of Matthew and Luke could be explained in terms of a tendency to emphasise the deity of Jesus ('einer Tendenz der Hervorhebung der Göttlichkeit Jesu') (vol. I, p. 90 (ET, vol. I, pp. 124–5)).

Thus, for example, the presentation of Jesus as 'Son of God' is much more important to Mark than to either Matthew or Luke. For example, he describes 'Son of God' (despite its absence from Mark 1.1, which he takes to be an interpolation from John) as the watchword of the whole book ('das Losungswort des Buchs'; vol. I, p. 90 (ET, vol. I, p. 124)). Jesus' personality is also more mysterious in

Mark: his words, thoughts, actions and the course of his life provoke reactions of amazement, fear and an awe-inspiring announcement of his divine greatness ('schreckensvolle Verkündigung seiner göttlichen Grösse'; vol. I, pp. 90–1 (ET, vol. I, p. 125)). Mark presents another picture of the Lord, compared with Matthew and even Luke: a declining humanity, a swelling deity in incarnate form ('. . . eine untergehende Menschheit, eine aufgehende Gottheit in Fleischgestalt . . .'; vol. I, p. 91(ET, vol. I, p. 125)). In the same context Keim suggests that Mark's image of Jesus approaches that preferred by some Gnostics; in a later passage he suggests that Mark's conception of Jesus as mysterious and divine is almost docetic (vol. II, pp. 522–4 (ET, vol. IV, pp. 231–3)). Keim also explicitly connects this dogmatic argument for the posteriority of Mark with the dogmatic tendencies of scribes (vol. I, p. 101 (ET, vol. I, p. 138)).

Two conclusions can be drawn from this historical survey. First that nineteenth-century defenders of the Griesbach hypothesis either used some form of christological argumentation to defend Mark's posteriority, or at least allowed that the principle was relevant to the redaction of gospel traditions. Secondly, there are numerous indications, specifically in Griesbach, Strauss, and Keim, that the principle was understood along the same lines as the accepted and related text-critical principle. Nevertheless it is noteworthy that when British scholars, in the following period, developed a widely influential christological argument for Markan priority they did so without reference to these discussions.

3. The christological argument for Markan priority

The gradual demise of the Griesbach hypothesis and the influence of Weisse, Ewald and Holtzmann made the 'primitivity' of Mark a popular argument for its substantial historicity. Matthean priority rapidly became a minority position, although it continued to be defended into the twentieth century by scholars such as A. Schlatter (*Die Theologie der Apostel*, 1922 and *Der Evangelist Matthäus*, six editions between 1895 and 1963); T. Zahn (*Das Evangelium des Matthäus*, 1903; cf. also *Einleitung in das Neue Testament*, vol. II, pp. 322–34; ET, vol. II, pp. 601–17: Mark drew upon prior Aramaic Matthew); E. W. Lummis (*How Luke Was Written*; 1915), H. G. Jameson (*The Origin of the Synoptic Gospels: A Revision of the Synoptic Problem*, 1922), and B. C. Butler (*The Originality of St Matthew: A Critique of the Two-Document Hypothesis*, 1951).

Many scholars echoed Weisse and Holtzmann in describing Mark as the most primitive of the gospels, the most faithful representation of the human Jesus, and thus the primary source for the study of the life of Jesus.[43] In 1879 E. A. Abbott emphasised the originality and extreme antiquity of Mark on the grounds that Mark 'contains many expressions which would be likely to be stumbling-blocks in the way of weak believers, so that they are omitted in the later Gospels' (citing Mark 6.5f; 1.32, 34; 3.20f; 10.35; 15.44; 3.15; 8.24; 11.21; 16.4).[44] Subsequently, the argument for Mark's originality and primitivity became associated with the christological argument, and this combination became a powerful force in English-speaking scholarship.[45]

While German scholars regarded Markan priority as settled by Holtzmann, Weiss, Wernle *et al.*, British scholars around the turn of this century generally maintained a sceptical distrust of 'modern German NT criticism', and were thus less susceptible to adopting Markan priority solely on the authority of German critics.[46] The focus of British gospel criticism was Sanday's Oxford Seminar, where an inductive method was adopted. This focussed on studying the texts themselves through Synopses and commentaries, rather than reading German works.[47] In this connection Farmer's assertion that British scholars at Oxford and Cambridge took over Markan priority *uncritically* from their German colleagues must be contested.[48] In fact the development of the christological argument provided additional, and primarily British, support for Markan priority.

It is noteworthy, but not entirely surprising, that British scholars should develop a christological argument for Markan priority. Stoldt's survey (*Geschichte und Kritik der Markus-hypothese*) of German synoptic criticism never mentions the christological argument, but Farmer's survey (*The Synoptic Problem: A Critical*

---

[43] See e. g. Schweitzer, *Geschichte der Leben-Jesu-Forschung*, pp. 202–4 (ET, pp. 202–4) and *passim*.

[44] Abbott, 'Gospels', pp. 801–3, citation from p. 802.

[45] Cf. Bruce, *With Open Face: or, Jesus Mirrored in Matthew, Mark, and Luke* (1896), pp. 25–9 also *The Synoptic Gospels* (1897), p. 33; Gore, *Jesus of Nazareth*, pp. 194–5.

[46] Sanday, *The Life of Christ in Recent Research*, pp. 41–2; cf. Morgan, 'Non angeli sed angli: Some Anglican reactions to Tübingen gospel criticism'; Sanders in Fuller, 'Review Article: *The Synoptic Problem*: After Ten Years', pp. 69–70.

[47] See Sanday, 'Introductory', esp. p. viii.

[48] Farmer, 'State *Interesse* and Marcan Primacy 1870–1914', pp. 2495–6.

Analysis), focussing on English scholars, discusses it at some length. Three reasons might be suggested for this. First, theologically speaking, the doctrine of the incarnation was more central to the work and faith of British scholars.[49] Secondly, the influence of kenoticism, focussing on the humanity of the incarnate Christ – his questions, ignorance and inabilities – was mediated at Oxford up until the turn of the century by the influential C. Gore, especially through his chapters in *Lux Mundi*, his *The Incarnation of the Son of God* (Bampton Lectures for 1891), and his *Dissertations on Subjects Connected with the Incarnation*.[50] Thirdly, the question of the historical reliability of the gospels, of which Mark was by then generally favoured as the earliest and most reliable, was of great importance (and remained so in the commentaries of Taylor and Cranfield).[51] These factors indicate that Sanday's Oxford Seminar is a likely source of the developed christological argument for Markan priority. Certainly the basic framework of this argument was expressed by participants in that seminar, particularly J. C. Hawkins, W. C. Allen and B. H. Streeter.[52]

Hawkins' *Horae Synopticae* (1899) includes in its discussion of Mark a listing of 'Passages seeming (a) to limit the power of Jesus Christ, or (b) to be otherwise derogatory to, or unworthy of, Him' (p. 96). He lists the following (pp. 96–8, indebted to Abbott, 'Gospels'):

(a)   Mark 1.32, 34; 4.36; 6.5; 7.32–7; 8.22–6; 11.20; 15.44f;

(b)   Mark 1.12; 3.5, 21; 6.3, 48; 10.14, 17f; 11.3, 13; 14.14 (the

---

49 Sanday, *The Life of Christ in Recent Research*, pp. 119–42 (also p. 40 where he mentions *Lux Mundi*); cf. Morgan, 'Non angeli sed angli'; 'Historical Criticism and Christology: England and Germany' .

50 On the influence of kenoticism see Sanday, *Outlines of the Life of Christ*, pp. 232–3; Streeter, 'The Historic Christ', p. 75; and (more generally) Smedes, *The Incarnation: Trends in Modern Anglican Thought*, pp. xi–xviii, 1–15; Lawton, *Conflict in Christology: A Study of British and American Christology from 1889–1914*; Langford, *In Search of Foundations: English Theology 1900–1920*, pp. 185–216.

51 See Allen, 'Modern Criticism and the New Testament'; Sanday, *Outlines of the Life of Christ*, pp. 213–16; Headlam, *The Life and Teaching of Jesus the Christ*, pp. 8–15; Burkitt, *The Gospel History and Its Transmission*, pp. 3, 33–104; also Morgan, 'Historical Criticism and Christology'; Smith, 'Comments on Taylor's Commentary on Mark'.

52 In addition to Sanday's own articles, 'A Survey of the Synoptic Problem' (1891); 'Gospels' (1893); other British statements in support of the two-source hypothesis in this period included Woods, 'The Origin and Mutual Relation of the Synoptic Gospels' (1890); Jackson, 'The Present State of the Synoptic Problem' (1909).

second edition adds Mark 1.11; 5.7; 7.9; 12.32; 14.58 to this list, 1909[2], pp. 117–21).

Hawkins, like Wernle and others before him, accepted the priority of Mark on other grounds, specifically Woods' arguments concerning the *matter, general form and order* of the synoptics (p. 94 referring to Woods, 'The Origin and Mutual Relation of the Synoptic Gospels') and measured Matthean redaction against Mark in this light.

A similar approach is also characteristic of **Allen's** ICC commentary on Matthew (1907), which regards Markan priority as 'the one solid result of literary criticism' (p. vii). The first sentence reads: 'Almost the entire substance of the second Gospel has been transferred to the first (p. xiii). Allen argued that Matthew altered Mark 'due to an increasing feeling of reverence for the person of Christ' (p. xxxi). This is not, therefore, an argument for Markan priority, rather an explanation of Matthew's redaction. Allen shows that Matthew omits references to:

(i)   Jesus' emotions (Mark 3.5; 1.41, 43; 3.21; 6.6; 8.12; 10.14, 21; 14.33);

(ii) Jesus' inability (Mark 1.45; 6.5, 48; 7.24; 9.30; 14.58; 11.13);

(iii) Jesus' questions (Mark 5.9, 30; 6.38; 8.12, 23; 9.12, 16, 21, 33; 10.3; 14.14); and

(iv) makes other alterations of a christological nature (Mark 6.3; 10.18; 13.32).

Allen also mentions Matthew's alterations to miracles (Matt. 9.22; 15.28; 17.18), his emphasis on the universalism of Jesus' activity (Matt. 8.16; 12.15), and the omission of Mark's unusual miracle stories (Mark 7.32–35; 8.22–5) (pp. xxxi–xxxiii; cf. also Allen, 'Modern Criticism and the New Testament' (1902), pp. 216–17).

In 1915 H. J. **White** called attention to the growing consensus concerning 'The "Dogmatic" Variations in Matthew'.[53] He argued that since Matthew regularly abbreviated Mark's accounts 'there is no need to postulate a special cause when the general cause (i. e. abbreviation) will do equally well' (p. 308). He also showed that Matthew does include references both to Jesus' emotions and to his questions, hence any dogmatic purpose is carried through inconsis-

---

[53] Headlam had already been critical of some discussions of the supposed tendency (*The Miracles of the New Testament* (1915), pp. 210–16).

tently (pp. 311–17). He further noted that reverence for Jesus in later years involved no shrinking from his humanity: 'the more Church writers insisted on the Divinity of the Saviour, the more they loved to emphasize the fact that He who was Creator and Lord of all had also become poor for our sakes' (p. 311; he refers to 2 Cor. 8.9; Phil. 2.7; Justin, *Dialogue with Trypho*, 88). The remaining cases, he argued, 'are few in number and do not imply an alteration in point of view, but rather a desire to prevent misconception' (p. 321). White did not deny the priority of Mark, indeed he presupposed it, but did make a helpful plea for moderation in the claims made about Matthew. His argument, however, has had little effect on the subsequent history of the debate.[54]

Of particular importance is **Streeter**'s *The Four Gospels: A Study of Origins. Treating of the manuscript tradition, sources, authorship, and dates* (1924), which represented probably the most significant work on the subject hitherto published in English. His defence of the priority of Mark consists of arguments concerning the content of Mark, the independent adaptation of Markan wording by Matthew and Luke, the originality of the Markan order and the primitivity of Markan theology, style and diction in relation to Matthew and Luke (pp. 159–62). In this latter connection he argued that Mark's gospel is shown to be more primitive by the 'constant tendency of Matthew and Luke – showing itself in minute alterations, sometimes by one, sometimes by the other, and often by both – to improve and refine Mark's version' (p. 162).

Of special interest is Streeter's assertion that 'of these small alterations many have a reverential motive' (p. 162). He gives two types of example:

(a) whereas in Mark Jesus is only addressed as 'Lord' (κύριε) once, this occurs nineteen times in Matthew and sixteen times in Luke (along with six uses of ἐπιστάτα);

(b) 'certain phrases [in Mark] which might cause offence or suggest difficulties are toned down or excised [in Matthew and/or Luke]' (specifically Mark 6.5 ‖ Matt. 13.58 and Mark 10.18 ‖ Matt. 19.17).[55]

---

[54] Hawkins had read White and annotated his *Horae* accordingly, but his overall reaction is unclear (Neirynck, *Hawkins's Additional Notes to his «Horae Synopticae»*, pp. 96–8).

[55] Streeter (*The Four Gospels*, p. 164) referred readers to Hawkins, *Horae Synopticae*, pp. 114–53 for a detailed collection of further examples.

Throughout the twentieth century the christological argument has functioned specifically as an argument for Markan priority in many studies, including those of F. C. Conybeare, E. Klostermann, G. M. Styler, R. H. Stein, W. D. Davies and D. C. Allison, and G. N. Stanton.[56] In addition many scholars have viewed Matthew's redaction of Mark as involving some measure of increased reverence; examples include G. H. Dalman, F. H. Chase, H. L. Jackson, A. Plummer, E. Klostermann, B. W. Bacon, F. W. Green, S. E. Johnson, G. Bornkamm, G. Barth, G. Strecker, G. M. Styler, R. E. Brown, W. Grundmann, B. Rigaux, W. F. Albright and C. S. Mann, A. Descamps, R. H. Gundry, G. N. Stanton and J. Gnilka.[57]

These two lists of scholars clearly represent two logically distinct types of argument: one group reading Matthean redaction on the basis of Markan priority (assumed) and the other attempting to establish Markan priority. Nevertheless there are grounds for suggesting that too sharp a distinction between the two types of this argument would be misleading. First, the same phenomena are adduced; that is both the same texts (especially Matt. 13.58 cf. Mark 6.5; Matt. 19.17f cf. Mark 10.18) and the same issues (Jesus' emotions, inability and questions) are repeatedly mentioned. Secondly, the discussions themselves overlap in many cases, with some scholars (e. g. Allen and Plummer) suggesting both types of the

---

[56] Conybeare, *History of New Testament Criticism* (1910) pp. 56–7 (following Robinson, *The Study of the Gospels*); Klostermann, 'Synoptische Evangelien' (1928) pp. 424–5 (his fourth point in support of Markan priority); Styler, 'The Priority of Mark' (1962) p. 228; Stein, *The Synoptic Problem* (1987) pp. 84–5; Davies & Allison, *Matthew* (1988) vol. I, pp. 104–5; Stanton, *The Gospels and Jesus* (1989) p. 37.

[57] Dalman, *Die Worte Jesu*, p. 277, n. 1 (ET, p. 337 n. 1); Chase, 'The Gospels in the light of Historical Criticism', pp. 387, 389–90; Jackson, 'The Present State of the Synoptic Problem', p. 446; Plummer, *Matthew*, pp. xiv–xv; Klostermann, *Matthäusevangelium*, pp. 20–1; Bacon, *Studies in Matthew*, pp. 87–9; F. W. Green, *Matthew*, p. 11; S. E. Johnson, 'Matthew', pp. 235–6; Bornkamm, 'Enderwartung und Kirche im Matthäusevangelium', pp. 35–40 (ET, pp. 38–44); Barth, 'Das Gesetzesverständnis des Evangelisten Matthäus', p. 117 and n. 1 (ET, p. 125 and n. 1); Strecker, *Der Weg der Gerechtigkeit*, pp. 123–6; Styler, 'Stages in the Christology in the Synoptic Gospels', pp. 404–6; R. E. Brown, *Jesus – God and Man: Modern Biblical Reflections*, pp. 45–6; Grundmann, *Matthäus*, pp. 24–6; Rigaux, *Témoinage de l'évangile de Matthieu*, pp. 250–5 (ET, pp. 181–5); Albright and Mann, *Matthew*, pp. CLIV–CLV; Descamps, 'Rédaction et christologie dans le récit matthéen de la Passion', pp. 396–7; Gundry, *Matthew*, *passim*; Stanton, 'The Origin and Purpose of Matthew's Gospel: Matthean Scholarship from 1945 to 1980', p. 1925; Gnilka, *Matthäusevangelium*, vol. I, p. 163.

argument in the same discussion; and others (such as Klostermann, Stanton and Styler) appearing in both lists due to different publications. Clearly such an argument will always have a double function (if true!) – to establish Markan priority and to highlight Matthew's redactional interests. This double function suggests that any discussion of this christological argument must take place within the framework of a redaction critical approach.

4. Responses to the christological argument

Defenders of Matthean priority have not offered any lengthy response to the christological argument in favour of Markan priority. B. C. **Butler** (*The Originality of St Matthew: A Critique of the Two-Document Hypothesis*, 1951) offered examples where Matthew appears 'primitive' in comparison with Mark, but did not address the christological argument directly (pp. 123–37). For example, he argued that Mark 6.3 can be explained as an alteration of Matthew; and that Mark's omission of 'Son of the living God' from Matthew 16.16 is simply 'casual', since Mark clearly believed Jesus was the Son of God (cf. 1.1; 13.32) (pp. 128–9, 131). More fundamentally, Butler argued against accepting any a priori 'historical order of theological development' since the literary sequence must be determined first, rather than the theological (p. 170). Theological primitivity, he argued, should not be correlated to chronological priority: 'the parish magazine is not necessarily of earlier date than the *Summa Theologica* of St Thomas' (p. 171).

W. R. **Farmer** (*The Synoptic Problem: A Critical Analysis*, 1964) deals more explicitly with Streeter's arguments concerning primitive christology and Markan priority, and with the theory of the christological argument (pp. 159–69, 230–2). He argues that 'there is no reliable way in which to adjudge the christology of Mark as earlier or later than that of Matthew or Luke' (p. 230). All three come from the post-Pauline period, during which christology was complex and highly developed, but

> there is no objective basis upon which to reconstruct a scheme of christological development in this period against which to measure the relative date of a specific christological reference in the Gospels. For this reason, the christology of a given passage offers no secure criteria by which

it can be judged primary or secondary to a related christology in a parallel passage.

(p. 230)[58]

Farmer also examines the passages regarded by Abbott and Streeter as foundational to the argument.[59] Streeter treated the christological argument as part of a broader argument for Mark's primitive character (including roughness of style and grammar, as well as the view of the disciples); and Farmer discusses several passages of interest. Throughout this discussion Farmer has several characteristic arguments. First, he often turns Streeter's argument around, asserting that the agreement of Matthew and Luke against Mark constitutes an argument against Markan priority (p. 163 on Mark 3.21; p. 165 on Mark 15.44; p. 167 on Mark 7.32–5; 8.22–6). The problem of the minor agreements is Farmer's main positive argument (pp. 74–117, 118–52). Secondly he argues that little is known about what constitutes a later, or more developed christological tradition, especially since Mark is sometimes followed by Luke if not Matthew (p. 160 on Mark 10.18; pp. 168–9 on Mark 16.4). Farmer, however, does not deal with the whole breadth of evidence in Allen which we summarised above, dealing with only five selected passages (Mark 6.5; 10.18; 1.32, 34; 3.21; 8.24).

In connection with Mark 6.5, Farmer shows that neither Matthew nor Mark deny that some miracles took place, but he does not address the issue of inability; Mark 10.18 is dismissed rapidly; and 3.21 is declared irrelevant (due to mistranslation). These passages shall be discussed later; suffice to say here that Farmer, while highlighting the lack of a christological scale against which the gospels can be measured, also acknowledged the general principle that the solution which can best 'give a credible account of the development of Christology in the biblical period' must be favoured.[60]

Other neo-Griesbachians can be discussed briefly. D. L. Dungan simply ridicules Streeter's ability 'to range the various Gospel texts in terms of earlier or later reverentialness' (*sic*), and does not consider a single example.[61] O. L. Cope argues that theological

---

[58] For a similar argument see Fuller, 'Review Article: *The Synoptic Problem*: After Ten Years', p. 64.

[59] Abbott, 'Gospels', pp. 801–3; Streeter, *The Four Gospels*, pp. 162–4, see our earlier discussion.

[60] Farmer, 'The Synoptic Problem: The Inadequacies of the Generally Accepted Solution', p. 24.

[61] Dungan, 'Mark – The Abridgement of Matthew and Luke', p. 65.

factors should be ignored until literary decisions are made, a position which is not representative of neo-Griesbachian approaches.[62] P. **Parker** makes a fuller attempt to show that Matthew contains primitive ideas about Jesus.[63] He mentions:

(i) the relationship between Jesus and John the Baptist, which depicts Jesus as dependent upon John (Matt. 3.13; 4.17 cf. 3.2; 23.33 cf. 3.7; 12.33 cf. 3.8; 7.19 cf. 3.10; 13.30 cf. 3.12);

(ii) the fact that Joseph is also called 'Son of David' (1.20);

(iii) the Curetonian version of Matthew 1.16.

In fact none of these is particularly forceful: the Curetonian variant at 1.16 is unlikely to be authentic;[64] the whole point of Matthew 1 is to relate Jesus' Davidic descent through Joseph (see below, chapters 8 and 10); and Matthew's comparison between Jesus and John the Baptist (admittedly important) is not necessarily indicative of literary primitivity. Indeed, the whole question of Jesus' relationship with John in Matthew (although it is not historically improbable) deserves fuller treatment taking account of the salvation-historical distinctions (Matt. 11.7–15) as well as the parallels. In fact only one of the passages addressed by Parker contains a Markan parallel: this is Matthew 9.8, which Parker takes as proving that 'son of man' includes all mankind for Matthew, a position subjected to christological revision in Mark 2.10; but this is an implausible suggestion which shall be picked up later (in chapter 12). T. R. W. Longstaff's study of Markan christology makes no attempt to analyse Markan redaction of Matthew and Luke, although he is tempted to make them exemplars of the views Mark wishes to reject (a position we shall also discuss later).[65]

It must be conceded that the efforts of the neo-Griesbachians have been focussed on dismantling other arguments for Markan priority, and only recently on explaining the redactional interests of Mark as the Griesbach hypothesis conceives him (henceforth: Griesbach-Mark). In addition, the christological argument for Markan priority has played a minor role in the history of debate. In

---

[62] Cope, 'The Argument Revolves: The Pivotal Evidence for Markan Priority Is Reversing Itself', pp. 150–1; cf. Farmer, 'The Two-Gospel Hypothesis: The Statement of the Hypothesis'.

[63] Parker, 'The Posteriority of Mark', pp. 93–4.

[64] See Head, 'Christology and Textual Transmission', pp. 116–17.

[65] Longstaff, 'Crisis and Christology: The Theology of Mark'; cf. Weeden, *Mark, Traditions in Conflict*; Kloppenborg, 'The Theological Stakes in the Synoptic Problem'.

any case, it does seem that no detailed examination of this christological argument has been attempted previously (on either side), and this book seeks to fill that gap. Before the method to be adopted in this examination is introduced (in chapter two), two related areas of discussion remain to be addressed.

The lack of a christological scale highlighted by Farmer is apparent in several recent studies. In the first case a comparison between the preaching of Acts, Mark, and Matthew and Luke has been used to suggest that christology developed backwards. In other words the fundamental christological *moment* which defined Jesus' identity moved from the resurrection (as Acts 2.36; 5.31; 13.32f; Rom. 1.3f; Phil. 2.8f), back to the baptism (Mark 1.11), then to the conception (Matt. 1.21, 23; Luke 1.35), and hence to pre-existence before creation (John 1.1).[66] What must be noted here is that the order of the synoptics is presupposed as a given, and the christological development is worked out subsequently; there is no independent verification of the direction of development.[67]

This, and more, might equally be said of **Styler**'s 'Stages in Christology in the Synoptic Gospels'. Here Matthew's advances on Mark are discussed in terms of explicitness, reverence and ontological interests (pp. 404–6). But the discussion is bedevilled (for our purposes), not only by the presupposition of Markan priority, but by the repeated caveat that perhaps Matthew does not make any 'advance' at all on Mark (p. 404 and n. 1, p. 405 and n. 8). Again, there is no external verification, and certainly no known scale against which the christological content of any particular passage can be graded.

5. Conclusions

It is noteworthy that modern defenders of the Griesbach hypothesis have not chosen to follow their predecessors in utilising a christological argument to support Markan posteriority. Indeed they have generally disputed the very principle, complaining that the nature

---

[66] R. E. Brown, *The Birth of the Messiah*, pp. 29–32, 135, 140–1. This type of argument goes back at least as far as Sanday (*The Life of Christ in Recent Research*, p. 133); also Drury, 'Who's in, Who's out?'; Grant, *Gods and the One God*, p. 99.

[67] The same problems are inherent in Dibelius, *Gospel Criticism and Christology*. Fuller, 'The Conception/Birth of Jesus as a Christological Moment' offers a general critique.

of christological development in the early period is not a 'known' against which the 'unknown' of synoptic relationships can be measured (Butler and Dungan). This complaint needs to be taken seriously, along with Farmer's assumption that in fact the major christological developments took place in the period *before* the writing of the synoptic gospels. The way in which the development is traced, however, depends upon so many factors (historical, theological and philosophical as much as textual) that great diversity remains.[68] Farmer here reflects an important (if somewhat brittle) consensus position, one particularly associated with Hengel.[69] If this consensus be granted, then the issue at stake, which was not recognised by the earlier generations of British scholars, is not whether Mark or Matthew is more primitive, original and a more authentic witness to a 'lower' christology; but the extent to which the developed christologies of the later period have shaped the gospel traditions represented in both Matthew and Mark.

This survey has also clarified the key passages and themes upon which the christological argument in support of Markan priority has been based. These discussions have tended to focus on the particular relationship between Matthew and Mark, an issue which is obviously basic to resolving the synoptic problem in general, although this relationship itself is only one part of the broader picture. The survey has also revealed issues which remain to be addressed and clarified: (i) the use, by defenders of the Griesbach hypothesis, of a comparison between Mark and the 'apocryphal' gospels;[70] and (ii) the apparent use of scribal tendencies to illustrate the tendencies of synoptic redactors. We shall return to all of these issues in the next chapter.

---

[68] Consider, for example, the differences between Casey, *From Jewish Prophet to Gentile God: The Origins and Development of New Testament Christology*; Dunn, *Christology in the Making: A New Testament Inquiry into the Origins of the Doctrine of the Incarnation* (cf. 'Foreword to Second Edition'); and Marshall, 'Incarnational Christology in the New Testament'.

[69] Hengel, *Der Sohn Gottes*; numerous essays in *Between Jesus and Paul*.

[70] The supposed connection between Mark and the apocryphal gospels goes back at least as far as Schleiermacher (*Einleitung ins neue Testament*, p. 313), and was taken up by Baur, Strauss and Keim (as noted above).

2

METHOD AND APPROACH

1. Introduction

The history of research discussed in the previous chapter makes
clear that arguments connecting the christology of the gospels to
the question of literary relationships characterised both the
nineteenth-century defenders of the Griesbach hypothesis and the
twentieth-century defenders of Markan priority and the two-source
hypothesis. The fact that both hypotheses have, in the past,
appealed to such an argument indicates the potential value of a
thorough assessment of the adequacy of the christological argument for Markan priority in relation to the contemporary debate
about synoptic relationships.

We have already noted the current perception that several of the
traditional arguments for Markan priority have broken down. This
perception has prompted the search for new methods and arguments, among which perhaps the most important new argument is
that which depends upon the redaction-critical usefulness of the
two-source hypothesis. In this chapter we shall suggest that a
comparative redaction-critical investigation is the most appropriate
method with which to assess the christological argument for
Markan priority. This conclusion will emerge from a discussion of
the methods proposed by *both* neo-Griesbachians *and* contemporary Markan priorists. In addition we shall suggest that a
redaction-critical method is:

(i) intrinsically appropriate in view of several aspects of
gospel christology, in particular the influence of christological factors on the gospel traditions in both the pre-gospel
and post-gospel environment;

(ii) able to break the circularity within the traditional
argument.

In addition to defending and clarifying such a method, this chapter will discuss both the material to be investigated and the investigation procedure to be followed in the remainder of the book.

2. Farmer's criteria of priority

Developing a proper method by which literary priority or posteriority can be determined is the obvious first step in addressing the synoptic problem. In fact lack of agreement on methodological issues is a major cause of diverse hypotheses to explain the synoptic phenomena. At one point patristic traditions were held to be reliable sources of information concerning the authorship, date, and place of composition of the gospels. With some exceptions the early Fathers regarded Mark as both dependent upon Peter's preaching and secondary to Matthew:

> Papias (in Eusebius, *Hist. eccl.* III. 39.15f);
> Irenaeus, *Adversus haereses* III. 1.1 (also in Eusebius, *Hist. eccl.* V. 8.2–4), III. 11.8;
> Clement, *Hypotyposeis* (in Eusebius, *Hist. eccl.* VI. 14.6f);
> Tertullian, *Adversus Marcionem* IV. 2, 5;
> Origen, *Homily on Matt.* 1 (= Eusebius, *Hist. eccl.* VI. 25.3–6);
> Eusebius, *Hist. eccl.* III. 24.5–7;
> Jerome, *De viris illustribus* III, VII, VIII; *Comm. on Matt.* Praef.;
> Augustine, *De consensu* I. 4.

The exceptions include Clement's statement that the gospels with genealogies were written first; and the possibility that Papias' testimony suggests Markan priority.[1]

Several methods were employed during the nineteenth century, including Baur's *Tendenzkritik* and the priority of the primitive (or non-mythological, as in Strauss), without any clear agreement being reached. A presupposition behind Streeter's arguments is that a secondary writer might be known by the improvements and refinements he makes to his source.[2] Form critics advocated 'laws of tradition' which predicted that later traditions were marked by

---

[1] Gundry, *Matthew*, p. 614. See further Orchard and Riley, *The Order of the Synoptics*, pp. 111–226.
[2] Streeter, *The Four Gospels*, p. 162.

such things as increased length and detail and fewer Semitisms. E. P. Sanders' examination of these proposed criteria of priority concluded that there was insufficient evidence to establish 'laws of tradition' on the basis of either length, narrative detail or the number of Semitisms; furthermore: *'dogmatic statements that a certain characteristic proves a certain passage to be earlier than another are never justified'.*[3]

In view of the lack of agreement, Farmer's attempt to establish a proper methodological basis for his discussion is to be applauded. In 1964 he set forth 'canons of criticism' which indicated secondary characteristics and which 'provide the most important guides necessary for a study of the history of the redaction of the Synoptic tradition at the hands of the canonical Evangelists'.[4]

Farmer begins with an earlier work by E. D. Burton (*Some Principles of Literary Criticism and Their Application to the Synoptic Problem*, 1904), who was concerned to provide a theoretical basis for his discussion of the synoptic problem (something he regarded as insufficiently considered despite the multitude of theories, p. 195). Burton's most general principle is adapted from textual criticism: 'that one [document in literary relationship] is to be accepted as, relatively speaking, the original which will explain the origin of the others, but cannot itself be explained as the product of the others' (p. 197). Burton also had six criteria for determining the secondary character of two documents in a literary relationship (pp. 196–8):

(1)   misunderstandings of source material;
(2)   insertions which interrupt the argument;
(3)   omission of material which destroys flow;
(4)   'insertion of matter the motive for which can be clearly seen in the light of the author's general aim, while no motive can be discovered for its omission by the other author if he had had it in his source';
(5)   the converse of this: 'omission of matter traceable to the motive natural to the writer when the insertion could not thus be accounted for'; and
(6)   'alterations of other kinds which conform the matter to the general method or tendency of the author'.

---

[3] Sanders, *Tendencies*, p. 272; cf. pp. 1–8 concerning 'the need for criteria'.
[4] Farmer, *The Synoptic Problem*, p. 229.

Burton stated these criteria without expansion or defence. The usefulness of the first three, however, depends entirely on the extent to which these features are regarded as 'manifest' or 'clear'. This is particularly problematic with (2) and (3) because the 'course of thought', 'connection' or flow of argument of material within the synoptic gospels can hardly be regarded as self-evident (or agreed). It is thus questionable whether these offer as secure a methodological foundation as Burton and Farmer claimed; note, for example, J. B. Tyson's comment that while the principles seem valid their application is 'a hazardous occupation'.[5] Furthermore, criteria (4), (5) and (6) are essentially the same and relate to the expectation that an author has identifiable motives which will be reflected in his addition (4), omission (5) and/or alteration (6) of source material. In other words these three criteria are specific examples of a more general principle relating to the redactional activity of the evangelist.

Burton's discussion suggests that inasmuch as a writer's motives, that is the perspective from which he redacts his material, are known, then one would expect his use of sources to conform to that perspective rather than not to conform to it. Explanations, he suggests, are more readily identified for additions and alterations than for omissions, for which there may be a number of possible reasons (pp. 203–4). This suggests that greater clarity will be provided by focussing on redactional additions and alterations. Burton seems to confirm this general understanding when he says: 'The tendency of a particular writer, if it can be determined, would in any case be the safest criterion' (p. 198).

Farmer added three more criteria (or 'canons') for determining secondary characteristics in the synoptics:[6]

(i) evidence of 'extra-Palestinian, or non-Jewish provenance';
(ii) the existence of 'explanatory redactional glosses, and expansions aimed to make the tradition more applicable to the needs of the Church';
(iii) the use of characteristically redactional phrasing or vocabulary. This last had a corollary to the effect that the

---

[5] Tyson, 'The Two-Source Hypothesis: A Critical Appraisal', p. 451.

[6] *The Synoptic Problem*, p. 228. Farmer's first edition included the additional 'canon' that the gospel traditions became more specific; this was subsequently withdrawn under the influence of Sanders, *Tendencies*. The three criteria have recently been restated in Farmer, 'The Two-Gospel Hypothesis: The Statement of the Hypothesis', p. 140.

appearance in one gospel (e. g. Mark) of language that is unequivocally redactional to the parallel passage of another (e. g. Matthew) is indicative of the priority of the latter (i. e. Matthew) to the former (i. e. Mark).

These principles, however, are not unequivocal, as even Farmer notes – 'no one of these canons of criticism is decisive in any given instance'. In particular both 'non-Jewish provenance' and the addition of 'explanatory glosses' reveal more about the general provenance of a work than its priority relative to another tradition.

If all our available gospel traditions reflect the historical movement from Jesus-tradition within Jewish Palestine to its later use within Gentile Christianity throughout the Mediterranean (as seems undeniable), then the evidence for a Jewish provenance of Matthew (to pick the obvious example) cannot be used as a conclusive argument for its priority. For example, H. Owen's argument that Matthew was written in Jerusalem around AD 38 for the purposes of instructing Jewish converts assumes that the Jesus-tradition never left a Palestinian Jewish environment.[7] Since Farmer clearly regards Matthew as essentially secondary to the life-setting of Jesus his attempt to revive the basic pattern of Owen's argument is problematic.[8]

Farmer's criterion (i), although having the advantage of simplicity, cannot distinguish between a re-appropriation of gospel traditions for a Jewish community and the presentation of material shaped within an early Jewish-Christian milieu.[9] Criterion (ii), concerning addition of glosses, suffers from analogous weaknesses. Evidence which highlights a certain provenance for a gospel must be taken as just that: evidence for a gospel's provenance. The question must then, of course, be asked more generally: what can be deduced about the date of the gospel from a study of its contents and provenance?

Farmer's criterion (iii) has been more widely recognised as a valuable indication of relative priority. Tuckett observed that many scholars in the past have 'appealed to the coherence or otherwise of some alleged redactional activity' (e. g. Wilke, Lachmann, Weiss,

---

[7] Owen, *Observations on the Four Gospels*, p. 115.
[8] See *The Synoptic Problem*, p. 18, p. 227 and, for revival of Owen, Farmer, 'The Two-Gospel Hypothesis: The Statement of the Hypothesis', pp. 147–56.
[9] Tuckett, *The Revival of the Griesbach Hypothesis*, pp. 10–11; Tyson, 'The Two-Source Hypothesis: A Critical Appraisal', p. 450.

Woods and Streeter and, from another perspective, Griesbach, Orchard, Longstaff and Dungan).[10] Broadly similar arguments (although phrased in terms of *Tendenz*) were used by members of the Tübingen school including E. Zeller in 1843, supporting the Griesbach hypothesis; A. Hilgenfeld in 1850, supporting an Augustinian position; and A. Ritschl in 1851, supporting Markan priority.

Zeller argued that Mark's use of vocabulary characteristic to Matthew and Luke was an indication of their priority to Mark.[11] His first example is ἀναχωρεῖν which occurs ten times in Matthew and once in Mark 3.7. This suggests to Zeller that Mark derived his use of the term from Matthew 12.15. It is readily apparent that the method in this form is a fairly blunt instrument, especially since Zeller's conclusion is far from self-evident even assuming the Griesbach hypothesis; and does not allow for numerous other possibilities such as the general use of common, non-technical, vocabulary.[12]

Hilgenfeld argued that Luke was secondary to Mark, since Luke's additional material conforms to his general *Tendenz*, and that Mark depended upon Matthew alone, since he altered this source according to his *Tendenz*. He opposed the Griesbach hypothesis by questioning why, if Mark followed Luke, he never reproduced passages expressing any peculiarly Lukan *Tendenz*.[13]

Ritschl drew attention to the confession of Peter at Caesarea Philippi (Matt. 16.16 || Mark 8.29), which Matthew treats as a new revelation (16.17–19; also implied in Mark). This suggested dependence upon Mark since Matthew 14.33 shows that this knowledge was already the property of the disciples.[14] The principle is clearly stated:

> It must count as a critical axiom that when elements which
> serve a total redactional perspective are found in the

---

[10] Tuckett, *The Revival of the Griesbach Hypothesis*, pp. 13 and 15.

[11] Zeller, 'Vergleichende Uebersicht über den Wörtervorrath der sämmtlichen neutestamentlichen Schriftsteller', pp. 527–36; cf. Tuckett, 'The Griesbach Hypothesis in the 19th Century', p. 44.

[12] Cf. for further criticisms Tuckett, 'The Griesbach Hypothesis in the 19th Century', n. 69 on p. 57.

[13] Hilgenfeld, *Das Markus-Evangelium nach seiner Composition, seiner Stellung in der Evangelien-Literatur, seinem Ursprung und Charakter*. For discussion see Fuller, 'Baur versus Hilgenfeld', pp. 360–2.

[14] Ritschl, 'Ueber den gegenwärtigen Stand der Kritik der synoptischen Evangelien', p. 515; cf. also Tuckett, *The Revival of the Griesbach Hypothesis*, p. 11.

context of a different presentation, and particularly so if they are contradictory with the idiosyncrasies of that other presentation, this is an indication of the dependence of the one upon the other.[15]

In more recent times this general principle has been reinforced. R. H. Fuller, who had earlier described Farmer's canons as 'a notable contribution', regarded the argument from redactional expectations to be a crucial 'non-reversible criterion' of continuing relevance.[16] Tuckett also accepted its importance, while noting the practical and theoretical difficulties in ascertaining and describing the redactional preferences of the evangelists.[17] Tuckett sought to escape these difficulties by appealing to the more general criteria of 'coherence' (to which we shall return below).

It seems clear, therefore, that the most important of these proposed criteria concerns a principle relating to the expected redactional tendencies of an author. This is the principle upon which Burton's (4), (5) and (6) are based; and the only one of Farmer's three proposals which is not obviously flawed. In the next section of this chapter we will show that a similar criterion has recently been developed, albeit along somewhat different lines, by defenders of the two-source hypothesis.

3.   A useful argument

Since the loss of confidence in many of the arguments that previous generations had used to 'establish' Markan priority, new arguments have been actively sought by the scholarly community. The Cambridge conference of 1979 resolved that 'recent criticism of it [the two-source hypothesis] has been so devastating that it now requires new critical foundations'.[18] One popular new foundation

---

[15] 'Dagegen muss als kritischer Grundsatz gelten, dass wenn Elemente, welche der einen Gesammtanschauung dienen, in dem Contexte der anderen Darstellung sich finden und zwar so, dass sie in sich, oder mit Eigenheiten der anderen Darstellung widersprechend sind, hierin ein Merkmal der Abhängigkeit dieser von jener vorliegt' (Ritschl, 'Ueber den gegenwärtigen Stand der Kritik der synoptischen Evangelien', p. 515).

[16] Fuller, 'Baur versus Hilgenfeld', pp. 369–70; cf. earlier: 'Review Article: *The Synoptic Problem*: After Ten Years', p. 64.

[17] Tuckett, *The Revival of the Griesbach Hypothesis*, pp. 11–12; cf. also Fuller, 'Baur versus Hilgenfeld', pp. 369–70.

[18] Dungan, 'The Jerusalem Symposium 1984', p. XIII. Farmer's introduction to the

was provided by arguing for the redaction-critical usefulness of Markan priority. According to J. M. Robinson:

> the success of *Redaktionsgeschichte* in clarifying the theologies of Matthew and Luke on the assumption of dependence on Mark is perhaps the most important new argument for Marcan priority, just as perhaps the main ingredient lacking in William R. Farmer's argument for Marcan dependence on the other written Gospels is a convincing *Redaktionsgeschichte* of Mark based on that assumption.[19]

This argument, based on both the usefulness (*Brauchbarkeit*) of Markan priority and the general success of redaction criticism, has been taken up in various ways in subsequent studies by scholars such as G. Strecker, H. B. Green, G. N. Stanton and J. S. Kloppenborg.[20] J. K. Elliott, for example, wrote: 'Stringent use of a redaction-critical approach to the gospels . . . enables the reader to assess the relative priority of the synoptic gospels as complete units.'[21]

In an important paper given at the same conference as Robinson's, which has come to be regarded as something of a 'classic' defence of the two-source hypothesis, J. A. Fitzmyer suggested that 'the *Brauchbarkeit* argument is a valuable, but extrinsic, criterion for judging the worth of the hypothesis'.[22] He argued that while arguments based on common subject-matter, order and wording are at an abstract or theoretical level inconclusive; when the texts are examined in the light of the redactional tendencies of the evangelists the two-source hypothesis yields an acceptable solution, whereas Markan activity (or his resulting theology) on the

---

proceedings phrases this differently ('Introduction', pp. xx–xxi; dependent on Powers, 'The Shaking of the Synoptics').

[19] J. M. Robinson, 'On the *Gattung* of Mark (and John)', pp. 101–2.

[20] E. g. Strecker, *Der Weg der Gerechtigkeit*, p. 11; Green, 'Review of Albright and Mann, *Matthew*', p. 482; Stanton, 'The Origin and Purpose of Matthew's Gospel', p. 1902 (cf. pp. 1899–900 for the principle); Kloppenborg: 'one argument in favor of the 2DH is its very *Brauchbarkeit* in accounting for the shape of Matthew and Luke' ('The Theological Stakes in the Synoptic Problem', pp. 93–4).

[21] J. K. Elliott, 'The Synoptic Problem and the Laws of Tradition', p. 152.

[22] Fitzmyer, 'The Priority of Mark and the "Q" Source in Luke', p. 134. See Fuller, 'Review Article: *The Synoptic Problem*: After Ten Years', p. 64; and cf. Farmer's response (below); Fitzmyer's essay was reprinted in Bellinzoni's 1985 collection *The Two-Source Hypothesis: A Critical Appraisal*, pp. 37–52.

Griesbach hypothesis is 'incomprehensible' or implausible.[23] In other words he applies the *Brauchbarkeit* principle to the Streeterian arguments concerning order and wording which had been criticised by Farmer.

The neo-Griesbachians have attempted, in various studies, to defend the Griesbach hypothesis against the charge that it fails to provide a convincing picture of Markan redaction. Thus we have attempts to explain the Markan redaction as consistent with other conflationary literature (Longstaff, *Evidence of Conflation in Mark?*); or as explicable in terms of a historically reminiscent Petrine redaction (Mann, *Mark*). It remains the case, however, that no thorough redaction-critical analysis of Mark on the Griesbach hypothesis has yet been published (Riley, *The Making of Mark*, does little analysis). Farmer himself devoted portions of two studies to respond to Fitzmyer.

In these studies Farmer maintained that the Griesbach hypothesis offers a more credible explanation for the order of pericopae than the two-source hypothesis on the grounds of internal simplicity and probability.[24] He argued that the theology of Griesbach-Mark is that of an irenic church theologian, uniting the emphases of Matthew and Luke in a historically credible manner.[25] And he sought to provide explanations for Griesbach-Mark's redactional behaviour in producing what might be described as a highly original free recomposition, 'an artistic literary achievement'.[26] The implication of Farmer's response is that the methodological point has been conceded: the theory which can offer the best explanation of the redactional activities of the evangelists is to be preferred.[27] Nevertheless Farmer warned of the dangers of circularity in the use of an argument from the redaction-critical usefulness of the two-

[23] Fitzmyer, 'The Priority of Mark and the "Q" Source in Luke', pp. 134–47. See particularly his six questions on pp. 134–5 for examples of the application of the 'usefulness' argument to the subject-matter of the gospels, and his repeated appeal to the relative plausibility of the different solutions (e. g. pp. 137, 138, 139). While 'extrinsic' could mean either 'non-essential' or 'external' (*OED* vol. III, p. 477), Fitzmyer is not intending to deny the use of the principle.

[24] Farmer, 'Modern Developments of Griesbach's Hypothesis', pp. 293–5; substantially repeated in 'Is Streeter's Fundamental Solution to the Synoptic Problem Still Valid?', pp. 153–5.

[25] Farmer, 'Modern Developments of Griesbach's Hypothesis', pp. 288–9.

[26] Quotation from Farmer, 'The Passion Prediction Passages and the Synoptic Problem', p. 558 n. 2; cf. also 'The *Minor Agreements* of Matthew and Luke Against Mark and the Two Gospel Hypothesis', p. 164.

[27] Cf. also Fee, 'Modern Text Criticism and the Synoptic Problem', pp. 168–9.

source hypothesis to support the very principle which redaction-critics have universally presupposed:

> It would be helpful if these critics were to carry through their redactional analyses of the Gospels on different source hypotheses, publish the results of their research, and then demonstrate that the two-source hypothesis produces more useful results than alternative source hypotheses.'[28]

This methodological agreement between Farmer and Fitzmyer, with respect to the value of the redaction-critical usefulness of the hypotheses, finds a parallel in the work of C. M. Tuckett and neo-Griesbachian response to it. Tuckett's criticisms of the Griesbach hypothesis, in both its nineteenth-century and modern forms, have focussed on the implausibility of the redactional procedure of Griesbach-Mark.[29] Tuckett's 'criterion of coherence' provides his basic method for comparing hypotheses:

> The extent to which an hypothesis gives a coherent, consistent picture of the redactional activity of each evangelist will then be a measure of its viability.[30]

In Tuckett's book this general criterion is applied at different levels, to 'small grammatical changes, the changes of words and phrases with wider theological implications, and the changes involving the choice and ordering of whole pericopes'.[31] A. J. McNicol, in a review of Tuckett's book, supports this approach: 'the Neo-Griesbachians can affirm Tuckett's methodology as a working principle'; and Tuckett in turn applauded this agreement in approach.[32] A further confirmation of this methodological agreement was probably the most significant of the agreed conclusions reached at the 1984 Jerusalem conference. The resolution stated:

> that a literary, historical and theological explanation of the

---

[28] Farmer, 'The Two-Document Hypothesis as a Methodological Criterion in Synoptic Research', p. 392.

[29] Tuckett, *The Revival of the Griesbach Hypothesis*, pp. 186–7; 'The Griesbach Hypothesis in the 19th Century', *passim* esp. p. 48.

[30] Tuckett, *The Revival of the Griesbach Hypothesis*, p. 13

[31] Ibid., p. 15.

[32] McNicol, 'The Two Gospel Hypothesis Under Scrutiny: A Response to C. M. Tuckett's Analysis of Recent Neo-Griesbachian Gospel Criticism', p. 7; Tuckett, 'The Two Gospel Hypothesis Under Scrutiny: A Response', p. 25.

evangelists' compositional activity, giving a coherent and reasonable picture of the whole of each Gospel, is the most important method of argumentation in defense of a source hypothesis.[33]

While it would be easy to overestimate the 'newness' of this argument – we have already seen that something like it was used in the Tübingen school, and is intrinsic to Burton's principles, not to mention the fact that placing the gospels in their literary, historical and theological milieu has been a prominent part of synoptic studies for over two hundred years – it is clear that the importance placed on the compositional or redactional activity of the evangelists reflects methodological advances made since World War II.

4.   Christological development as a law of tradition

The question remains how to relate the christological argument for Markan priority to the argument from redaction-critical plausibility. One possible answer to this question would be to consider christological development as a given law of tradition. Take, for example, the following statement:

> The general direction of early Christology cannot be gainsaid. It was from the lesser to the greater. The passing of time incontrovertibly saw a development; there was an enhancing of feelings of reverence, an increase in Jesus' position and status. Hence, because Matthew possesses a higher Christology than Mark, and because he lacks certain details which make Jesus more human, all presumption is against Matthean priority.[34]

Here christological development appears as the first of W. D. Davies and D. L. Allison's arguments from the tendencies of the synoptic tradition. The authors stand within the Oxford Seminar tradition which was identified in chapter one and the passages and issues they cite are substantially the same as those discussed by Hawkins and Allen (chapter 1 section 3). But no attempt is made to defend the use of christological development as a criterion of priority, and Davies and Allison make only the most general assertion about the nature of that development. The assumption of

---

[33] Dungan, *The Interrelations of the Gospels*, p. 609.
[34] Davies and Allison, *Matthew*, vol. I, p. 104.

the Oxford Seminar tradition was that christological development could be measured in relation to the presentation of the humanity of Jesus in the gospels. Essentially this presupposed a high degree of continuity in the way in which the Jesus tradition was handled between pre-gospel and gospel-composition situations.

By way of comparison, a common characteristic of nineteenth-century defenders of the Griesbach hypothesis was the assertion that the christology of Griesbach-Mark, expressed in his alterations and expansions to Matthew and Luke, could be related to the later christological presentations of the apocryphal gospels and later scribal traditions. These scholars used christological development as a criterion of Markan posteriority, drawing their comparisons from a later period and presupposing a high degree of continuity in the way in which Jesus-tradition was handled between gospel-composition and post-gospel situations.

For example, F. E. D. Schleiermacher suggested that in terms of Markan expansion and artificial verisimilitude ('künstliche hervorgebrachter äusserer Schönheit') the gospel displays an inclination towards apocryphal characteristics, representing a later period of written composition.[35] This assessment was supported by T. Keim, who argued that Mark represented a modernising of Matthew–Luke and contained implausible and secretive apocryphal characteristics.[36] F. C. Baur argued that the Markan miracle traditions were close to those of apocryphal gospels.[37] Hilgenfeld suggested that the walking on water in Mark had a mysterious, even magical, character.[38] Even some Markan priorists have been sympathetic to this sort of argument.[39]

Elements of this view have also found recent exposure in Farmer's *The Synoptic Problem*. He maintains, referring specifically to Schleiermacher, that certain features of Mark are similar to features prominent in apocryphal gospels; specifically noting the

---

[35] Schleiermacher, *Einleitung ins Neue Testament*, pp. 314–15 (and n. 1 on p. 315).

[36] *Geschichte Jesu von Nazara*, vol. I, p. 100 (ET, vol. I, pp. 137–8); cf. also vol. II, pp. 522–3 (ET, vol. IV, pp. 231–3); vol. III, pp. 39–40 (ET, vol. VI, p. 47). Keim also included scribal tendencies (vol. 1, p. 101 (ET, vol. I, p. 138)).

[37] Baur, *Kritische Untersuchungen über die kanonischen Evangelien*, p. 562: cf. above, chapter 1 section 2.

[38] Hilgenfeld, *Das Markus-Evangelium*, p. 58; cf. *Die Evangelien*, pp. 149–50.

[39] Wrede, *Das Messiasgeheimnis in den Evangelien*, pp. 146–8 (ET, pp. 146–8) (cf. below, chapter 13); Bultmann, *Die Geschichte der synoptischen Tradition*, pp. 373–4 (ET, p. 348); *Theologie des Neuen Testaments*, pp. 470–1 (ET, vol. II, pp. 124–6).

incorporation of numbers (p. 116), grammatical and vocabulary 'barbarisms' (pp. 122 and 130), and the addition of minor details (p. 134).[40] More recently he has specifically included theological tendencies in this category, arguing that Mark, like John, shares characteristics and theological tendencies with non-canonical gospels.[41]

The fact that both sides of the debate have appealed to different aspects of the process of transmission of gospel traditions in support of their 'christological arguments', albeit with little attention given to actually evaluating the available evidence, might suggest that little is to be gained by direct appeal to christological development as a criterion of priority or 'law of tradition'. This impression is strengthened by two considerations. First, although christological development of various sorts influenced the Jesus-tradition in the pre-gospel stage, the nature of this development is disputed and discussions of this period are, for our purposes, over-dependent upon prior decisions concerning the synoptic problem. Secondly, although there are clear indications of christological development in the post-gospel use of gospel traditions (to be discussed shortly), the actual facts of the matter challenge the common use of terms such as 'lesser' and 'higher' christology in this connection. In particular it must be noted that evidence of a shift away from the humanness of Jesus (his emotions, limitations etc.) is ambiguous and cannot be said to be characteristic of the reuse of gospel traditions in the later period.

Available evidence of the utilisation of gospel traditions occurs in non-canonical gospels, in individual projects which appropriate canonical material, and in scribal alterations to the gospel texts. With respect to this evidence no additional indications of Jesus' humanity are present in *Gos. Pet.* or *Gos. Thom.*, nor can such evidence be found in Marcion's redaction of Luke. On the other hand, *P. Eg. 2* includes an additional reference to Jesus' indignation (ἐμβρειμησάμενος; line 51); *Sec. Gos. Mark* incorporates a reference to Jesus' anger (col. 2, line 25); numerous manuscripts add a reference to Jesus' anger at Luke 6.10 (esp. D X f¹ f¹³ it¹⁰mss etc., harmonising with Mark 3.5), and the Arabic *Diatessaron* incorporates an additional reference to Jesus' fear (48.16f). The ignorance

---

[40] Cf. also his comments in 'The Two-Document Hypothesis as a Methodological Criterion', p. 390.

[41] Farmer, 'The Two-Gospel Hypothesis: The Statement of the Hypothesis', pp. 146–7.

of Jesus is referred to in *Gos. Naz.* 2; enhanced in some manuscripts at Mark 13.32 (where $\Delta \Theta f^{13}$ 565 cop etc. add μονος); and Tatian follows Mark's rather than Matthew's version of the rejection at Nazareth (*Diat.* 17.36–53, esp. v. 28) and the question about calling Jesus good (*Diat.* 28.42–51). Passages concerning the birth and family of Jesus were subject to vigorous redaction, but in different directions. Even such popular devices as increasing the impact of Jesus upon the people, and an increased frequency of reverential titles (particularly 'the Lord'), are found to be non-uniform, and exceptions to both are readily available.[42]

These problems suggest that the use of a supposed christological tendency by which to measure the christological 'level' of the synoptics is fraught with danger, not only because of the danger of circularity to which Farmer pointed, but because there is no scale! Instead of appealing to a distinct tendency whose trajectory can be measured, an approach which is able to integrate christological concerns with the now accepted method relating to assessing redaction-critical plausibility must be implemented.

5. The christological argument and redactional plausibility

In this section we shall propose a reorientation of the christological argument along new lines. This reorientation is appropriate to the christological argument as formulated in chapter one; to the christological interests of the evangelists; and to what can be known about the christological interests of later gospel redactors. Taking these in reverse order it seems quite clear that during both the pre-gospel stage and the post-gospel stage of the transmission of the gospel traditions the available material was shaped, filtered and arranged in relation to the christological convictions of those who handled the tradition. This lends support to the presumption that something similar was true at the stage of writing.[43]

The clearest examples of christological shaping, filtering and altering are found in various types of post-gospel redaction of gospel traditions. A survey of this material reveals that later redactors often betray their own particular christological position in and through their redaction of received traditions. As the gospel

---

[42] For further discussion of the evidence relevant to Tatian and the manuscript tradition see Head, 'Tatian's Christology' and 'Christology and Textual Transmission', pp. 114–23.

[43] Cf. also Sanders, *Tendencies*, pp. 8 and 282–3.

traditions are received and passed on they pass through the grid, and receive the imprint, of the redactor's christology. This is clearly true of *some* scribes involved in the copying of gospel texts.[44] It is also true, often more manifestly so, in the alterations of gospel material involved in the composition of several of the early non-canonical gospels.

With regard to this material it seems to be the case that the longer the document, the more clear this tendency appears. *Gos. Thom.* shifts the material in a gnosticising direction in a variety of ways: by the overall shaping of the document, particularly the opening (1–2); the introduction of new material (e. g. 28, 61, 77) and the alteration of synoptic traditions (e. g. 13, 30).[45] The *Gos. Pet.* offers a redaction of synoptic tradition in an apocalyptic and sensational direction.[46] Although less survives of other non-canonical gospels or papyrus fragments of gospel traditions the available evidence points to similar patterns in this literature.

P. Oxy. 840, a fourth-century manuscript, contains a conversation between Jesus and a chief priest in the Temple, in which Jesus is consistently designated as σωτήρ (lines 12, 30).[47] In P. Oxy. 1081, a fourth-century manuscript containing a Greek version of a portion of *Soph. Jes. Chr.*, the disciples address Jesus as κυριέ, while the narrator uses σωτήρ (lines 25–7).[48] P. Berlin 11710, a sixth-century non-canonical gospel fragment, contains numerous specific christological confessions.[49] In *Gos. Naz.* 'Lord' appears as the dominant narrative designation for Jesus (2; 15a (‖ Matt. 18.21f, but shifted from Peter's question to the narrative); 16; 24; 28; 32; 34 (these last four medieval)), with 'Jesus' appearing only once (10 ‖ Matt. 12.13), and 'Master' once (16).[50] *Gos. Heb.* appears to have been more clearly Gnostic than other Jewish-Christian gospels, with its talk of 'powers' (1) and its adoptionist tendencies; 'Lord' was the standard narrative designation (2, 5,

[44] Ehrman, *The Orthodox Corruption of Scripture*; Head, 'Christology and Textual Transmission'.
[45] We cannot here defend the strangely unfashionable view that *Gos. Thom.* is secondary to the synoptic gospels, see Tuckett, 'Thomas and the Synoptics' and Neirynck, 'The Apocryphal Gospels and the Gospel of Mark', pp. 133–9 for recent support; and Dehandschutter, 'The Gospel of Thomas and the Synoptics', and Fallon and Cameron, 'The Gospel of Thomas', for surveys.
[46] Discussed fully in Head, 'On the Christology of the Gospel of Peter'.
[47] Grenfell and Hunt (eds.), *The Oxyrhychus Papyri* V (1908) 1–10.
[48] Grenfell and Hunt (eds.), *The Oxyrhychus Papyri*, VII (1911) 16–19.
[49] Lietzmann, *ZNW* 22 (1923) 153–4.
[50] *NTA*, vol. I, pp. 146–53; cf. Klostermann, *Apocrypha* vol. II, pp. 3–8.

7(ter)).[51] The *Gos. Eb.* both omits the virgin birth (3) and includes an explicit account of the entry of the Holy Spirit into Jesus at his baptism (4),[52] a doctrine characteristic of Ebionite christology, in which the union of the Holy Spirit with the man Jesus produced the Christ.

> Irenaeus, *Adversus haereses* III. 11.7 (they distinguish between Jesus and the Christ); Tertullian, *Praescriptio* 33.11 (did not believe that Jesus was the Son of God); Tertullian, *De carne Christi* 14 (Jesus is a mere man and only the seed of David); Hippolytus, *Refutatio* VII. 34.1f (Christ and Jesus; a man like us all); Epiphanius, *Panarion* 30.3.3–6 (differences among Ebionites re when heavenly being united with Jesus); 30.14.4 (Jesus was really a man, Christ came into being in him after descent of dove).

In the case of the two individual redactors of the second century it appears that both Marcion and Tatian had particular and personal christological interests which shaped their redaction of the gospel traditions. Marcion rearranged, omitted and reinterpreted his Lukan source material in the light of his docetism.[53] Although he is by no means as radical as Marcion there are also sufficient indications in Tatian's editorial practices to suppose that 'he filtered the gospel texts through his own christological grid.'[54]

In all of these cases 'christological redaction' can be seen to have taken place and diverse techniques (addition, omission, conflation, alteration, restructuring etc.) were employed by authors, scribes and redactors with the result that the final product becomes a vehicle for the expression of a characteristic christology. Thus, it is not a matter of isolated changes to 'elevate' Jesus; rather it involves a representation of traditional material in view of a new situation and different christological beliefs and priorities.

It is not only the post-gospel redactors who give indications of such editorial interests; the nature of the gospels themselves, and specifically the clear christological interests of the evangelists, suggests that we should be able to detect such interests in the composition and arrangement of the gospels and in the alterations that are made to their sources. Recent studies have emphasised the importance of christology for all the synoptic evangelists.[55] The

---

[51] *NTA*, vol. I, pp. 163–5; cf. Klostermann, *Apocrypha* vol. II, pp. 3–8.
[52] *NTA*, vol. I, pp. 156–8; cf. Klostermann, *Apocrypha* vol. II, pp. 8–11 (all from Epiphanius, *Panarion*, 30).
[53] Head, 'Marcion's Gospel Redaction'.
[54] Head, 'Tatian's Christology', quote from p. 137.
[55] Guelich, *Mark*, pp. xxxviii–xl; Stanton, 'The Origin and Purpose of Matthew's Gospel', pp. 1922–5; Evans, *Luke*, pp. 64–84.

source hypothesis which is able to account for the evangelist's redactional behaviour by appeal to clear christological interests will obviously be highly favoured.

Finally then, a reorientation of the christological argument along the lines of redactional plausibility would parallel recent attempts to restate arguments from order, wording and content in terms of the redactional plausibility (or otherwise) of the different hypotheses.[56] In addition, the nature of the christological argument itself, as outlined in the previous chapter, lends itself to an investigation focussing on its 'usefulness' in explaining redactional perspectives. That is, the argument was found to function on two levels: both as a 'proof' of Markan priority and as an indication of Matthean redactional interests. This suggests that the logical method of approaching the christological material is by investigating and assessing the nature of the redactional behaviour predicted by the two major hypotheses.

6. Our approach

The task before us is therefore to compare the ways in which the two-source hypothesis and the Griesbach hypothesis account for the material surveyed in the traditional christological argument for Markan priority. In some ways Davies and Allison suggest such a procedure when they write that

> we find it perplexing to suppose that an early Christian writer with Matthew's text before him would almost systematically set out to highlight Jesus' ignorance and make him a much more emotional figure. But the reverse procedure is quite intelligible.[57]

Here the authors are utilising, albeit in a rudimentary way, a comparative-redactional method. That is, the evidence is viewed from two perspectives – Matthean or Markan priority – and the respective redactional procedure is assessed for plausibility. The aim of this work is to answer Farmer's plea for critics 'to carry through their redactional analyses of the Gospels on different source hypotheses' before determining which hypothesis 'produces

---

[56] Cf. Styler, 'The Priority of Mark', pp. 290–1; Tuckett, *The Revival of the Griesbach Hypothesis*, pp. 186–7.
[57] Davies and Allison, *Matthew*, vol. I, p. 105.

more useful results'.[58] But how can the relative 'plausibility' of different approaches be measured?

We cited earlier the resolution agreed by the Jerusalem conference:

> that a literary, historical and theological explanation of the evangelists' compositional activity, giving a *coherent and reasonable picture* of the whole of each Gospel, is the most important method of argumentation in defense of a source hypothesis.[59]

This statement suggests that a crucial element is an overall explanation of the compositional (or redactional) activity of the evangelist on each theory. Therefore the more *'coherent and reasonable picture'* of that activity in light of the whole gospel (here shifting slightly the sense of the statement), the more plausible the hypothesis upon which the explication of redactional activity is based, especially if comparison shows one to be more plausible (i. e. more coherent and more reasonable) than the other. These two terms, 'coherent' and 'reasonable', are here taken to relate to two fields of evidence upon which arguments about the plausibility of various envisaged redactional activity can be measured.

'Coherent' is taken to refer to internal matters, and this feature will be measured using traditional redaction-critical methods, looking especially for favoured terminology, vocabulary and common theological themes in the alterations made to sources. As D. R. Catchpole has said: 'when a writer changes a text we would normally expect the change to be in harmony, rather than disharmony, with the writer's theological outlook and intention, and with such evidence as we have from a reading of his work as a whole concerning its setting and purpose'.[60]

'Reasonable' is taken to refer to external matters, as an indicator of the plausibility of the model in relation to external tests. This might be taken as 'reasonable to this commentator', but the reasons why it should be found reasonable to the commentator still should be capable of statement. For example, generalisations about what the evangelists were likely to do with gospel traditions in the first

---

[58] Farmer, 'The Two-Document Hypothesis as a Methodological Criterion', p. 392 (cited in full earlier).
[59] Dungan, *The Interrelations of the Gospels*, p. 609. My emphasis.
[60] Catchpole, *Quest for Q*, p. 3; cf. also Sanders, *Tendencies*, p. 272; Neirynck, 'Synoptic Problem', pp. 592–3.

century can be compared with second-century examples of the redaction of gospel traditions, suggested techniques can be tested in analogous contemporary literature or in contemporary discussions of literary criticism, parallels in contemporary literature might explicate the reasons behind alterations and so on.

The method to be followed will therefore be to compare the redactional procedure and perspective envisaged by the two major hypotheses, the two-source hypothesis on the one hand, and the Griesbach hypothesis on the other. Since the so-called christological argument for Markan priority has focussed primarily upon the relationship between Matthew and Mark, the crucial element of the synoptic problem in general, we shall be comparing the redactional activity of Matthew (assuming Markan priority) with that of Mark (assuming the Griesbach hypothesis). Although the discussion will depend on countless historical judgements we shall not be concerned with judgements on the historicity of the gospel accounts as such, but on the comparison between two different hypotheses. In comparing the redactional activity of the evangelists on the two different hypotheses alterations made by the later evangelist to his source which contain little evidence of deriving from some alternative source material will generally be labelled redactional, as is customary among gospel critics (particularly Markan priorists in relation to Matthean redaction). This form of labelling should not be taken to imply that no significant tradition history could lie behind the material so designated, since any sensible hypothesis ought to allow for the possibility of oral traditions or recollections influencing the redactional activity of a later evangelist. Nevertheless, it will normally designate material which, on either hypothesis, is so congruent with the evangelist's style as to make the recovery of any pre-evangelical tradition problematic.

The aim is to perform the investigation by adopting the hypothesis-testing exercise of imagining the truth of the alternative theories: one has to assume the truth of the hypothesis in order to test its coherence and reasonableness; at times this might require a self-conscious suspension of disbelief, or, in Farmer's words, 'an act of self transcendence'.[61] We might compare J. A. T. Robinson's comment, in a different connection: 'Like any hypothesis it can be tested – let alone established – only *a posteriori*, by adopting it and

[61] Farmer, 'Luke's Use of Matthew', p. 40; cf. also Tuckett, *The Revival of the Griesbach Hypothesis*, p. 14.

then seeing whether it yields a more adequate explanation of the data.[62]

In his 1991 dissertation S. R. Llewelyn pointed to the use of redaction criticism as a means of resolving the synoptic problem. He argued that both coherence and some external reference would be needed to secure such a resolution.[63] A somewhat similar method has been defended recently by S. E. Johnson who has argued that it is precisely redaction criticism, with its interest in the theology of the evangelists, which enables the source critic to compare the theological phenomena of the synoptic gospels. Thus for example he proposes that the Griesbach hypothesis be tested 'by studying Mark from this point of view with as great sympathy as possible.'[64] In the application of this method, however, Johnson tends towards a literary-compositional approach rather than a strictly redaction-critical one. In fact he does not discuss the redactional procedure in detail, and this diminishes the impact of his work. His chapter on christology highlights the differences between Mark's secrecy motif and the clear presentations of Matthew and Luke (a subject to which we shall return at some length in chapter twelve).[65]

In terms of content and approach the following chapters can be classified in three sections. The first of these (chapters three to five) deals with exegetical and redactional studies of single passages of interest. Chapters three and four contain investigations of two passages which have dominated discussion of the christological argument (focussing on the 'why do you call me good?' of Mark 10.17 and the account of Jesus' rejection at Nazareth). Chapter five focusses on a passage of christological importance found only in Matthew and Mark (Jesus' walking on water). In these three chapters we shall undertake redactional studies of the passages from the two perspectives (two-source hypothesis and Griesbach hypothesis) with a view to describing and evaluating the plausibility of the redactional processes envisaged by each theory. We shall begin with the two-source hypothesis, since this is where the argument begins, before turning to the Griesbach hypothesis.

[62] J. A. T. Robinson, *The Priority of John*, p. 9.
[63] Llewelyn, 'A Stylometric Analysis of Parallel Sections of the Synoptic Gospels', pp. 121–2.
[64] Johnson, *The Griesbach Hypothesis and Redaction Criticism*, p. 3.
[65] A broadly similar comparative approach is also characteristic of New, *Old Testament Quotations in the Synoptic Gospels and the Two-Document Hypothesis*.

The second section comprises an investigation of other aspects of the christological argument for Markan priority. Chapter six focusses on purported omissions by Matthew of material in Mark considered inappropriate or irreverent (Jesus' emotions, questions which suggest his ignorance and his inability). Chapter seven focusses on purported additions and alterations made by Matthew to Mark in the interests of christological reverence (the worship of Jesus, additions to the passion narrative and other additions). Although in each case we shall consider the perspectives of both the two-source hypothesis and the Griesbach hypothesis, the focus of attention in these chapters is on evaluating the Matthean intention which is suggested by the christological argument for Markan priority, hence we shall look first and critically at the two-source hypothesis and then, more briefly, at the Griesbach hypothesis.

The third section (chapters eight to twelve) seeks to broaden the basis of comparison by investigating the use of various christological titles and related themes in both Matthew and Mark (again using the perspectives provided by the competing hypotheses). The major christological titles – Messiah, Son of David, Teacher, Lord, Son of Man, Son of God – will be studied, as well as the so-called 'Messianic Secret'. In these chapters earlier procedure shall be reversed and the investigations will begin with the Griesbach hypothesis. This procedure will thus focus initially on thematic overviews of Griesbachian material, on which relatively little has been written, and subsequently on the more fully researched area of Matthean theology on the two-source hypothesis. Our concern throughout is to attempt an even-handed analysis of the two competing hypotheses. Chapter twelve will focus almost entirely on investigating the secrecy material from the perspective of the Griesbach hypothesis.

3

THE RICH YOUNG RULER (MATT. 19.16–22; MARK 10.17–22; LUKE 18.18–23)

1. Introduction

The two passages which have been most prominent in the formation and use of the christological argument for Markan priority have involved the Matthean parallels to Mark 10.17f and 6.5f (chapter one, section 3). This chapter is devoted to an analysis of the first of these, probably the passage most often cited in this connection, concerning the 'rich young ruler' – a traditional designation which in fact conflates elements from the triple tradition: all three evangelists refer to wealth, Matthew identifies the man as ὁ νεανίσκος (Matt. 19.20), and Luke as an ἄρχων (Luke 18.18).

> For Matthew 19.16–17a we follow the text of NA27 = UBS4 (also Aland, *Synopsis*; Orchard, *Synopsis*; Huck–Greeven, *Synopsis*; and all modern commentators). Despite the arguments of Wenham ('Why do you ask me about the good? A Study of the Relation between Text and Source Criticism') and some earlier scholars (e.g. Scrivener, *A Plain Introduction to the Criticism of the New Testament*, pp. 327–9; Burgon, *The Traditional Text of the Holy Gospels*, pp. 259–78; cf. Strauss, *Das Leben Jesu für das deutsche Volk*, p. 118 (ET, p. 156)), the critical text is to be preferred as the more difficult reading over against the *textus receptus* which has been harmonised to Mark and Luke at this point (discussed further in Tregelles, *An Account of the Printed Text of the Greek New Testament*, pp. 133–8; Hort, 'Notes on Select Readings', in Westcott and Hort, *New Testament*, vol. II, pp. 14–15; Metzger, *Textual Commentary*, p. 49). Conybeare's attempt to reconstruct an earlier form of Jesus' response: μή με λέγε ἀγαθόν ('call me not good') from the evidence of Marcion, Clementine Homilies, Didymus and Ephraem ('Three Early Doctrinal Modifications of the Text of the Gospels', pp. 108–12) has not commanded assent (see esp. Warfield, 'Jesus' Alleged Confession of Sin', pp. 142–45).

This passage has often been regarded as a mainstay of the christological argument for Markan priority, which suggests a christological explanation for the difference between the question of Jesus in Mark: 'Why do you call me good?' and that in Matthew: 'Why do you ask me about the good?' In other words, Matthew alters Mark's text with a view to 'correcting', or, at least, protecting from possible misunderstanding, the implicit suggestion in Mark's potentially embarrassing account, that Jesus is not good (and not God).[1] Other possibilities have been suggested: E. Lohmeyer argued that the differences between the accounts derived from divergent translations of an Aramaic source, and conservative scholars in particular have tended to minimise the perception of christological differences between the two accounts.[2] The majority of commentators have, however, generally agreed that a christological motivation explains Matthew's alteration of Mark here.[3] Indeed, for many scholars there could be no clearer proof of Markan priority; hence F. W. Beare's comment: 'it is totally inconceivable that the Matthean form [of Matthew 19.17] could arise except as a theologically-motivated correction of the Markan text'.[4]

It is also often asserted that Matthew's correction attempt has not been a total success, and results in a less than fully coherent narrative.[5] D. R. Catchpole's brief discussion of this passage highlights the 'tensions' in Matthew's account but concludes that Matthew is secondary to Mark primarily on the grounds of a traditio-historical principle relating to christological development.[6] Nevertheless, the mere existence of such 'tensions' is inconclusive in terms of priority and arguments about priority must derive from the process by which such tensions arose, not simply from their existence. In addition, 'clarity' and 'coherence' are somewhat subjective notions and in any case it is not necessary that an unclear narrative will be later than a clear one. In fact one might argue the opposite: Matthew's rather unclear formulation has been clarified

---

[1] Cf. Gaechter, *Matthäusevangelium*, p. 621.

[2] Lohmeyer, *Matthäus*, pp. 284–5; cf. Warfield, 'Jesus' Alleged Confession of Sin'; Stonehouse, *Origins of the Synoptic Gospels*, pp. 93–112; Carson, 'Matthew', pp. 421–3; 'Redaction Criticism', pp. 135–6.

[3] For a list of scholars see Luck, 'Die Frage nach dem Guten', p. 283.

[4] Beare, 'Review of W. R. Farmer, *The Synoptic Problem*', p. 297; cf. also the firm language of Schweizer, *Matthäus*, pp. 252–3 (ET, p. 387); Grundmann: 'the opposite course is inconceivable' (*TDNT*, vol. I, p. 16).

[5] E.g. Beare, *Matthew*, p. 394; Conybeare: 'bit of botching', attributed to an ancient 'corrector', 'Three Early Doctrinal Modifications of the Text of the Gospels', p. 109.

[6] Catchpole, 'The Synoptic Divorce Material', p. 96; cf. also his 'Tradition History', p. 167.

in the versions of Luke and Mark. Or a different approach might
be pursued (with O. L. Cope): Matthew's narrative presupposes a
certain exegetical background which renders its intention and
meaning clear; Mark and Luke, lacking a knowledge of this background, have simplified the account, and therefore obscured the
meaning of the passage.[7]

In what follows we shall first investigate Matthew's redactional
procedure assuming Markan priority. This will focus on the overall
intentions of the Matthean redaction as well as the christological
question. We shall then make a corresponding analysis of Markan
redaction of Matthew and Luke assuming the Griesbach hypothesis. The initial purpose is to assess the plausibility of this type of
redaction according to the criteria discussed in chapter two. In
both cases the passage will be considered in relation to the
following teaching about discipleship and wealth, which is closely
related to the story of the rich young ruler in all three synoptic
gospels.[8]

2. Matthew's redaction of Mark assuming Markan priority

In this passage the Matthew–Luke agreements against Mark are
minimal, consisting primarily in the agreed omission of some
Markan details, and could not be used to justify a substantial
Mark–Q overlap.[9] Therefore, from the perspective of the two-
source hypothesis, the investigation has to deal with Matthew's
redaction of Mark since there is no evidence for the existence of
additional source material. Matthew's redaction of Mark involves,
despite the omission of many uniquely Markan details, a slight
lengthening of the pericope (116–110–92 words). The overall structure of Matthew's version is similar to Mark's and leads into the
following discussion about discipleship, where Matthew's version is
substantially shorter than Mark's.

The extent to which the overall purpose of the passage is similar in
Matthew and Mark is variously assessed by commentators. B. B.
Warfield, on the one hand, makes them substantially identical; while
U. Luck, on the other hand, detects a fundamental theological-

---

[7] Cope, *Matthew: A Scribe Trained for the Kingdom of Heaven*, pp. 111–19; 'The
Argument Revolves' (discussed below).
[8] Walter, 'Zur Analyse von Mark 10:17–31'; Taylor, *Mark*, p. 425.
[9] Neirynck, *The Minor Agreements of Matthew and Luke Against Mark*, pp. 135–6.

ethical difference between the two accounts.[10] While several of our observations will count against Warfield, Luck also exaggerates the significance of Matthew's omission of the eschatological specificity of Mark 10.30 ('now in this age . . . in the coming age').

As is common, Matthew's introduction includes several favourite 'Matthean' terms, with the result that Matthew's redaction of Mark results in vocabulary that conforms to Matthean preferences.[11] Note, for example, the following:

> ἰδοὺ (62–7–57; for καὶ ἰδού : 2.9; 3.16, 17; 4.11; 8.2, 24, 29, 32, 34; 9.2, 10, 20; 12.10, 41, 42; 15.22; 17.3, 5; 19.16; 20.30; 26.51; 27.51; 28.2, 7, 9, 20);
>
> προσέρχομαι (51–5–10);
>
> εἶπον with a dative (84 times cf. 49 in Mark, not often in this word order; Mark's ἐπηρώτα is less common in Matthew (8–25–17)).

Mark's description of the man's approach and kneeling before Jesus has been described as a 'sign of reverence' which might, by application of a principle of christological development, indicate Matthean priority;[12] but this does not follow: Matthew's presentation of reverential approaches to Jesus is essentially more nuanced than Mark's (see chapter seven); and Matthew consistently omits Markan openings.

Other examples which show Matthew's tendency to omit or significantly abbreviate Markan openings and approaches include Matthew 8.2 || Mark 1.40; Matthew 9.1f || Mark 2.1–4; Matthew 15.21 || Mark 7.24; Matthew 15.32 || Mark 8.1; Matthew 16.24 || Mark 8.34; Matthew 17.22 || Mark 9.30; Matthew 20.17 || Mark 10.32 (whole verses of this type omitted by Matthew include Mark 2.13; 3.20f; 5.21; 6.31). This should probably be regarded as but one aspect of Matthew's general tendency to abbreviate the Markan account of its non-essential (to Matthew!) details. Although Luke does not appear to share the same general tendency to abbreviate, in this case Luke 18.18 agrees with Matthew in omitting the Markan opening.

Matthew also makes significant alterations (underlined) to the man's question and Jesus' response:

---

[10] Warfield, 'Jesus' Alleged Confession of Sin', p. 103; Luck, 'Die Frage nach dem Guten'.
[11] Schnackenburg, *Matthäusevangelium*, p. 183.
[12] Sanders and Davies, *Studying the Synoptic Gospels*, p. 98.

Matthew 19.16f

Διδάσκαλε,
τί ἀγαθὸν ποιήσω
ἵνα σχῶ ζωὴν αἰώνιον;
ὁ δὲ εἶπεν αὐτῷ,
Τί με ἐρωτᾷς περὶ τοῦ ἀγαθοῦ;
εἷς ἐστιν ὁ ἀγαθός.
εἰ δὲ θέλεις εἰς τὴν ζωὴν εἰσελθεῖν,
τήρησον τὰς ἐντολάς.

Mark 10.17–19a

Διδάσκαλε ἀγαθέ,
τί ποιήσω
ἵνα ζωὴν αἰώνιον κληρονομήσω;
ὁ δὲ Ἰησοῦς εἶπεν αὐτῷ,
Τί με λέγεις ἀγαθόν;
οὐδεὶς ἀγαθὸς εἰ μὴ εἷς ὁ θεός.
τὰς ἐντολὰς οἶδας.

Assessing the significance of these alterations is not straightforward. Matthew's alterations in this exchange do not fall into measurable Matthean vocabulary preferences: ἐρωτάω (4–3–16); ἔχω (74–71–78); περί (28–23–45); εἰμι (289–192–361). Furthermore, the transition from the man's question concerning 'a good thing' that he should do, to Jesus' counter-question concerning 'the good', and then to Jesus' statement, 'One is the good', is difficult and obscure. Note especially the transfer from the neuter form used in the two questions, ἀγαθόν, τὸ ἀγαθόν, to the masculine in Jesus' statement, ὁ ἀγαθός. Defenders of the two-source hypothesis find in this process convincing evidence of Matthew's use of Mark: if he were not following Mark why would he introduce such a difficulty? Matthew's Jesus might be accused of missing the question.[13] In addition the sense of a contrast between Jesus and God, often regarded as the problem in the Markan account, is actually retained in Matthew.[14]

Warfield argued that there was no contrast between Jesus and the one who is Good, since the accounts use an enclitic (unaccented) με which might as well be omitted.[15] This approach, however, is not convincing: accentuation of such pronouns is generally an editorial decision (since accents were not in common use before the third century AD), and the use of the shorter enclitic form does not preclude emphasis or at least a positive syntactical function in the sentence.[16]

Thus the Matthean alterations fail the test of vocabulary con-

[13] Wellhausen, *Matthaei*, p. 98.
[14] Hill, *Matthew*, p. 64.
[15] Warfield, 'Jesus' Alleged Confession of Sin', pp. 104–5; cf. also Weiss, *Matthäus-Evangelium*, pp. 339–40.
[16] Robertson, *A Grammar of the Greek New Testament*, pp. 231–3, 682; Winer, *A Treatise on the Grammar of New Testament Greek*, pp. 62–3.

sistency and, at this level, pose a problem for the two-source hypothesis.

Matthew's major alterations emphasise the question of the function of the law since the man's questions, both in v. 16b and v. 18a, suggest that he seeks one specific good work which would bring eternal life. R. J. Banks argued that this one good work is related to Jewish teaching about good works over and above the law.[17] Although a possible conclusion it should be noted, first that the sources refer to plural deeds (*m'śym ṭwbym, b. Ber.* 32b, *b. Sanh.* 99a; *Midr. Qoh.* 2.24; 3.12f; 5.17; 8.15 etc.); secondly that these are not meant to be good deeds 'over and above the law' (Banks' phrase), but alongside, and presumably in obedience to, the law; and thirdly that these 'good deeds' were not in themselves thought sufficient to guarantee entry into the life to come (cf. *b. Sanh.* 99a).

Jesus' response to the man, 'Why do you ask me about the good?', is, as Luck has argued, a question which directs attention to God's requirements (e.g., 'the good' of Amos 5.14f; Mic. 6.8 etc.). Luck, following W. Wagner, noted that the commentators' reflex attribution of Matthean alterations to christological causes has hindered recognition of other elements of Matthew's presentation. He focussed attention on the connection between 'life' and 'good' in the OT (e.g. Deut. 30.15–20; the connection between 'the good way' of Prov. 2.9, 20 and 'the way of life' of Prov. 2.19; 5.6; 6.23; 15.24; 16.17).[18] In particular, he argued, 'One is good' echoes the *shema* (Deut. 6.4), which symbolises, for Israel, the assumption of the yoke of the Torah. Since God alone is good (cf. also Philo, *De mutatione nominum,* 7; *De somniis,* I.149) the question of the availability of life (the good, righteousness) arises. Thus Matthew maintains the same thrust as Mark, but focusses the issue more closely: Jesus directs the man to God's requirements as laid down in the law. In this connection A. Schlatter emphasised the predictability of Jesus' response: God's will for Israel is not a riddle, it is clear.[19]

In the following text Matthew continues the dialogue, adding to

---

[17] Banks, *Jesus and the Law in Synoptic Tradition,* p. 160 (citing Str-B, vol. I, pp. 808ff, vol. IV, pp. 536ff, 559ff).

[18] Luck, 'Die Frage nach dem Guten'; cf. Wagner, 'In welchem Sinne hat Jesus das Prädikat ΑΓΑΘΟΣ von sich abgewiesen?'.

[19] *Der Evangelist Matthäus,* p. 577; cf. also Moore, *Judaism,* vol. II, p. 321. This interpretation is anticipated in Tertullian, *Adversus Marcionem* IV.36.

Jesus' response a further question; formally the resultant narrative could be described as a *Schulegespräche*, a scholastic dialogue.[20]

Such transformation of narrative into direct speech is relatively common in Matthew (cf. Matt. 3.2 // Mark 1.4; Matt. 6.31 // Luke 12.29; Matt. 8.6 // Luke 7.2; Matt. 8.32 // Mark 5.13; Matt. 10.9–10 // Mark 6.8–9; Matt. 12.10 // Mark 3.2; Matt. 13.10 // Mark 4.10; Matt. 14.2 // Mark 6.14 (although cf. *v.l.*); Matt. 15.15 // Mark 7.17; Matt. 15.22 and 25 // Mark 7.25–6; Matt. 17.9 // Mark 9.9; Matt. 18.1 // Mark 9.34; Matt. 26.1–2 // Mark 14.1; Matt. 26.15 // Mark 14.10; Matt. 26.27 // Mark 14.23; Matt. 26.66 // Mark 14.64; Matt. 27.23 // Mark 15.14).[21]

The effect of these additions is to reinforce and interpret the man's initial question. By repeating the man's goal in slightly different terms – εἰσελθεῖν εἰς τὴν ζωὴν is the equivalent of 'having eternal life' or participating in the world to come[22] Matthew emphasises the clear statement which follows: τήρησον τὰς ἐντολάς (τηρέω: 6–1–0), a form of expression which is common in the OT (e.g. Gen. 26.5; Exod. 20.6; Lev. 18.4; Deut. 4.2; 26.18; 1 Kings 2.3; 1 Chron. 28.7; Ps. 119.4ff). Jesus then directs the man to specific commandments, adding love of neighbour to Mark's account. Matthew's version (οὐ + future) is closer to the LXX of Exodus 20.13–16 and Deuteronomy 5.17–20 (and *Didache* 2.1) than Mark's. The omission of μὴ ἀποστερήσῃς by both Matthew and Luke (and some mss of Mark) is presumably due to its absence from the decalogue list.[23] This addition *is* characteristic of Matthew's overall presentation (cf. 5.43ff; 22.39; cf. Lev. 19.18).

Matthew also restructures Jesus' response in v. 21 (note the relatively unusual transformation of a word of Jesus into a question from the man: τί ἔτι ὑστερῶ;). This restructuring creates a parallel with v17: Εἰ θέλεις εἶναι ... Several of these terms reflect Matthean preferences: φημί (16–6–8); θέλω (42–25–28); τέλειος (3–0–0). The 'perfection' of which Matthew speaks is not a higher plane of discipleship,[24] but refers to attaining 'eternal life' through following Jesus: the man's question 'what do I still lack?' relates back to entering into eternal life, his failure and sadness are not due

---

[20] Bultmann, *Die Geschichte der synoptischen Tradition*, p. 57 (ET, p. 54).

[21] Cf. Sanders, *Tendencies*, pp. 260–1.

[22] Cf. Mark 9.43–5; Matt. 7.14; 18.8; Dan. 12.2; *Pss. Sol.* 3.12; 13.11; 14.10; 15.15; 1 Enoch 58.3; 103.4; 2 Enoch 50.2; 2 Macc. 7.9, 36; 4 Macc 15.3; *T. Jud.* 25.1; CD 3.20; 1QS 4.7; Moore, *Judaism*, vol. II, p. 94; Bultmann, *TDNT*, vol. II, p. 859.

[23] On the order of the commandments see McNeile, *Matthew*, p. 278.

[24] Against many earlier commentators (e.g. Wellhausen, *Matthaei*, p. 98; Klostermann, *Matthäusevangelium*, p. 158; Holtzmann, *Die Synoptiker*, p. 268) and Cope, *Matthew: A Scribe Trained for the Kingdom of Heaven*, p. 116.

to missing out on an elite discipleship; rather, as Matthew shows, following Jesus is a requirement for inheriting eternal life (v. 29).[25] 'Perfection' in Matthew (as at Qumran) 'is the decisive character-istic of the new community'.[26] Thus θησαυρὸν ἐν οὐρανοῖς, although here picked up from Mark, is already defined in Matthew 6.19f, as the antithesis of earthly treasure: 'treasure in heaven' was a well-known description of the rewards of obedience to God's commands, and is, in several places, a concept that is parallel to 'life' – a further indication that Matthew is not interested in presenting a two-stage approach to perfection.

> Parallels include: 'Lay up your treasure according to the commandments of the Most High, and it will profit you more than gold' (Sir. 29.11); cf. Ezra's 'treasure of works' (4 Ezra 7.77; cf. 8.33); the 'store of good works' (2 Bar. 14.12; 24.1). It is often (as in Matthew) associated predominantly with almsgiving (cf. Tob. 4.8f; Hauck, *TDNT* vol. III, p. 137). Note also *Pss. Sol.* 9.5: 'He that does righteousness lays up (θησαυρίζει) for himself life with the Lord'; cf. 2 Bar 14.13; 24.1. An instructive parallel is offered in *m. Pe'a* 1.1: 'These are the things whose fruits a man enjoys in this world while the capital is laid up for him in the world to come: honouring father and mother, deeds of loving-kindness, making peace between a man and his fellow; and the study of the Law is equal to them all.' Here participation in fruits of *h'wlm hb'* is for those who obey the command-ments (the same ones that Jesus selects).

As Luck has argued, whatever legitimacy might attach to the christological theory of Matthean redaction, it does not provide a *sufficient* explanation for *all* of the changes introduced by Matthew and the overall emphasis of the passage.[27] From the evidence adduced by Luck it becomes clear that Matthew's sharper focus on 'the good' can be explained as arising from his concern to empha-sise God's requirement of obedience to the law. This in turn may not provide a complete explanation for the Matthean redaction, and it is certainly possible that Matthew also saw the advantage of avoiding the christological conclusion that might (in his view

---

[25] See further Barth, 'Das Gesetzesverständnis des Evangelisten Matthäus', pp. 89–93 (ET, pp. 96–9); Trilling, *Das wahre Israel*, pp. 192–4; Davies, *The Setting of the Sermon on the Mount*, pp. 210–13; du Plessis, *ΤΕΛΕΙΟΣ: The Idea of Perfection in the New Testament*, p. 172; Ridderbos, *The Coming of the Kingdom*, p. 293; Schweizer, *Matthäus*, p. 253 (ET, p. 388).

[26] Barth, 'Das Gesetzesverständnis des Evangelisten Matthäus', p. 93 (ET, p. 99); cf. the well-known passages in 1QS 1.8f; 2.2; 4.22; 8.1, 20; 9.19 (cited by Barth), see further du Plessis, *ΤΕΛΕΙΟΣ: The Idea of Perfection in the New Testament*, pp. 104–15; Schnackenburg, 'Die Vollkommenheit des Christen nach den Evangelien'; Gnilka, 'Die Kirche des Matthäus und die Gemeinde von Qumran', pp. 57–62.

[27] Luck, 'Die Frage nach dem Guten', p. 284; also Banks, *Jesus and the Law in Synoptic Tradition*, pp. 160–4.

wrongly) be drawn from Mark's account. Nevertheless, it is clear that the christological explanation is neither a necessary nor a sufficient means of accounting for the Matthean redaction according to the two-source hypothesis.

The explanation based on highlighting the place of the law has the advantage of offering a common explanation for many of the redactional features of Matthew's account. In addition it is an explanation which is in harmony with other aspects of Matthew's gospel; and with at least one later redactor of Matthew, as the version of this story in *Gos. Naz.*, which is probably a revision of Matthew, also displays a redactional interest in the Law, explaining the command to go and sell all as an application of Leviticus 19.18.[28]

3. Griesbach-Mark's redaction of Matthew and Luke

According to Griesbach, Mark at this point followed Matthew, but had Luke at hand as well.[29] Evidence from the triple tradition makes it clear that Griesbach-Mark should be envisaged as having knowledge of both his sources, with sequential parallels between both Mark and Luke (fourteen words in Mark 10.18: Τί με λέγεις ἀγαθόν; οὐδεὶς ἀγαθὸς εἰ μὴ εἷς ὁ θεός τὰς ἐντολὰς οἶδας, note also the preceding pericope Mark 10.15 // Luke 18.17: eighteen identical words); and, to a lesser degree, between Mark and Matthew (thirteen words in Mark 10.21: καὶ δὺς [τοῖς] πτωχοῖς, καὶ ἕξεις θησαυρὸν ἐν οὐρανῷ, καὶ δεῦρο ἀκολούθει μοι, and seven words in Mark 10.22: ἀπῆλθεν λυπούμενος, ἦν γὰρ ἔχων κτήματα πολλά).

A superficial examination might suggest that Mark shifts from following Luke at the beginning of the pericope to Matthew at the end, but there is additional evidence against this conclusion. Griesbach-Mark reproduces words that are found only in Matthew in v. 17 (εἰς, ἵνα), v. 20 (αὐτῷ), as well as v. 21f (ὑστερεῖ is loosely paralleled in Matthew, as is τῷ λόγῳ). In addition he reproduces words found only in Luke in v. 17 (ἐπηρώτα [Luke: ἐπηρώτησέν] αὐτόν), v. 18 ('Ιησοῦς), v. 19 (four uses of μή, verb endings parallel, σου), v. 20 (ὁ δὲ, ἐκ νεότητός), v. 21 (εἶπεν, ἕν, ὅσα ἔχεις).

---

28 Origen, *Comm. on Matt.* XV.14 (Latin), cf. *NTA*, vol. I, pp. 148–9; see further Klijn, 'The Question of the Rich Young Man in a Jewish-Christian Gospel'.

29 Griesbach, 'Demonstration', n. 35, p. 211.

In terms of the order of this and the surrounding passages Mark agrees with both Matthew and Luke. In terms of wording we must reckon with a fairly complex redactional process. Griesbach-Mark makes no major omissions of material common to Matthew and Luke, although he does omit details from one or the other. In terms of additions, material unique to Mark, there are several noteworthy phrases.

Mark's introduction contains an expanded version of the man's approach to Jesus: ἐκπορευομένου αὐτοῦ εἰς ὁδὸν προσδραμὼν εἰς καὶ γονυπετήσας αὐτόν.[30] This expansion contains typically Markan vocabulary – ἐκπορεύομαι (6–11–3); ὁδός (22–16–20); προστρέχω (0–2–0); γονυπετέω (2–2–0) – and grammatical forms: Griesbach-Mark regularly uses the genitive absolute in redactional additions to either Matthew or Luke when introducing a new story/ pericope (cf. 4.35; 5.2, 21; 6.2, 54; 8.1; 10.17; 10.46 (diff. Matt. 20.29); 11.11b, 12, 27; 13.1; 14.3, 66). In other introductions he reproduces a genitive absolute found in one or both of his sources (5.35; 9.9; 13.3; 14.22, 43; 15.42).[31] The new introduction serves to link this passage more tightly into Mark's 'Way' narrative (8.27– 10.45: characterised by passion predictions and teaching about discipleship 'on the way' to Jerusalem). Indeed, on the Griesbach hypothesis, while features of this section of Mark's narrative are derived from Matthew, the consistent use of ἐν τῇ ὁδῷ throughout (8.27; 9.33, 34 (v.l.); 10.32 (here fronted in relation to Matthew's use in 20.17); 10.52) is a distinctly Markan device, perhaps deriving ultimately from Exodus 23.20 or Isaiah 40.3 (cf. Mark 1.2f).[32] The action of kneeling is a mark of reverence but since in this case the man fails to respond to Jesus (and does not join him 'in the way') it should not be taken as an indication of the man's faith (cf. 10.22). A popular interpretation of the passage involves the suggestion that Mark's description of the man's approach reveals that he was insincerely flattering Jesus.[33] A difficulty with this view is that in

[30] Best: the first five words are redactional (*Following Jesus*, p. 110); cf. Bultmann, *Die Geschichte der synoptischen Tradition*, p. 20 (ET, p. 22).

[31] See also Pryke, *Redactional Style in the Marcan Gospel*, pp. 62–3; and (less clearly) Peabody, *Mark as Composer*, p. 93 (§177), p. 103 (§217), p. 105 (§227).

[32] For discussion see Swartley, 'The Structural Function of the Term "Way" (*Hodos*) in Mark's Gospel' (with bibliographical survey); Watts, 'The Influence of the Isaianic New Exodus on the Gospel of Mark', pp. 61–4; Marcus, *The Way of the Lord*, pp. 31–41.

[33] Stonehouse, *Origins of the Synoptic Gospels*, p. 107; Dalman, *Die Worte Jesu*, p. 277 (cf. ET, p. 337), particularly re 'good teacher'.

other places Mark clearly indicates an insincere enquirer, often stating the motives behind certain actions (3.2; 8.11; 12.13ff). Mark's addition of his favoured διδάσκαλε in v. 20 (11–12–14) could be taken, not as an addition of great christological importance, but as a device to link the two statements made by the man.

Two other additions occur in the second part of the passage. Firstly, the description of Jesus' love for the man: ὁ δὲ Ἰησοῦς ἐμβλέψας αὐτῶ ἠγάπησεν αὐτὸν καὶ εἶπεν αὐτῷ (10.21 Markan additions underlined). Secondly, the description of the man's response: ὁ δὲ στυγνάσας ἐπὶ τῷ λόγῳ (10.22). While these additions might all contribute to Markan verisimilitude,[34] there is no indication that they contribute specifically to the christological intention of the author. Among the neo-Griesbachians Mann thinks that Mark had another (Petrine) source in addition to Matthew and Luke; while Farmer regards this type of addition as 'characteristic of second century Apocryphal Gospel literature' and thus as evidence that Mark is later than Matthew and Luke.[35]

For the crucial initial dialogue between the man and Jesus Griesbach-Mark follows Luke rather than Matthew. Mark's narrative forms a relatively coherent whole which is normally classified as a typical apophthegm, or pronouncement story.[36] The man's approach, and initial statement, utilises the practically unprecedented 'good teacher' – there is only one parallel in the Talmud (*b. Ta'an* 24b, fourth or fifth century), although 'good man' appears in the OT (Prov. 12.2; 14.14; Eccl. 9.2; cf. also *T. Sim* 4.4; *T. Dan*. 1.4; *T. Ash*. 4.1), and elsewhere in Jesus' teaching (Matt. 12.35; Luke 6.45). This statement receives a response from Jesus that takes up that unusual designation and redirects the man's attention to God and his commandments. The progress of the narrative shows that the discussion focusses, not on Jesus himself, but on ἀγαθός and the requirements for entry into life.[37] In other words, as most commentators now insist, the questions of Jesus' moral goodness, or deity, are not raised in Mark. Some support for this position could be drawn from J. Jeremias' argument that the

---

[34] Best, *Following Jesus*, p. 115, n. 6.
[35] Mann, *Mark*, p. 399; Farmer, *The Synoptic Problem*, p. 134.
[36] Bultmann, *Die Geschichte der synoptischen Tradition*, p. 20–1 (ET, pp. 21–2); Taylor, *The Formation of the Gospel Tradition*, p. 64; Dibelius classified it as a less than pure form, designated as 'paradigm', *Der Formgeschichte des Evangeliums*, p. 40 (ET, p. 43).
[37] Bishop, 'A Suggestion', p. 365.

antithetic parallelism of question and response places the stress on the second part of Jesus' answer.[38]

Nevertheless a degree of contrast between Jesus on the one hand and God and his law on the other cannot be discounted, and is essential to the argument of the passage.[39] There is a positive christological point in that the ultimate requirement for eternal life is following Jesus (10.21) and v. 30 brings the teaching that follows to conclusion with a form of *inclusio*: eternal life is guaranteed for those who forsake all for Jesus' sake. Jesus directs the man's attention firstly to the requirements of God's law and subsequently to the further requirement of following Jesus. In the following verses Griesbach-Mark intensifies the difficulty, even impossibility, of entering life (10.24) in order to emphasise the grace of God at work among those who follow Jesus (10.26). The main point of the passage, revealed in the conclusion in v. 30f, is the nature of discipleship.

Beyond those things mentioned above there is no indication that Griesbach-Mark has imposed any particular perspective on the material by his redactional activity. In addition, although many of the additions conform to vocabulary preferences, and Mark's tendency to add details, there is no obvious overall christological point. That is not to say that Markan additions might not reflect his own christological perspective, rather it suggests that Griesbach-Mark's redaction does not clearly reveal that perspective.

Griesbach-Mark's decision to follow the Lukan rather than Matthean version of the man's question and Jesus' reply is readily defensible. In the first place Luke's account is arguably clearer than Matthew's, and Mark's choice corresponds to that made by Tatian, who chose the Mark–Luke version over against the Matthean for inclusion in the *Diatessaron* (see Arabic 28.42–51 also present in Ephraem's commentary and the Persian).[40] This is also true of a wide range of NT manuscripts which alter Matthew's version in order to bring it into conformity with the Mark-Luke version (these include at Matt. 19.17: C W Δ E F G H etc. fam[13] syr[p] cop[sa]

---

[38] Jeremias, *Neutestamentliche Theologie 1*, pp. 28–9 (ET, pp. 18–19); see Mark 3.33f parallels; 8.12; 11.17; Matt 7.3–5 parallels; 10.23 parallels; 12.27 parallels; Luke 12.51; 22.35.

[39] Taylor, *Mark*, p. 426; Banks, *Jesus and the Law*, p. 161; Cope, *Matthew: A Scribe Trained for the Kingdom of Heaven*, p. 111; Stonehouse, *Origins of the Synoptic Gospels*, pp. 93–108; Lane, *Mark*, pp. 365–6.

[40] Ephraem XV.1f (in both Syriac and Armenian) Persian (II.39), see further Head, 'Tatian's Christology', pp. 134–5 and n. 61.

cop^{bo(pt)}; Irenaeus).[41] Granted that Matthew's text tended to dominate in harmonising variants this is a remarkable and early series of witnesses to scribes who also chose the Mark–Luke version of the question of Jesus. A further witness to such a choice might be Justin (*Apology* I. 16.7), who appears to know Matthew's introduction to the narrative (καὶ προσελθόντος αὐτῷ τινος καὶ εἰπόντος . . .) but gives a form of the man's question and Jesus' answer which is closer to Mark–Luke (διδάσκαλε ἀγαθέ . . . οὐδεὶς ἀγαθὸς εἰ μὴ μόνος ὁ θεός . . .).[42]

This evidence shows that the choice made by Griesbach-Mark between the available alternatives corresponds exactly with analogous choices made during the second century by other editors of the gospels. Furthermore, a survey of patristic comments on this passage suggests that the problem provoked by the passage was not so much the sinlessness of Jesus (from 'Why do you call me good?'), but the contrast drawn between Jesus and God, summed up in the phrase: 'None is good save one, even God.' Certainly it was this contrast, which is common to both Matthew and Mark–Luke, which needed explanation.

> See Clement, *Paed.*, I. viii (p. 227); Origen, *Contra Celsum* V.11, *Comm. on John* II.7 (cf. IX.28); Macarius Magnes, *Apocriticus* II.ix (Crafer, pp. 34–5); Chrysostom, *Hom. on Matt.* LXIII; Gregory of Nyssa, *Against Eunomius* XI.2. The issue of Jesus' goodness is, of course, raised on occasion, particularly by Marcion (acc. Hippolytus, *Haer*. VII.31.19; Origen, *First Principles* II.v.1; cf. also *Clem. Hom.* XVIII.1–3; Augustine, *Sermon* XL).

Before any preliminary conclusions can be drawn from this discussion we must turn briefly to an alternative description of a Griesbachian approach to this pericope.

4. O. L. Cope on Matthew 19.16–22 and parallels

Cope has recently argued for the priority of Matthew 19.16–22 in relation to Mark and Luke on the grounds that Matthew's version follows an existing exegetical tradition relating to the function of

---

[41] Also noticed by Cope, *Matthew: A Scribe Trained for the Kingdom of Heaven*, p. 119 n. 56; 'The Argument Revolves', p. 153.

[42] Cf. also Justin, *Dialogue with Trypho*, 101 (quoting the same passage). Massaux suggested that Justin combined elements of Matthew and Luke (*Influence de l'Evangile de saint Matthien sur la littérature chrétienne avant saint Irénée* , p. 486 (ET, vol. III, pp. 28–9)).

Torah and utilising texts from Proverbs 3.35–4.4.[43] On this basis Matthean priority is more probable because the versions of Mark and Luke are ignorant of the subtle allusions involved. In this way Cope seeks to bypass the christological argument: 'the theological importance of the passage, whether attractive or offensive, ought to play no role in the decision about the issue of literary priority' ('The Argument Revolves', p. 151).

Cope observes that the passage encompasses discussion of a number of key concepts: entrance into the life to come, the good, the commandments and the perfect. He suggests that 'there is good evidence that this particular combination of ideas stems from Jewish discussions of the function of the Torah in connection with Prov 3:35–4:4' (*Matthew: A Scribe Trained for the Kingdom of Heaven*, p. 112). He argues that *m. 'Abot* 6.3 attests precisely such an exegetical tradition in which honour = good; good = the law; therefore honour = the law:

> And 'honour' is naught else than 'the Law', for it is written, *The wise shall inherit honour*, and *The perfect shall inherit good*; and 'good' is naught else than 'the Law', for it is written, *For I give you good doctrine; forsake ye not my Law*.

Cope's argument, however, is fraught with problems. First, this tradition is probably very late, since it is generally agreed that the sixth chapter of *m. 'Abot* was not part of the earliest collection.[44] Cope suggests four reasons why this particular tradition should be regarded as ancient:

(i)   it is connected with either R. Meir (AD 140–65), or R. Joshua b. Levi (AD 240–70);

> However, while *m. 'Abot* 6.1 is connected with R. Meir and 6.2 is attributed to R. Joshua b. Levi, this does not mean that 6.3 should be connected with either of these. There is no statement of continuation (such as that normally used to continue attribution from a previous saying 'he used to say . . .' *m. 'Abot* 1.13, 14; 2.4, 6, 9, 16; 3.11, 15, 17; 4.3, 8, 17, 22; 5.21); rather 6.3 is the first of five passages which are not connected with any particular individual. In other words the passage is an unattributed saying in a document that could well be dated after AD 1000.

---

[43]   Cope, *Matthew: A Scribe Trained for the Kingdom of Heaven*, pp. 111–19; 'The Argument Revolves'; supported by Farmer, 'Introduction', pp. xxv–xxvi.

[44]   Danby, *The Mishnah*, p. 458, n. 12; Herford, *Pirke Aboth*, pp. 149–50 (citing Rashi and Maimonides); Strack and Stemberger, *Introduction to the Talmud and Midrash*, p. 129.

(ii)   a similar tradition associated with R. Johanan (*c.* AD 200)
       appears in *b. Ber.* 5a;

> However, the parallel in *b. Ber.* 5a is not a substantial one; in a discussion
> of Psalm 39.3 R. Johanan explains: ' "The good thing" refers only to the
> Torah, as it is said *For I give you good doctrine; forsake ye not My
> teaching.*' A similar tradition (interpreting the 'good doctrine' of Prov. 4.2
> as the Torah) is also found in the following saying (R. Zera, although
> some say R. Hanina b. Papa, *c.* AD 300). Clearly, there is no mention of
> the other themes (life, inheritance etc.), the conclusion to be drawn is
> simply that the Rabbis had read Proverbs 4.2 in Hebrew and drew the
> conclusion that the 'good precepts' (*lqh twb*) given to Israel in the first
> phrase were to be identified with 'my teaching' (*trwty*, lit. 'my Torah') in
> the second, parallel phrase.

(iii) the basic equations that Cope focusses on (i.e. honour = -
       good, good = law, honour = law) appear (in *m. 'Abot* 6.3) as
       independent (and therefore pre-existing) traditions ap-
       pended to the discussion;

> This is unsupported assertion and is hardly self-evident.

(iv)   the parallels with Matthew suggest the early existence of
       this tradition.

> This is a circular argument and depends on assuming what Cope is trying
> to prove.

Cope's argument depends not on the general conviction that the
Torah was good, nor even on the possibility of the more general
parallel 'the good = the Torah' (cf. Prov. 28.10: *ynhlw twb*), but on
the more extensive progression he outlined. As this cannot be
established as an early tradition Cope's attempt to list parallels
between Matthew and this tradition ('the good', 'the law', 'inheritance', 'perfect') falls into a type of 'parallelomania': many of the
parallels he suggests are conceptually quite different. For example,
in the exegetical tradition of *m. 'Abot* 6.3 the inheritance is received
in this life in the form of Torah, but in Matthew the inheritance is
eternal life (in the age to come). Further the whole nature of the
discussions in each of the two places is widely divergent.[45]

Thus Cope's particular argument that Matthew's ὁ ἀγαθός refers
to the Torah has not been established (he translates: 'The Good
[the Torah] is one'; *Matthew: A Scribe Trained for the Kingdom of
Heaven*, p. 114). While he rightly acknowledges the importance of

---

[45] Sandmel: 'two passages may sound the same in splendid isolation from their
context, but when seen in context reflect difference rather than similarity'
('Parallelomania', p. 2).

passages such as Proverbs 4.4; Deuteronomy 30.15; Psalm 119.39 (see our discussion), this does not establish the coherence of Matthew's account over against Mark and Luke. Cope argues that it is more likely that Mark and/or Luke had difficulty with the passage, and in ignorance of the exegetical tradition altered it, than that Matthew found the elements of the story in Mark and constructed his version from it:

> Faced with Matthew's version, ignorant of its subtle allusions and puzzled by a grammatical difficulty, either Mark or Luke revised the introduction to the passage and thus destroyed the exegetical tradition, the logic of the story, and the formal structure.
>
> ('The Argument Revolves', p. 153; less forcefully in *Matthew: A Scribe Trained for the Kingdom of Heaven*, p. 118)

The evidence he has adduced for this conclusion is, however, insubstantial and unpersuasive.

5.   Conclusion

It does not seem that the high value placed on this passage as a proof of Markan priority has been fully substantiated by our discussion. First, on the Griesbach hypothesis, Mark's redactional choices are explicable and, on the basis of other similar choices, broadly plausible, and in general occur within recognisably 'Markan' parameters. The two-source hypothesis can also readily explain the phenomena of this passage as also generally within recognisably 'Matthean' parameters, although the importance of Matthew's interest in the law in his redaction of the passage has probably been underplayed in many recent treatments, perhaps as a result of scholarly preoccupation with the christological questions. Within the broader context of the whole passage neither hypothesis demands or even suggests that christological factors have been particularly important. The common assumption that Matthew's alteration of Jesus' response to the man (Matt. 19.17) is a redactional evasion of the christological implications of Mark 10.18 does not cohere with the positive emphasis within Matthew's version of the account or with comparative evidence of later preferences in the manuscripts and Tatian. Once Markan priority became established it was natural to read Matthew's changes as significant, but these changes do not yield a conclusive argument for Markan priority unless certain other conditions about the development of christology (which is not otherwise in evidence) are assumed. Thus in our opinion this passage does not yield firm conclusions in support of one or other of the hypotheses.

4

JESUS' REJECTION AT NAZARETH (MATT. 13.53–8; MARK 6.1–6a)

1. Introduction

This passage has often been cited in connection with the christological argument for Markan priority because of the difference between Mark's statement: 'he could do no mighty work there . . . and he marvelled because of their unbelief' (6.5–6a), which suggests that Jesus was *unable* to perform miracles in Nazareth; and Matthew's: 'he did not do many mighty works there, because of their unbelief' (13.58), which avoids the implication of Jesus' *inability*.[1]

In addition, defenders of the Griesbach hypothesis have cited another part of the same pericope; suggesting that Mark 6.3, 'is this not the carpenter, the son of Mary . . .', is a christological revision of Matthew's description of Jesus as 'son of the carpenter' (13.55) in order to make the statement compatible with the virgin birth. F. Bleek, for example, argued that Mark 'shrank, upon reverential and religious grounds, from putting into the mouth of even unbelieving Jews a description of Jesus [as in Matthew and Luke] which represented Him as merely the son of an earthly father'.[2] S. Davidson, supported by Farmer, argued that Mark's version agreed better with the virgin birth than does either Matthew or Luke.[3] More recently E. P. Sanders and M. Davies made the general comment that 'Matthew here looks less pious [than Mark]'.[4]

---

[1] Hawkins, *Horae Synopticae*, p. 96; Allen, *Matthew*, pp. xxxi–xxxii; Streeter, *The Four Gospels*, p. 162; cf. above chapter one, section three.

[2] Bleek, *Einleitung in das Neuen Testament*, p. 192 (cited from ET, vol. I, p. 266).

[3] Davidson, *An Introduction to the Study of the New Testament*, pp. 499–500; Farmer, *The Synoptic Problem*, p. 231.

[4] Sanders and Davies, *Studying the Synoptic Gospels*, p. 98.

2. Matthew's redaction of Mark assuming Markan priority

Although it is possible that portions of Luke 4.16–30 came from Q,[5] there is little evidence, with the possible exception of Matthew 13.55a // Luke 4.22c, that this has influenced Matthew here. Our investigation will therefore have to regard Matthew as a revision of Mark as no additional source seems likely. E. Grässer seems representative in arguing that although oral tradition exerted an influence 'the story shaped by Mark represents the starting point for his co-redactors'.[6]

Matthew's general procedure is relatively clear. He has abbreviated the three miracle stories which immediately precede this account (Mark 4.35–5.43) and grouped them together with others in chapters 8 and 9. After that departure, Matthew returns to Mark's order at this point. Indeed, with the exception of Mark 6.6b–13 (which Matthew includes in ch. 10), Matthew will now follow Mark's order more or less faithfully for the remainder of the gospel. Thus the placement of the story in Matthew, the last of his significant rearrangements of the Markan order, might be significant, showing that failure to understand owing to 'hardness of heart' (as reflected in the parables of Matt. 13) leads directly to rejection.[7] Matthew thus prepares his readers for opposition to Jesus from those represented in this passage.

Matthew 13.53–8 is shorter than Mark 6.1–6a (107—125 words), and this abbreviation has been accompanied by a restructuring of the passage, although the basic outline of events (which is essentially the same story of rejection by Jesus' own πατρίς) remains the same.

Many of Matthew's alterations to Mark are explicable in terms of his clear stylistic and literary preferences. Verse 53 functions as a link-verse, concluding the parables (τὰς παραβολὰς ταύτας) and signalling the beginning of a new section (as do the other such links in 7.28; 11.1 with μετέβη ἐκεῖθεν; 19.1 with μετῆρεν; and 26.1).[8] Rather than Mark's ἐξῆλθεν Matthew uses μετῆρεν (a term which

---

[5] Tuckett, 'Luke 4,16–30, Isaiah and Q' (vv. 16–21, 23, 25–7); cf. Schürmann, *Lukasevangelium*, vol. I, pp. 241–4; Marshall, *Luke*, p. 179.

[6] Grässer, 'Jesus in Nazareth (Mark VI. 1–6a)', p. 7.

[7] Cf. Davies and Allison, *Matthew*, vol. II, p. 453.

[8] So originally Streeter, *The Four Gospels*, p. 252; also Bultmann, *Die Geschichte der synoptischen Tradition*, p. 359 (ET, p. 334): Matthew uses them as transitions from Q back to Mark; Kingsbury, *Matthew: Structure, Christology, Kingdom*, pp. 6–7; Bauer, *The Structure of Matthew's Gospel*, p. 129.

in the NT only occurs in Matt. 13.53 and 19.1; cf. also μεταβαίνω, another verb of motion compounded with μετα- : (5–0–0)); and substitutes ἐλθών for Mark's ἔρχεται (cf. similar alterations from historic present to aorist participle in Matt. 8.2: προσελθών; 9.18, 23; 21.23; and to an aorist indicative: 8.34; 14.25; 19.2; 21.12, 23; 22.23; 26.69; 28.1).

Matthew also omits Mark's phrase: καὶ ἀκολουθοῦσιν αὐτῷ οἱ μαθηταὶ αὐτοῦ. This is unusual, as in several other places Matthew redactionally introduces 'the disciples' (8.23; 9.19, 37; 10.1; 11.1 etc.). There are two possible explanations for this omission. First, it has been suggested that Matthew wanted to emphasise the isolation of Jesus at the moment of rejection: 'Matthew sets Jesus by himself, in the face of a hostile audience.'[9] A difficulty with this view is that Matthew elsewhere specifically signals the isolation of Jesus (14.23; 26.44). Even in 14.13 it is probable that the disciples are understood to be with Jesus (cf. 14.15);[10] furthermore κατ' ἰδίαν means 'privately' (17.1, 19; 20.17; 24.3; Acts 23.19; Gal. 2.2; 2 Macc. 14.21), rather than 'alone', and is the opposite of 'publicly' (κατὰ κοινόν, Josephus, Antiquities IV.310; 2 Macc. 4.5; cf. BAGD, p. 370). Since the flow of Matthew's narrative indicates the presence of the disciples in 13.36 and 51 it is difficult to be persuaded of this explanation (only those who read Matthew alongside Mark could get the point).

A second possible explanation arises from the observation that it is not common for Matthew to describe the disciples as 'following' Jesus (only once, in 8.23); generally they come to Jesus (προσέρχομαι 5.1; 13.10, 36; 14.12, 15; 15.12, 23; 17.19; 18.1; 24.1, 3), and the crowd(s) or other individuals 'follow' Jesus (ἀκολουθέω 4.25; 8.1; 9.9, 19, 27; 12.15; 14.13; 19.2; 20.29, 34; 21.9; 27.55). The twelve (οἱ μαθηταὶ αὐτοῦ) have followed Jesus in the sense that they have entered into a particular relationship with him (4.20, 22; 9.9; cf. 19.27f; 10.1–4), while Jesus' call to 'follow me' is directed to those outside (8.22; 9.9; 19.21). In other words, it is possible that Matthew chose to avoid a mode of expression that was not particularly appropriate after chapter 10. Thus it is not enough simply to count occurrences of words (μαθητής: 73–46–37; ἀκολουθέω: 25–18–17), one must consider the Matthean usage of such words.

---

[9] Beare, Matthew, p. 319; also Oberlinner, Historische Überlieferung und christologische Aussage, p. 352.
[10] So, for example, Davies and Allison, Matthew, vol. II, p. 486.

Matthew's other alterations can be understood in the light of his tendency to omit non-essential items (e.g. 'on the sabbath'). Matthew characteristically adds αὐτῶν to 'the synagogue' (cf. 4.23; 9.35; 10.17; 12.9 cf. Mark 3.1; 13.54 cf. Mark 6.2; 23.34[11]). He abbreviates the first question (v.54b), although he balances this by reintroducing a similar question in v.56 (πόθεν οὖν τούτῳ ταῦτα πάντα;). This results in a neatly structured account,[12] which focusses more closely the identity of Jesus and the source of his teaching and miraculous activity, which suggests that the central section (v.55, 56a) was regarded as important for Matthew. Notably, it is only in these verses that Matthew does not abbreviate Mark's version but expands it (34–28 words).

These central verses contain two significant differences from Mark: first, Jesus is called ὁ τοῦ τέκτονος υἱός (rather than ὁ τέκτων ὁ υἱός), a reading which is textually relatively secure, certainly in comparison with Mark, although some scribes identified Jesus' father by name; syr[s] substitutes 'Joseph' for τέκτονος, syr[c] and OL – 'the son of Joseph the carpenter'. Secondly, instead of 'the son of Mary', Matthew has a further question: οὐχ ἡ μήτηρ αὐτοῦ λέγεται Μαριάμ; These alterations have often been attributed to Matthew's christological concerns, but the nature of these concerns has been variously described since, as U. Luz notes, the reasons for the alterations are not clear.[13] A number of possibilities have been suggested.

First, a number of scholars have argued that 'son of Mary' was offensive, perhaps implying that Jesus was illegitimate.[14] However, both H. K. McArthur and T. Ilan have offered decisive evidence *against* the assumption that identification by the mother's name 'conferred an air of odium on the man so designated'.[15]

Secondly, some scholars have argued Matthew wanted to avoid the description of Jesus as a carpenter.[16] This has the advantage of

[11] Segbroeck, 'Jésus rejeté par sa patrie (Mt 13,54–58)', pp. 173–4.
[12] Segbroeck, 'Jésus rejeté par sa patrie (Mt 13,54–58)'; Luz, *Matthäus*, vol. II, pp. 383–4; Davies and Allison, *Matthew*, vol. II, pp. 451–2; Lagrange, *Matthieu*, p. 284 notes the *inclusio*.
[13] Luz, *Matthäus*, vol. II, p. 384.
[14] E.g. Beare, *Matthew*, p. 319; Klostermann, *Matthäusevangelium*, p. 126; Stauffer, 'Jeschu ben Mirjam'.
[15] McArthur, 'Son of Mary'; Ilan, ' "Man Born of Woman . . ." ' (Job 14:1). The Phenomenon of Men Bearing Metronymes at the Time of Jesus' (quotation from p. 24).
[16] Holtzmann, *Die synoptischen Evangelien*, p. 52; Allen, *Matthew*, p. 155; BAGD, p. 809; Gnilka, *Matthäusevangelium*, p. 514.

coherence with scribal alterations of Mark's text away from the identification of Jesus as a carpenter.
There are two (related) variant readings to the preferred reading at Mark 6.3 (. . . ὁ τέκτων, ὁ υἱὸς τῆς Μαρίας . . .):

(a) ο του τεκτονος υιος και της Μαριας (f[13] 33 700 it[a, aur, b, c,] e, i, rl cop[bo(mss)] arm Origen); and

(b) ο του τεκτονος υιος της Μαριας (P[45] (which reads: τεκτον]ος ο υ[ιος) 565 (1253 2148 omit του) it[e] (l[10 and 547] offer partial support).

These variants to Mark probably arose from harmonisation to Matthew.[17] It is possible that negative attitudes towards manual labour, which were characteristic among the élite of the Greco-Roman world (cf. Cicero, *De off.* I.42.150; Seneca, *Ep.* 88.21; Plutarch, *Per.* 2.1), may have influenced Christians in a later period (note especially the jibe against Jesus the carpenter from Celsus recorded in Origen, *Contra Celsum*, VI.34).[18] Evidence is lacking, however, that Matthew shared such a prejudice against physical labour, especially considering the positive view of Jewish traditions about the nature of work and the practice of many Rabbis.[19] Among pre-70 'Rabbis' Hillel (b. *Yoma* 35b), Shammai (b. *Šabb.* 31a) and Abba Hilkiah (b. *Ta'an* 23a-b) are all said to have worked; cf. *m. 'Abot* 2.2: 'excellent is the study of the Torah combined with a worldly occupation for the toil involved in both makes sin to be forgiven'.[20] This is not therefore particularly compelling as an explanation of Matthew's redaction.

Thirdly, W. Grundmann argued that since both Matthew and his readers know that Jesus was legally the son of Joseph and also by *Geist-Erzeugung* (Spirit-generation) the son of Mary, Matthew's alterations highlight the distance between true and false understandings of Jesus' identity and thus emphasise the error of the Nazaraeans: they know nothing about Jesus' true nature.[21]

Fourthly, a number of scholars have argued that the alteration was made on the basis of further information, possibly some

[17] See further Head, 'Christology and Textual Transmission', pp. 118–19.
[18] See further Geoghegan, *The Attitude to Labor in Early Christianity and Ancient Culture*; Burford, *Craftsmen in Greek and Roman Society*; Moseé, *The Ancient World of Work*. Justin is rather more positive in *Dialogue with Trypho*, 88.
[19] Luz, *Matthäus*, vol. II, p. 385, n. 11.
[20] Cf. further 'Labor', *EncJud* 10 (1972) 1322–3; also passages cited by Str-B, vol. II, pp. 10–11 (on Mark 6.3) and pp. 745–47 (on Acts 18.3).
[21] Grundmann, *Matthäus*, p. 359; cf. also Schweizer, *Matthäus*, p. 205 (ET, p. 315).

independent tradition. Some support for the existence of additional independent tradition can be drawn from Luke 4.22b which has οὐχὶ υἱός ἐστιν ᾿Ιωσὴφ οὗτος; (cf. also John 6.42).[22] Ilan's suggestion, that Matthew changed Mark's designation on the basis of further information concerning Joseph, including the genealogical connection with David (shared, albeit in different form by Luke 3.23–38), is possible, but does not explain why Matthew uses 'son of the carpenter' rather than 'son of Joseph' since this would connect much better with the birth narratives, cf. 1.18–25.[23] It is also possible that Matthew's statement relies on either additional information about Joseph or deduction from common practice,[24] but this does not explain the motivation behind the alteration. Clearly, it has proved difficult for redaction critics to ascertain Matthew's motivation at this point. Thus, although there are several possible explanations for Matthean practice at this point, no single explanation commands acceptance.

The second significant alteration made by Matthew in this passage occurs in v. 58. Here Matthew offers an abbreviated version of Mark's text, omitting the details of the healings, and Jesus' marvelling. He merges the two aspects of Mark's statement ('not able to do any . . . except a few') into one statement: καὶ οὐκ ἐποίησεν ἐκεῖ δυνάμεις πολλάς. Matthew also adds a reason for this (from Mark 6.6a): διὰ τὴν ἀπιστίαν αὐτῶν. According to many commentators Matthew's version removes any thought of Jesus' inability: 'Inability has become refusal; Jesus is indisputably in charge.'[25] This view, however, must assume that Matthew speaks of 'refusal' at this point. While the unbelief of the people provides the reason for the lack of many miracles, it is not stated that this is due to Jesus' decision. Equally possible is the view that, even according to Matthew, Jesus' activity is constrained (or curtailed) by the

---

[22] Schürmann argued that the Lukan form is independent of Mark 6.3, *Lukasevangelium*, pp. 235–6.

[23] Ilan, 'The Phenomenon of Men Bearing Metronymes at the Time of Jesus', p. 45.

[24] Augustine, *De consensu* II.42; Lohmeyer, *Matthäus*, p. 231: the differences between Matthew and Mark arise from different ways to account for the unusual appearance of Jesus ('die Aussergewöhnlichkeit des Auftretens Jesu'); Schlatter, *Der Evangelist Matthäus*, p. 455: traditional Jewish method of giving work of the father.

[25] Davies and Allison, *Matthew*, vol. II, p. 460; cf. similarly Luz, *Matthäusevangelium*, vol. II, p. 386; Beare, *Matthew*, p. 320; Gundry, *Matthew*, p. 284; Klostermann, *Matthäusevangelium*, p. 126: Matthew omits offensive material.

unbelieving response, as A. H. McNeile noted, 'οὐκ ἐποίησεν might mean either inability or refusal'.[26]

Another approach to the Matthean redaction would be to suggest that Matthew is clarifying what he regarded as the implications of Mark's account. Thus it is Matthew who explains that it was because of unbelief that there were few miracles. This connection is not specified in Mark, although it might be implied.[27] This would be an expression of Matthew's interest in asserting the importance of faith for receiving the benefits of Jesus' miraculous ministry; an interest which, although not unique to Matthew (see e.g. Mark 5.34 // Matt. 9.22// Luke 8.48; Mark 10.52 // Luke 18.42; Luke 7.50; 17.19), does appear in numerous redactional comments, e.g. Matthew 8.13; 9.29; 15.28.[28] This approach coheres with Matthew's placement of the passage after the parables: it provides an example of those who 'see without seeing and hear without hearing' (13.13; cf. 13.54), and it links with 12.46–50 to show that geo-social connections are of no more value (for understanding Jesus' ministry) than family ties.[29]

In this context the omission of ἐδύνατο could be due to Matthew's preference for the simple form ἐποίησεν in place of Mark's ἐδύνατο . . . ποιῆσαι. While the use of an auxiliary verb is characteristic of Mark, especially with periphrastic constructions, and the use of ἄρχομαι, δύναμαι, θέλω, or ἔχω with a following infinitive,[30] it is less common in Matthew, where the Markan form is often simplified by omission of the non-essential verb.

> With ἄρχομαι: Matthew 8.34 // Mark 5.17; Matthew 13.54 // Mark 6.2; Matthew 14.35 // Mark 6.55; Matthew 16.1 // Mark 8.11 (?); Matthew 19.27 // Mark 10.28; Matthew 20.17 // Mark 10.32; Matthew 20.24 // Mark 10.41; Matthew 20.30 // Mark 10.47; Matthew 21.12 // Mark 11.15; Matthew 24.4 // Mark 13.5; Matthew 26.67 // Mark 14.65; Matthew 26.71 // Mark 14.69; Matthew 27.29 // Mark 15.18 (?). With δύναμαι: Matthew 12.25b // Mark 3.25b; Matthew 12.26b // Mark 3.26b; Matthew 15.11 // Mark 7.15. Matthew does use the auxiliary form on occasion (see Turner for details), but the examples listed here show that Matthew made similar alterations fairly often (it is a natural way to abbreviate material without losing content).

Thus it is possible to explain Matthean redaction of Mark on the basis of two complementary interests: first the necessity of faith for

---

[26] McNeile, *Matthew*, p. 207.
[27] Held, ' Matthäus als Interpret der Wundergeschichten', p. 265 (ET, pp. 277–8).
[28] Ibid., pp. 227–8 (ET, pp. 239–41).
[29] Davies and Allison, *Matthew*, vol. II, p. 470.
[30] See Turner, 'Marcan Usage: VIII. (*sic*) Auxiliary verbs', pp. 349–60.

the working of miracles, and secondly Matthew's tendency to simplify Mark's auxiliary verbs. These two interests suggest that it is not necessary to appeal to christological alteration for an explanation of the Matthean redaction. Among commentators both D. Hill and E. Schweizer have expressed some scepticism in relation to the idea of christological redaction here.[31]

In general, with the important exception of 'son of the carpenter', we have found that Matthean redaction of Mark is explicable within the parameters of lexical and syntactical preferences and theological principles apparent throughout the gospel. The christological argument does not appear to be a necessary deduction from the redactional processes observed in this passage. Thus, while the material investigated is generally amenable on the two-source hypothesis, the christological argument is not a necessary part of this hypothesis.

3.   Griesbach-Mark's redaction of Matthew (and Luke)

According to the Griesbach hypothesis Mark's placement of Jesus' rejection at Nazareth in Mark 6.1–6a does not follow the immediate order of either of his sources. Luke's similar episode occurs at the beginning of Jesus' ministry (Luke 4), and Matthew's closely parallel account concludes his parable chapter (Matt. 13). One must reckon with Griesbach-Mark having followed Luke's ordering of the material up to this point for:

(a)   the storm-stilling (Mark 4.35–41//Luke 8.22–5),
(b)   the 'Gerasene' demoniac (Mark 5.1–20//Luke 8.26–39),
(c)   Jairus' daughter and woman with haemorrhage (Mark 5.21–43//Luke 8.40–56).

Unlike Mark and Luke, Matthew does not have these stories in consecutive order, moreover there are clear indications in some of these passages that Mark parallels Luke's wording more closely than Matthew's (e.g. Mark 5.3f, 8–10, 15f, 18–20, 22, 25, 29–31, 35–37, 41). At this point (Mark 6.1–6a), Griesbach-Mark follows neither Luke nor Matthew in terms of order, although he returns to Luke in Mark 6.6b-13 and 14–16 // Luke 9.1–6 and 7–9; and will then begin to follow Matthew's order from Mark 6.14–16 // Matthew 14.1f for the remainder of the gospel.

From the perspective of the Griesbach hypothesis this state of

---

[31]   Hill, *Matthew*, p. 242; Schweizer, *Matthäus*, p. 205 (ET, p. 316).

affairs is normally explained as follows: Griesbach-Mark followed Matthew up until Matthew 13 (the parables), then followed Luke's order of material after the parables, before returning to the point where he had left Matthew.[32] This explanation loses some of its force, however, when it is recalled that even in those passages where Mark appears to be following Luke closely, there is also evidence of his dependence upon Matthew (e.g. Mark 4.37f, 40f; 5.1f, 17, 23f, 28, 38).[33] Thus the hypothesis that Griesbach-Mark left Matthew open at 13.53 and returned to it only after having followed Luke 8.22–56 cannot be correct: whichever source Mark followed he appears to have made the effort to consult the alternative as well.

In this passage (6.1–6a) it is clear that in terms of wording Griesbach-Mark is primarily dependent upon Matthew. There are several close and apparently significant parallels with Matthew, especially in Mark 6.3 where, although he leaves out some words from Matthew 13.55f, we find that every word except four in Mark – i.e. twenty-seven out of thirty-one – are from Matthew; a similar thing could be argued from 6.4. Mark has only four words in common with Luke and not Matthew: καί (6.1 cf. Luke 4.16); σάββατον (6.2 cf. Luke 4.16: ἐν τῇ ἡμέρᾳ τῶν σαββάτων); ὅτι (6.4 cf. Luke 4.24 introducing the proverb); αὐτοῦ (6.4 cf. Luke 4.24: ἐν τῇ πατρίδι αὐτοῦ[34]).

The first agreement with Luke is hardly significant in view of the disagreement of the verbal augment (Mark begins: καὶ ἐξῆλθεν, cf. Luke: καὶ ἦλθεν); in addition, Mark regularly begins passages without, on Griesbach hypothesis, an exemplar with a καί (NB Matt. 13.54 also begins with καί, Mark 6.1 has two). Since the last two word-parallels (and the manuscript variants) suggest the influence of slightly different forms of a common proverb (also known from John 4.44; *Gos. Thom.* 31; P. Oxy. 1.5; suggested by Dio Chrysostom 47.6; cf. the sentiments of Apollonius of Tyana, *Ep.* 44; Pindar, *Olym.* 12.13–16; Pliny, *Ep.* VIII.20 and Epictetus, *Disc.* III.16.11),[35]

---

[32] Griesbach, 'Demonstration', n. 27 and n. 30, p. 211; Farmer, *The Synoptic Problem*, pp. 240–1 (who emphasises the 'positive correlation between agreement in order and agreement in wording'; cf. pp. 217–19); Riley, *The Making of Mark*, p. 66.

[33] Against Griesbach, 'Demonstration', n. 29, p. 211.

[34] For this term at Luke 4.24 several mss read ἑαυτοῦ (ℵ D W cop^sah cop^bo(pt)). Some mss of Mark also use ἑαυτοῦ (ℵ* Θ).

[35] Cf. Wettstein, *Novum Testamentum Graecum*, vol. I, p. 409; Bultmann, *Die Geschichte der synoptischen Tradition*, p. 30, n. 2 (ET, p. 31); Davies and Allison, *Matthew*, vol. II, pp. 459–60.

and the reference to the sabbath is a possible deduction from Matthew's account, it is probably fair to suggest that Griesbach-Mark was following Matthew alone in this passage.[36]

Griesbach-Mark passes over Matthew's linking phrase, ἐγένετο ὅτε ἐτέλεσεν ὁ Ἰησοῦς τὰς παραβολὰς ταύτας, as he does with each of the other occurrences of this phrase (Matt. 7.28; 11.1; 19.1; 26.1). This is not surprising considering the fact that Mark records few of the discourses, and, particularly on the Griesbach hypothesis, is manifestly uninterested in recording a large amount of the contents of Jesus' teaching.[37] He alters Matthew's μετῆρεν for the more common ἐξῆλθεν (43–39–44), and reshapes the sentence around his preferred historic present (ἔρχεται – Mark has 39 presents cf. 35 aorists (of ἔρχομαι); Matthew has 27:83).

After following Matthew's phrase εἰς τὴν πατρίδα αὐτοῦ, Mark adds: καὶ ἀκολουθοῦσιν αὐτῷ οἱ μαθηταὶ αὐτοῦ. This addition is necessary within the Markan narrative in order to re-include all the disciples since in 5.37 Jesus had only allowed three disciples – Peter, James and John – to follow him into the home of the synagogue ruler. Although not mentioned in this passage, the disciples have been present since Matthew 13.36, 51f (cf. Matt. 4.23f which only mentions Jesus but presupposes the presence of the disciples, cf. 4.22; 5.1; also other passages where Jesus alone is mentioned but Matthew probably assumes the presence of the disciples, e.g. 8.5–9, cf. v. 10; 9.35f, cf. v. 37; 12.9–13). Note that in Matthew ἐκεῖθεν refers to the house of 13.36 (cf. 9.10, 28; 12.46 (?); 13.1) which apparently belonged to either Peter (cf. 8.14; 17.25), Jesus (cf. Mark 2.15), or perhaps Matthew (cf. Luke 5.29). In Mark on the other hand ἐκεῖθεν refers to the house of the synagogue ruler (5.38).[38] Mark also has a redactional interest in the presence of the disciples in preparation for 6.6b–13. This is analogous to his practice at 3.7 of specifying and emphasising the presence of his disciples (cf. Matt. 12.15; Luke 6.17) in preparation for 3.13–19 (both pivotal passages in Mark's presentation of the twelve).[39]

In Mark 6.2 Griesbach-Mark adds a favoured genitive absolute,

---

[36] So also de Wette, *Einleitung*, p. 189 (ET, p. 168); Farmer, *The Synoptic Problem*, p. 241; Riley, *The Making of Mark*, p. 66.

[37] Cf. already Dibelius, *Die Formgeschichte des Evangeliums*, p. 237 (cf. ET, pp. 235–6).

[38] For discussion see Davies and Allison, *Matthew*, vol. II, pp. 99–100; Malbon, 'τῇ οἰκίᾳ αὐτοῦ: Mark 2.15 in Context'.

[39] See Lohmeyer, *Markus*, p. 109; Grässer, 'Jesus in Nazareth (Mark VI. 1–6a)', p. 11 and n. 4.

identifying the occasion as a sabbath. In an earlier passage Gries-bach-Mark derived 'on the sabbath' from Luke (Mark 1.21 // Luke 4.31); his other references to the timing of events on the sabbath are common to the triple tradition (2.23; 3.2; 16.1f).

> Markan examples of genitive absolute with γίνομαι include 1.32 (// Matt. 8.16); 4.17 (// Matt. 13.21); 4.35; 6.21, 35 (partial // Matt. 14.15), 6.47 (// Matt. 14.23); 14.17 (// Matt. 26.20); 15.33, 42 (// Matt. 27.57). On the Griesbach hypothesis Mark has picked these up from Matthew; in fact he probably uses all those available in his (Matthean) source (cf. 16.2 (v.l. which Mark, assuming Griesbach hypothesis, may not have known, cf. Mark 8.11–13 which skips over the doubtful portion of Matt.); 20.8 (unique to Matt.); 26.6 (Mark 14.3 uses a gentive absolute with ὄντος)).

Griesbach-Mark also alters Matthew's imperfect (ἐδίδασκεν) to ἤρξατο διδάσκειν (ἄρχω: 13–27–31; the simple construction of aor. mid. with present infinitive: 10–26–18).[40] These changes do not materially affect the sense of the passage, but they do cohere with Markan preferences, as understood by the Griesbach hypothesis. This is also true of the omission of αὐτῶν from Matthew 13.54 ('their synagogue'); comparable omissions are found in Mark 3.1 (cf. Matt. 12.9); 13.9 (cf. Matt. 10.17); cf. also Matthew 9.35; 23.34 (no parallel in Mark). Nevertheless Mark maintains the first of these occurrences: Mark 1.39 // Matthew 4.23. This is slightly inconsistent (but not impossible) behaviour; on the other hand according to the two-source hypothesis Matthew follows Mark's first version ('their synagogue', 1.21, 39) and then uses this phrase consistently throughout.

Mark also changes the way in which the response is introduced; having omitted Matthew's pronouns he identifies the subject of the response: καὶ πολλοὶ ἀκούοντες (πολύς: 60–61–60). Although there is evidence that scribes often added phrases or words like this which intensify the effect Jesus had on observers, in this case Mark's alteration to Matthew does not actually intensify the reaction (see below).[41] He also expands their astonished comments into a three-fold question (parallels with Matthew underlined):

Πόθεν τούτῳ ταῦτα,[42]

---

[40] Turner, 'Marcan Usage: VIII. (sic) Auxiliary verbs', pp. 352–3.
[41] See the variants to Matt. 7.28; 8.18; 9.35; 15.30; Mark 1.34; Luke 4.32, 36, 40; 5.17; 6.18; 9.11; 11.14 listed and discussed briefly in Head, 'Christology and Textual Transmission', pp. 119–20.
[42] ℵ C and some other mss add πάντα, presumably under the influence of Matt. 13.56.

καὶ τίς ἡ σοφία ἡ δοθεῖσα τούτῳ
καὶ αἱ δυνάμεις τοιαῦται διὰ τῶν χειρῶν αὐτοῦ γινόμεναι;

In doing this Griesbach-Mark destroys the structure of Matthew's account. Matthew had two questions beginning with πόθεν . . . (vv. 54, 56b) surrounding the question about the identity of Jesus; Mark gives approximately equal space to the two aspects of the question in succession. From πόθεν to γινόμεναι Mark has nineteen words (thirty-five syllables), then from οὐχ to Σίμωνος eighteen words (thirty-three syllables), then nine words (fifteen syllables) in the final part of the question (from καί to αὐτῷ). The expansion results in an introductory question, 'Where did this man get these?' followed by a further question which explains the ταῦτα by enquiring into the nature of Jesus' σοφία and δυνάμεις. While the phraseology of the expansion to Matthew's question is not particularly Markan (e.g., οὗτος: 149–79–229; τίς: 91–72–114; δίδωμι: 56–39–60; τοιοῦτος: 3–6–2; χείρ: 24–25–26; γίνομαι: 75–55–131), the use of αἱ δυνάμεις τοιαῦται probably refers back to the previous miracles (Mark 4.35–5.43).[43]

Thus the fact that Jesus has not previously performed miracles in Nazareth would not, perhaps, impact strongly on Mark's readers; especially since, in Mark's narrative, the reader has been prepared to expect a universal awareness of Jesus' activity throughout Galilee (see 1.28, 39, 45; 2.1f; 3.7f, 19f; 5.14). This aspect of the account is more emphatic in Mark than in Matthew or Luke, especially in connection with Galilee (Mark 1.28 // Luke 4.37; Mark 1.45 // Luke 5.15f; Mark 2.1f // Luke 5.17; Mark 3.7f // Luke 6.17). In addition, Mark often mentions crowds that came to Jesus, emphasising that Jesus was well known publicly (1.32f; 2.2, 13; 3.8, 20; 4.1; 5.21, 24; 6.31, 55f; 8.1).[44] Mark's addition of καὶ ἐν τοῖς συγγενεῦσιν αὐτοῦ (v. 4) reflects their knowledge of his activity (cf. 3.21). This suggestion seems a better explanation (at the level of Griesbach-Markan redaction) than Riley's comment that Mark's version is less appropriate than Matthew's.[45]

There are a number of narrative tensions within this account, including:

(i) Jesus comes εἰς τὴν πατρίδα αὐτοῦ (v. 1) but the proverb in v. 4 relates also to his συγγενεῖς and his οἰκία;

---

[43] With Guelich, *Mark*, p. 309. This might be supported by the reference to Jesus' laying on hands in 5.23, 41.

[44] Bultmann, *Die Geschichte der synoptischen Tradition*, pp. 367–8 (ET, pp. 342–3); Grässer, 'Jesus in Nazareth (Mark VI. 1–6a)', p. 12.

[45] Riley, *The Making of Mark*, p. 66.

(ii) his disciples are with him (v. 1) but are not mentioned again;
(iii) he is teaching, but the crowd question his mighty works (δυνάμεις, v. 2);
(iv) the two responses, astonishment (v. 2), and offence (v. 3) are in tension;
(v)   the statement in v. 5 that Jesus can do no mighty works (5a) is immediately modified by the mention of a few healings (5b);
(vi) Jesus marvels at the lack of faith (v. 6), even though he has used a well known proverb which explains his lack of honour (v. 4).

Despite the confidence with which some scholars, assuming Markan priority, have used these tensions in order to question the unity of Mark's sources,[46] the fact that both the two-source hypothesis and the Griesbach hypothesis require that a secondary writer has maintained these tensions from his source (they are just as much a part of Matthew's version as Mark's) suggests that such tensions alone are not proof of posteriority.

While the initial questions concern the source of Jesus' wisdom and miraculous deeds, the second set of questions (Mark 6.3) concern the identity of Jesus. Matthew has three questions (οὐχ . . . οὐχ . . . οὐχὶ . . .), which Mark summarises in two (Matt: 33 words; Mark: 27). In the first question Griesbach-Mark changes Matthew's 'son of the carpenter' to 'the carpenter' and brings together 'son' and the reference to Mary in Matthew's following phrase, resulting in: οὐχ οὗτός ἐστιν ὁ τέκτων, ὁ υἱὸς τῆς Μαρίας (Mark 6.3a). The following alterations are minor and bring the list of brothers and mention of sisters into line with the initial question.

The consensus explanation of this alteration, from the Griesbachian perspective, is that Mark, who does not mention Joseph at all, desired to protect the doctrine of the virgin birth and so Jesus could not be regarded as the son of a human father.[47] This explanation, however, is not without problems. First, Griesbach-Mark had access to both birth narratives but did not include even the briefest mention of the virgin birth. Secondly, his alteration results in the very unusual 'son of Mary' (cf. our previous discussion). Thirdly, this argument assumes that Mark expects his readers to know and accept the traditions which he omits from Matthew and Luke despite the fact that in other places Griesbach-Mark

---

[46] E.g. Grässer, 'Jesus in Nazareth (Mark VI. 1–6a)'; Mayer, 'Überlieferungs- und redaktionsgeschichtliche Über-legungen zu Mk 6, 1–6a'; Betz, 'Jesus in Nazareth. Bemerkungen zu Markus 6, 1–6'; Oberlinner, *Historische Überlieferung und Christologische Aussage.*

[47] Davidson, *Introduction*, pp. 499–500; Bleek, *Einleitung*, p. 192 (ET, vol. I, p. 266); Farmer, *The Synoptic Problem*, p. 231; Riley, *The Making of Mark*, p. 67 (cf. Klostermann, *Markusevangelium*, p. 55).

seems to differ from his sources. Fourthly, the question of the villagers is part of the astonished, unbelieving response to Jesus' activity and should be so regarded in Mark, rather than as safeguarding a Christian position.

McArthur argued, on the basis of matriarchal identifications in the OT and Judaism, that 'son of Mary' carried no particular connotation. This is all the more likely since, as he notes, patristic writers made nothing of the phrase, focussing rather on the description of Jesus as a carpenter.[48] Ilan has provided additional evidence of 'men bearing metronymes'. There is no evidence for the use of the mother's name as an indication of illegitimacy, but it is common when the mother was more prominent than the father.[49] Thus despite the prominence which this passage has in defences of the Griesbach hypothesis – Stoldt claimed that it provided '*ein sicherer Beweis für die Posteriorität des Markus*' (a secure proof for the posteriority of Mark)[50] – there is little evidence which guarantees the secondary status of Mark's account. Since Matthew, who does include the virgin-birth tradition, presumably saw no problem with the account in this form – and in his account distinguishes between Jesus' being 'son of the carpenter' and 'his mother called Mary' – it is somewhat surprising that it should be thought a problem for Mark.

Another possible explanation would be to argue that 'son of the carpenter' was the original text of Mark.[51] The evidence, however, does not favour this position. The reading ὁ τέκτων, ὁ υἱὸς τῆς Μαρίας has a substantial weight of external support (ℵ A B C D K L W Δ Θ Π f¹ 28 892 1071 etc. it $^{d\ f\ ff2\ l\ q}$ Vg syr$^{p,\ h}$ cop$^{sa,\ bo}$). The alternative readings are, to various degrees, much closer to Matthew (see above, p. 70), and also avoid the difficulties in the shorter variant: the unusual 'son of Mary', and calling Jesus ὁ τέκτων. As we have already noted, second-century evidence suggests that the description of Jesus as a carpenter was contentious in some circles (Origen, *Contra Celsum*, VI.34–6).[52] In addition, the

---

[48] McArthur, 'Son of Mary'.

[49] Ilan supports Markan priority: both Matthew and Luke claimed that Joseph was of royal descent and thus changed Mark's description, Ilan, 'The Phenomenon of Men Bearing Metronymes at the Time of Jesus'.

[50] Stoldt, *Geschichte und Kritik der Markus-hypothese*, p. 192 (ET, p. 20).

[51] Klostermann, *Markusevangelium*, p. 63; Taylor, *Mark*, p. 300; McArthur, 'Son of Mary', pp. 47–52 (against Blinzler, *Die Brüder und Schwestern Jesu*, pp. 28–30).

[52] For Origen's knowledge of a text lacking 'carpenter' see Chadwick, *Origen: Contra Celsum*, p. 352. For background on ancient carpentry see Höpfl, 'Nonne

reading of ὁ τέκτων, ὁ υἱὸς τῆς Μαρίας would provide an explanation for all the other variations if it were original. Furthermore, harmonisation with the text of Matthew is one of the most powerful factors affecting scribes of Mark, otherwise how would one explain that the text of Matthew was not changed at all? For these reasons it does not seem reasonable to offer this as a solution to the problem of Markan redaction here.[53]

Thus while there are two possibilities which would satisfactorily describe Markan redaction on the Griesbach hypothesis, neither is fully persuasive. The Griesbach hypothesis will probably continue to press the explanation involving Markan interest in the virgin birth, but there appears to be little independent evidence to support this position.

In the succeeding verse Griesbach-Mark follows Matthew quite closely (except for omitting Matthew's reprise: πόθεν οὖν τούτῳ ταῦτα πάντα;), summarising the response of the people in the phrase καὶ ἐσκανδαλίζοντο ἐν αὐτῷ. Mark expands the proverb of Jesus (καὶ ἐν τοῖς συγγενεῦσιν αὐτοῦ, although this phrase is not present in ‭א‬*). In the final editorial comment Mark makes several significant alterations and additions to Matthew in order to provide a different explanation for the absence of miracles: καὶ οὐκ ἐδύνατο ἐκεῖ ποιῆσαι οὐδεμίαν δύναμιν.

The vocabulary of this new material is, with a notable exception, not markedly Markan: δύναμαι: (27–33–26); ὀλίγος: (6–4–7); οὐδείς: (19–26–33); ἄρρωστος: (1–3–0); θεραπεύω: (16–5–14); ἐπιτίθημι: (7–8–5). The exception, which is characteristic of Markan style especially inasmuch as he differs from Matthew and Luke, involves the use of a negated form of δύναμαι in narrative formulations: Mark 1.45 (narrative comment); 2.4 (narr. comm.), 19b; 3.20 (narr. comm.), 24, 25, 26, 27; 5.3 (narr. comm.); 6.19 (narr. comm.); 7.18, 24 (narr. comm.); 9.3 (narr. comm.), 28 (// Matt. 17.19), 29; 15.31 (// Matt. 27.42). The large number of unparalleled examples of this construction, particularly in narrative comments, distinguish it as characteristically Markan, although present in other gospels.

hic est fabri filius?'; McCown, 'ὁ τέκτων'; Furfey, 'Christ as *Tektōn*' (cf. also Batey, 'Is not this the Carpenter?'; Buchanan, 'Jesus and the Upper Class'; Vermes, *Jesus the Jew*, pp. 21–2).

53 Scribal alterations owing to an interest in the virgin birth did occur (e.g., Matt. 1.16 and other passages discussed in Globe, 'Some Doctrinal Variants in Matthew 1 and Luke 2'; Tatian omits references to Jesus' father, Head, 'Tatian's Christology', p. 128). What is lacking is evidence (or arguments) that 'son of Mary' did connote the virgin birth.

Neither Matthew nor Luke ever uses this form with Jesus as the subject.

> In Matthew (in addition to those just noted in parallel with Mark) we find it in sayings of Jesus (Matt. 5.14, 36; 6.24(bis); 7.18; 10.28; 16.3; 26.42); in a question (9.15 // Mark 2.19a // Luke 5.34); in narrative comments concerning the disciples (17.16//Luke 9.40) and the Pharisees (22.46). In Luke it is also predominantly in Jesus' teaching and parables (6.39; 11.7; 14.20, 26, 27, 33; 16.1, 13, 26; 21.15); in narrative comments it is also found in 1.20, 22 (Zechariah); 8.19 (Jesus' mother); 19.3 (Zacchaeus).

Mark, on the other hand, uses it four times with Jesus as the subject (1.45; 6.5; 7.24 and 3.20). On the other three occasions the 'inability' refers to something forced upon Jesus by external constraints: Jesus' inability to enter a town quietly – 1.45; or to hide away quietly – 7.24; or to eat – 3.20 (with his disciples) because of his fame.

This is also true of the other narrative uses in Mark. In 2.4 the men found it impossible to approach Jesus because of the crowd (a temporary constraint); in 5.3 no one could bind the demoniac; in 6.19 Herodias was not able to kill John because he was protected by Herod (also temporary!); in 9.3 the phrase is used as an illustration of the whiteness of Jesus' transfigured appearance.[54] In 1.45 (ὥστε μηκέτι αὐτὸν δύνασθαι φανερῶς εἰς πόλιν εἰσελθεῖν) it is really a statement of Jesus' unwillingness to enter a town (rather than 'inability' as such, cf. also Luke 11.7); in 7.24 the verb is in a passive form, so strictly speaking it is not about Jesus' 'inability', but about the inability of his disciples (or those in the house?) to hide him. In 3.20 it refers to the constraint placed upon Jesus and his disciples by the coming of the crowd. In any case it is clear that Mark's statement in 6.5 is not a totally isolated one.

It remains difficult, however, to explain Mark's text as a redaction of Matthew: the reason for the constraint which is provided by Matthew (unbelief) is not related directly to the lack of miracles; the mention of some healings (Mark 6.5b) cannot be understood (as in the other passages just noted) as the resolution of a temporary constraint (the syntax prohibits this); and the starkness of the negative statement is in a high degree of tension with the following exception clause.[55]

The final phrase (most commentators divide the passage after v.

---

[54] Cf. Turner, 'Marcan Usage: VIII. (*sic*) Auxiliary verbs', pp. 354–5.
[55] Codex W replaces ἐκεῖ with οὐκέτι, introducing a smoother text, with a different temporal resolution (Hurtado, *Codex W in the Gospel of Mark*, p. 78).

6a) does introduce (from Matthew) the factor of the unbelief of the crowd: καὶ ἐθαύμαζεν διὰ τὴν ἀπιστίαν αὐτῶν. Griesbach-Mark has, however, obscured the connection between this unbelief and the lack of miracles. This despite the facts that the connection is so clear in Matthew and that other Markan passages with δύναμαι and a negative often provide the reason for the 'inability': Mark 2.4 and 5.3f use a διά clause directly following the negative; 6.19f uses a γάρ clause directly following the negative; 3.20 places the negative information in a result clause (Mark 9.3 is an exception to this rule). It is not clear that compelling explanations of Mark's redaction of Matthew can be made at this point. It is notable that Tatian's *Diatessaron* follows Mark's form (conflating 'many' from Matthew): 'he could not do many mighty works there', but adds Matthew's explanation: 'because of their unbelief' (Arabic, 17.48).[56] This might suggest, in addition to the lack of textual variations in Mark, that it was not the οὐκ ἐδύνατο that was particularly problematic in the later period; this certainly seems to be the case among patristic writers. Origen quotes both forms agreeably in his argument that 'among unbelievers . . . mighty works . . . were not even able to operate'. He argues that both Matthew and Mark here 'set forth the supreme greatness of the divine power, viz. that it can act even in unbelief'.[57]

In general it is clear what Griesbach-Mark must have done in order to get from his source to his text, and it is noteworthy that many of these 'alterations' are explicable in terms of otherwise known Markan preferences. There are, however, difficulties for the Griesbach hypothesis in explaining Mark's behaviour, and the christological explanation of Mark's redaction on the Griesbach hypothesis is unpersuasive.

4. Conclusion

The conclusions to be drawn from our investigation of this passage are as follows: first, difficulties remain for either hypothesis. This does not mean that neither hypothesis is correct, although repeated difficulties would cast doubt on the ability of either to explain the synoptic phenomena. It might mean that more light could be shed

---

[56] Cf. Head, 'Tatian's Christology', p. 134 for other versions.
[57] Origen, *Comm. on Matt.* X.16; quoted from Smith, *Ante-Nicene Exegesis of the Gospels*, vol. 3, pp. 57–8.

on the basis of fuller information, or it could mean that no redactor made a fully explicable redaction of his exemplar; in other words there is no process of redaction of sources which will yield a fully explicable analysis of the motivation of the editor. Secondly, the christological explanations for Matthean redaction are not the most compelling explanations available. In other words, even though the two-source hypothesis yields a generally adequate view of the phenomena, Matthew's motivation is adequately understood apart from the supposition of 'reverential alterations'. Thirdly, Markan redaction (on the Griesbach hypothesis) can yield relatively plausible explanations for many of the synoptic phenomena. The aspects of Griesbach-Markan redaction which, in our opinion, do not seem plausible may yield to further exploration of the Griesbach hypothesis.

The two most commonly cited passages in support of the christological argument for Markan priority do not seem able to bear the weight which this argument has placed upon them. In neither case is the revisionary aspect of 'christological redaction' really necessary in order to explain the redactional activity of Matthew on the two-source hypothesis.

5

WALKING ON WATER (MATT. 14.22–33; MARK 6.45–52)

1. Introduction

In the previous chapters the two passages which were highlighted by the history of research as of great importance for the christological argument for Markan priority were investigated. This chapter contains a similar investigation of the synoptic account of Jesus' walking on the sea (Matt. 14.22–33 // Mark 6.45–52). This account is clearly of great christological significance for the evangelists and this, together with the utility of no Lukan parallel, justifies its inclusion here. While it does not contain 'christological embarrassments' characteristic of the christological argument for Markan priority, there are significant indications of redactional activity on the part of the evangelists in relation to the miracle-working activity of Jesus (an area significantly underplayed in the history of research of this particular argument). As previously the aim of this chapter is to describe the type of redactional processes envisaged on both the two-source hypothesis and the Griesbach hypothesis with a view to assessing the coherence and plausibility of these respective procedures.

This passage occurs within the long section, parallel (in terms of content and order) in Matthew and Mark, but absent from Luke (Mark 6.45–8.21 // Matt. 14.22–16.12), which has often been described as Luke's 'Great Omission'.

> Assuming Luke knew of this material (either from Mark, with the two-source hypothesis, as demonstrated by Schürmann, *Lukasevangelium*, vol. I, p. 527; or from Matthew, as most forms of Griesbach hypothesis) its absence can be explained in view of one or more of the following factors:
>
> (i)   Luke's tendency to avoid doublets (Creed, *Luke*, p. lxi);
> (ii)   Luke's interest in confining Jesus' ministry to Galilee (Fitzmyer, *Luke*, vol. I, pp. 770–1);
> (iii) Luke's desire to connect the feeding miracle more closely with Peter's confession (perhaps he knew the tradition behind John 6; Marshall, *Luke*, p. 364);

(iv)   Luke's recognition that this material, in Mark 7.1–8.21, represents 'Mark's Gentile Mission' and was thus inappropriate in his first volume (Drury, *Tradition and Design in Luke's Gospel*, pp. 96–102).

These chapters provide an ideal opportunity to compare the Griesbach view of Markan redactional techniques with the two-source hypothesis view of Matthean redaction: since there are no parallels in Luke, the alternatives suggested by the two hypotheses are simple: either Matthew has used Mark or Mark has used Matthew. Although, on the two-source hypothesis, the influence of Q *might* be discernible at various places within this larger block of material (e.g. Matt. 15.14 // Luke 6.39; Matt. 16.3 // Luke 12.56; and the agreements between Matt. and Luke at Matt. 15.27 // Luke 16.21; Matt. 16.4 // Luke 11.29; Matt. 16.5 // Luke 12.1), there is no evidence for such influence in Matthew 14.22–33. On the other hand, evidence for the influence of Luke upon Mark's wording (Griesbach hypothesis) is confined to Mark 8.11f // Luke 11.29. The detailed investigation can therefore proceed without the added complication of dealing with the influence of either Luke or Q.

Evidence for literary dependence between the Markan and Matthean accounts is very strong, especially in the opening sequence and common material in the story itself. The introduction (Matt. 14.22 // Mark 6.45) contains twelve out of fourteen words in common;[1] Matthew 14.24b–7 parallels Mark in forty out of fifty words; and Mark 6.48–50 parallels Matthew in forty out of fifty-nine words (including sequences of five, six, six and five words). Literary dependence is not generally denied, although the place of the Johannine parallel (John 6.16–21) which appears to represent an independent and primitive tradition remains disputed.[2]

2.   Matthew's redaction of Mark assuming Markan priority

Matthew and Mark are in agreement as regards the order of the accounts. From the perspective of Markan priority Matthew's redaction in this passage comprises a major addition (14.28–31, seventy-seven words), and many minor alterations, resulting in a slight abbreviation of Mark's material. These alterations have two

---

[1] So Aland, *Synopsis*, with NA27; the text of Orchard, *Synopsis*, offers a fourteen-word sequence (including αυτου in Matt. and αυτον in Mark). Note also the variant reading at Matt. 14.24: μέσον τῆς θαλάσσης ἦν, which is much closer to Mark than the text of NA27 (this variant discussed below).

[2] R. E. Brown, *John*, vol. I, pp. 252–4.

main effects: first, Matthew introduces numerous resonances with other passages within the gospel. J. P. Heil, whose work offers a fuller exegesis than is available in the commentaries, argues that in Matthew the walking-on-water episode answers the question of Jesus' identity raised by the storm-stilling (8.18–27) and anticipates the confession of Peter (16.13–20).[3] Secondly, the new material in verses 28–31 is carefully related to the preceding passage in such a way as to create two parallel statements:[4]

(i) *Jesus walks on the sea (v. 25) and Peter walks on the water (v. 29):*

v. 25: ['Ιησοῦς]   ἦλθεν πρὸς αὐτοὺς
                          περιπατῶν ἐπὶ τὴν θάλασσαν.
v. 29: Πέτρος   περιεπάτησεν ἐπὶ τὰ ὕδατα
           καὶ ἦλθεν πρὸς τὸν 'Ιησοῦν.

(ii) *the situation of the men in the boat (v. 26f) and that of Peter sinking (vv. 30f):*

v. 26f: ἰδόντες . . . λέγοντες . . . φόβου ἔκραξαν.(v. 27) εὐθὺς δὲ ἐλάλησεν [ὁ 'Ιησοῦς]
v. 30f: βλέπων . . . ἐφοβήθη . . . ἔκραξεν λέγων (v. 31) εὐθέως δὲ ὁ 'Ιησοῦς . . . λέγει.

This has resulted in a restructuring of the pericope such that Jesus' words, Θαρσεῖτε, ἐγώ εἰμι· μὴ φοβεῖσθε (v. 27), become the mid-point of the story; and the worship and confession of the disciples (v. 33) is the final climax.[5] The general point is that Matthew's additional material is carefully placed within a restructured account.[6] This restructured account will be examined in four sections.

2.1   Introduction and setting (Matt. 14.22f)

Here many of the alterations reflect characteristic Matthean preferences, without affecting the sense of the passage: for example, the spelling εὐθέως (consistently preferred by Matthew) and the

---

[3] Heil, *Jesus Walking on the Sea*, pp. 85–111.   [4] Ibid., pp. 17–18.
[5] Sibinga, 'Matthew 14:22–33 – Text and Composition', p. 33.
[6] Davies and Allison, *Matthew*, vol. II, p. 496; Gerhardsson, *The Mighty Acts of Jesus*, p. 57; Luz, *Matthäus*, vol. II, pp. 404–5.

absolute τοὺς μαθητάς (thirty-four out of seventy-five occurrences in Matthew lack identifying pronoun, but cf. many *v.l.*). Among other changes Matthew has added αὐτόν, omitted πρὸς βηθσαϊδάν (thus removing the geographical difficulty from Mark's account), and altered Mark's ἕως αὐτὸς ἀπολύει τὸν ὄχλον to ἕως οὗ ἀπολύσῃ τοὺς ὄχλους. The use of ἕως οὗ is characteristically Matthean (1.25; 13.33; 14.22; 17.9; 18.34; 26.36), for a parallel with subjunctive meaning 'while' rather than 'until' cf. 26.36 (BAGD, p. 335; BDF, #216, 383). The significance of some of these changes should not be exaggerated, for example, Matthew's use of the plural form οἱ ὄχλοι (in v. 22 and v. 23) should probably be regarded as a stylistic alteration.

> Gundry regards the use of the plural as significant: 'Matthew pluralizes [*sic*] Mark's crowd in order to emphasize their numbers as representing the largeness of the church' (*Matthew*, p. 296). But this is uncontrolled! While Mark prefers the singular (thirty-seven times cf. two plural), Matthew has a more marginal preference for the plural (nineteen times singular cf. thirty-one plural). These figures confirm that Matthew often does use the singular (both in parallel with Mark: cf. Matt. 13.2; 14.14; 15.10, 32, 35; 17.14; 20.29; 21.26; 26.47; and in redactional additions to Mark: cf. Matt. 8.18; 9.23, 25; 14.5; 15.31, 33; 20.31; 21.8; 27.15, 24). In light of passages which alternate between singular and plural (13.2; 14.13–15; 15.30–39; 21.8f) it seems unlikely that a distinction in meaning is intended (also Minear, 'The Disciples and the Crowds in the Gospel of Matthew', p. 29).

In v. 23 Matthew introduces a repetitious element, preferring ἀπολύσας τοὺς ὄχλους to Mark's ἀποταξάμενος αὐτοῖς (Matt. uses ἀπολύω twenty times, cf. Mark twelve times, and Matt. never uses ἀποτάσσομαι, cf. Mark only here, also in Luke 9.61; 14.33). This alteration clarifies the ambiguous pronoun of Mark, and is characteristic of this section of Matthew (cf. 14.15, 22; 15.39).[7] Matthew has also changed Mark's verb from ἀπῆλθεν to ἀνέβη. The resultant construction (ἀναβαίνω + εἰς τὸ ὄρος) is used twice elsewhere (Matt. 5.1 and 15.29, cf. Mark 3.13) and is taken by some scholars to be an indication that Matthew is intending to make a connection between Jesus and Moses (Jesus is also alone on the mountain praying, cf. Exod. 24.2; 32.31f; 33.12–23; 34.8f etc.).[8] A difficulty with this argument is that the rest of the pericope does not make any use of this theme; it is perhaps more likely that this

---

[7] Davies and Allison, *Matthew*, vol. II, p. 501.
[8] Gundry, *Matthew*, p. 297; Davies and Allison, *Matthew*, vol. II, p. 502 (against Donaldson, *Jesus on the Mountain*, p. 12).

alteration can be explained in terms of linguistic preferences.⁹ The
Matthean emphasis in v. 23b is on Jesus' isolation (κατ' ἰδίαν . . .
μόνος ἦν ἐκεῖ), although the significance of this is unclear (for κατ'
ἰδίαν cf. Matt. 14.13, 23; 17.1, 19; 20.17; 24.3).

2.2   The storm and the epiphany of Jesus (vv. 24–7)

In v. 24 Matthew emphasises the distance of the boat from the
land: ἤδη σταδίους πολλοὺς ἀπὸ τῆς γῆς ἀπεῖχεν (v. 24a). This
involves an alteration of Mark 6.47 ('in the midst of the sea') which
does not use characteristically Matthean vocabulary: 'Neither
στάδιον nor ἀπο τῆς γῆς is attested elsewhere in the First Gospel,
and ἀπέχω is not otherwise redactional.'¹⁰ For this reason Davies
and Allison prefer the variant reading μέσον τῆς θαλάσσης ἦν
(with א C L W f¹ it Maj etc., also read by Greeven, *Synopsis*). This
view, however, takes insufficient acount of the possibility of scribal
harmonisation to the parallel text in Mark and the strength of the
external support for the reading of NA27 given above (B (θ 700) f¹³
syr cop).¹¹

Matthew also omits a few words from Mark and adds a new
clause resulting in βασανιζόμενον ὑπὸ τῶν κυμάτων. This addition
is the first of several which increase the parallelism between this
account and the stilling of the storm (Matt 8.23–7); in this case ὑπὸ
τῶν κυμάτων is also found in 8.24, where the boat was being
swamped by the waves.¹² Matthew's account focusses attention on
the boat throughout v. 24 – as the object of the passive verb
βασανιζόμενον and the referent of ἐναντίος – and tends to increase
the severity of the problem, which in Mark is effectively limited to
difficulty in rowing. These alterations align Matthew more closely
to the 'distress at sea' motif discussed by Heil and prepare for the

---

⁹ Gnilka, *Matthäusevangelium*, vol. II, p. 12 (cf. also Pesch, *Markusevangelium*, vol.
I, p. 360) suggests that the mountain is part of a theophany motif; but the
passages cited, Deut. 33.2 and Hab. 3.3, do not speak of ascent, and, unlike here,
specify the mountain.
¹⁰ Davies and Allison, *Matthew*, vol. II, p. 503, n. 26. But cf. Gundry who describes
the changes, if not the vocabulary, as typical of Matthew's redactional behaviour
(*Matthew*, p. 297).
¹¹ Also supported by Aland, *Synopsis*, p. 210; Metzger, *Textual Commentary*, p. 37;
Gnilka, *Matthäusevangelium*, vol. II, pp. 12–13; Luz, *Matthäusevangelium*, vol. II,
p. 406.
¹² Cf. 1QH 3.6, 12–18; 6.22–5; 7.4f where 'the image of the storm-tossed ship
metaphorically describes the eschatological oppression of the righteous' (Davies
and Allison, *Matthew*, vol. II, p. 69).

christological point which Matthew will press: God alone can rescue from the sea and 'distress *at sea* implies rescue *by God*'.[13]

The report of Jesus' coming, walking on the sea, is very similar to that of Mark. This plays an important role in the christological focus of the whole pericope, particularly in light of the OT background concerning Yahweh walking on seas (Job 9.8; Hab. 3.15; Ps. 77.19; cf. Isa. 43.16; 51.9f; *Frg. Tg.* Exod. 15.11). Matthew omits the enigmatic statement of Mark 6.48: καὶ ἤθελεν παρελθεῖν αὐτούς. Although some argue that Matthew omitted this phrase because it seemed to imply that Jesus was not able to do what he wanted,[14] a simpler and more obvious reason is that for Matthew, unlike Mark, παρελθεῖν normally means 'to pass away' (5.18; 24.34f; 26.39, 42).[15]

Matthew slightly rearranges Mark's description of the disciples' response (v. 26): inserting μαθηταί, shifting ἐταράχθησαν from a later phrase in Mark 6.50, changing Mark's ἔδοξαν το λέγοντες, and adding ἀπὸ τοῦ φόβου; resulting in οἱ δὲ μαθηταὶ ἰδόντες αὐτὸν ἐπὶ τῆς θαλάσσης περιπατοῦντα ἐταράχθησαν λέγοντες ὅτι Φάντασμά ἐστιν, καὶ ἀπὸ τοῦ φόβου ἔκραξαν. This combination of fear and being troubled echoes Psalm 76.16LXX: εἴδοσάν σε ὕδατα, ὁ θεός εἴδοσάν σε ὕδατα καὶ ἐφοβήθησαν, καὶ ἐταράχθησαν ἄβυσσοι, πλῆθος ἤχους ὑδάτων ('When the waters saw thee, O God, when the waters saw thee, they were afraid, yea, the deep trembled'). Thus it might be said that Matthew revises Mark in light of the OT background (as also in vv. 30f). In v. 27 in response to the disciples' cry Jesus identifies himself, in words identical to Mark: Θαρσεῖτε, ἐγώ εἰμι· μὴ φοβεῖσθε. In view of Matthew's interest in the OT it is probably right to take this not only as an identification formula (as in Luke 1.19; 24.39; Acts 9.5; 22.8; 26.15) but also as revelatory, theophanic statement, echoing the ἐγώ εἰμι language of Exodus 3.14; Isaiah 41.4; 43.10; 47.8, 10; and the μὴ φοβεῖσθε language of Genesis 15.1; 26.14; 28.13; 46.3; Isaiah 41.13; 43.1–3; Revelation 1.7 (cf. *Apoc. Abr.* 9.2f; 2 Enoch 1.8).[16]

---

[13] Heil, *Jesus Walking on the Sea*, p. 36. He discusses Exod. 14.10–15.21; Ps. 107.23–32; John 1.1–16; Wis. 14.2–4; 1QH 3.6, 12–18; 6.22–5; 7.4f; *T. Naph.* 6.1–10 (pp. 17–37).

[14] Davies and Allison, *Matthew*, vol. II, p. 505.

[15] Gundry, *Matthew*, p. 298.

[16] Zimmermann, 'Das absolute Ἐγώ εἰμί als die neutestamentliche Offenbarungsformel'; Davies and Allison, *Matthew*, vol. II, p. 506; Gundry, *Matthew*, p. 299; Luz, *Matthäus*, vol. II, p. 408; Gnilka, *Matthäusevangelium*, vol. II, p. 13.

2.3   Peter walking on the water (vv. 28–31)

Matthew's long addition fits well into this context, with a parallel between Jesus' coming to the boat (v. 25) and Peter's later coming to Jesus (v. 29). As already noted, many of the terms used in this account echo Matthean preferences (particularly phrases in the stilling of the storm of Matt. 8.23–7): Peter's use of the vocative Κύριε (vv. 2a, 30b; cf. 8.25b), particularly Κύριε, σῶσόν με (v. 30b; cf. 8.25b: Κύριε, σῶσον); Jesus' use of ὀλιγόπιστος (v. 31b, cf. 8.26); and the use of κελεύω (14.28 cf. 8.18). As for the story itself we cannot attempt a complete analysis.[17] It is noteworthy that Peter's dilemma (v. 30) is provoked by the wind (linking with vv. 24 and 32), and is expressed in terms reminiscent of Psalm 69.1–3 (Ps. 68 LXX):

> Save me (σῶσόν με), O God! For the waters (ὕδατα) have
>   come up to my neck.
> I sink in deep mire, where there is no foothold;
> I have come into deep waters (θαλάσσης),
>   and the flood sweeps over me (κατεπόντισέν με).
> I am weary with my crying (κράζων); my throat is parched.
> My eyes grow dim with waiting for my God.[18]

It is also noteworthy that Jesus' saving action involves stretching out his hand (cf. also 8.3; 12.49; 26.51), which is allusive of OT rescue passages such as Psalm 18.17f; 144.7f: 'Stretch forth thy hand from on high, rescue me and deliver me from the many waters . . .' Therefore, although the insertion readily provides teaching about discipleship (cf. Peter's role elsewhere in Matt.), it is also of a piece with the overall christological impact of the passage.[19]

2.4   Conclusion and confession (vv. 32–33)

Matthew returns to Mark's account (v. 32) but makes major alterations to the conclusion. He omits Mark's phrase λίαν [ἐκ περισσοῦ] ἐν ἑαυτοῖς ἐξίσταντο – Matthew uses the term ἐξίστημι only once, in 12.23; elsewhere, where Mark uses it Matthew prefers another word: in 9.8 (// Mark 2.12) he uses ἐφοβήθησαν in a

---

[17] See Heil, *Jesus Walking on the Sea*, pp. 60–4; Lövestam, 'Wunder und Symbolhandlung. Eine Studie über Matthäus 14, 28–31'.
[18] Heil, *Jesus Walking on the Sea*, p. 61; NB also Ps. 69.14–16.
[19] Davies and Allison, *Matthew*, vol. II, pp. 497–8.

positive context; he omits Mark 3.21; in 9.25 he has massively abbreviated Mark's account (5.42). Matthew may not have regarded ἐξίστημι as a very positive term and substitutes a typically Matthean statement, οἱ δὲ ἐν τῷ πλοίῳ προσεκύνησαν αὐτῷ, and a climactic confession: Ἀληθῶς θεοῦ υἱὸς εἶ. This is the only time in Matthew (before 28.17) that the disciples 'worship' Jesus, and the confession anticipates 27.54 (as well as 16.16). The theophanic allusions throughout the story suggest that 'Son of God' here is not primarily concerned with Jesus' royal-messianic status, but with a divine status.[20]

In conclusion we note that Matthew's redaction of Mark serves to highlight christological issues of importance throughout Matthew, and in particular uses Matthean vocabulary to do so. Matthew's tendency to adapt the Markan wording to his own preferences is also seen in the brief sequel where 14.35b is expressed in the same way as 4.24 (cf. also 14.36 // 9.20f).

3. Mark's redaction of Matthew according to the Griesbach hypothesis

Markan redaction of Matthew, on the Griesbach hypothesis, will obviously entail the reverse of what we have just seen. Nevertheless, it will be necessary to make the attempt to assess Markan redaction within the broader context of the Griesbachian perspective. Farmer asserted that Mark 'changed a story created to serve the needs of Christian preaching . . . and converted it into a wonder story concentrating attention on Jesus' lordship over nature'.[21] According to the Griesbach hypothesis Mark has omitted Matthew's account of Peter's walk on the sea (14.28–31; 77 words), but otherwise slightly fills out Matthew's version (Matt.: 132 words; Mark: 148). Other than the one major omission, Mark's alterations are fairly minor (adding or omitting a few words), and we shall survey the more significant in what follows.

Some of the less significant alterations result in a conformity with Markan preferences, for example, in 6.45: the alteration from εὐθέως to εὐθύς, the addition of αὐτοῦ to τοὺς μαθητάς (while Matt. often has the absolute form οἱ μαθηταί, Mark prefers an identifying pronoun or other identifier in forty-one out of forty-six

---

[20] Kingsbury, *Matthew: Structure, Christology, Kingdom*, pp. 66–7.
[21] *The Synoptic Problem*, p. 242.

occurrences; the exceptions are: 8.1 (cf. *v.l.*); 9.14; 10.10 (cf. *v.l.*), 10.13; 14.16 (cf. *v.l.*)); in 6.47: changing δέ into καί. Other minor changes include: the omission of αὐτόν; the alteration of ἕως οὗ ἀπολύσῃ τοὺς ὄχλους to ἕως αὐτὸς ἀπολύει τὸν ὄχλον (Matt. 14.22 // Mark 6.45); the alteration of ἀπολύσας τοὺς ὄχλους to ἀποταξάμενος αὐτοῖς; the alteration of ἀνέβη to ἀπῆλθεν (εἰς τὸ ὄρος); and the omission of κατ' ἰδίαν (Matt. 14.23 // Mark 6.46).

Among other changes to the introductory verses Griesbach-Mark introduces a geographical element: Jesus sends the disciples πρὸς Βηθσαϊδάν. This could not be deduced solely from the information in Matthew (cf. Matt. 14.34); but if Mark drew this from Luke 9.10 (likely assuming Griesbach hypothesis) he appears to have confused the geographical information.[22] Griesbach-Mark then removes the repetition – 'he dismissed the crowds' – from Matthew 14.22b–23a. It is not clear, however, why Mark used ἀποτάσσομαι in the second phrase (he only uses the word here, but in both occurrences in Luke 9.61 and 14.33 it has connotations of renunciation inappropriate for this context).

Griesbach-Mark also alters the wording of Jesus' ascent to the mountain (aorist forms of ἀπέρχομαι are common Markan vocabulary: twenty-three times), and omits Matthew's κατ' ἰδίαν, although Jesus remains alone. Although κατ' ἰδίαν is a common phrase in Mark (4.34; 6.31, 32; 7.33; 9.2, 28; 13.3) in each case it presumes the presence of the disciples rather than their absence, as in Matthew's usage here, 14.23; hence the omission. In the description that follows Mark places the relative positions of the disciples in the boat and Jesus on land in a more deliberate contrast than Matthew: ἦν τὸ πλοῖον ἐν μέσῳ τῆς θαλάσσης, καὶ αὐτὸς μόνος ἐπὶ τῆς γῆς (v. 47). In this Mark has changed Matthew's description to place the boat in the middle of the sea; thus emphasising both the separation of Jesus from the disciples and their precarious position.

Griesbach-Mark's restructuring of Matthew's account creates a more clear-cut distinction between the introduction and setting (Mark 6.45–7) and his statement of the problem (v. 48 prepared for in v. 47). The link between the two is achieved by the addition of καὶ ἰδὼν αὐτούς (v. 48): Jesus sees the disciples in their distress and

---

[22] Pesch (*Markusevangelium*, vol. I, p. 359) suggests that the phrase gives a directional indication (*Richtungsangabe*) rather than a destination (*Zielangabe*), as in 8.22 (supported by Guelich, *Mark*, p. 348).

this prompts his coming to their aid (cf. the previous story in 6.34 where Jesus' seeing (εἶδεν) leads to compassion and aid).[23] While in Matthew the focus is on the boat, in Mark the focus is on the disciples: the wind is against them (αὐτοῖς) and they are 'harassed in rowing'.

> This translation preserves the ambiguity of βασανιζομένους ἐν τῷ ἐλαύνειν (cf. Heil, *Jesus Walking on the Sea*, p. 5). Since the next clause begins with γάρ, supplying a reason for the first clause, it seems likely that βασανιζομένους ἐν τῷ ἐλαύνειν should be understood as a single unit of meaning. Since ἐλαύνω can refer both to making progress and to rowing (BAGD, p. 248), most translations fall into one of two categories: (i) 'they were making headway painfully' (RSV); or (ii) 'straining at the oars' (NASB, cf. Pesch, *Markusevangelium*, vol. I, p. 357: 'sie sich quälen beim Rudern').

At this point, however, Mark's refocussing on the disciples results in a diminishing of the scale of the problem. In particular by omitting the mention of waves (cf. Mark 4.37), he presents this less as a potential sea-going disaster, or even as a tempest; and more like a transportation difficulty.[24]

Griesbach-Mark follows Matthew's report that Jesus came to the disciples 'walking on the sea', and adds καὶ ἤθελεν παρελθεῖν αὐτούς (v. 48). J. S. Sibinga's observation that the phrase ἔρχεται πρὸς αὐτοὺς περιπατῶν ἐπὶ τῆς θαλάσσης· καὶ ἤθελεν παρελθεῖν αὐτούς stands exactly in the centre of the Markan pericope (sixty-four words in vv. 45–7a, eleven here, sixty-four words in vv. 49–52) may support the contention that this is the key to Mark's interpretation.[25] This much discussed phrase has two main interpretative possibilities.[26] Many commentators have regarded this as an expression of the frustrated intention of Jesus – he wanted to pass by and keep going, but was stopped by the disciples' cries.[27] D. F. Strauss argued that Mark intended to suggest that Jesus habitually walked on water simply as a normal means of travel. Thus 'this particular of Mark's presents itself as one of the most striking

---

[23] Heil, *Jesus Walking on the Sea*, pp. 68–9.
[24] Lagrange, *Marc*, p. 173: 'il n'est point question d'une tempête'; Pesch, *Markusevangelium*, vol. I, p. 360.
[25] Sibinga, 'Matthew 14:22–33 – Text and Composition', p. 33, n. 47.
[26] Cf. Snoy, 'Mark 6,48: « . . . et il voulait les dépasser.» Proposition pour la solution d'une énigme'; Fleddermann, '"And He Wanted to Pass by Them" (Mark 6:48c)'.
[27] Wellhausen, *Marci*, p. 52; Gould, *Mark*, p. 122; Swete, *Mark*, p. 138: a 'feigned purpose' designed to strengthen faith; Taylor, *Mark*, p. 329; Turner, 'Markan Usage: VIII. [*sic*] Auxiliary . . . verbs', p. 356.

among those by which the second Evangelist now and then approaches to the exaggerations of the apocryphal gospels'.[28] T. Snoy regards this as part of Mark's messianic secret motif because in the two other occasions where Mark uses ἤθελεν (7.24; 9.30) it expresses Jesus' desire to remain hidden; thus on this occasion Jesus approached the disciples, but then intended to withdraw.[29]

A more recent and plausible interpretation sees the phrase καὶ ἤθελεν παρελθεῖν αὐτούς as a conscious allusion, on the part of Mark, to the epiphany language of the LXX (e.g. Gen. 32.31f; Exod. 33.19–23; 34.5f; 1 Kings 19.11; Dan. 12.1).[30] H. Fledder-mann, although not wishing to deny the epiphanic nature of Mark's presentation, argued for a background in LXX Amos 7.8; 8.2 where παρελθεῖν means 'to rescue from disaster'.[31] These OT parallels offer a perspective which fits the account well and could be regarded as accounting for several somewhat puzzling features in Griesbach-Mark's alteration of Matthew: he downplays the storm element, and omits the account of Peter's walking on the sea, in order to emphasise the epiphanic appearance of Jesus: 'He wants to "pass by them" while walking on the sea so that they can see him performing this glorious and majestic divine action, which leads to their rescue.'[32]

Griesbach-Mark continues to follow Matthew in his description of the disciples' reaction to this event. He omits μαθηταί – they have been in view throughout, and need no reintroduction; changes their response from saying to thinking (ἔδοξαν) he was a phantom (Mark only uses the verb δοκέω in one other place, 10.42; Matthew uses it ten times); and rearranges the word order and omits ἀπὸ τοῦ φόβου ('they cried out from fear'). Although φοβέομαι is common in Mark (twelve times), the noun is used only once (Mark 4.41, in an unusual construction). Mark probably assumes this fear (cf.

---

[28] Strauss, *Das Leben Jesu*, vol. II, p. 186 (cited from ET, p. 501).

[29] Snoy, 'Mark 6,48: «. . . et il voulait les dépasser.» Proposition pour la solution d'une énigme', pp. 360–1.

[30] Lohmeyer, 'Und Jesus ging vorüber' (cf. his commentary); Heil, *Jesus Walking on the Sea*, p. 71; Guelich, *Mark*, p. 350; Pesch, *Markusevangelium*, vol. I, p. 361; Lane, *Mark*, p. 236; Theissen, *Urchristliche Wundergeschichten*, pp. 186–7 (ET, pp. 186–7).

[31] Fleddermann, '"And He Wanted to Pass by Them" (Mark 6:48c)', pp. 393–4. Snoy noted several differences from OT theophanies, where the glory is not generally revealed clearly ('Mark 6,48: «. . . et il voulait les dépasser.» Proposi-tion pour la solution d'une énigme', p. 360).

[32] Heil, *Jesus Walking on the Sea*, p. 71.

Jesus' statement of reassurance in 6.50b; and his use of the passive of ταράσσω, which often connotes fear, BAGD, p. 805). He also adds πάντες γὰρ αὐτὸν εἶδον, emphasising that all those present saw Jesus (6.50, implied in Matt. 14.33).

The passage about Peter (Matt. 14.28–31) is omitted; perhaps because he wanted to emphasise the uniqueness of Jesus, or because of Petrine reticence? Griesbach-Mark largely follows Matthew's report that Jesus entered the boat and the wind stopped, but after that point the conclusion to the pericope is decisively different. He omits Matthew's christological climax and replaces it with a negative response: καὶ λίαν [ἐκ περισσοῦ] ἐν ἑαυτοῖς ἐξίσταντο. Although Mark uses ἐξίστημι elsewhere to describe apparently positive reactions to the ministry of Jesus (2.12; 5.42), here (and in 3.21) it is used negatively (cf. a similar term θαυμάζω used positively in 5.20; 6.6; and neutrally perhaps negatively in 12.17; 15.5, 44).

There are two textual problems in Mark 6.52:

> (i) ἐκ περισσοῦ absent from ℵ B (L) Δ 892 (syr^{s.p}) co; while other witnesses lack λίαν (primarily D (W, f¹, 28) 565 700; but also in other ways Θ). The longer text is supported by A f¹³, Maj it syr^h. If these words were original they would signal an even greater emphasis on the astonishment of the disciples.
>
> (ii) many manuscripts add καὶ ἐθαυμάζον at the end of the verse (square brackets in UBS4). The early weight of manuscripts (ℵ B) and versions (it syr cop) speaks in favour of the shorter reading here; a scribe may have remembered Acts 2.7 (cf. Metzger, *Textual Commentary*, pp. 92–3).

In the following verse Mark explains the reason for the disciples' astonishment: οὐ γὰρ συνῆκαν ἐπὶ τοῖς ἄρτοις, ἀλλ' ἦν αὐτῶν ἡ καρδία πεπωρωμένη. This redactional statement changes the disciples from models of Christian confession (in Matthew), into a position that is no different from those who opposed Jesus (whose hearts are hardened, 3.5; cf. 8.17). This conclusion serves to place the whole passage in the broader framework of Mark's bread motif (cf. esp. 8.14–21), emphasising the links between the two feeding miracles and the passages which link them (note also the mention of the boat in 6.54). Heil defends the view that Mark's statement refers to a lack of understanding concerning the identity of Jesus: 'they did not understand on the basis of the loaves'.[33] This links with the immediately prior episode (so M. D. Hooker), but refers to

---

[33] Ibid., p. 6 and n. 13; against Quesnell, *The Mind of Mark*, p. 58.

misunderstanding the purpose of this episode, which was to reveal the identity of Jesus.[34]

4. Conclusion

In this case it becomes apparent that although many of Mark's alterations to Matthew (on the Griesbach hypothesis) *can* be explained in terms of Markan interests and vocabulary preferences (perhaps more than defenders of the two-source hypothesis have been prepared to accept), there are nevertheless specific indications that the two-source hypothesis offers a more coherent and plausible explanation for the redactional behaviour of the evangelists. In particular Matthew's redaction regularly involves repeated use of Matthew's favourite (and significant) phrases, especially in the way in which the walking-on-water account is expressed in terms reminiscent of the stilling-of-the-storm pericope. In addition, the two-source hypothesis understanding of Matthean redaction of Mark results in a plausible and consistent understanding of Matthean christology (so far!). Markan redaction of Matthew (on the other hand) is sometimes (but inconsistently) reactionary, for example in omitting the disciples' worship of Jesus and confession of him as 'Son of God'.

The positive conclusion reached in this chapter contrasts somewhat with the negative conclusions reached in our previous two chapters. In this chapter the positive christological emphases of Matthew have provided a plausible explanation for his redaction of Mark. The previous passages were more concerned with a negatively oriented argument. This argument was focussed in Matthew's avoidance of various peculiarities of the Markan account. In the next chapter we shall investigate several topics highlighted by the christological argument for Markan priority (as expounded in chapter one, section three).

---

[34] Heil, *Jesus Walking on the Sea*, pp. 73–4, and esp. n. 108; Hooker, *Mark*, pp. 169–70.

6

ARGUMENTS CONCERNING JESUS' EMOTIONS, 'INABILITY' AND QUESTIONS

1. Introduction

The area in which the christological argument for Markan priority most clearly reflects its historical and theological origins is in the argument that Matthew omitted from Mark passages concerning Jesus' emotions, inability and questions owing to christological embarrassment. This argument was particularly important to scholars influenced by the British kenotic movement with its theological emphasis on the limited human consciousness of Jesus (cf. chapter one, section three). Scholars such as W. Sanday, J. C. Hawkins and W. C. Allen appear to have been heavily influenced by this movement which regarded traditional orthodox dogmatic christology as somewhat docetic. In reaction to this, the Markan presentation of Jesus as a feeling, questioning, human being was esteemed as providing access to the real historical Jesus. Matthew's omissions of references to Jesus' emotions, inability and questions which assume Jesus' ignorance were regarded as an indication of his posteriority in relation to Mark in view of the generally docetic trend of later gospel writers.[1]

The passages in view in this chapter are linked not only by this common historical origin, but also on source-critical grounds in that they all involve, according to the two-source hypothesis, Matthean omissions from Mark. They thus involve redaction by omission, a practice which is characteristic of 'reactionary writing', to borrow D. Dungan's term, and is well attested, as a general category, in the redaction of gospel traditions in the second century. The clearest example is Marcion whose criticism by omission is well known and apparently pervasive (cf. Irenaeus,

---

[1] Hawkins, *Horae Synopticae*, pp. 117–21; Allen, *Matthew*, pp. xxxi–xxxiii; Davies and Allison, *Matthew*, vol. I, pp. 104–5.

Adversus haereses I.27.2–4; Tertullian, *Adversus Marcionem* I.1.5);[2] Tatian's omission of the genealogies might be another, albeit less clear example; and numerous examples could be found of deliberate omission on the part of scribes.[3] Nevertheless there is an inherent difficulty involved in attributing definite motives to redactional omissions, a difficulty that is especially apparent in the case of Matthew's relationship with the generally fuller passages in Mark: on the two-source hypothesis abbreviations may be due not to embarrassment but to a general desire to abbreviate and focus the accounts.[4]

In this chapter we shall investigate numerous passages with the aim of assessing the value of the argument concerning christological embarrassment for the two-source hypothesis. Hence we shall begin with the two-source hypothesis perspective for the passage, asking in particular whether the alleged embarrassment provides the best explanation for Matthean redaction of Mark. For each passage we shall also examine, from the other perspective, the redactional behaviour of Griesbach-Mark. The results shall be summarised briefly after each section. Clearly the christological argument for Markan priority focussed almost entirely on the relationship between Matthew and Mark (see chapter one). In the following sections evidence from Luke will be adduced first in connection with the two-source hypothesis for comparative purposes; and secondly in connection with the Griesbach hypothesis as a source and subject for Mark's redaction.

2.   The emotions of Jesus

Table 6.1 lists the synoptic references to Jesus' emotions. This table shows that with the exception of 'compassion' terminology, where Matthew has four references to Mark's two, there *are* fewer references to Jesus' emotions in Matthew than in Mark. In particular there are five passages where Matthew is closely parallel to

---

[2] Head, 'Marcion's Gospel Redaction'.
[3] See further Head, 'Tatian's Christology', esp. pp. 131–2 (on the omission of the genealogies); Head, 'Christology and Textual Transmission', esp. pp. 120–6 (on Mark 13.32; Matt. 24.36; Luke 22.43f), for a different perspective on Luke 22.43f see Ehrman, *The Orthodox Corruption of Scripture*, pp. 187–94, who nevertheless supports the general principle (see, e.g. pp. 91–2 on Matt. 24.36).
[4] White, 'The "Dogmatic" Variations in Matthew', p. 308; cf. Burton, *Some Principles of Literary Criticism and Their Application to the Synoptic Problem*, pp. 203–4.

Table 6.1   *Synoptic references to Jesus' emotion*

Mark	Matthew	Luke
1.41a καὶ <u>ὀργισθεὶς</u> ἐκτείνας τὴν χεῖρα αὐτοῦ ἥψατο . . .	8.3a καὶ ἐκτείνας τὴν χεῖρα ἥψατο αὐτοῦ . . .	5.13a καὶ ἐκτείνας τὴν χεῖρα ἥψατο αὐτοῦ . . .
1.43 καὶ <u>ἐμβριμησάμενος</u> αὐτῷ εὐθὺς ἐξέβαλεν αὐτόν,	8.4a καὶ λέγει αὐτῷ ὁ Ἰησοῦς,	5.14a καὶ αὐτὸς παρήγγειλεν αὐτῷ
no parallel	8.10 ἀκούσας δὲ ὁ Ἰησοῦς <u>ἐθαύμασεν</u> καὶ εἶπεν τοῖς ἀκολουθοῦσιν, . . .	7.9 ἀκούσας δὲ ταῦτα ὁ Ἰησοῦς <u>ἐθαύμασεν</u> αὐτόν, καὶ στραφεὶς τῷ ἀκολουθοῦντι αὐτῷ ὄχλῳ εἶπεν, . . .
no parallel to Matt. 9.30f (cf. Mark 10.46–52)	9.30 καὶ <u>ἐνεβριμήθη</u> αὐτοῖς ὁ Ἰησοῦς λέγων,	no parallel to Matt. 9.30f (cf. Luke 18.35–43)
cf. 6.34 cited below	9.36 Ἰδὼν δὲ τοὺς ὄχλους <u>ἐσπλαγχνίσθη</u> περὶ αὐτῶν ὅτι ἦσαν ἐσκυλμένοι καὶ ἐρριμμένοι . . .	no parallel
3.5 καὶ περιβλεψάμενος αὐτοὺς <u>μετ' ὀργῆς,</u> <u>συλλυπούμενος</u> ἐπὶ τῇ πωρώσει τῆς καρδίας αὐτῶν, λέγει τῷ ἀνθρώπῳ, . . .	12.13 τότε λέγει τῷ ἀνθρώπῳ, . . .	6.10 καὶ περιβλεψάμενος πάντας αὐτοὺς εἶπεν αὐτῷ, . . .
6.6a καὶ <u>ἐθαύμαζεν</u> διὰ τὴν ἀπιστίαν αὐτῶν.	13.58 καὶ οὐκ ἐποίησεν ἐκεῖ δυνάμεις πολλὰς διὰ τὴν ἀπιστίαν αὐτῶν.	no parallel (cf. 4.16–30)
6.34 . . . καὶ <u>ἐσπλαγχνίσθη</u> ἐπ' αὐτοὺς ὅτι ἦσαν ὡς πρόβατα μὴ ἔχοντα ποιμένα,	14.14 . . . καὶ <u>ἐσπλαγχνίσθη</u> ἐπ' αὐτοῖς . . .	phrase not found in 9.10b–17
7.34 καὶ ἀναβλέψας εἰς τὸν οὐρανὸν <u>ἐστέναξεν,</u> καὶ λέγει αὐτῷ, Εφφαθα, . . .	no parallel	no parallel
8.2 <u>Σπλαγχνίζομαι</u> ἐπὶ τὸν ὄχλον . . .	15.32 <u>Σπλαγχνίζομαι</u> ἐπὶ τὸν ὄχλον, . . .	no parallel

Table 6.1   *contd*

Mark	Matthew	Luke
8.12 καὶ ἀναστενάξας τῷ πνεύματι αὐτοῦ λέγει, . . .	no parallel (cf. 16.1–4)	no parallel (cf. 11.16, 29)
10.14 ἰδὼν δὲ ὁ Ἰησοῦς ἠγανάκτησεν καὶ εἶπεν αὐτοῖς,	19.14 ὁ δὲ Ἰησοῦς εἶπεν, . . .	18.16 ὁ δὲ Ἰησοῦς προσεκαλέσατο αὐτὰ λέγων, . . .
10.21 ὁ δὲ Ἰησοῦς ἐμβλέψας αὐτῷ ἠγάπησεν αὐτὸν καὶ εἶπεν αὐτῷ, . . .	19.21 ἔφη αὐτῷ ὁ Ἰησοῦς, . . .	18.22 ἀκούσας δὲ ὁ Ἰησοῦς εἶπεν αὐτῷ, . . .
phrase not found in 10.51f	20.34 σπλαγχνισθεὶς δὲ ὁ Ἰησοῦς ἥψατο τῶν ὀμμάτων αὐτῶν, . . .	phrase not found in 18.41f
14.33b καὶ ἤρξατο ἐκθαμβεῖσθαι καὶ ἀδημονεῖν,	26.37 ἤρξατο λυπεῖσθαι καὶ ἀδημονεῖν.	phrase not found in 22.40f
14.34a καὶ λέγει αὐτοῖς, Περίλυπός ἐστιν ἡ ψυχή μου . . .	26.38a τότε λέγει αὐτοῖς, Περίλυπός ἐστιν ἡ ψυχή μου . . .	phrase not found in 22.40f

Mark except for the key word or phrase involved (Matt. 8.3, 4; 13.58; 19.14, 21). Both W. C. Allen and W. D. Davies and D. C. Allison gave a prominent place in their support for Markan priority to the argument that Matthew has omitted references to Jesus' emotions because of christological reverence.[5] Their discussions, however, exhibit a common weakness in simply listing the relevant passages, without any critical discussion. It cannot be assumed without argument that theirs is the best explanation for Matthean redaction according to the two-source hypothesis.

By way of perspective it is noteworthy that if account is taken of all the emotions attributed to all the other characters, not including Jesus, Mark has forty-one references while Matthew has thirty-three (see Appendix 6.A, p. 121). This involves, given the greater length of Matthew, a ratio proportional to length of over two to one (2.1:1). In other words, Mark has twice as many references as

[5] Allen, *Matthew*, p. xxxi; Davies and Allison, *Matthew*, vol. I, pp. 104–5.

Matthew to any sort of human emotion. Matthew is not opposed in principle to recording human emotions (cf. Matt. 2.3, 10, 16, 22), but it does seem that he is less interested in such matters than Mark. In addition, many of these Markan emotions occur in passages which are heavily abbreviated in Matthew (e.g. Mark 1.26, 27; 5.15, 33, 42; 6.19, 20b). Either of these two observations might also help to explain the relative lack of Jesus' emotions in Matthew. Other observations might also be noted in view of the evidence laid out in the appendix:

(i)   Matthew tends to make the subject of the emotion explicit, whereas Mark often leaves it to be inferred from the narrative;
(ii) Mark's five occurrences of θαμβέομαι are all unparalleled in Matthew;
(iii) Matthew favours θαυμάζω;
(iv) Mark occasionally uses an unparalleled intensifying ἐκ prefix (9.6, 15; 12.17; 16.5).

In the following section our investigation shall begin with those passages in which Matthew and Mark are most closely parallel (Matt. 8.3, 4; 13.58; 19.14, 21), before looking at the other passages recording emotions of Jesus.

In his account of the cleansing of the leper (Mark 1.40–5 // Matt. 8.1–4 // Luke 5.12–16) Mark refers both to the anger of Jesus (ὀργισθείς, v. 41) and to his agitation (ἐμβριμησάμενος, v. 43; BAGD, p. 254).

> Although a significant number of scholars, as reflected in NA27 = UBS4, follow the externally well-attested reading of σπλαγχνισθείς at Mark 1.41 (with ℵ A B C L W etc. f¹ f¹³ syr cop etc.), the majority of commentators have preferred the more difficult, albeit less well-attested, reading of ὀργισθείς (D it ᵃ ᵈ ᶠᶠ² ʳ¹ Ephraem). See Turner, 'A Textual Commentary on Mark 1', p. 147; Taylor, *Mark*, p. 187; Hooker, *Mark*, p. 79; Head, 'Christology and Textual Transmission', pp. 122–3; Gnilka, *Markus*, vol. I, pp. 92–3; Pesch, *Markusevangelium*, vol. I, p. 141, note c. In support of σπλαγχνισθείς see Haenchen, *Der Weg Jesu*, p. 96; Metzger, *Textual Commentary*, p. 70; Gundry, *Mark*, pp. 102–3.

Matthew's version is shorter than Mark's (sixty-two words cf. ninety-nine); this remains true without the introductory and concluding comments: 52–70–62 (Matt. 8.2–4; Mark 1.40–4; Luke 5.12ab–14). The parallels in wording between Matthew and Mark are close, and they share a nine-word sequence except for Matthew's omission of ὀργισθείς. The placement of the passage in

Matthew might be explained as a link between the Sermon on the Mount and the series of miracles in chapters 8 and 9, possibly placed because of the reference to fulfilling the law.[6] Commentators have also shown that Matthew's alterations involve the introduction of Matthean vocabulary, particularly in 8.2: καὶ ἰδοὺ λεπρὸς <u>προσελθὼν</u> <u>προσεκύνει</u> αὐτῷ λέγων, <u>Κύριε</u>, . . .[7] Matthew's omissions also highlight key elements within the account.[8] Within the broader Matthean context it is possible that a reference to Jesus' anger would be in a degree of tension with 5.22. Thus, assuming the two-source hypothesis, Matthew's redaction of Mark coheres with elements of his procedure elsewhere. In addition, the omission of Jesus' anger is characteristic of the scribal tradition at this point and is also rendered plausible by the difficulty in accounting for Jesus' anger within the Markan account.

At least four possibilites have been advocated:

(i)   Jesus was angry at the man for approaching him and thus violating the Torah regulations for segregation (cf. Lev. 13.45f; Rawlinson, *Mark*, pp. 21–2);

(ii)   Jesus' anger represents the ritual agitation of a miracle worker (cf. Pesch, *Markusevangelium*, vol. I, p. 144; Gnilka, *Markus*, vol. I, p. 93);

(iii) Jesus was angry at the interruption of his mission (so G. B. Telford, 'Mark 1:40–45');

(iv)   Jesus' anger was directed at the root cause of the man's problem, the forces of evil behind the distorting disease (e.g. Taylor, *Mark*, p. 188; Grundmann, *Markus*, p. 51; Guelich, *Mark*, p. 74).

For some scholars the difficulty is so intense as to provide evidence that the account is incoherent and must have originated from the conflation of two separate stories (so Lohmeyer, *Markus*, pp. 44–6; Cave, 'The Leper: Mark 1:40–45').

While these considerations render the two-source hypothesis view of Matthean redaction both plausible and coherent, they do not *demand* the conclusion that Matthew's redaction is motivated by christological embarrassment with Jesus' anger *per se*. Indeed, the exegetical difficulty in understanding the reason for Jesus' anger provides a more appropriate rationale for the omission than the supposed theological difficulty. In particular, we should note both

---

[6] For the arrangement of Matt. 8 and 9 see Thompson, 'Reflections on the Composition of Mt 8:1–9:34'; Kingsbury, 'Observations on the "Miracle Chapters" of Matthew 8–9'; Burger, 'Jesus Taten nach Matthäus 8 und 9'.

[7] Gundry, *Matthew*, p. 139; Grundmann, *Matthäus*, pp. 247–8; cf. esp. Matt. 9.18.

[8] Held, 'Matthäus als Interpret der Wundergeschichten', pp. 202–4 (ET, pp. 214–15); cf. pp. 221–4 (ET. pp. 233–7) on Matthew's tendency to highlight the conversational element in miracle stories.

Matthew's later use of ἐμβριμάομαι in connection with Jesus (9.30); and that in two kingdom parables Matthew uses ὀργίζομαι of the king or lord in the parable of the talents (18.34) and the king in the parable of the vineyard (22.7). This suggests (along with other judgement passages, e.g. 25.31ff) that Matthew expected the wrath or anger of the Son of Man to be exercised in judgement.

Griesbach-hypothesis analysis of this passage suggests that Mark is primarily following Luke at this point, although parallels noted above demand the influence of Matthew on the wording.[9] The account links the 'day-in-the-life' block of stories in Mark 1.21–39 with the conflict stories of 2.1–3.6. F. Bleek, followed by other scholars, appealed to Mark 1.42 as evidence of conflation of Matthew and Luke: 'Matthew adds, καὶ εὐθέως ἐκαθαρίσθη αὐτοῦ ἡ λέπρα; Luke adds, καὶ εὐθέως ἡ λέπρα ἀπῆλθεν ἀπ' αὐτοῦ; and Mark writes, καὶ εὐθέως ἀπῆλθεν ἀπ' αὐτοῦ ἡ λέπρα ἐκαθαρίσθη.'[10] The issue of Jesus' emotions has not, however, been addressed by Griesbachian scholars. Although Griesbachians have appealed to the eighteen-word 'minor agreement' of Matthew 8.2b–3 // Luke 5.12d–13 as evidence against the two-source hypothesis and for Luke's use of Matthew, it is nevertheless not easy to explain Griesbach-Mark's alteration of this material.[11] With his two sources agreed Griesbach-Mark nevertheless omits κύριε, adds ὀργισθείς and makes several other minor changes. It is hardly surprising that neo-Griesbachians prefer to read σπλαγχνισθείς here, as this might be felt to cohere with other occurrences of the term in Mark (6.34; 8.2; 9.22).[12] But even this would not result in a consistent redactional behaviour because at Matthew 20.23 // Mark 10.51f Griesbach-Mark passes over an occurrence of the term in his source, and in any case Mark 1.41 would be the only place where it was redactionally added. Nor is the use of ἐμβριμάομαι particularly characteristic of Griesbach-Mark (1–2–0–2). There is thus little evidence to suggest that the redactional activity envisaged for Mark by the Griesbach hypothesis produces a consistent picture.

---

[9] Griesbach, 'Demonstration', pp. 108–9, 209; Bleek, *Einleitung*, p. 251 (ET, vol. I, p. 268); de Wette, *Einleitung*, pp. 187–8 (ET, p. 166); Farmer, *The Synoptic Problem*, p. 238.

[10] Bleek, *Einleitung*, p. 245 (cited from ET, vol. I, p. 261).

[11] Farmer, *The Synoptic Problem*, pp. 144–5; cf. also, supporting Luke's knowledge of Matthew, Gundry, *Matthew*, p. 139; Goulder, *Luke*, vol. I, p. 329.

[12] Orchard, *Synopsis*, p. 47; Mann, *Mark*, p. 218 (although the notes on p. 219 suggest a preference for ὀργισθείς as the harder reading).

This eighteen word agreement between Matthew 8.2b–3 and Luke 5.12d–13 is the largest of the 'minor agreements' of Matthew and Luke against Mark. Few two-source hypothesis scholars have suggested a Mark–Q overlap here. The agreement is generally held to be the result of coincidental independent alterations by both Matthew and Luke (e.g. Streeter, *The Four Gospels*, pp. 309–10; Neirynck, *The Minor Agreements*, pp. 65–6; Davies and Allison, *Matthew*, vol. II, pp. 12–13; Fitzmyer, *Luke*, vol. I, p. 574). Another possibility is the existence of additional sources either written (Schramm, *Der Markus-Stoff bei Lukas*, pp. 91–9) or oral (Marshall, *Luke*, pp. 206 and 209).

The account of Jesus' rejection at Nazareth has already been discussed at some length (chapter 4). Mark 6.6a refers to Jesus' marvelling, καὶ ἐθαύμαζεν διὰ τὴν ἀπιστίαν αὐτῶν, which is not found in the parallel account in Matt. 13.58. On the two-source hypothesis it is hardly likely that difficulties with attributing this attitude to Jesus motivated its omission, since Matthew, although most often using it of the reaction of the crowd or the disciples (see 8.27; 9.33; 15.31; 21.20; 22.22; 27.14), does elsewhere use the same verb in describing Jesus' reaction to the centurion's faith (Matt. 8.10Q). On the other hand, on the Griesbach hypothesis, the introduction of the verb does not correspond to Markan vocabulary preferences (7–4–13), nor is the attribution of this attitude to Jesus paralleled in any other Markan account, despite the presence of Matthew 8.10 // Luke 7.9 in his source material.

In two places surrounding the passage concerning the 'rich young ruler' Mark includes an indication of Jesus' emotional experience which Matthew lacks. As already noted in chapter three, indications of literary dependence between Matthew and Mark in this context are strong, and in both places Matthew simply lacks the 'emotional' term: ἠγανάκτησεν ('be indignant' in Mark 10.14); and the phrase ὁ δὲ Ἰησοῦς ἐμβλέψας αὐτῷ ἠγάπησεν αὐτὸν (Mark 10.21). The use of these omissions as an argument for the priority of Mark is, however, quite problematic. Although Matthew nowhere else uses the term ἀγανακτέω of Jesus, he does not scruple to view Jesus as indignant without using the term (cf. ch. 23). In addition, it is difficult to see how the omission of a reference to Jesus' love would be omitted from a feeling of 'reverence' to Jesus. From the Griesbach hypothesis it is sufficient to observe that the additions that Mark makes to his sources do not correspond to general Markan vocabulary preferences: ἀγανακτέω (3–3–1); ἀγαπάω (8–5–13).

Matthew's version of the healing of the man with the withered hand begins and ends closely parallel to Mark (Matt. 12:9f // Mark

3.1f; Matt. 12.13f // Mark 3.5bf). The central section of the passage is quite different in Matthew, with the addition in vv.11–12a of the argument *qal wahomer*: 'of how much more value is a man than a sheep' (this same example is found in similar discussions including CD 11.13–17, where rescue is rejected; and *b. Šabb.* 128b, defending a milder view). Matthew's narrative is much simpler than Mark's: in Mark attention is divided between Jesus on the one hand and the man and the opponents in turn (man, v. 1; opponents, v. 2; man, v. 3; opponents, vv. 4, 5a; man, v. 5b; opponents, v. 6). Matthew has a simpler structure (man, v. 10a; opponents, vv. 10b, 11, 12; man, v. 13; opponents, v. 14). While Mark records various aspects of Jesus' interaction with the characters (vv. 3, 4c; 5ab), Matthew, with the exception of the initial statement concerning the motive of Jesus' opponents (v. 10b) and the concluding statement concerning the plotting against Jesus (v. 14), simply records the statements made (note the verbalising of the opponents' challenge in v. 10).

These alterations, assuming the two-source hypothesis, indicate Matthew's concerns: first, with Jesus' positive teaching on attitudes to the sabbath (the additional material in vv. 11f) of which the healing becomes an illustration;[13] secondly, on the growing opposition to Jesus (as also in Mark). Where Mark's account is vivid and lively, and full of dramatic interest, Matthew's is simple and straightforward. It is this general context which must inform our assessment of Matthew's omission of the reference to Jesus' anger and grief in Mark 3.5. As we mentioned above, there is little evidence that Jesus' anger against his opponents should cause embarrassment to Matthew in view of his general presentation of the controversies and Jesus as judge. The two-source hypothesis does not need the category of 'christological embarrassment' to explain Matthean redaction.

On the Griesbach hypothesis Mark's redaction involves both a process of selecting phrases from Matthew and Luke,[14] and the addition of new material. Of this new material two key terms are not found elsewhere in Mark: ὀργή and συλλυπέομαι (a NT hapax). The final phrase of Mark's additional material in v. 5, ἐπὶ τῇ πωρώσει τῆς καρδίας αὐτῶν, approximates to other Markan vocabulary preferences – cf. the use of the verbal form πωρόω in

---

[13] Verseput, *The Rejection of the Humble Messianic King*, p. 179.
[14] de Wette, *Einleitung*, p. 188 (ET, p. 167); Bleek, *Einleitung*, p. 251 (ET, vol. I, p. 268); Davidson, *Introduction*, p. 471; Farmer, *The Synoptic Problem*, p. 238.

6.52 and 8.17 – although in the latter two passages the disciples' obtuseness and insensibility are apparently in view, whereas in 3.5 it is difficult to exclude the idea of hardness and obstinacy.[15] There is thus little indication of redactional consistency of vocabulary here. Two more passages involve Mark's use of (ἀνα)στενάζω, the only occurrences in the gospels. The first is Mark 7.32–5, the healing of a deaf mute by Jesus, a passage unique to Mark. The second passage is Mark 8.12, in the report of the Pharisees' approach to Jesus in order to seek a sign (Mark 8.11–13 // Matt. 16.1–4). In this passage the Matthean version is not very close to Mark (furthermore the Lukan parallels are split up in Luke 11.16; 12.54–6; 11.29; while Mark 11.12f // Matt. 16.4 is also closely paralleled in Matt. 12.38f). While the key words in the introduction (οἱ Φαρισαῖοι, πειράζοντες, σημεῖον), in Jesus' rebuke (γενεά, σημεῖον, δοθήσεται, σημεῖον), and in the transitional comments between this and the next pericope (Mark 8.13 // Matt. 16.4b–5a) are closely parallel, there are also significant differences between the accounts: Matthew's extra material in 16.2f; the description of the generation as πονηρὰ καὶ μοιχαλὶς; and the identification of the sign to be given as the sign of Jonah. In other words, Matthew has treated the whole account fairly loosely, thus making it more difficult to maintain an argument which depends on selective omissions. Nevertheless, Matthew does lack Mark's phrase καὶ ἀναστενάξας τῷ πνεύματι αὐτοῦ λέγει, and he places Jesus more firmly in opposition to the Pharisees, hence the addition of 'evil and adulterous generation'. Jesus' exasperation at the Pharisees is somewhat sharpened in Matthew's version. It is likely, however, that factors other than christological embarrassment are more important in explaining Matthean redaction here. The Markan question (3.4) has been replaced by the Matthean pronouncement (12.11f); hence Matthew omits the Pharisees' silence, which is what prompts Jesus' anger and grief in Mark.[16] In other words, the emotional responses of Jesus are omitted as part of a broader pattern of alteration.[17]

These investigations have cast some doubt upon the theory that

---

[15] J. A. Robinson argued that πώρωσις generally conveyed obtuseness, insensibility or moral blindness rather than hardness or obstinacy (*Ephesians*, pp. 264–74; cf. also BAGD, p. 732).

[16] Guelich, *Mark*, p. 137.

[17] Gundry, *Matthew*, p. 227; Gnilka, *Matthäusevangelium*, vol. I, p. 447; Banks, *Jesus and the Law*, pp. 126–8. It is notable that commentators such as Davies and Allison do not appeal to the principle of christological embarrassment in their comments here.

Matthew wished to avoid attributing emotions to Jesus owing to christological embarrassment, and this is further supported by passages where Matthew explicitly predicates such emotions of Jesus. In one of these Matthew follows Mark (Mark 14.32–42 // Matt. 26.36–46): καὶ ἤρξατο ἐκθαμβεῖσθαι καὶ ἀδημονεῖν, καὶ λέγει αὐτοῖς, Περίλυπός ἐστιν ἡ ψυχή μου ἕως θανάτου (Mark 14.33b–4a cf. Matt. 26.37b–8a). Notwithstanding some differences in the wording, the accounts are closely parallel. The differences in wording are mainly stylistic: the addition of 'Jesus' at the beginning of a paragraph; use of λεγόμενος (Matt.: 13, Mark: 1); reference to 'sons of Zebedee' without names (Matt.: 3, Mark: 0); use of τότε (Matt.: 89; Mark: 6). Matthew also has λυπέω where Mark has ἐκθαμβέω. This might be regarded as a softening of the emotions on Matthew's part, since in collocation with ἀδημονέω, which itself can mean 'be in anxiety' or 'be distressed' (BAGD, p. 16), the meaning becomes something more akin to 'be in grief-stricken anxiety', whereas Mark's version may perhaps best be understood as 'experience distressed amazement'. Descamps thus suggested that Matthew wanted to avoid the attribution to Jesus of the terror of a mere mortal.[18] Other factors, however, cannot be discounted. The first factor is stylistic: Matthew never uses ἐκθαμβέω – ἐκθαμβέω and θαμβέω are found only in Mark in the NT (9.15; 14.33; 16.5 and 1.27; 10.24; 10.32 respectively); secondly, assimilation to the OT background of Jesus' statement could explain the alteration (Ps. 41.6, 12; 42.5 LXX). Matthew does not shy away from Jesus' experience of emotions *per se*, even if here he slightly modifies the Markan account.

There are two other passages (already mentioned) where Matthew predicates emotions of Jesus. Matthew 8.10 (// Luke 7.9) uses θαυμάζω to describe Jesus' response to the faith of the centurion. This passage indeed implies that Jesus was surprised by that faith. The other passage to note is Matthew 9.30: at the close of the story after Jesus heals the two blind men, he 'sternly charges them' (ἐνεβριμήθη αὐτοῖς) not to make the event known.

Summary

It is not clear that Matthew's fewer references to Jesus' emotions are due to 'christological redaction'. Even assuming the two-source

---

[18] Descamps, 'Rédaction et christologie dans le récit matthéen de la Passion', p. 396.

hypothesis the occasional explicit mention of such emotions, the availability of other explanations, Matthew's general acceptance of the humanity of Jesus, and his habitual abbreviation of Markan narratives, all call into question the role of such arguments in support of Markan priority. This is certainly not a consistent characteristic of Matthew, nor is it necessarily plausible since there is no evidence of any second-century tendency to omit Jesus' emotions *per se*, indeed, at times they are introduced (cf. above p. 40). Since Matthew also omits recorded emotions of other human characters in the narrative of Mark, his lack of interest in Jesus' emotions does not necessarily indicate a christological *Tendenz*. In short, the use of this aspect of the argument for Markan priority is extremely weak. In any case White's argument, that even the NT books with the 'highest' christologies also present a real humanity and references to Jesus' emotional activity (e.g. John 11.33, 38; Heb. 5.7) is still relevant.[19]

On the other hand we have encountered several difficulties in considering the Griesbach-hypothesis approach to these passages. From this perspective the addition of emotions (not only to Jesus, but also to other characters) should probably be regarded as a subset of Mark's general tendency to add enlivening details to the narratives. In this Mark often maintains a distinctive vocabulary, emphasising, in particular, reactions to Jesus' activity. It is unlikely that specifically 'christological' factors were involved. It might be thought of as an example of an anti-docetic tendency or polemic but this would be radically unlike any other form of such polemic, which is much more straightforward. If Griesbach-Mark's redactional activity is attributed to verisimilitude, the difficulty remains that Mark does not use characteristic vocabulary. In addition in the only two places where Matthew presents him with a clear exemplar for Jesus' emotions, he ignores it.

Excursus 6.1. Jesus' compassion in Matthew

One emotion that Matthew clearly treats positively is that expressed by the verb σπλαγχνίζεσθαι – 'to have compassion'. In the NT this verb occurs only in the synoptic gospels – a total of eleven times (Matt. 9.36; 14.14; 15.32; 18.27; 20.34; Mark 6.34; 8.2; 9.22; Luke 7.13; 10.33; 15.20). In the two places where it is found in Mark it is

---

[19] White, 'The "Dogmatic" Variations in Matthew'.

also found in Matthew, as well as in two additional passages. According to H. Koester, a semantic shift occured in the first-century usage of 'compassion' terminology. The Hebrew terms *rḥm* and *nḥm* are reasonably common in the Masoretic Text, where they are used, among other meanings, to express the idea of 'compassion', especially in relation to Yahweh's dealings with Israel (e.g. Deut. 13.17; 30.3; Isa. 14.1; 49.13; 54.7–10; Mic. 7.19). In the LXX these are, however, never rendered with σπλαγχνίζεσθαι (which only occurs in Prov 17.5 and 2 Macc. 6.8), but with various constructions, most often using ἐλεήσει σε or οἰκτείρω (cf. Rom. 9.15, the only NT occurrence of οἰκτείρω, which combines these two terms). Koester finds in both the NT and the *Testaments of the Twelve Patriarchs* evidence of a semantic shift in which σπλαγχνί-ζεσθαι takes over from οἰκτείρω as the translation of *rḥm*.[20] Thus background of the NT usage of term is apparently not found in the LXX, nor in classical literature, but in contemporary Judaism.[21]

For this usage see *T. Zeb.* 6.4; 7.1, 2; 8.3; cf. also (parallel to NT usage): *The Life of Adam & Eve* 9.3; 27.2; 29.9; *T. Abr.* 12.12, 13; *T. Zeb.* 4.2; 8.1, 4; 4 Baruch 6.18 (6.21 in ET: 'the Lord had compassion and remembered his covenant with Abraham'); *Apoc. Sedrach* 13.2; *T. Job* 26.5.

Especially interesting is the *Testament of Zebulun*, the full title of which is 'The Testament of Zebulun concerning Compassion and Mercy'. In 8.1–4, compassion is presented as both ethical in intent – 'have compassion toward every person, . . . in order that the Lord may be compassionate and merciful to you' (8.1) – and as characteristic of God's acts in the last days: 'In the last days God will send his compassion (τὸ σπλάγχνον αὐτοῦ) on the earth, and whenever he finds compassionate mercy (σπλάγχνα ἐλέους), in that person he will dwell' (8.2).

The usage in Jesus' parables is somewhat similar (e.g. Matt. 18.27; Luke 10.33; 15.20); σπλαγχνίζεσθαι is used to describe both the attitude of the 'good Samaritan' (Luke 10.33), and the characteristic of those who represent God in the parables (Matt. 18.27; Luke 15.20). Of these, as well as the following passages, it could be said that it does not denote the mere 'emotion' but 'it expresses the guiding inner disposition which leads to mercy.'[22]

An example of Matthew's use of σπλαγχνίζεσθαι can be seen in

---

[20] Koester, *TDNT*, vol. VII, p. 552; Hollander and de Jonge, *The Testaments of the Twelve Patriarchs*, p. 255.
[21] So also Lightfoot, *Philippians*, p. 86.
[22] Koester, *TDNT*, vol. VII, p. 551 (here in connection with *T. Zeb.*).

9.36 where Matthew sums up the continued activity of Jesus (9.35) along the lines of the progression from the previous summary statement in 4.23: word and deed (chapters 5–7, 8–9). The themes of christology and discipleship which are prominent in chapters 8 and 9 come together. Jesus' compassion is directed towards the crowds, who have been prominent in the entire section: 4.25; 5.1; 7.28; 8.1, 18; 9.8, 23, 25, 33 ('disciples' are mostly present only in the interludes between miracles in chapters 8 and 9: 8.21, 23; 9.10, 11, 14 (bis), 19). This compassion is based in part on the lack of qualified leaders: the people are 'like sheep without a shepherd' (9.36; cf. Num. 27.17; 1 Kings 22.17 // 2 Chron. 18.16; Ezek. 34; Zech. 10.2f; 11.4–17; Jdt. 11.19). Implicit is the claim that Jesus is the messianic shepherd (cf. Ezek. 34.23; 37.24). The compassion of Jesus is then directed towards mission (hence the sending out of the twelve follows in chapter 10).

It seems apparent that Matthew's interest in depicting Jesus' compassion is part and parcel with his positive christological aim. It involves 'a Messianic characterisation of Jesus rather than the mere depiction of an emotion'.[23] This is borne out in the other places where Matthew uses the term: in connection with Jesus' healing of the sick (14.14); his provision of bread (15.32); and the giving of sight to the blind (20.34). As such, the use of 'compassion' terminology should be related to the broader scheme of Matthew's presentation. In addition the frequency of 'mercy' cognates, much more frequent in Matthew than in Mark (ἐλεέω (7–3–4 + 0); ἔλεος (3–0–6 + 0)), should be noted. Especially prominent are the repeated requests to Jesus as Messiah/Son of David, ἐλέησον με/ ἡμᾶς (Matt. 9.27; 15.22; 17.15; 20.30, 31); and the double quotation of Hosea 6.6, Ἔλεος θέλω καὶ οὐ θυσίαν (Matt. 9.13; 12.7).[24] In this area Matthew appears to stand in proximity to *T. Zeb.*: the last days have come, the one in whom mercy and compassion are to be found is Jesus the Messiah, the one in whom God's presence is also found (Immanuel).

> The dating of *T. 12 Patr.* is, of course, too uncertain to postulate dependence. At its most basic the debate concerns whether the clearly Christian interpolations (so e.g. *T. Jos.* 19.6; *T. Ben.* 3.8) require a Christian provenance for the whole work (so de Jonge, *The Testaments of the Twelve Patriarchs*, pp. 121–8; 'Christian Influence in the Testaments of

---

[23] Koester, *TDNT*, vol. VII, p. 554.
[24] See Gerhardsson, 'Sacrificial Service and Atonement in the Gospel of Matthew'; Hill, 'On the Use and Meaning of Hosea VI.6 in Matthew's Gospel'.

the Twelve Patriarchs'; 'The Interpretation of the Testaments of the Twelve Patriarchs in Recent Years' (dating the work *c.* AD 200)); or whether they should be regarded as interpolations into an already existing hellenistic Jewish work (Kee, in *OTP* vol. I, pp. 777–8 (Maccabean with interpolations); Schürer (rev.), *The History of the Jewish People*, vol. III, pp. 767–781 (with bibliography), esp. p. 774 (100–63 BC plus interpolations)); see further Slingerland, *The Testaments of the Twelve Patriarchs*; Charlesworth, 'Reflections on the SNTS Pseudepigrapha Seminar at Duke on the Testaments of the Twelve Patriarchs' and *The New Testament Apocrypha and Pseudepigrapha*, pp. 211–20.

Matthew's Jesus exercises his messianic authority through meekness and gentleness (Matt. 11.29; 12.15–21 (Isa. 42.1–4); 21.5 (Zech. 9.9)).[25] Whatever view is taken of the source-critical question, in this case it appears that Matthew adapts and uses a particular 'emotion' for a christological purpose.

3. The questions of Jesus

Another category which was prominent in the christological argument for Markan priority outlined in chapter one concerned the ignorance of Jesus. Here too the influence of kenotic theology, particularly that of Charles Gore, appears evident. Passages and questions which imply Jesus' ignorance are said to be omitted by Matthew owing to reverence for Jesus.[26] The relevant passages are Mark 5.9, 30; 6.38; 9.16, 21. Davies and Allison included a number of additional questions which, for various reasons, are not particularly relevant: these include Mark 8.12 and 9.33, which are not properly interrogative (see below); 8.23, which is only one part of a larger omission; and 14.14, which is not in the same category, since it is part of Jesus' instructions to the disciples.

There is evidence to suggest that in some parts of the manuscript tradition passages which specifically attribute ignorance to Jesus (i.e. Mark 13.32 // Matt. 24.36) were altered to avoid such an implication (although there is no evidence that Jesus' questions were similarly altered). It is also clear that some parts of the 'orthodox' patristic tradition regarded Jesus' ignorance as problematic (e.g. Hilary, *De Trinitate* 9. esp. 59–75; Augustine, *De*

---

[25] For further developments along these lines see Schlatter, *Die Theologie der Apostel*, p. 81; Barth, 'Das Gesetzesverständnis des Evangelisten Matthäus', pp. 117–22 (ET, pp. 125–31); Verseput, *The Rejection of the Humble Messianic King*, esp. pp. 150, 304–5.

[26] Lawton, *Conflict in Christology*, p. 66; Streeter, *The Four Gospels*, pp. 162–3; Davies and Allison *Matthew*, vol. I, p. 105.

Trinitate I.12.23; Athanasius, *Orationes contra Arianos*, III.42ff).[27] These facts suggest that the possibility of an evangelist shying away from questions implying Jesus' ignorance must be investigated. Nevertheless, it will be necessary first of all to define the nature of the questions upon which the argument depends and then investigate the relevant texts in Mark.

According to all four canonical gospels, much of Jesus' teaching ministry involved the asking of questions, indeed the number of such questions, notwithstanding some punctuational uncertainties, are impressive: Matthew has ninety-four; Mark fifty-nine; Luke eighty-two; John forty-nine.[28] Matthew's Sermon on the Mount, for example, contains sixteen questions. Many if not most of these questions are, however, purely rhetorical or instructional, asked in order to prompt listeners/readers to thought. Such questions must be carefully distinguished from those which are asked in order to obtain knowledge otherwise not possessed.

In other words, grammatical form is not identical with meaning and function: not all questions have the same semantic force.[29] Grammatically speaking sentences can be classified as either declarative, interrogative, or imperative.[30] J. Lyons draws a helpful distinction between the meaning of sentences, or the grammatical form, and the meaning of utterances. The utterance, 'abstract entities which are context-independent', is related to the sentence by what is called 'characteristic use'.[31] For example, the characteristic use of an interrogative sentence is to ask a question. This does not mean, however, that this is the most common use of that utterance:

> on any given occasion, a speaker might use an expression to mean something different from the meaning that it has by virtue of its lexical and grammatical meaning. But he cannot always do this. Nor is he free to use an expression with any meaning that he chooses to give it. Unless he has come to some prior agreement with the addressee about the intended interpretation of an expression, what he means by it must be systematically related to its inherent

---

[27] See Gore, *Dissertations on Subjects Connected with the Incarnation*, pp. 98–179.
[28] Navone provides a list in 'The Dynamic of the Question in the Gospel Narrative'.
[29] Cf. Thiselton, 'Semantics and New Testament Interpretation' pp. 76–7.
[30] Palmer, *Semantics*, p. 150.
[31] Lyons, *Language and Linguistics*, p. 164.

meaning. And its inherent meaning is determined by its characteristic use.[32]

Lyons notes elsewhere that distinctions between questions and statements are often 'drawn solely in the non-verbal component of utterances', that is, the difference is associated with an intonation pattern, or some 'paralinguistic modulation' which expresses the speaker's doubt.[33]

The issue for us is not therefore to determine the grammatical form of Jesus' questions, but to ascertain whether they include what Lyons describes as 'one of the felicity-conditions attaching to the appropriate utterance of questions', that is 'that the speaker should not know the answer to his question'.[34] In these terms we need to ask whether Jesus' words, although grammatically inter-rogative, are properly called questions at all. It is, however, precisely in the area of 'paralinguistic modulation' that the exegete is stymied. We do not know and cannot recover either the gestures or modulation with which either Jesus, or the first readers of the gospels, accompanied the words. This means we must pay very close attention to any contextual indications of the nature of the question.

Mark 5:9: 'What is your name?'

It is not clear that this question *necessarily* implies that Jesus did not know the answer. The background to the question is the belief that knowledge of a name gave one power over the named person (examples include *T. Sol.* 2.1; 3.6; 4.3f; 5.1, 6f; *b. Me'il* 17b; *PGM* I.161f; IV.3037ff; XIII.242ff).[35] If the purpose of this episode is to underline Mark's assertion that Jesus is the powerful one (cf. Mark 1.7; 3.27), then the demand for a name is part of a power struggle which provides an opportunity for Jesus to reveal his power as greater than the demons: *even if Jesus had known the name, the demon must be made to speak.*[36] Thus this passage does

---

[32] Ibid., pp. 167–8.   [33] Lyons, *Semantics*, vol. II, p. 754.
[34] Ibid., vol. II, p. 754.
[35] Taylor, *Mark*, p. 281; Bietenhard, *TDNT*, vol. V, pp. 280–1; Hull, *Hellenistic Magic and the Synoptic Tradition*, p. 70; Twelftree, *Christ Triumphant: Exorcism Then and Now*, pp. 62–5 and *Jesus the Exorcist*, p. 84; Hooker, *Mark*, p. 143; Gundry, *Mark*, p. 251.
[36] Hull, *Magic*, p. 70; Twelftree, *Christ Triumphant*, pp. 62–5; Deissmann, *Licht von Osten*, p. 223, n. 8 (ET, p. 260).

not meet the 'felicity-condition' required to demonstrate the ignorance of the Markan Jesus. In any case, Matthew's version of Jesus' dealings with the demoniac is drastically abbreviated compared with Mark's (Matt. 8.28–34: 135 words; Mark 5.1–20: 324 words). Even assuming Markan priority, Matthew's omission of many details from the narrative simplifies the whole structure of the meeting between Jesus and the demons with the result that in Matthew Jesus does not speak until the simple command of v. 32: ὑπάγετε. This process of abbreviation is an adequate explanation for the Matthean redaction which does not require a more specific rationale.

Mark 5:30: 'Who touched my garments?'

In this case Mark's account gives many indications that real ignorance is assumed. The description of the crowd jostling Jesus (συνέθλιβον αὐτόν, v. 24, cf. 3.9); the approach of the woman from behind (ὄπισθεν, v. 27), and the incredulous reaction of the disciples (v. 31) all contribute to the impression of real ignorance on the Markan Jesus' part, even when juxtaposed with the knowledge that 'power had come out from him', v. 30. It is, however, possible to interpret the whole episode in Mark as a demonstration of Jesus' 'supernatural knowledge' – he knows that power has gone out, he knows it went to someone behind him, by the touching of his garments, and he knows it was a woman. For R. H. Gundry, the disciples' remark in v. 31 is simply 'a foil that makes Jesus' supernatural knowledge stand out in bold relief'.[37] This interpretation illustrates the extent to which 'questions' are capable of varying interpretations, and the difficulty in establishing whether such a passage meets the 'felicity-conditions'. Nevertheless, the phrasing of Jesus' question in Mark (as in Luke 8.46) could plausibly suggest ignorance of the identity of the person. The account in Matthew is, however, severely abbreviated (Matt. 9.20–2: 48 words; Mark 5.25–34: 153 words), involving the simplification of the narrative, and focussing on the words of Jesus as the source of her healing/salvation. This, in addition to the fact that Matthew omits Mark 5.29–33 *in toto*, provides little grounds for us to find a specifically christological reason in the omission of the question.

[37] Gundry, *Mark*, p. 270.

Mark 6.38: 'How many loaves have you?'

It is probable but not certain that this question functions as an interrogative in Mark. Considerations which might weigh against the interrogative nature of the question include the fact that Mark uses the feeding miracles to draw attention to the identity of Jesus (Mark 6.52; 8.17–21), and the parallel in John which presents the whole event as orchestrated by Jesus as a test (John 6.6).[38] It is difficult, however, to claim that Matthew's omission of the question, coming as it does in the midst of a much longer omission of twenty-four words from Mark 6.37b–8a, is due to christological redaction; particularly since in Matthew 15.34 the question in Mark 8.5, πόσους ἔχετε ἄρτους, is reproduced with only a change of word order.

Mark 9.16: 'What are you discussing with them?' 9.21: 'How long has he had this?'

The first question does seem to function in Mark as a request for information: Jesus has been absent and, upon returning to the disciples, he finds a crowd and an argument (vv. 14f). The question is addressed generally, and the answer (vv. 17f) provides Jesus with the information to which he responds (vv. 19f). By way of contrast a similar question, which appears to be non-interrogative, is Mark 9.33: 'What were you discussing on the way?' This question is really an invitation to discussion, since although the disciples are silent, not answering the question (v. 34), Jesus addresses exactly the issue which they had been discussing (9.35ff). The function of the second question (Mark 9.21) is not clear in the context. Curiosity, emphasis, compassion, might all be suggested,[39] but since it is not developed in the context it is extremely difficult to establish its function.

Once more Matthew's version of this episode is much shorter than Mark's (Matt. 17.14–21: 133 words; Mark 9.14–29: 270 words). Mark has all the detail of a dramatic power encounter, in which the terms of the struggle are evident (9.17f, 20, 22, 25f) and Jesus' victory and power are ascribed to prayer (v. 29). Matthew omits both questions as he abbreviates the details of the lad's condition (17.15), passes relatively smoothly over the exorcism (v. 18), and applies the lesson of faith (v. 20).

---

[38] Cf. Quesnell, *The Mind of Mark*, and Lane, *Mark*, p. 228 respectively.
[39] Lane, *Mark*, pp. 332–3.

Summary

It is notable that none of these questions unambiguously give every indication of satisfying the original 'felicity-condition' – that they are asked in order to provide information that was not otherwise known. Nevertheless, none of the three questions which most nearly satisfy this 'felicity-condition', Mark 5.30; 9.16, 21, appear in Matthew. There are too many other factors involved in the redactional process to draw any firm conclusions concerning the possibility of Matthew's christological redaction, even assuming Markan priority. Since Matthew does include an explicit affirmation of Jesus' ignorance (Matt. 24.36) and since the omission of these questions can be accounted for on other grounds it cannot be said that this category offers conclusive evidence for Markan priority.

We have not attempted to assess the Griesbach-hypothesis view of each of these passages, as our concern has been to assess an oft-used argument for the two-source hypothesis. Nevertheless, on the assumption of the Griesbach hypothesis, the Markan additions are more likely to have been motivated by Mark's (apparently) general desire to include details, dialogue and other enlivening elements in his accounts. The questions are designed (at least on a literary level) to elicit information important to the progress of the story. Christological factors, such as a Markan attempt at emphasising the humanity of Jesus, seem unlikely.

4. The 'inability' of Jesus

This category relates to several Markan passages, not found in Matthew, which suggest that Jesus was unable to do various things: Mark 1.45; 6.5, 48; 7.24; 11.13 are listed by Davies and Allison.[40] These, it is suggested, were deliberately omitted by Matthew because of christological embarrassment. This category is probably the weakest of the three surveyed in this chapter, there is no indication that this issue was of concern to later redactors of gospel traditions, and we shall make only brief comments on each passage.

Mark 1.45 (cf. Matt. 8.4).   It is not apparent that this verse refers to an inability of Jesus. The inability relates to him entering

---

[40] Davies and Allison, *Matthew*, vol. I, p. 105.

φανερῶς, not entering in any absolute sense. Mark 7.24 is a similar case, not strictly about some inability of Jesus. Both these passages have more to do with Mark's secrecy/disclosure motif (on which see chapter twelve). In addition Matthew regularly omits Markan connecting links throughout the collection of miracles in chapters 8 and 9 (Matt. 8.14 // Mark 1.29; Matt. 8.23 // Mark 4.35f; Matt. 8.34 // Mark 5.18–20; Matt. 9.1 // Mark 2.1f; Matt. 9.9 // Mark 2.13; Matt. 9.18 // Mark 5.21). If we assume Markan priority then this practice provides the most plausible explanation for the omission of Mark 1.45 by Matthew.

Mark 6.5 (cf. Matt. 13.58). This is probably the only true 'inability' in all the passages under consideration. Nevertheless we argued previously (chapter four) that Matthean embarrassment at the inability of Jesus was not the most likely explanation for the difference between the accounts. Matthew's preference for simple verbs rather than auxiliaries combined with his emphasis on the necessity of faith provide reasonably plausible alternatives to the christological explanation for the difference.

Mark 6.48 (cf. Matt. 14.25). This passage has also been discussed already (chapter five). There we argued that Mark's καὶ ἤθελεν παρελθεῖν αὐτούς should not be taken as an indication of Jesus' inability, but as an indication of the epiphanic nature of Jesus' walking on the sea. Hence Matthew's omission of the admittedly enigmatic phrase should not necessarily be understood as an avoidance of Jesus' inability, since this is not in any case what Mark is about.

Mark 11.13 (cf. Matt. 21.18f). While Matthew's version of the whole incident is quite different from Mark's, the distinction is not based on the inability of Jesus to find fruit. The failure is that of the tree, and in any case is equally true in Matthew as in Mark.

The aspect of the christological argument which focusses on the inability of Jesus has, in our view, little value in proving the priority of Mark over against Matthew. In general the two-source hypothesis can readily and plausibly explain the alterations made by Matthew without appeal to the principle of embarrassment with Mark's presentation of the humanity of Jesus.

5.   General comments on omissions

In the three preceding sections of this chapter we have investigated passages which, it has been argued, Matthew omitted from Mark because of their presentation of Jesus' emotions, ignorance or inability to do certain things. Before concluding this chapter attention shall be given to some other passages in Mark concerning which scholars have made the claim that they were omitted by Matthew because of their christological implications.

W. C. Allen, followed by other scholars, suggested that Matthew (and Luke) may have omitted Mark 3.20f because of some unease that Jesus' family, οἱ παρ' αὐτοῦ, should accuse Jesus of madness, ἐξέστη.[41] It has also been suggested that the healing miracles unique to Mark (Mark 7.33–6; 8.22–6) were omitted because of Jesus' use of physical means and the partial result of the second one.[42] Furthermore, Allen suggested that two other passages, Mark 1.23–38 and 9.20–4, were omitted because Matthew wanted 'to avoid descriptions of bodily anguish after Christ's healing word'.[43]

These arguments illustrate the difficulties involved in arguments about the motivation behind omissions (rather than alterations or additions). The suggestions are not necessarily implausible, they are simply unverifiable. Furthermore, it is not clear that the use of physical means of healing caused any general difficulty, cf. John 9.6; Luke 22.51; and the addition of a reference to Jesus spitting *on his fingers* before the healing in Mark 7.33 in the Arabic *Diatessaron* 21.3.[44] They can have little role in a general argument for Markan priority except to point to possible and plausible explanations for Matthew's omissions from Mark. In any case, the limited number of these omissions, and their non-central nature – they do not contain any of the basic christological themes in Mark – implies that according to the two-source hypothesis, Matthew should not be regarded as 'reactionary' in his relationship with Mark.

It is obvious that, according to the Griesbach hypothesis, Mark

---

[41] Allen, *Matthew*, p. xxxi; Hawkins, *Horae Synopticae*, p. 119; Streeter, *The Four Gospels*, p. 171; Davies and Allison, *Matthew*, vol. I, p. 105. Taking the Markan sandwich (3.20f cf. 31–5) as indicating that Jesus' family is the subject (with e.g. Guelich, *Mark*, p. 172 and Gundry, *Mark*, p. 180; against Wansbrough, 'Mark 3,21 – Was Jesus out of His Mind?', pp. 234–5; Wenham, 'The Meaning of Mark iii.21', pp. 296–7).

[42] Allen, *Matthew*, p. xxxii; Hawkins, *Horae Synopticae*, p. 118.

[43] Allen, *Matthew*, p. xxxiii.

[44] Head, 'Tatian's Christology', p. 134.

omitted a great deal of material from both Matthew and Luke. According to Griesbach himself, Mark 'sought brevity, as one who wanted to write a book of small compass', he 'omitted things that did not pertain to the office of Teacher, which the Lord publicly exercised' (Matt. 1 and 2; Luke 1 and 2) and the longer discourses of Christ (so Matt. 5–7, portions of chapters 10, 11, 12 ,13, 18, 20, 22, 23, 24, 25 and the bulk of Luke 10–18); he also omitted some things 'that concerned Jews alone' (so e.g. Luke 4.16–30 and many OT quotations).[45] It has proven difficult, however, to explain the motivation behind Griesbach-Mark's many omissions; especially the combination of large-scale omission and small-scale addition of minor details. D. L. Dungan suggested that Griesbach-Mark is somewhat reactionary in relation to Matthew and Mark, like Marcion, but unlike Farmer's picture of Griesbach-Mark as an irenic church theologian.[46] Nevertheless, it is universally difficult to ascribe motives to the omission of material, and the Griesbach hypothesis should not necessarily be criticised for failing to deliver compelling explanations at every point. Far more important for the Griesbach hypothesis is to be able to explain the positive redactional emphases of Griesbach-Mark.

6. Conclusion

In this chapter we have investigated those parts of the christological argument for Markan priority which most clearly betray the historical and theological origins of the theory. It must be concluded that the arguments concerning the emotions, ignorance and inability of Jesus do not provide compelling evidence of the type required to prove Markan priority. This is due, in part, to the fact that arguments based on the motivation behind the supposed omission of certain passages, phrases, or words are extremely precarious. This was already noted by White and others (chapter one), and should be re-emphasised strongly. When other plausible reasons for these omissions can be supplied, and christological factors cannot explain all the phenomena, there seems little to be gained from the continuing use of such argumentation. There is so

---

[45] Griesbach, 'Demonstration', pp. 106–7. See also Dungan, 'Mark – The Abridgement of Matthew and Luke'.

[46] Dungan, 'Reactionary Trends in the Gospel Producing Activity of the Early Church: Marcion, Tatian, Mark'; cf. Farmer, 'The Two-Gospel Hypothesis: The Statement of the Hypothesis', pp. 155–6.

much we do not know concerning the redactional activities of the evangelists (on any model) that we must hesitate before identifying motives on the basis of insufficient evidence.

Although some qualified support for the two-source hypothesis continues to be provided by the plausibility of Matthean redaction on that model, the argument concerning Matthean embarrassment with details of Mark's narrative cannot be sustained. The over-confident statements of some scholars concerning the nature of the christological argument should be modified in this light. In the next chapter we shall investigate the other side of the coin, focussing on Matthean alterations and additions which, it is often claimed, enhance the christology presented therein.

Appendix 6.A. Reported emotions in Matthew and Mark[1]

Ref.	Mark text	Subject	Reason	Ref.	Matthew text	Subject	Reason	Luke info.	Comments
1.22	ἐξεπλήσσοντο ἐπὶ τῇ διδαχῇ αὐτοῦ.	C (syn)	JT	7.28	ἐξεπλήσσοντο οἱ ὄχλοι ...	C (inc D)	JT		
6.2	πολλοὶ ἀκούοντες ἐξεπλήσσοντο	C (syn)	JT	13.54	ὥστε ἐκπλήσσεσθαι αὐτοὺς	C (syn)	JT		
7.37	ὑπερπερισσῶς ἐξεπλήσσοντο	C	JM	15.31	ὥστε τὸν ὄχλον θαυμάσαι	C	JM		
10.26	οἱ δὲ περισσῶς ἐξεπλήσσοντο	D	JT	19.25	οἱ μαθηταὶ ἐξεπλήσσοντο σφόδρα	D	JT		
11.18	πᾶς γὰρ ὁ ὄχλος ἐξεπλήσσετο ἐπὶ τῇ διδαχῇ αὐτοῦ.	C	JT	22.33	οἱ ὄχλοι ἐξεπλήσσοντο ἐπὶ τῇ διδαχῇ αὐτοῦ	C	JT		different context
1.27	καὶ ἐθαμβήθησαν ἅπαντες,	C (syn)	JT/JM		no parallel			4.36: θάμβος	
9.15	πᾶς ὁ ὄχλος ἰδόντες αὐτοῦ ἐξεθαμβήθησαν,	C	JP		no parallel				cf. Mark 14.33
10.24	οἱ δὲ μαθηταὶ ἐθαμβοῦντο ἐπὶ τοῖς λόγοις αὐτοῦ.	D	JT		no parallel				
10.32	καὶ ἐθαμβοῦντο,	D (?)	JT (?)		no parallel				see below
16.5	καὶ ἐξεθαμβήθησαν.	women	angel					24.5: ἐμφόβων	cf. Mark 16.6
5.20	καὶ πάντες ἐθαύμαζον	C	JM		no parallel				
12.17	καὶ ἐξεθαύμαζον ἐπ' αὐτῷ	Phar	JT	22.22	καὶ ἀκούσαντες ἐθαύμασαν	Phar etc.	JT		Mark: NT hapax

Appendix 6.A. (*contd*)

Ref.	Mark text	Subject	Reason	Ref.	Matthew text	Subject	Reason	Luke info.	Comments
15.5	ὥστε θαυμάζειν τὸν Πιλᾶτον	Pilate	J silence	27.14	ὥστε θαυμάζειν τὸν ἡγεμόνα λίαν.	gov (i.e. Pilate)	J silence		
15.44	ὁ δὲ Πιλᾶτος ἐθαύμασεν εἰ ἤδη τέθνηκεν,	Pilate	J dead		no parallel				
4.41	καὶ ἐφοβήθησαν φόβον μέγαν,	D	JM	8.27	οἱ δὲ ἄνθρωποι ἐθαύμασαν	D	JM		intros saying
	no parallel			9.33	καὶ ἐθαύμασαν οἱ ὄχλοι	C	JM	11.14 // Matt.	intros saying
	11.21: no mention			21.20	καὶ ἰδόντες οἱ μαθηταὶ ἐθαύμασαν	D	JM		intros saying
				2.22	ἐφοβήθη ἐκεῖ ἀπελθεῖν·	Joseph	Archel.		
5.15	καὶ ἐφοβήθησαν.	C	JM		not in abbv report			8.35: ἐφοβ.	
5.33	ἡ δὲ γυνὴ φοβηθεῖσα καὶ τρέμουσα,	woman	JM		not in abbv report			8.47: τρέμουσα ἦλθεν	
6.20	ὁ γὰρ Ἡρῴδης ἐφοβεῖτο τὸν Ἰωάννην,	Herod	JB	14.5	ἐφοβήθη τὸν ὄχλον,	Herod	C		
	not mentioned			14.30	βλέπων δὲ τὸν ἄνεμον [ἰσχυρὸν] ἐφοβήθη,	Peter	wind		
9.6	ἔκφοβοι γὰρ ἐγένοντο.	D (PJ)	JP - trans	17.6	καὶ ἐφοβήθησαν σφόδρα.	D	Voice		gospel hapax
	not mentioned, cf. 9.6								

Mark ref	Mark text			Matt ref	Matt text			Parallels / notes
9.32	καὶ ἐφοβοῦντο αὐτὸν ἐπερωτῆσαι.	D		17.23	καὶ ἐλυπήθησαν σφόδρα.	D	JT - passion	9.45: ἐφοβοῦντο ἐρωτῆσαι — second listing in this verse
10.32	οἱ δὲ ἀκολουθοῦντες ἐφοβοῦντο.	D	general		not in abbv report	D	JT (?)	
11.18	ἐφοβοῦντο γὰρ αὐτόν,	CP	JT		no parallel	CP	JT	
11.32	ἐφοβοῦντο τὸν ὄχλον,	CP	C	21.26	φοβούμεθα τὸν ὄχλον,	CP etc.	C	
12.12	καὶ ἐφοβήθησαν τὸν ὄχλον	CP	C	21.46	ἐφοβήθησαν τοὺς ὄχλους,	CP	C	20.19: ἐφοβ.
				27.54	ἐφοβήθησαν σφόδρα,	Cent etc.	J death	
				28.4	ἀπὸ δὲ τοῦ φόβου αὐτοῦ ἐσείσθησαν	guards	angel	
16.8	ἐφοβοῦντο γάρ.	women	JP - res		cf. Matt. 28.8 below			
6.50	πάντες γὰρ αὐτὸν εἶδον καὶ ἐταράχθησαν.	D	JP - walk on water	14.26	καὶ ἀπὸ τοῦ φόβου. ἔκραξαν	D	JP	John 6.19: ἐφοβήθησαν
				2.3	Ἡρῴδης ἐταράχθη	Herod	JP star etc.	
				9.8	οἱ ὄχλοι ἐφοβήθησαν	D		
2.12	ὥστε ἐξίστασθαι πάντας	C	JM			C	JM	5.26: ἔκστασις
5.42	ἐξέστησαν ἐκστάσει μεγάλῃ.	C	JM		not in abbv report	C	JM	8.56: ἐξέστησαν
6.51	λίαν ἐν ἑαυτοῖς ἐξίσταντο,	D	JM	12.23	καὶ ἐξίσταντο πάντες οἱ ὄχλοι	C	JM	cf. Matt. 9.33

Appendix 6.A. *(contd)*

Ref.	Mark text	Subject	Reason	Ref.	Matthew text	Subject	Reason	Luke info.	Comments
16.8	εἶχεν γὰρ αὐτὰς τρόμος καὶ ἔκστασις	women	JP - res	28.8	μετὰ φόβου καὶ χαρᾶς μεγάλης	women	JP - res	24.9: event no emotion	
1.26	σπαράξαν αὐτὸν . . . φωνῆσαν φωνῇ μεγάλῃ ἐξῆλθεν	unclean spirit	JP/JT		no parallel				
9.26	καὶ κράξας καὶ πολλὰ σπαράξας ἐξῆλθεν	unclean spirit	JP/JT	17.18	καὶ ἐξῆλθεν ἀπ' αὐτοῦ τὸ δαιμόνιον·				
6.19	ἡ δὲ Ἡρῳδιὰς ἐνεῖχεν αὐτῷ	Herod	JB						
6.20	ἀκούσας αὐτοῦ πολλὰ ἠπόρει	Herod	JB						
6.26	περίλυπος γενόμενος	Herod	JB's head	14.9	λυπηθείς	Herod	JB's head	no parallel	
				17.23	καὶ ἐλυπήθησαν σφόδρα	D	JT		cf. Matt. 18.31
10.22	ὁ δὲ στυγνάσας ἐπὶ τῷ λόγῳ ἀπῆλθεν λυπούμενος,	rich yng man	JT	19.22	ἀκούσας δὲ ὁ νεανίσκος τὸν λόγον ἀπῆλθεν λυπούμενος,	rich yng man	JT	18.23: περίλυπος ἐγενήθη	
14.19	ἤρξαντο λυπεῖσθαι	D	JT	26.22	λυπούμενοι σφόδρα ἤρξαντο	D	JT	no parallel	
14.72	καὶ ἐπιβαλὼν ἔκλαιεν.	Peter	denial	26.75	ἔκλαυσεν πικρῶς.	Peter	denial	22.62 // Matt.	

	Greek	Subject	Note	Parallel
	2.16 Ἡρῴδης ἰδὼν ὅτι ἐνεπαίχθη ὑπὸ τῶν μάγων ἐθυμώθη λίαν	Herod	tricked	cf. Mark 10.14
10.41 οἱ δέκα ἤρξαντο ἀγανακτεῖν	Ja & Joh 20.24 οἱ δέκα ἠγανάκτησαν	D		Ja & Joh no parallel
	21.15 ἠγανάκτησαν	CP etc.	JM & Hosanna	
14.4 ἦσαν δέ τινες ἀγανακτοῦντες πρὸς ἑαυτούς,	ointment 26.8 οἱ μαθηταὶ ἠγανάκτησαν	D	ointment no parallel; but cf. 13.14	
	2.10 ἰδόντες δὲ τὸν ἀστέρα ἐχάρησαν χαρὰν μεγάλην σφόδρα.	wise men star		13.17; 19.6 37; 23.8 (cf. 15.5)
14.11 οἱ δὲ ἀκούσαντες ἐχάρησαν	26 15 Judas	CP	no emotion	22.5: ἐχάρησαν

Note: [1] Abbreviations: JT = Jesus' teaching; JM = Jesus' miracle; JP = Jesus' presence; C = crowd (or people); D = disciples; JB = John the Baptist; CP = chief priests; Phar = Pharisees; syn = synagogue; gov = governor; trans = transfiguration; res = resurrection (others should be reasonably clear).

7

THE WORSHIP OF JESUS AND THE PASSION NARRATIVES

1. Introduction

In this chapter two further areas in which scholars have detected christological factors involved in Matthew's redaction of Mark will be investigated. These in turn have functioned as part of a general christological argument in favour of Markan priority. These two areas were not much discussed in the history of research, in part at least because the type of investigation offered in defence of these positions post-dates the influence of redaction criticism. While the subjects covered in the previous chapter cohered around the omission of material from Mark, the topics covered in this chapter involve Matthew's alterations and additions to Mark and in particular the suggestion that this redactional activity reflects a different, and later, subsequent, posterior, christological position. In view of this common factor we shall conclude the chapter with a brief discussion of other additional material (on each hypothesis).

The first section will deal with some terminology of 'approach' and 'worship' directed to Jesus. Since this is primarily the product of redaction-critical approaches to Matthew we shall concentrate on evaluating the arguments presented in defence of the view that Matthew uses special terminology with the connotation that Jesus is approached or worshipped in the same terms as God. A second area in which Matthew's christological interests have been commonly observed by redaction critics is in the passion narrative. Without entering into a detailed analysis of the whole accounts we shall compare Matthean redaction on the two-source hypothesis with Markan redaction on the Griesbach hypothesis, particularly in terms of additions and positive alterations made to their respective sources.

2. 'Worship' and 'approach' terminology

Recent studies have drawn attention to the possibility that Matthew's preference for the προσκυνεῖν and προσέρχεσθαι word-groups is an outcome of his reverent attitude towards Jesus. H. J. Held, for example, argued that προσκυνεῖν was used by Matthew 'only in the sense of genuine worship of Jesus'.[1] In addition J. R. Edwards has recently argued that 'προσέρχεσθαι is a signal pointing to the messianic character of Jesus in the First Gospel'.[2]

No doubt both terms *are* clearly favoured by Matthew (προσέρχεσθαι (52–4–11), προσκυνεῖν (13–2–3)),[3] but to interpret either as a christologically technical term goes far beyond what the available evidence allows. In connection with the more common term, προσέρχεσθαι ('to approach'), Edwards argued that προσέρχεσθαι 'carries unmistakable cultic connotations' – of approach to God, particularly for some ritual or cultic purpose. In Matthew these cultic connotations of the term are transferred to Jesus in order to emphasise 'his unique, messianic character' (p. 65).

Clearly προσέρχεσθαι was often used of approaching a deity, both in the LXX (e.g. Exod. 16.9; 22.7; Lev. 9.5; Deut. 5.27; Sir. 1.27, 30; 2.1) and elsewhere (Dio Cassius 56.9.2; Porphyry, *Abstinentia* 2.47; Philo, *Quod Deus immutabilis sit*, 8; *De sacrificiis Abelis et Caini*, 12; P. Giess. 1.20, 24), as the major lexicons attest.[4] Nevertheless the word is far from being a technical term and has numerous other common meanings, from the very general – 'to come', 'to go', 'to approach', 'to visit', 'to appear' – to the more unusual senses such as 'to attack' (e.g. Xenophon, *Cynegeticus*, VI.2.16), 'to surrender' (Thucydides, *Hist.* III.59) and even 'to have sexual intercourse' (Hippocrates, *Epid.* VI.3.14).[5] In view of this breadth of meaning, the appeal to a technical cultic usage must be approached with caution.

---

[1] Held, 'Matthäus als Interpret der Wundergeschichten', p. 217 (cited from ET, p. 229); similarly Gundry, *Matthew*, p. 27.

[2] Edwards, 'The Use of ΠΡΟΣΕΡΧΕΣΘΑΙ in the Gospel of Matthew', p. 73; similarly Kingsbury, *The Parables of Jesus in Matthew 13*, p. 41; Beare, *Matthew*, pp. 108–9.

[3] Held, 'Matthäus als Interpret der Wundergeschichten', pp. 214–17 (ET, pp. 226–30); Schenk, *Die Sprache des Matthäus*, pp. 258 and 421–2.

[4] BAGD, p. 713; MM, p. 547; Schneider, *TDNT*, vol. II, pp. 683–4; *PGL*, p. 1169; cf. Edwards, pp. 65–7.

[5] MM, p. 547; Schneider, *TDNT*, vol. II, p. 683; LSJ, p. 1511; BAGD, p. 713; *PGL*, p. 1169.

Furthermore, Matthew gives little evidence of imposing a consistent pattern in his use of the term. Although it is often used of people approaching Jesus, on ten occasions those 'approaching' Jesus are his opponents, who come with neither reverence nor awe, but to test or entrap him (4.3 (the devil); 15.1; 16.1; 19.3; 21.23; 22.23 (Jewish leaders); 26.49 (Judas), 50 (soldiers), 60 (bis, false witnesses)). Edwards forces these references through a predetermined, but essentially arbitrary, grid: 'even in these adversarial approaches, Matthew demonstrates that Jesus' opponents come to him because he has authority and that in every instance the authority of Jesus is vindicated' (p. 68).

On two occasions Jesus 'approaches' the disciples (Matt. 17.7; 28.18) and on a further five occasions people 'approach' someone other than Jesus: Matthew 14.12 (the disciples approach the body of John); 17.24 (tax-collectors approach Peter); 26.69 (the maid approaches Peter), 73 (bystanders approach Peter); 27.58 (Joseph approaches Pilate). Edwards suggests that Peter functions as a representative of Jesus (hardly the case in 26.69 and 73!), that John the Baptist was a holy man and that the term is used of Pilate because of his authority over Jesus' body (p. 69). These exceptions clearly indicate that even *if* Matthew occasionally uses προσέρχεσθαι in a technical or quasi-technical sense connoting the approach of a petitioner to his deity, a possibility enhanced by the collocation of προσέρχεσθαι with either προσκυνεῖν (Matt. 8.2; 9.18; 20.20; 28.9) or κύριε (8.2, 5, 25; 13.27; 17.14; 18.21; 25.20) (with Edwards, p. 67), his usage cannot be strait-jacketed in the manner advocated by Edwards.

An analysis of Matthew's use of the term in relation to his sources (on the two-source hypothesis) suggests that it was regularly added by Matthew, since Mark uses the verb only five times (three of which are paralleled in Matthew, Mark 6.35; 10.2; 14.45; the other two are 1.31; 12.28). There are numerous occasions when it might be explained in terms of stylistic preference, especially when Mark uses a simple verb with a separate πρός (Mark 1.40 // Matt. 8.1; Mark 7.1 // Matt. 15.1; Mark 10.50 // Matt. 9.28; Mark 11.27 // Matt. 21.23; Mark 12.18 // Matt. 22.23; Mark 15.43 // Matt. 27.58; cf. also Luke 9.57 // Matt. 8.19). At other times Matthew introduces προσέρχεσθαι when Mark uses a simple verb (Mark 2.18; 5.27; 6.29; 14.3; 14.66 (although *v.l.* add προς αυτον)), or a related compound term (Mark 9.14: προστρέχοντες // Matt. 17.14: προσῆλθεν; Mark 10.17: προσδραμών // Matt. 19.16: προσελθών; Mark 10.35: προσπορεύονται // Matt. 20.20: προσῆλθεν).

If Matthew's use of the term is both more varied than allowed for by Edwards and explicable as a stylistic rather than a theological preference, then although the Matthean pattern is perfectly explicable on the two-source hypothesis it cannot be regarded as a technical aspect of Matthean christology.

The other word under consideration is προσκυνεῖν. In general this term was 'used to designate the custom of prostrating oneself before a person and kissing his feet, the hem of his garment, the ground, etc.'[6] Other terms or phrases could be used to refer to this act of prostration which is basic to the meaning of προσκυνεῖν, the synoptics themselves offer two alternatives, for example:

(i) γονυπετέω in Mark 1.40 (*v.l.*), parallels: προσελθὼν προ-σεκύνει, Matthew 8.2; πεσὼν ἐπὶ πρόσωπον, Luke 5.12; Mark 10.47, parallel: προσελθών, Matthew 19.16; Matthew 17.14 (no parallels); 27.29 (see in following);

(ii) τιθέναι τὰ γόνατα (Mark 15.19: καὶ τιθέντες τὰ γόνατα προσεκύνουν αὐτῷ, parallel Matt. 27.29: γονυπετήσαντες ἔμπροσθεν αὐτοῦ, and characteristic in Luke as an attitude of prayer: Luke 22.41; Acts 7.60; 9.40; 20.36; 21.5).

It is in this exercise of lexical choice that Matthew, according to many scholars, chose to use προσκυνεῖν in order to emphasise the connotation that the recipient of such respect was divine.[7] This conclusion can only be drawn, however, by emphasising one side of the evidence for contemporary use of προσκυνεῖν. The same term was used in a wide variety of less 'loaded' contexts for various types of respectful greetings, e.g. 'to kiss' (LXX 1 Kings 19.18; Job 31.27Σ; BGU 423.15; P. Giess. 22.5, both AD II) or 'to greet', 'to welcome respectfully' or 'to respect' (LXX Gen. 47.31; Exod. 18.7; 1 Sam. 20.41; 1 Kings 1.47; 2.19; Josephus, *Antiquities*, VIII.331; Philo, *De Iosepho*, 164; *De opificio mundi*, 83; BGU 615.8; P. Giess. 17.11; P. Oxy. 237 vi.37; P. Teb. 286.22 these four AD II).[8] It seems most probable that προσκυνεῖν differs from other terms for

---

[6] BAGD, p. 716; Greeven, *TDNT*, vol. VI, pp. 759–63; Reicke, 'Some Reflections on Worship in the New Testament', p. 195; cf. LSJ, p. 1518: 'make obeisance . . . fall down and worship . . . prostrating oneself before kings and superiors'.

[7] Greeven, *TDNT*, vol. VI, pp. 763–4; Held, 'Matthäus als Interpret der Wunder-geschichten', p. 217 (ET, p. 229) cited earlier; Gundry, *Matthew*, p. 27.

[8] See Greeven, *TDNT*, vol. VI, pp. 760–3; LSJ, p. 1518; MM, p. 549; *NewDocs* vol. I, pp. 56–7; *PGL*, pp. 1174–6.

worship 'in emphasizing more the semantic component of position or attitude involved' (LN, p. 540). We should also note that prostration of some sort was a mark of respect in Rabbinic circles (*b. Ketub* 63a: two people prostrate themselves before Akiba; *b. Sanh.* 27b: Bar Hama kissed R. Papi's feet).

Moreover, Matthew himself uses the term προσκυνεῖν for a variety of different types of supplication, including not only the respectful approach of a servant to his master (18.26),[9] and the submissive attitudes of various supplicants (2.2, 11: magi; 8.2: leper; 9.18: the ruler; 15.25: the woman) and disciples (14.33; 28.9); but also the insincere worship of Herod (2.8; cf. 4.9), the scheming and ill-informed attitude of the mother of the sons of Zebedee (20.20), and the hesitatant or doubting worship of the disciples (28.17). Matthew, on the two-source hypothesis, clearly favours προσκυνεῖν as a description of approach, either adding it (20.20), or substituting it for another related term (8.2 cf. Mark 1.40: γονυπετῶν; 9.18: cf. Mark 5.22 πίπτει πρὸς τοὺς πόδας αὐτοῦ; 15.25 cf. Mark 7.25: προσέπεσεν πρὸς τοὺς πόδας αὐτοῦ).[10] These three passages, however, suggest that Matthew may use the term in order to translate the physical gesture of Mark. If this is so, then, although Matthew's usage can be plausibly accounted for on the basis of his redactional preferences, there is insufficient evidence to establish that the term was a christologically loaded expression connoting the worship of Jesus as divine.

> E. E. Lemcio has suggested that at various points Matthew's use of προσκυνεῖν (with respect to the Canaanite woman, 15.25; the magi and Herod, 2.2, 8, 11; the mother of the sons of Zebedee, 20.20f) evokes a royal connotation: 'προσκυνεῖν expresses the proper attitude towards royalty'. He concludes that for Matthew 'the προσκυνεῖν of Jesus may be something more than reverence/obeisance but less than worship *per se*' (*The Past of Jesus in the Gospels*, pp. 67–8).

In neither of these cases are we able to conclude that Matthew regards the terminology as technical and connotative of Jesus' receipt of divine honours. Nevertheless, it is noteworthy that Matthew's text is amenable to such a 'reading'. It is probably fair to assume that even if not at the time of Matthew's writing at least by the turn of the first century, Christian readers would have

---

[9] Even if the Lord of the parable represents God, it must presumably have been comprehensible as a human transaction.

[10] Matt. 4.9 and 10 parallels Luke 4.7 and 8 (Q). Other occurrences are unique to Matt. (2.2, 8, 11; 18.26; 28.9, 17).

accepted the worship of Jesus as divine and would have then appreciated the significance of Matthew's record.

Pliny refers to Christians singing 'a hymn to Christ, as to a god' (*Ep* X.96. AD 112). Recent studies have described 'the worship of Jesus' in various forms of early Christianity (Bauckham, 'The Worship of Jesus in Apocalyptic Christianity'; France, 'The Worship of Jesus: A Neglected Factor in Christological Debate?'); the many (pre-)Pauline 'hymns' reflect a stage prior to that suggested by Pliny (cf. Rom. 1.3f; Phil. 2.6–11; Col. 1.15–20 etc. see J. T. Sanders, *The New Testament Christological Hymns*; Hengel, *Between Jesus and Paul*, pp. 78–96 (188–90)).

But this is a suggestion at the level of *Wirkungsgeschichte* rather than *Redaktionsgeschichte* and it would be unfair to charge Matthew with anachronism, when it could be argued that he is cleverly exploiting an ambiguity inherent within his chosen terminology.[11]

In general it would appear that in this area Matthean redaction of Mark, on the two-source hypothesis, is both coherent and plausible. It is coherent in the sense that it conforms with his otherwise determinable redactional and vocabulary preferences and it is plausible in the sense of fitting with other aspects of Matthean christology as well as with comparative material in which ambiguity may be exploited in the redaction of gospel traditions.[12] Matthew might be regarded as an example of the adaptation of gospel traditions to later prevailing conditions and beliefs.

If the two-source hypothesis can account well for the positive aspects of Matthean redaction, it is not so clear that the Griesbach hypothesis can account for Markan redaction of his sources in connection with the use of this terminology of approach and worship. On the vocabulary level Griesbach-Mark would have to introduce προσκυνέω on two occasions, Mark 5.6 and 15.19, which both relate to less than full understanding on the part of the demoniacs and the soldiers, and then prefer other vocabulary in his parallels to Matthean passages containing the term. This, of course, is not impossible, but nor is it predictable or explicable in terms of Mark's general christological presentation. Riley accepts that Matthew's account of the approach of the leper, καὶ ἰδοὺ λεπρὸς προσελθὼν προσεκύνει αὐτῷ λέγων, Κύριε, κ.τ.λ. (8.2), is 'a statement of reverential approach to Jesus' and argues that this is

---

[11] Cf. Carson, 'Christological Ambiguities in the Gospel of Matthew'.
[12] This has been suggested in connection with the language of *Gos. Pet.* 10 and 19 in Head, 'On the Christology of the Gospel of Peter'.

progressively toned down by Luke (5.12, altering Matthew's προ-σελθών προσεκύνει) and then by Mark (1.40, omitting κύριε).[13] But this assessment is not particularly plausible (since Mark is clearly interested in people approaching Jesus with faith), and will lead to a view of Griesbach-Mark as in some degree reactionary *vis-à-vis* his sources. In addition, we found above that Mark's omission of the material in Matthew 14.33 is difficult to account for on the Griesbach hypothesis without constructing a possible scenario for this in Mark's secrecy motif – Jesus was not truly 'worshipped' until his messianic sonship was revealed on the cross (Mark 15.39). Whether such an overall scenario is amenable to the Griesbach hypothesis we shall investigate in chapter twelve.

3. Christological redaction in the passion narratives

Many scholars have argued, from the two-source hypothesis perspective, that one of the most important factors influencing Matthew's redaction of the passion narrative was christological. For example, X. Léon-Dufour argued that the whole narrative was modified according to 'une perspective christologique', and D. P. Senior refers to the death scene in particular as 'charged with christology'.[14] An oft-quoted phrase suggests that Matthew presents the passion and death of Jesus 'als christologische Offenbarung' (as a christological revelation).[15] The main features of Matthew's redaction, especially additional material in relation to Mark, will be surveyed in what follows. The neo-Griesbachians have not presented a detailed redaction-critical analysis of Mark's use of Matthew and Luke in the passion narrative; in the second

---

[13] Riley, *The Making of Mark*, pp. 18–19.
[14] Léon-Dufour, 'Récits de la Passion', p. 1475; Senior, *The Passion Narrative according to Matthew*, p. 337; see Stanton, 'The Origin and Purpose of Matthew's Gospel', p. 1925; cf. also Vanhoye, 'Structure et théologie des récits de la Passion dans les évangiles synoptiques'; Conzelmann, 'Historie und Theologie in den synoptischen Passionsberichten'; Dahl, 'Die Passionsgeschichte bei Matthäus'; Descamps, 'Rédaction et christologie dans le récit matthéen de la Passion'.
[15] Vielhauer, 'Zu W. Anderson', p. 482; subsequently quoted by Barth, 'Das Gesetzesverständnis des Evangelisten Matthäus', p. 137 (ET, p. 146) (who also refers to Lightfoot, *History and Interpretation in the Gospels*, p. 164: 'a revelation of the true Messiah'); Schulz, *Die Stunde der Botschaft*, p. 202, and Descamps, 'Rédaction et christologie dans le récit matthéen de la Passion', p. 410 (who both quote Dibelius, *Die Formgeschichte des Evangeliums*, p. 199: 'So wird die Leidensgeschichte des Matthäus zur christologischen Offenbarung' (ET, p. 198)); Senior, *The Passion Narrative*, p. 4.

subsection we shall discuss whether such an approach might offer a coherent and plausible understanding.

3.1 Matthew's passion narrative (two-source hypothesis)

Advocates of the two-source hypothesis have generally agreed that Matthew depends throughout the passion primarily upon Mark and not at all upon Q.[16] Although this 'primarily' extends in some scholars' views to 'totally' or 'solely' (for example D. P. Senior's *The Passion Narrative according to Matthew*), other scholars, notably R. E. Brown in *The Death of the Messiah*, have attributed the additional material to an additional source, either written or oral.[17] A. Descamps analysed Matthew's modifications of Mark as falling into three categories: formal; historical; and christological.[18] However, the alterations and additions which Matthew makes to Mark reflect, in the view of many scholars, interests which go beyond the christological emphases to which we shall shortly turn, and include a broad range of interests such as the following:

(i)   the exemplary nature of Jesus' passion (e.g. Senior, *The Passion Narrative according to Matthew*, pp. 338–9; Strecker, *Der Weg der Gerechtigkeit*, pp. 182–4; Gerhardsson, 'Jésus livré et abandonné d'après la Passion selon Saint Matthieu');

(ii) the explanation of the 'Grundlegung der Kirche' (the foundation-laying of the church) (e.g. Schneider, *Die Passion Jesu*, pp. 159–64; Dahl, 'Die Passiongeschichte bei Matthäus', p. 27);

(iii) the detailing of Jewish responsibility for Jesus' death (esp. 26.3–5, 14–16, 57–68; 27.3–10, 25; e.g. Senior, 'Matthew's Special Material in the Passion Story', pp. 285–9; Fitzmyer, 'Anti-Semitism and the Cry of "All the People" '; van Tilborg, *The Jewish Leaders in Matthew*, pp. 73–98; Trilling, *Das wahre Israel*, pp. 66–74; Mora, *Le refus d'Israël. Matthieu 27,25*; Brown, *The Death of the Messiah*, vol. I, pp. 29–30).

(iv) N. A. Dahl attempted to bring some coherence to the discussion, arguing that the relationship between church

---

[16] Despite Hirsch, *Frühgeschichte des Evangeliums*, vol. II, pp. 236–49.
[17] R. E. Brown, *The Death of the Messiah*, vol. I, pp. 59–61.
[18] Descamps, 'Rédaction et christologie dans le récit matthéen de la Passion'.

and synagogue is the main issue behind the Matthean redaction ('Die Passiongeschichte bei Matthäus').

In terms of the contribution of the Matthean redaction to his christological emphases three aspects in particular deserve attention. Notably, in each case Matthew draws upon material already present in Mark in order to highlight the point.

1. Jesus' name appears in seventeen additional places in the passion narrative (Matt. 26.1, 4, 6, 19, 26, 36, 49, 50, 52, 71; 27.11, 17, 20, 27, 37, 54, 55, 57; cf. 26.21 omitted from Mark 14.18) This focusses attention on the main character who is also depicted as being in total control of events (e.g. 26.18: 'my time is near'; 26.50: 'do that for which you have come'; 26.52–4: legions of angels; 26.61: 'I can destroy the temple . . .').[19] In particular Jesus' death is presented as the result of his clear will to give up his life despite the possibility of rescue at his command (e.g. 26.42: 'may your will be done'; 26.53: the legions of angels), emphasised by Matthew's phrasing at the end: 'he gave up the spirit' (27.50).[20] This is signalled at the very outset of Matthew's passion narrative by the juxtaposition of Jesus' statement, that the Son of Man would be crucified during the Passover (26.2), with the desires of the Jewish leaders, 'not during the feast' (26.5): Jesus dies at the time of his own choosing, not that of his opponents. While the statement of the Jewish leaders is present in Mark 14.2, and the contrast is clearly implicit in Mark's account (they have been seeking his death since 3.6), it is made clearer in Matthew's redaction by the addition of the statement echoing Jesus' passion predictions: καὶ ὁ υἱὸς τοῦ ἀνθρώπου παραδίδοται εἰς τὸ σταυρωθῆναι (26.2; cf. esp. 20.18f).

2. The OT background of the passion, already present in Mark's account (general statements: Mark 14.21 // Matt. 26.24; Mark 14.49 // Matt. 26.56; quotations: Mark 14.27 // Matt. 26.31; Mark 15.34 // Matt. 27.46) is made much more specific in Matthew (e.g.

---

[19] So also Dibelius, *Die Formgeschichte des Evangeliums*, pp. 198–9 (ET, pp. 197–8); Gerhardsson, 'Jésus livré et abandonné d'après la Passion selon Saint Matthieu', pp. 211–12; Fischer, 'Redaktionsgeschichtliche Bemerkungen zur Passionsgeschichte des Matthäus', pp. 109–15; Descamps, 'Rédaction et christologie dans le récit matthéen de la Passion', pp. 401–2; Verseput, 'The Role and Meaning of the "Son of God" Title in Matthew's Gospel', pp. 547–8; Barth, 'Das Gesetzesverständnis des Evangelisten Matthäus', pp. 134–5 (ET, pp. 143–4); Brown, *The Death of the Messiah*, vol. I, p. 29.

[20] Klostermann, *Matthäusevangelium*, p. 224; Verseput, 'The Role and Meaning of the "Son of God" Title in Matthew's Gospel', p. 547; Brown, *The Death of the Messiah*, vol. II, p. 1081.

the general statement of 26.54; also quotations in 27.9f from Jer. 32.7 and Zech. 11.12; 27.43, 50 from Ps. 22).[21] A related category is that Jesus is referred to more explicitly as Messiah (26.68; 27.17, 22). This results in and coheres with a greater emphasis on the eschatological significance of Jesus' death in Matthew (particularly in 27.51–3, but also 26.52–4; 27.3–10, 19).

> The eschatological significance of this material is exaggerated by H.-W. Bartsch who concluded from Matthew 27.51–54: 'Erdbeben und Aufer-stehung der Toten sind nicht Zeichen, sondern sie gehören selbst bereits zu den Ereignissen der mit Sterben Jesu beginnenden Parusie!' (The earthquake and resurrection of the dead are not signs, rather they belong to the parousia which has already begun with the death of Jesus) ('Die Passions- und Ostergeschichten bei Matthäus. Ein Beitrag zur Redak-tionsgeschichte des Evangeliums', p. 86). For a critique (Bartsch assesses only Matthew's special material) see Senior, *The Passion Narrative according to Matthew*, pp. 307–23.

3. Matthew emphasises 'Son of God' by adding it to the narrative several times (27.40, 43 – the mockery, cf. also 26.63 – reshapes Mark).[22] In several additional places Matthew adds a reference to 'my Father' to Jesus' words (26.29, 39, 42).[23] A related category is Matthew's additional references to Jesus being 'with' the disciples or vice versa (26.29: in the future; v. 36: 'Jesus went with them', vv. 38 and 40: watching 'with me'; v. 51: swordsman identified as one of those 'with Jesus', cf. also v. 71); this may be related to Matthew's presence christology (cf. 1.23; 18.20; 28.20).

In relation to these alterations it has been suggested that Matthew presents a transcendent and de-historicised picture of Christ. Descamps, for example, compares Matthew's Christ with that of the Byzantine mosaics.[24] Senior offers a less extreme conclusion but still sees the result of these alterations as a 'heigh-tened *christological* portrait' whereby Matthew enhances

the figure of the Messiah – even at a moment of suffering

---

[21] Gerhardsson, 'Jésus livré et abandonné d'après la Passion selon Saint Matthieu'; Descamps, 'Rédaction et christologie dans le récit matthéen de la Passion', pp. 402–4; Gundry, *The Use of the Old Testament in St Matthew's Gospel*, pp. 201–4. Cf. generally Moo, *The Old Testament in the Gospel Passion Narratives*, and, for Mark, Suhl, *Die Funktion der alttestamentlichen Zitate und Anspielungen im Markusevangelium*, pp. 26–66.

[22] Senior, *The Passion Narrative*, pp. 337 and 283–4, 327–8 (on Matt. 27.40 and 54 respectively); de Kruijf, *Der Sohn des lebendigen Gottes*, pp. 95–104.

[23] Descamps, 'Rédaction et christologie dans le récit matthéen de la Passion', pp. 395–6.

[24] Ibid., pp. 414–15.

and humiliation. Throughout the narrative, the impression is given that acknowledgement of Jesus as Messiah, as Son of God, is the basic message the redactor (inspired by Mark) wishes to proclaim.[25]

This conclusion is not generally considered to be part of an argument for Markan priority, but the result of redaction-critical studies which *presuppose* Markan priority. Nevertheless Senior does suggest that although he has presupposed Markan priority from the beginning this theory is supported by his investigation.[26] Of course, inasmuch as Matthean redaction of Mark provides a plausible and coherent picture of his redactional behaviour then it can be used to support Markan priority, but only if the converse is not true. Despite the language of *heightened* christology present in several discussions, there is little in the way of sure directional indicators by which Matthew's christology at this point might be measured as later and secondary to that of Mark.

Differences such as Matthew's more explicit use of the OT, and emphasis on Jesus as Messiah, may plausibly be regarded as owing more to the personality and situation of the author than to later developments. For example, Senior discusses the different use of 'Son of God' in Matthew and Mark and concludes that while in Mark the term comes as a sudden revelation (Mark 15.39 never used previously in the same form), in Matthew it has been at the forefront of discussion (Matt. 26.62; 27.40, 43) and echoes previous confessions (Matt. 14.33; 16.16), and so it involves for Matthew the confirmation of Jesus' identity as 'Son of God' rather than a radical revelation of that identity.[27] But this is not automatically an argument for Markan priority, since the Griesbach hypothesis might suggest that Mark has harnessed his sources deliberately in order to arrange this final climax. So this argument cannot be elevated over the more general argument from redactional plausibility. For example, when Dahl argues that the pattern of additions of special Matthean traditions 'secondarily inserted into the Marcan order' points towards Markan priority he is also making an argument from literary and redactional plausibility.[28] Such

---

[25] Senior, *The Passion Narrative*, p. 337.
[26] Ibid., pp. 5–8, 339–41; cf. also Dahl, 'Die Passiongeschichte bei Matthäus', pp. 17–18 (ET, pp. 42–3).
[27] Senior, *The Passion Narrative*, pp. 327–8 and compare our discussion below.
[28] Dahl, 'Die Passiongeschichte bei Matthäus', p. 18 (cited from ET, p. 43).

arguments, however, necessitate the comparative examination of the material from the perspective of the Griesbach hypothesis.

3.2   Mark's passion narrative (Griesbach hypothesis)

While most studies of the Markan passion narrative have assumed Markan priority and focussed on the nature of Mark's sources, defenders of the Griesbach hypothesis have so far failed to offer a redaction-critical study of Mark's use of Matthew and Luke in the passion narratives (notwithstanding some very brief comments in C. S. Mann, *Mark*, e.g. p. 543).[29]

> For surveys of studies in the Markan passion narrative, most of which focus on the question of whether a pre-Markan source existed and if so what it contained, see J. B. Green, *The Death of Jesus*, pp. 9–14 and Pesch, *Markusevangelium*, vol. II, pp. 7–10; Soards, 'The Question of a PreMarcan Passion Narrative'. Most scholars, including Green, Pesch and Soards assent to the existence of a pre-Markan account (also Dibelius, *Die Formgeschichte des Evangeliums*, pp. 178–218 (ET, pp. 178–217); Bultmann, *Die Geschichte der synoptischen Tradition*, pp. 297–308 (ET, pp. 275–84)); although debate continues on its extent and content and some scholars deny the existence of a continuous pre-Markan narrative source (e.g. Linnemann, *Studien zur Passionsgeschichte*, pp. 54–68; Kelber, *The Oral and Written Gospel*, pp. 187–99).

In terms of both order and content Griesbach-Mark follows Matthew more closely than Luke. On the Griesbach hypothesis, Lukan influence on the wording of Mark can be seen in a few places, but these tend to be limited to a single word or short phrase, supplementing the Matthean account (Mark 14.1, 11, 13, 15; 15.1, 21, 26, 33, 42f, 46). Griesbach-Mark nowhere includes a distinctly Lukan passage (e.g. Luke 22.15–18, 21–30, 31f, 35–8, 43f, 52, 67–71; 23.4f, 6–12, 13–16, 27–32, 40–3). Nor does he select only passages which Matthew and Luke both attest (Mark 14.3–9, 27–31, 38b–42, 55–64; 15.7–10, 16–20, 29–31, 34–6, 38). In short we are justified in seeing Griesbach-Mark as primarily dependent upon Matthew, with a relatively less significant dependence upon Luke.[30]

---

[29] Some attention to the distinctives of the Markan account (in addition to the commentaries) can be found in Senior, *The Passion of Jesus in Mark*; Matera, *The Kingship of Jesus: Composition and Theology in Mark 15*; Schneider, *Die Passion Jesu nach den drei älteren Evangelien*, pp. 155–9; Dormeyer, *Die Passion Jesu als Verhaltensmodel*, pp. 276–81; Brown, *The Death of the Messiah*.

[30] Griesbach, 'Demonstration', p. 109; Bleek, *Einleitung*, pp. 256–7 (ET, pp. 273–4); Davidson, *Introduction*, p. 476; Mann, *Mark*, p. 543; Riley, *The Making of Mark*, pp. 179–94; Farmer *et al.*, 'Narrative Outline of the Markan Composition According to the Two Gospel Hypothesis', pp. 235–8.

Griesbach-Mark adds little to Matthew, only the passage concerning the young man (Mark 14.51f), the reference to Pilate's questioning whether Jesus had died (15.44), and an additional temporal indicator (15.25). He alters Matthew's wording in many places and omits several passages (Matt. 26.25, 42b, 44, 52–4; 27.3–10, 19, 21, 24f, 51b–3, 62–6).

While not as emphatic as his sources, since Mark does not contain all the explicit OT citations of Matthew (or Luke 22.37), Mark does contain general statements (Mark 14.21: 'the Son of Man goes as it is written of him' // Matt. 26.24; 14.49: 'let the scriptures be fulfilled' // Matt. 26.56), explicit citations (Mark 14.27 cf. Zech. 13.7 // Matt. 26.31), and clear allusions (particularly to Ps. 22 in 15.24, 29a, 34).[31] Griesbach-Mark's avoidance of explicit citations with introductory formulae is consistent throughout the gospel and could be explained in various ways; it could, for example, be attributed to a non-Jewish audience and/or the allusive/parabolic nature of Mark's presentation.

Griesbach-Mark does omit three statements from Matthew which imply Jesus' innocence (Matt. 27.4: Judas; v. 19: Pilate's wife; vv. 24f: Pilate). These omissions are unusual in view of Luke's emphasis on the same point (Luke 23.4: Pilate; vv. 14f; v. 22: Pilate; v. 41: criminal; v. 47: centurion). Thus Griesbach-Mark omits similar material from both his sources. On the other hand his additions to the Sanhedrin trial emphasise the disagreements of the 'false witnesses' (Mark 14.56b, 57, 59) and thus suggest that Mark also thought that Jesus was not guilty.

At both 15.9 and 12 Griesbach-Mark adds 'the King of the Jews' to Matthew, and elsewhere Mark parallels Matthew's use of the phrase (15.2, 18, 26, 32 ('king of Israel')). In the series of mockings Mark takes the first (by the soldiers) largely intact from Matthew as a royal mocking (Mark 15.16–20 // Matt. 27.27–31). Within this passage, Griesbach-Mark alters the term χλαμύδα κοκκίνην ('scarlet robe', Matt. 27.28) to πορφύραν ('purple cloak', Mark 15.17). This change *could* be motivated by a 'kingly' interest, since ἡ πορφύρα can refer to the royal purple garment.

> For ἡ πορφύρα as a royal garment see BAGD, p. 694, citing Dio Chrysostom, 4.71 (which implies that kings normally were associated with

---

[31] See Moo, *The Old Testament in the Gospel Passion Narratives*, pp. 252–8, 264–75; also Suhl, *Die Funktion der alttestamentlichen Zitate und Anspielungen im Markusevangelium*, pp. 45–56.

the purple garment); Josephus, *Ant.*, XI.256f (esp 257: ἐνδύεται τὴν πορφύραν ἥν ὁ βασιλεὺς φορῶν ἀεὶ διετέλει); 1 Macc. 10.62; cf. also Josephus, *Ant.*, XVII.197 (King Herod's body wrapped in purple for his funeral); *Tg. Onq.* Gen. 49.11: 'let his raiment be of fine purple' (for the royal Messiah); *Tg. Esth. I* 6.8 refers to 'the purple robe with which they dressed the king on the day he came to his reign' [MT 'royal' = Targum 'purple']. On the other hand, the two terms (κόκκινος and πορφύρα) are often used in collocation (Exod. 39.12; 2 Chron. 2.6; Rev. 17.4, BAGD, p. 440), and the difference in meaning may be negligible (in addition to its royal connotations purple robes functioned as a more general status symbol; Reinhold, *History of Purple as a Status Symbol in Antiquity*).

In addition Mark has reoriented the second mockery, by those passing while Jesus was on the cross (Mark 15.27–32), more fully around the title 'King of the Jews' (present in the Matthean account), by omitting Matthew's two references to Jesus as 'the Son of God' (Matt. 27.40, 43). Thus the second mocking, like the first, is a mocking of Jesus as King. This coheres with Matera's conclusion that 'the overall theme of chapter 15 is the "Kingship of Jesus"'.[32]

Matera tends to transform Mark's quite specific 'King of the Jews' into a more absolute 'Kingship' without allowing for the particularity of the title. He does, however, attempt to integrate the 'Kingship' theme with the climax – Mark 15.39: Jesus as Son of God (i.e. messianic king); Matera, *The Kingship of Jesus: Composition and Theology in Mark 15*, pp. 125–45; cf. also Donahue, 'Temple, Trial, and Royal Christology (Mark 14:53–65)'.

In his account of the crucifixion and death of Jesus (Mark 15.20b–41), Griesbach-Mark follows Matthew closely, and little of significance is altered until the centurion's 'confession'. Mark omits Matthew's earthquake, opening tombs and resurrected saints and thus focusses attention much more closely on the tearing of the veil (15.38). These omissions require some reshaping of v. 39 to the effect that it is Jesus' death rather than the miraculous events in Matthew 27.54 which prompt the confession from the centurion alone: Ἀληθῶς οὗτος ὁ ἄνθρωπος υἱὸς θεοῦ ἦν. Mark has omitted 'Son of God' from Matthew twice in this chapter (Matt. 27.40, 43), and used a different form in Mark 14.61 ('the Son of the Blessed' cf. Matt. 26.63: 'Son of God'). This has the dramatic effect of withholding the title until the unveiling of the messianic secret is complete.

Thus there are indications, from the Griesbach-hypothesis per-

---

[32] Matera, *The Kingship of Jesus: Composition and Theology in Mark 15*, p. 61.

spective, that the Markan passion narrative could be regarded as a 'christological redaction' of the Matthean narrative. The suggestions made are tentative, but serve to show that there is nothing in the narrative which *demands* that Mark could not have been secondary to Matthew. Mark's presentation is simply different, and it could be that further investigation by defenders of the Griesbach hypothesis could explicate the possibilities more fully. Explaining Mark's omissions from Matthew, and from Luke, remains a difficulty for the Griesbach hypothesis, but our concern in this chapter has largely been with additional material and positive alterations. In these terms the Griesbach hypothesis can provide a relatively plausible analysis of the Markan passion narrative.

4.   General comments on additions

Since, as has already been noted, the topics covered in this chapter all involve Matthew's alterations and additions to Mark, this section will offer brief discussion of some of the other additional material used by the evangelists. A list of additional material is presented in Appendix 7.A ('Matthean "Additions" to Mark': passages added by Matthew to Mark assuming Markan priority; where Lukan parallels or 'Q' material are also noted) and Appendix 7.B ('Markan "Additions" to Matthew': passages added by Mark to Matthew assuming Matthean priority).

4.1   Matthew's additions to Mark

Assuming Markan priority, Matthew's additions to Mark amount to something like half of the gospel. Much of this additional material is clearly incorporated from other sources, whether 'Q' or some other source. It is worth noting, however, additional material which is clearly phrased in Matthean redactional terminology and would be regarded as Matthean additions by many defenders of the two-source hypothesis. The most important additions form the gospel's introduction (chapters 1 and 2) and conclusion (28.16–20), and both are crucially important for Matthew's christology.

As K. Stendahl has argued, chapters 1 and 2 introduce the Matthean Jesus by answering the questions '*Who* is Jesus?' and '*Where* does he come *from*?'; this is a widely accepted analysis, sometimes extended to four sections: Who? (1.1–17); How? (1.18–25); Where? (2.1–12); Whence? (2.13–23).[33] Throughout this section the christological focus never shifts, identifying Jesus by titles such as υἱοῦ Δαυὶδ, υἱοῦ Ἀβραάμ (1.1), Χριστός (1.16f), Ἐμμανουήλ (1.23), τὸν υἱόν μου (2.15); and placing his advent at the pinnacle of God's dealings with Israel as the one who fulfils the OT promises (particularly 1.22; 2.5, 15, 17, 23), as the offspring of David's line (1.1–17), and as the one whom Gentiles seek to worship (2.2, 8, 11).[34]

Matthew's conclusion (28.16–20) has also received a great deal of attention recently, especially since O. Michel argued that '*Matt. 28:18–20 is the key to the understanding of the whole book.*'[35] Numerous discussions have focussed on its important place in Matthew's christological presentation.[36] The debate concerning whether the passage should be regarded as signalling the fulfilment of Daniel 7.13f ('all authority . . .'),[37] the exaltation of Jesus as κύριος,[38] or as cohering primarily around Matthew's Son-christology,[39] must be viewed with some caution, especially when phrased in an entirely disjunctive manner. Stanton suggests that '28.16–20 contains a cluster of related Matthean themes' and 'a *grand finale* in which the evangelist summarises his main points', and this seems to be the most sensible way to approach the passage.[40] Studies have also pointed out the presence of Matthean vocabulary (e.g. προσκύνησαν, προσελθών, ἐξουσία,

---

[33] Stendahl, 'Quis et Unde? An Analysis of Mt 1–2'; on the extension see Brown, *The Birth of the Messiah*, pp. 53–4 (following Paul, *L'évangile de l'enfance selon saint Matthieu*, p. 96; cf. Davies and Allison, *Matthew*, vol. I, p. 219).

[34] Detailed studies include Tatum, *The Matthean Infancy Stories*; '"The Origin of Jesus Messiah" (Matt. 1:1, 18a): Matthew's Use of the Infancy Traditions'; Soares Prabhu, *The Formula Quotations in the Infancy Narrative of Matthew*; Nolan, *The Royal Son of God*; Brown, *The Birth of the Messiah*, pp. 45–232.

[35] Michel, 'Der Abschluß des Matthäusevangeliums', p. 21 (cited from ET, p. 35).

[36] See Stanton, 'The Origin and Purpose of Matthew's Gospel', pp. 1922–3; Donaldson, *Jesus on the Mountain*, pp. 275–6 (note to p. 171) for bibliography.

[37] Michel, 'Der Abschluß des Matthäusevangeliums'; Barth, 'Das Gesetzesverständnis des Evangelisten Matthäus', pp. 124–5 (ET, p. 133); Ellis, *Matthew: His Mind and His Message*, pp. 23–4; Frankemölle, *Jahwebund und Kirche Christi*, pp. 61–6; Lange, *Das Erscheinen des Auferstandenen im Evangelium nach Matthäus*, pp. 211–17; France, *Matthew: Evangelist and Teacher*, pp. 313–316.

[38] Hahn, *Das Verständnis der Mission im neuen Testament*, pp. 54–7 (ET, pp. 65–8).

[39] Kingsbury, 'The Composition and Christology of Matt 28:16–20' and elsewhere.

[40] Stanton, 'The Origin and Purpose of Matthew's Gospel', p. 1923; 'Matthew as a Creative Interpreter of the Sayings of Jesus', p. 287, n. 37; cf. similarly Gundry, *Matthew*, p. 593.

μαθητεύσατε, διδάσκοντες),[41] themes such as the authority and teaching of Jesus, the Zion-Mountain motif, and the presence motif; parallels to 11.27 and extensive parallels to the birth narratives.[42]

On this last point note, for example, Jesus' presence (1.23 cf. 28.20); Gentiles (2.1–12 cf. 28.19); the angel of the Lord (1.20, 24; 2.13, 19 cf. 28.2, 5); the trinitarian content (1.18, 20; 2.15 cf. 28.19), for more examples and discussion see Frankemölle, *Jahwebund und Kirche Christi*, pp. 321–5; Soares-Prabhu, *The Formula Quotations in the Infancy Narrative of Matthew*, pp. 173–6 (cf. the critical comments by Nolan, *The Royal Son of God*, pp. 107–8).

For the moment we are not concerned with the actual christological content of these passages. The obvious point is simply that Matthew's additions (assuming the two-source hypothesis) are of a strongly christological nature. The passages take up and focus christological themes of great importance for our evangelist. This is noteworthy in view of the importance of beginnings and endings in ancient literature. For Aristotle the prologue or proem had an introductory role to 'pave the way for what is to come', while the epilogue recapitulated what had gone before (Aristotle, *Rhetoric* III.1414b–15a and 1419b–20).[43] A similar christological interest is also exhibited in later forms of gospel redaction: the introduction to *Gos. Thom.* shapes the interpretation of what follows; Tatian's introduction, a skilful combination of Johannine and synoptic thought, placed a significant christological interpretation on what followed; and the dramatic opening of Marcion's gospel was understood to be indicative of his unorthodox views. Matthew's action, as understood by the two-source hypothesis, thus seems both coherent (internally) and plausible (externally); it is possible to speak of Matthew bracketing Mark by *inclusio* with key passages of christological importance.

[41] See Gundry, *Matthew*, pp. 593–7; Kingsbury, 'The Composition and Christology of Matt 28:16–20', pp. 575–9; Hubbard, *The Matthean Redaction of a Primitive Apostolic Commissioning*, pp. 73–98.

[42] Cf. Brooks, 'Matthew xxviii 16–20 and the Design of the First Gospel' (on the authority of Jesus); Donaldson, *Jesus on the Mountain*, pp. 174–90; Danker, ' "God With Us": Hellenistic Christological Perspectives in Matthew'; Lange suggested that 28.16–20 should be regarded as 'einer Neuauflage von Mt 11,27/Lk 10,22' (*Das Erscheinen des Auferstandenen im Evangelium nach Matthäus*, p. 488).

[43] See Russell and Winterbottom, *Ancient Literary Criticism*, pp. 158 and 169–70. Cf. also Horace, *Poetry*, *ll*140–52 (p. 283); Quintillian, *Controversia* 338 (pp. 344–5); Lucian, *History* 52–4 (p. 545); see Earl, 'Prologue-form in Ancient Historiography', and Robbins, 'Prefaces in Greco-Roman Biography and Luke–Acts'.

4.2   *Mark's additions to Matthew (Griesbach hypothesis)*

If the Griesbach hypothesis is assumed, then Mark's additions to Matthew and Luke, although relatively few, can be investigated (see Appendix 7.B). It is noteworthy that there are very few such passages and that none of them have the christological importance we saw in the previous section. In particular Griesbach-Mark has added little by way of prologue or epilogue. Many of the additions are of details (as has been previously noted and widely recognised). Two of the three healing miracles unique to Mark (7.33–6; 8.22–6) are quite similar involving: withdrawal from the crowd or village; the use of spittle; a secrecy command. Their addition helps two themes in Mark: the secrecy motif and the (mis)understanding motif, which could explain their addition according to the Griesbach hypothesis.[44] Nevertheless, none of the additions seem to offer any distinctive christological content. Indeed, of all Griesbach hypothesis defenders D. F. Strauss alone found any christological interests in these passages, arguing that Mark's accounts 'give dramatic effect to the scene' by means of the details of the narrative, the partial cure, the magical potency of the saliva, 'the exaggerated description of the astonishment of the people', and the magical significance of the Aramaic.[45] By contrast, modern Griesbachians tend to ascribe the passages to a Markan source.[46]

5.   Conclusion

In this chapter we have found that although Matthean use of 'worship' and 'approach' terminology can be regarded as compatible with his redactional vocabulary preferences, a clear christological argument for Markan priority has not been vindicated within this material. In connection with the passion narratives both the two-source hypothesis and the Griesbach hypothesis could provide relatively plausible and coherent explanations for the redactional behaviour envisaged. Matthean redaction (assuming Markan priority) coheres well with other recognised Matthean emphases,

---

[44] Riley, *The Making of Mark*, p. 96. According to both Griesbach ('Demonstration', p. 109) and Farmer (*The Synoptic Problem*, p. 242), Mark was following Matthew (rather than Luke) at both these points – the first passage can be explained as an expansion of Matt. 15.30 (Farmer, *The Synoptic Problem*, p. 244).

[45] Strauss, *Das Leben Jesu*, vol. II, pp. 74–7 (citation from ET, pp. 447–9).

[46] Farmer, *The Synoptic Problem*, p. 242; Mann, *Mark*, p. 336.

and in several respects is similar to aspects of the post-gospel transmission of gospel traditions. Griesbach-Markan redaction of the passion narratives can also be described in a relatively straightforward, and christologically informed, manner. In connection with the general category of additions, the Griesbach hypothesis loses out somewhat in comparison with the two-source hypothesis in terms of the plausibility and coherence of the additions.

Our investigation has so far followed the pattern laid down by the originators of the christological argument for Markan priority. On several occasions we have suggested that a broader base for comparison is still desirable and in the following chapters we shall continue our investigation by looking at the use of several themes and categories organised around the christological titles.

Appendix 7.A. Matthean 'additions' to Mark
Passages added by Matthew to Mark (assuming Markan priority)

Matthew	Contents	Luke
1.1–2.23	birth and infancy narratives	
3.7–10	John the Baptist – preaching repentance	3.7–9
3.12	John the Baptist – winnowing etc. (judgement)	3.17
3.14, 15	Jesus' baptism: 'fulfil all righteousness'	
4.3–10	temptation: Son of God	4.1–13
4.14–16	Isaiah quotation (Isa. 8.23–9.1)	
4.23b, 24	summary statement (cf. 9.35)	
5.1–7.28a	Sermon on Mount (slight parallels with Mark)	6.17–49
8.1	link with 5.1 and 4.25 re coming down from mountain	
8.5–13	Centurion's servant	7.1–10
8.17	Isaiah quotation (Isa. 53.4, 11)	
8.18–22	on discipleship etc.	9.57–60
9.32, 33	dumb demoniac	11.14, 15
9.37, 38	harvest saying	10.2
10.5–8	commission to Israel	9.2 (?)
10.12, 13	greeting of peace	10.6 (?)
10.15	Sodom and Gomorrah	
10.16	lambs and wolves	10.3
10.23–5	Son of Man coming; disciples and servants	6.40 (?)
10.26–33	exhortation to fearless confession	12.2–9
10.34–6	household divisions	12.51–3
10.37–9	discipleship, life etc.	14.25–7
10.40–1	receiving disciples etc.	
11.1	summary re end of discourse	
11.2–6	question of John the Baptist	7.18–23
11.7–19	Jesus concerning John the Baptist	7.24–35
11.20–4	woes on cities	10.12–15
11.25–7	thanksgiving	10.21, 22
11.28–30	'Come unto me . . .'	
12.17–21	quotation of Isaiah	42.1–4
12.22–30	Beelzebul etc. (cf. Luke and Mark, complex!)	11.14f, 17–23
12.33–5	good fruit etc.	6.43–5
12.36, 37	careless words	
12.40–2	sign of Jonah	11.30–2
12.43–5	return of evil spirit	11.24–6
13.14–15	quotation from Isaiah 6.9ff	
13.16–17	blessedness of disciples	10.23, 24
13.24–30	parable of tares	
13.33	parable of leaven	13.20f
13.35	citation of Psalm 78.2 re parables	
13.36–43	interpretation of parable of tares	
13.44–6	parable of hidden treasure and pearl	

Appendix 7.A. *(contd)*

Matthew	Contents	Luke
13.47–50	parable of the net	
13.51, 52	scribe trained for KoH	
14.28–31	Peter walks on water	
16.17–19	Peter blessed	
17.24–7	payment of temple tax	
18.10–14	parable of lost sheep	15.3–7
18.15–18	challenging a brother	
18.19, 20	two or more	
18.21, 22	forgive seven times	17.4
18.23–35	parable of the unforgiving servant	
19.10–12	eunuchs	
19.28	twelve thrones	22.30
20.1–16	parable of labourers in vineyard	
21.4, 5	quotation from Isaiah 62.11 and Zechariah 9.9	
21.14–16	healing in Temple, Hosanna, quotation from Psalm 8.3	
21.28–32	parable of two sons	
22.1–14	parable of great supper (partial Luke parallel)	14.15–24
23.1–36	woes to scribes and Pharisees (parallels in Mark and Luke)	
23.37–9	lament over Jerusalem	13.34f
24.10–12	false prophets	
24.14	preaching of gospel	
24.26–8	Son of Man	17.24, 37 (?)
24.37–41	days of Noah	17.26–36
24.42–4	watchful householder	12.39f
24.45–51	faithful and wise servant	12.41–6
25.1–13	parable of ten maidens	
25.14–30	parable of talents	19.11–27
25.31–46	last judgement	
26.52–4	appeal to Father, scriptures fulfilled	
27.3–10	death of Judas	
27.24, 25	Pilate washes hands	
27.51b–3	apocalyptic events in city at Jesus' death	
27.62–6	guard placed at tomb	
28.2–4	description of angel at tomb	
28.9, 10	women meet Jesus, worship him etc.	
28.11–15	bribing of the soldiers	
28.16–20	great commission	

Appendix 7.B. Markan 'additions' to Matthew
Passages added by Mark to Matthew (assuming Matthean priority)

Mark	Contents	Luke
1.1	beginning	
[1.23–8	exorcism in synagogue	4.33–7]
[1.35–8	early action, departure for Capernaum	4.42–3]
[1.45	conclusion of healing of leper	5.15f]
[3.8b–11	healing multitudes	6.17b–19]
3.20, 21	those with Jesus think he's mad	
[4.21–4	he who has ears . . . (some parallels)	8.16–18]
4.26–9	parable of seed growing secretly	
5.3–5 [8–10, 15, 16, 18–20]	details in the Gerasene demoniac account	[8.26–39]
5.21, 26 [29–33, 35–7, 43]	details in the account of the healing of Jairus' daughter and the bleeding woman	[8.40–56]
[6.15,16	opinions about Jesus	9.8f]
6.20–5 (parts of)	some details in account of John the Baptist's death	
6.[30] 31	return of apostles	[9.10]
7.2–4	explanation of Jewish customs	
7.33–6	healing of deaf mute	
8.22–6	blind man healed	
9.20–4	details in healing of possessed boy cf. 9.42	
[11.18, 19	chief priests plot against Jesus	19.47f]
12.32–4	extra conversation with scribe re KoG	
[12.41–4	the widow's mite	21.1–4]
13.33–7	take heed (some parallels with Matthew and Luke)	
14.51, 52	young man runs away naked	
[16.3, 4	at the tomb	24.2]

8

CHRISTOLOGY AND TITLES: JESUS AS TEACHER AND LORD

1. Introduction: 'titles' and gospel christology

In the next four chapters we shall investigate the way in which the two hypotheses under investigation account for and explain important christological themes within the gospels. In particular the aim is to examine the use of various titular christological categories in Matthew and Mark in the hope that this will offer the opportunity for a comparison between the gospels based on broader themes and christological concerns.

Historical interests have dominated the investigation of NT christology since the nineteenth century and Baur's *Tendenzkritik* (discussed in chapter one), and christological titles have played a prominent role within these discussions. Until recently much of the agenda was set by Bousset's *Kyrios Christos* (1913) which summed up the basic thrusts of both the *religionsgeschichtliche Schule* and the old liberal school.[1] The crucial problems addressed by Bousset were the question of the (dis?)continuity between the historical Jesus and the faith of the church, and the transformation of Jesus' message into Christianity among Gentile Christians, a transformation which was 'the great and decisive turning point in the development of Christianity'.[2] Bousset's investigation focussed on christological titles (especially κύριος); in particular he argued that apocalyptic Jewish Christianity created a Son-of-Man christology, and that hellenistic Christianity created a cultic Kyrios christology. The mapping of historical developments, understood as central to

---

[1] Perrin, 'Reflections on the Publication in English of Bousset's *Kyrios Christos*', p. 342 (citing Bousset, *Kyrios Christos*, ET, pp. 116–18). Note the subtitle (in ET): *A History of the Belief in Christ from the Beginnings of Christianity to Irenaeus.*
[2] Bousset, *Kyrios Christos*, p. VI (cited from ET, p. 12).

the study of NT christology, has been characteristic of most subsequent discussions.[3]

This mapping has normally been oriented around the diachronic analysis of various christological titles, understood as 'foci' for christological analysis.[4] Since the 1950s the study of NT christology has, for good or ill, been dominated by a titular approach. Works such as V. Taylor's *The Names of Jesus*, O. Cullmann's *Die Christologie des Neuen Testaments*, F. Hahn's *Christologische Hoheitstitel, Ihre Geschichte im frühen Christentum* and R. H. Fuller's *The Foundations of New Testament Christology* have all analysed the various facets of NT christology by analysing the history and use of christological titles.[5] A notable recent example is J. D. G. Dunn's *Christology in the Making*; the aim of the work is historical, to study the origins of the incarnation doctrine; and the approach consists of chapters on 'Son of God', 'Son of Man', 'Adam', 'Angel'/'Spirit', 'Wisdom', 'Word' (note also his 'Foreword to Second Edition').

This general approach, focussing on historical concerns through titles, has recently been subjected to important criticism. L. E. Keck, in particular, has argued that preoccupation with the history of christology and christological titles has left Jesus' place in NT christology insecure. This concentration misses much of the relevant material, tends to transcendentalise the presentation of Jesus, and fails to provide access to 'the dynamic struggle of NT Christology with early Christian theology'.[6] In a later publication he is more forceful: 'Probably no other factor has contributed more to the current aridity of the discipline than this fascination with the palaeontology of christological titles.'[7] He also attacks the (mistaken) view that meaning resides in words rather than sentences;

---

[3] Boers, 'Jesus and the Christian Faith: New Testament Christology Since Bousset's *Kyrios Christos*'; Hurtado, 'New Testament Christology: A Critique of Bousset's Influence'.

[4] See Foakes-Jackson and Lake, *Beginnings of Christianity*, vol. I, pp. 345–418 (esp. p. 346 on titles as 'foci'); other early studies include Burton, *Galatians*, pp. 392–417; Dalman, *Die Worte Jesu*, pp. 191–280 (ET, pp. 234–340).

[5] Fuller, although more aware than most of the limitations of the titular approach (e.g. *The Foundations of New Testament Christology*, p. 16), built on his earlier comment that titles provide 'the raw materials of Christology' (*The Mission and Achievement of Jesus*, p. 79).

[6] Keck, 'Jesus in New Testament Christology', p. 14.

[7] Keck, 'Toward the Renewal of New Testament Christology', p. 368.

and shows how the emphasis on titles has hampered the study of NT christology.[8]

As yet, however, no acceptable alternative method has been worked out. Keck himself is unclear concerning the organising principles to be used. In 'Jesus in New Testament Christology' he takes the titles as 'metaphors'; but in 'Toward the Renewal of New Testament Christology' he suggests 'respecting the grammar of christological discourse', focussing on NT texts and juxtaposing diverse canonical christologies. For resolution of these difficulties we await his book, *Jesus in New Testament Christology.*[9] Meanwhile, for the purposes of this discussion, which are primarily historical and comparative, organising the discussion around christological titles and using them to compare aspects of the evangelists' christological presentation remains the simplest approach. In any case the prominence of christological titles in the gospels – numerically and structurally – is surely indicative of their importance to the evangelists. Note, for example, the use of christological titles at structurally important locations such as in the titles and/or prologues (Matt. 1.1; Mark 1.1; John 1.1); apparently decisive junctures (Mark 8.29 and parallel; Mark 15.39 and parallel); and conclusions (Matt. 28.19; John 20.31). Thus, while the focus of attention in these chapters remains the texts of Matthew and Mark, the approach and organising principle depend on an analysis of the use of certain christological titles by the evangelists.

We have compiled (in Table 8.1) a list of the major christological titles used in the gospels (the same list with references is provided in Appendix 8.A). Obviously a simple chart like Table 8.1 may obscure a number of things. For example, there is no information concerning important issues such as the structural placing of the titles (e.g. the clustering of 'Son of God' in Luke 2–4 or John 5) and their narrative context (important, e.g. in Mark 12.35–7 and parallel), and the speaker's identities are also not identified. In addition the number of references to a title cannot be assumed to relate to its importance for an evangelist; ultimately only exegetical investigation of evangelical usage will allow any firm conclusions.

---

[8] Ibid., pp. 368–70. For other criticisms cf. Balz, *Methodische Probleme der neutestamentlichen Christologie*, e.g., p. 46; Hurtado, 'New Testament Christology: Retrospect and Prospect', p. 23; Jeremias, *Neutestamentliche Theologie 1*, pp. 239–40 (ET, pp. 250–1).

[9] Referred to in Keck, 'Toward the Renewal of New Testament Christology', p. 375, n. 9.

Table 8.1   *Christological titles in the gospels*

Christological title	Matthew	Mark	Luke (+ Acts)	John
Son of God	9	4	6 (+ 1)	9
the Son, my Son etc.	8	3	6 (+ 1)	20
Son of Man	30	14	25 (+ 1)	13
Son of David	9	4	4 (+ 0)	0
Christ	16	7	12 (+ 28)	19
Lord	27	7	41 (+ > 50)	44
Teacher	11	12	14 (+ 0)	6
Master (ἐπιστάτα)	0	0	6	0

Nevertheless the information in Table 8.1 does allow certain features of the gospels to emerge, even if a number of these will require modification. The features in Luke which are highlighted include the obvious propensity to 'Lord' as well as 'Master', and an apparently marginal interest in 'Son of David'. With respect to John's gospel the table highlights his use of 'Son' absolutely, as well as the common use of 'Lord', and a high proportion of occurrences of 'Christ'. In terms of a comparison between Matthew and Mark we could note that Matthew uses 'Lord' almost four times as often as Mark. Of the other titles Matthew seems to use all except one of them in slightly higher frequencies than Mark (based on a *pro rata* calculation of the relative lengths of Mark:Matthew as 1:1.67). Matthew uses 'Son of David' in six additional places, including one in the first verse. Mark's four uses are confined to two passages: in one of these Matthew has a different arrangement, leaving out one of the occurrences, but actually highlighting the Davidic sonship of Jesus; he then has five other places where he uses the term. 'Son of God', 'Son of Man' and 'Christ' are all only marginally more prominent in Matthew than in Mark. The exception is 'teacher' which Mark uses more often than Matthew.

This view of the use of christological titles could, at a superficial level, support the view of a primitive Mark – using 'teacher' and 'Son of Man' as his main titles – and a later, more developed Matthew – focussing on Jesus as 'Lord' and 'Son of God'; with Luke in particular using 'Lord' a great deal and John using 'Son' terminology and 'Lord' more than all the others. Whether this is supported by a closer examination is a major interest in what follows. No logical constraints impinge on the order in which these topics are dealt with. This chapter shall begin with the 'Lord' and 'teacher' terminology; according to the list these have the most divergent frequencies. The following chapter (chapter nine) will deal with 'Christ' and 'Son of David' terminology and then chapter ten with 'Son of God', another messianic term. Chapter eleven will deal with 'Son of Man'. In each case we shall begin with some introductory remarks concerning the use of the term, then investigate the Griesbach-hypothesis perspective of Markan redaction. Since in these chapters the investigation departs from material associated with the 'classical' christological argument for Markan priority it seems reasonable, not least in the interests of fair play, to begin the investigations from the Griesbach-hypothesis perspective before turning to the two-source hypothesis. This decision is not greatly significant and the argument would still hold if the alternative procedure was adopted.

2.   Jesus as teacher

2.1   Introduction

That Jesus was widely regarded as a teacher is the common assumption of all four canonical gospels, as well as Jewish sources such as Josephus, *Antiquities* XVIII.63 and *b. Sanh.* 43a. The terminology, in Hebrew and Aramaic as well as in Greek, is varied and interrelated. The major Semitic terms, *Rabbi* and *Mari,* can be used of someone who is a teacher, a Rabbi, or the master of a slave.

> The Rabbis favoured either one of the 'rab' forms ((*rb, rb', rnwn, rbwn'*) or a 'Mar' term (*mr'*). *mr'* has a varied usage and can be used of 'the master of slaves, the owner of goods, the master of the soul' as well as as a polite form of address, with the personal pronoun, for superiors or equals (Foerster, *TDNT* vol. III, p. 1084). *r^{a}b* is commonly used for a religious teacher (*m. 'Abot* 1.6, 16: *'śh lq rb*: 'Provide thyself with a *r^{a}b'*). The term with suffix: *rby* (e.g *m. Roš. Haš.* 2.9) became, in the second century, a title conferred on an officially recognised teacher: 'Rabbi' (*b. Sanh.* 13b; Moore, *Judaism,* vol. III, p. 15). In Rabbinic schools: 'Rabbi is greater than Rab; Rabban is greater than Rabbi; and greater than Rabban is the man's bare name' (Moore, *Judaism,* vol. III, p. 15). In the OT, however, *rb* means 'chief' and in many places in the Mishnah it is used of a master over against a slave (*m. Sukk.* 2.9; *m. Git.* 4.4, 5; *m. 'Ed.* 1.13; *m. 'Abot* 1.3; Schürer (rev.), *The History of the Jewish People,* vol. II, p. 325).

The NT terms, διδάσκαλος, ῥαββί, ῥαββουνί, κύριος, ἐπιστάτης, are all semantically related (LN, p. 416). Examples of some of these interrelations can be seen in triple-tradition passages, where each

Table 8.2   *'Teacher' and 'teaching' in the synoptic gospels*

	Matthew		Mark		Luke	
διδάσκαλος	12	11	12	12	16	14
διδάσκω	14	9	17	15	17	15
διδαχή	3	2	5	5	1	1

evangelist chooses a different term: διδάσκαλε (Mark 4.38), κύριε
(Matt. 8.25), ἐπιστάτα (Luke 8.24); and at the transfiguration:
ῥαββί (Mark 9.5), κύριε (Matt. 17.4), ἐπιστάτα (Luke 9.33); cf.
also John 1.38: ῥαββί, ὅ λέγεται μεθερμηνευόμενον διδάσκαλε.
Overlaps within the semantic ranges of these terms provide a range
of lexical choices for the evangelists. Mark has a proportionally
greater number of occurrences of 'teacher' terms applied to Jesus
than either Matthew or Luke. This also applies to cognate terms (in
Table 8.2 the left hand number gives the total, the right-hand
number those which refer to Jesus).

Luke has the most varied pattern, with disciples, approachers,
and Jews all calling Jesus διδάσκαλε (Luke 7.40; 9.38; 10.25; 11.45;
12.13; 18.18; 19.39; 20.21, 28, 29; 21.7), six uses of ἐπιστάτα, and
κύριε on the lips of disciples, approachers and potential disciples.
Mark has διδάσκαλε ten times (and in addition uses ῥαββί three
times and ῥαββουνί once) on the lips of all: disciples (4.38; 9.38;
10.35; 13.1), people approaching Jesus for help (9.17; 10.17, 20) and
Jewish figures (12.14, 19, 32). Matthew uses διδάσκαλε six times
(and ῥαββί twice) and restricts it to Jewish leaders (8.19; 12.38;
22.16, 24, 36) and the young man who does not follow Jesus
(19.16), with κύριε in sixteen places used by disciples and other
sympathisers. With a broad lexical choice available, such *relatively*
firm patterns may be significant. The use of ῥαββί is very similar
with Peter (9.5; 11.21) and Judas (14.45) using it in Mark (cf. the
blind man using ῥαββουνί in 10.51). In Matthew only Judas uses
the term (Matt. 26.25, 49).

2.2   *Jesus as 'teacher' in Griesbach-Mark*

Mark's interest in Jesus as teacher goes beyond the use of the noun
διδάσκαλος and includes an obvious preference for the verb as
well. Recently this interest has been recognised as an important

theme of Mark's gospel, especially in view of the prominence of teaching terminology in the seams or linking passages, for which, assuming Markan priority, Mark himself is generally held responsible.[10] In terms of content it should be noted that Mark's gospel contains a large amount of Jesus' teaching, more than is often assumed.[11] The focus of Jesus' teaching is on the way of the cross; as R. P. Meye has put it, the basic content of the 'Messianic Didache' is that the messianic way is the way of the cross (cf. 8.31; 9.31; 10.33f).[12]

Griesbach-Mark first introduces the theme of Jesus' teaching in 1.21–7, a passage derived from Luke 4.31–7. Jesus' teaching provokes astonishment because it is ὡς ἐξουσίαν ἔχων and not like the scribes (v. 22, this phrase parallels Matt. 7.29 but omitting αὐτῶν). The authority manifested in his teaching is also shown to be characteristic of the exorcism: Τί ἐστιν τοῦτο; διδαχὴ καινὴ κατ' ἐξουσίαν· καὶ τοῖς πνεύμασι τοῖς ἀκαθάρτοις ἐπιτάσσει, καὶ ὑπακούουσιν αὐτῷ (v. 27). Mark links the contents of the miracle story, and the response of the crowd, with the general statement in v. 22, described in both cases in terms of teaching (v. 22: ἦν γὰρ διδάσκων αὐτοὺς κ.τ.λ.; v. 27: διδαχὴ καινὴ κατ' ἐξουσίαν κ.τ.λ.). Luke had already made the link using different terminology, emphasising the authority of Jesus' word (λόγος) in 4.32 and 36. On the Griesbach hypothesis Mark adapts this link to his own terminology (derived from Matthew). This is a cumbersome procedure but not impossible.

> The many textual variants to 1.27 render the text rather uncertain (UBS4 lists six variants, along with numerous sub-variants). The UBS4 text and punctuation given here seems preferable on the grounds of attestation (ℵ B L 33) and awkwardness (Metzger, *Textual Commentary*, p. 75 (briefly); Pesch, *Markusevangelium*, vol. I, p. 118; Kuthirakkattel, *The Beginning of Jesus' Ministry According to Mark's Gospel (1,14–3,6)*, p. 116 n. 1; Guelich, *Mark*, p. 58; Gundry, *Mark*, p. 85). Some scholars support the longer reading: Τί ἐστιν τοῦτο; τίς ἡ διδαχὴ καινὴ αὕτη· ὅτι κατ' ἐξουσίαν καί . . .[C K Δ Π etc.] (Kilpatrick, 'Some Problems in New Testament Text and Language', pp. 198–201; cf. Elliott, 'An Eclectic Textual Commentary on the Greek Text of Mark's Gospel', pp. 50–1).

This introductory passage suggests that Mark links the teaching

---

[10] So especially Stein, 'The *Redaktionsgeschichtlich* Investigation of a Markan Seam (Mc 1,21f)'; Best, *The Temptation and the Passion*, pp. 71–2; cf. also Achtemeier, '"He Taught Them Many Things": Reflections on Marcan Christology'; Robbins, *Jesus the Teacher*.

[11] France, 'Mark and the Teaching of Jesus'.

[12] Meye, 'Messianic Secret and Messianic Didache in Mark's Gospel', p. 63.

activity of Jesus to his authoritative demonstration of the presence of the Kingdom. This suggestion receives support from Mark 6.34 where the compassion of Jesus is expressed in the fact that 'he began to teach them many things', whereas Griesbach-Mark's sources had spoken of Jesus' healing ministry (Matt. 14.14 // Luke 9.11). While Luke also has 'he spoke to them about the kingdom of God', the close parallels between Matthew and Mark in the surrounding context suggest a primary dependence upon Matthew at this point.[13]

Mark refers to Jesus teaching the crowds in parables, for example in 4.1f where he adds three references to 'teaching' to Matthew 13.1–3, and to Jesus teaching the disciples he had chosen to be with him (8.31; 9.31). In these two passages Griesbach-Mark uses διδάσκω where his sources use more general speaking or showing terms (Matt. 16.21: δεικνύειν // Luke 9.22: εἰπών; Matt. 17.22 // Luke 9.43b: εἶπεν). This procedure is not followed in the third passion prediction where all three use 'speaking' verbs (Mark 10.32: ἤρξατο . . . λέγειν; Matt. 20.17 // Luke 18.31: εἶπεν).

With one exception only Jesus is described, using διδάσκω, as teaching (the exception is 6.30 referring to the teaching of the disciples in extending Jesus' teaching ministry, cf. 6.7–12). On the other hand, many people are described, using κηρύσσω, as preaching: 1.4 and 7 (John the baptist); 1.14, 38f (Jesus); 1.45 (healed leper); 3.14 (twelve); 5.20 (healed demoniac); 6.12 (disciples); 7.36 (people in response to healing deaf and dumb man); 13.10 and 14.9 (future 'Christians'). In other places Mark uses the phrase ἐν τῇ διδαχῇ αὐτοῦ (4.2; 12.38) to place the teaching of Jesus which is cited into the context of a much larger amount of 'teaching' that is only alluded to (4.2, 33f).

The use of διδάσκαλε by petitioners of Jesus is consistent with the rest of Mark's presentation (for a list see Appendix 8.B). This vocative occurs ten times in Mark compared with six in Matthew and eleven in Luke; and it is the regular, but not exclusive term used by most of those who approach Jesus (κύριε appears once in 7.28; ῥαββί three times in 9.5; 11.21; 14.45; and ῥαββουνί once – 10.51; and Υἱὲ Δαυὶδ twice – 10.47f): the disciples (4.38; 9.38; 10.35; 13.1), the father of the boy with an unclean spirit (9.17), the rich young man (10.17, 20), the Pharisees and Sadducees (12.14, 19)

---

[13] So de Wette, *Einleitung*, p. 189 (ET, p. 168); Bleek, *Einleitung*, p. 254 (ET, vol. I, p. 271); Farmer, *The Synoptic Problem*, p. 242.

and the scribes (12.32). In other words, the characters in Mark's gospel, without distinction, call Jesus 'teacher' as they come to him, whether for a discussion about a point of teaching, or for healing or other help. διδάσκαλος also occurs in Mark 14.14 (as Matt. 26.18 // Luke 22.11), where Jesus uses ὁ διδάσκαλος of himself, suggesting that the disciples use the title to identify him to the owner of the upper room.

R. H. Stein suggested that the Markan presentation, especially of 1.21f, is based upon the belief that the messianic age, and the Messiah, would bring a new teaching.[14] Evidence for an association of teaching with the coming of the Messiah is extensive, although an explicit expectation of a 'teaching Messiah' is not specifically attested, and the vocabulary used is most commonly that of wisdom and knowledge rather than 'teaching'.

> Note, for example, the general statement of *Tg. Isa.* 12.3: 'you shall receive new instruction (*'lpn ḥdt*) with joy from the chosen of righteousness (*mbḥyry ṣdq*)' (cf. also *Tg. Isa.* 53.5: . . . by his teaching . . . (*b'lpnyh*) 11: . . . by his wisdom . . . (*bḥkmtyh*)); *Tg. Onq.* Gen. 49.11: 'they that carry out the Law shall be with him in study', NB Grossfeld, *Aramaic Bible*, vol. VI, pp. 164–5, note 29). In 1 Enoch the abundance of wisdom in the messianic age (expressed generally in 1 Enoch 5.8; 48.1; cf. also 2 Ba. 44.14) is associated explicitly with the messianic agent, the Son of Man who will open the hidden storerooms (46.3), and the Elect One in whom dwells the spirit of wisdom (49.1–4), 'from the conscience of his mouth shall come out all the secrets of wisdom' (51.3; cf. 91.10). Similar expectations of messianic wisdom (based, like those in 1 Enoch, on echoes of Isa. 11.2) are found in Qumran literature such as 1Q28b (= 1QSb) 5.25 (*rwḥ d't*); 4Q215 (*T. Naph.*) (the earth will be full of knowledge etc.); 4Q536 (Mess ar) 3 i 4–11 (re the wisdom, counsel and knowledge of the Elect of God); 4Q 381 15.7–9 (the Messiah makes known and teaches). Other passages link the announcement of glad tidings (Isa. 52.7) with the Messiah, e.g. 11Q13 (= Melch.) 2.18–20; 4Q521 12. In addition the expectation of a messianic interpreter of the law (possibly the priestly Messiah) is found in CD 6.11; 7.18; 4Q174 (Florilegium) 1.11; 4Q175 (Testimonia) 5–8 (cf. Deut. 18.18 and Hos. 10.12; and 1 Macc. 14.41; see further Collins, *The Scepter and the Star*, pp. 102–35); for an expectation of a new law see *Sib. Or.* III.758 (cf. Davies, *The Setting of the Sermon on the Mount*, pp. 109–90). Somewhat similar expectations are found in a range of other literature, e.g. *T. Levi* 18.2–6 (echoing both Num. 24.17 and Isa. 11.9); *Midr. Ps.* 21.1 (R. Tanhuma (IV) said: 'The king Messiah will come for no other purpose than to teach the nations of the earth thirty precepts'), similarly *Gen. Rab.* 98.9 on Genesis 49.11, naming R. Hanin and R. Johanan (III) (cf. *y.* '*Abod. Zar.* 2.1, discussing Zech. 11.12 and 30 Noachide commands); in Samaritan expectation, e.g. *Memar Markah* IV.12 (tenth statement) (Taheb as 'great in wisdom', 'filled with

---

[14] Stein, 'The *Redaktionsgeschichtlich* Investigation of a Markan Seam (Mc 1,21f)', p. 91; followed by France, 'Mark and the Teaching of Jesus', p. 111.

knowledge', coming to manifest the Truth; on Taheb as Moses *redivivus*
see *Memar Markah* III.3 etc.; cf. John 4.25, cf. further MacDonald, *The
Theology of the Samaritans*, pp. 359–71, III–IV AD). On the subject in
general see Riesner, *Jesus als Lehrer*, pp. 304–30.

V. K. Robbins argued that Jesus' role as 'teacher-Messiah' is
fundamental to Mark, the most basic christological feature to
which other attributes are added.[15] But this is a rather one-sided
approach; R. T. France appears to be on more solid ground in
emphasising the multi-faceted christological presentation of Mark,
of which 'Jesus the Teacher was a not unimportant theme'.[16]

Clearly much of what can be said of Griesbach-Mark could be
said of Mark on any hypothesis. In comparing the process of
achieving the final form with the major themes and interests of that
final form, two problems emerge in relation to the plausibility of
the Griesbach-Mark redaction. The first problem is that if Mark's
concentration on Jesus as teacher is to be attributed to an appreciation of various strands of Jewish messianic thought, this stands in
some degree of tension with other aspects of the Markan presentation in relation to Matthew and Luke. This relates specifically to
the lack of OT allusion in numerous passages in Mark compared
with Matthew, and other indications that readers would not be
familiar with Jewish thought (e.g., Mark 7.3–4 cf. Matt. 15.1f).

The second problem with the Griesbach hypothesis is that Mark's
obvious interest in Jesus as teacher is not matched by a concern to
include as much of the content of Jesus' teaching as either Matthew
or Luke. Some passages peculiar to Mark, in particular 4.33f and
12.38, suggest that the author acknowledges the existence of more
teaching without including it. These passages could refer to additional parable material (in both Matthew and Luke) and to the
warnings of Matthew 23 and would therefore make good sense on
the Griesbach hypothesis as in both cases Griesbach-Mark had
access to more teaching of Jesus on the subject. Nevertheless Mark
does not consistently point to such extra material, particularly with
respect to the Sermon on the Mount.

2.3   Jesus as 'teacher' in Matthew

In terms of the number of occurrences of terms such as διδάχη and
διδάσκω, Matthew shows less interest than Mark in presenting

---

[15] Robbins, *Jesus the Teacher*, p. 48.
[16] France, 'Mark and the Teaching of Jesus', p. 128.

Jesus as 'teacher'. In addition, Matthew is more willing to speak of others as teaching, not restricting it to Jesus. Nevertheless, Matthew presents a much fuller account of both the content and the style of Jesus' teaching, including clear indications of Jesus' role as authoritative teacher. The discourses of Matt. 5–7; 10; 13; 18; 24f are obvious examples, marked off not only by the well-known concluding formula: Καὶ ἐγένετο ὅτε ἐτέλεσεν ὁ Ἰησοῦς (7.28; 11.1; 13.53; 19.1; 26.1), but also by formulaic introductions which emphasise the teaching character of Jesus (5.1f; 10.1; 13.1f; 18.1f; 24.1–3).[17] In some respects, at least in terms of the vocabulary of teaching, Matthew exhibits a different attitude from Mark.

Matthew's summary statements categorise Jesus' teaching activity as one part of his broader ministry: διδάσκων ἐν ταῖς συναγωγαῖς αὐτῶν καὶ κηρύσσων τὸ εὐαγγέλιον τῆς βασιλείας καὶ θεραπεύων πᾶσαν νόσον καὶ πᾶσαν μαλακίαν (4.23; 9.35; both expansions of a briefer passage in Mark 1.39; 6.6b). Whereas Mark is willing to use 'teaching' as a summary covering the whole of Jesus' ministry, Matthew uses the terms more specifically to describe verbal communication. The saying of the crowd about Jesus teaching with authority is located by Matthew after the Sermon on the Mount (7.29, cf. 5.2). In other passages Matthew locates Jesus' teaching in particular situations ('in their cities' 11.1; 'in their synagogues' 13.54; 'in the temple' 26.55) where Mark was more ready to use the term absolutely. When in 28.20 the risen Jesus commissions his disciples to teach, the content is verbal: 'everything that I commanded you'.

In his use of the noun διδάσκαλος Matthew shows more reticence. Matthew's favourite form of address is κύριε (nineteen times), while διδάσκαλε occurs only six times, and ῥαββί twice. The disciples and people approaching in faith invariably use κύριε. Whereas Mark has the disciples (4.38) or a petitioner (9.17) use διδάσκαλε (or Peter use ῥαββί 9.5; or a blind man use ῥαββουνί 10.51), Matthew consistently uses κύριε (Matt. 8.25; 17.15; 17.4; 20.33 respectively). Where Mark reports a Jewish leader or a petitioner of little faith using διδάσκαλε, the Matthean parallel also has διδάσκαλε. In Matthew's unique material the same distinction is maintained.

For Matthew it is the scribe who says, Διδάσκαλε, ἀκολουθήσω σοι ὅπου ἐὰν ἀπέρχῃ (8.19), who receives an implicit warning from Jesus. It is the scribes and Pharisees, representatives of 'this evil

---

[17] Keegan, 'Introductory Formulae for Matthean Discourses'.

generation', who say to Jesus: Διδάσκαλε, θέλομεν ἀπὸ σοῦ σημεῖον ἰδεῖν (12.38). It is the wealthy young man, eventually discovered to be unwilling to give up his possessions, who asks Jesus: Διδάσκαλε, τί ἀγαθὸν ποιήσω ἵνα σχῶ ζωὴν αἰώνιον; (19.16). In the controversy stories in chapter 22 we find firstly the Pharisees and Herodians (v. 16), then the Sadducees (v. 24), and finally a lawyer (representing the Pharisees, v. 36) all approach Jesus with: Διδάσκαλε, . . . Other representatives of Jesus' opponents, including the Pharisees in 9.11 and the collectors of temple tax in 17.24, refer to Jesus, when speaking to his disciples, as ὁ διδάσκαλος ὑμῶν. Similarly, Matthew reserves the use of the title ῥαββί for Judas' use (26.25, 49).

It is this evidence which has suggested to some scholars that Matthew regarded the address διδάσκαλε as characteristic of Jesus' opponents, as in some way inadequate, and even as derogatory.[18] It is, however, impossible that Matthew was against the designation of Jesus as teacher; references within Jesus' sayings in Matthew preclude this; the term occurs in a general proverb in 10.24f, which assumes that Jesus taught his disciples; note also 26.18 (which parallels Mark 14.14 in identifying Jesus) and 23.8–10. This passage introduces, by a link with ῥαββί in v. 7, a parenthetical discussion concerning the disciples' attitudes to titles of respect. The passage is chiastic in structure: the outside brackets, defined by the passive verbs, designate Jesus as 'teacher' (διδάσκαλος) and 'private tutor' (καθηγητής).[19] In contrast to the scribes and Pharisees, the disciples of Jesus should not seek the titles of respect ('Ραββί, καθηγηταί). Matthew's reluctance may be a response to the use of the term 'teacher' among contemporary Jewish leaders.[20]

While Matthew is probably not, therefore, intending some covert criticism of Jesus as teacher, it does seem likely that he has imposed a system for using vocative forms of address to Jesus. This system distinguishes between those on the inside, who use κύριε, and those on the outside, who use διδάσκαλε. This coheres in any case with Matthew's overall purpose – it is Jesus the Lord whose teaching he has recorded – and is matched by a similar phenomenon in Luke.

---

[18] E.g. France, 'Mark and the Teaching of Jesus', p. 109.
[19] Most lexicons regard καθηγητής as synonymous with διδάσκαλος (e.g. BAGD, p. 388–9); but a clear case has recently been made in favour of 'a personal teacher' (Glucker, *Antiochus and the Late Academy*, pp. 127–34; Winter, 'The Messiah as the Tutor'; cf. also *NewDocs* 4 (1979)156–7).
[20] So Davies and Allison, *Matthew*, vol. II, p. 41.

Here sympathisers, that is the disciples, and in one case the ten lepers, address Jesus as ἐπιστάτα, while outsiders use διδάσκαλε. As J. Nolland noted, 'for Luke διδάσκαλε is an objective description while ἐπιστάτα involves a personal recognition of Jesus' authority'.[21]

> For ἐπιστάτα see Luke 5.5 (Peter); 8.24; 8.45 (Peter); 9.33 (Peter); 9.49 (John); 17.13 (lepers). For διδάσκαλε see Luke 7.40 (Simon the Pharisee); 9.38 (man from crowd); 10.25; 11.45 (lawyers); 12.13 (one of multitude); 18.18 (rich ruler); 19.39 (Pharisees); 20.21 (spies); 20.28 (Sadducees); 20.39 (scribes); 21.7 (they? could be disciples: parallels and context: 20.45; but not specified); cf. also 8.49.

Matthew's pattern suggests that we examine the use of κύριος terminology (used twenty-seven times in Matthew) before summarising our conclusions.

3. Jesus as 'Lord'

3.1 Introduction and background

Κύριος had a broad range of meaning in the first century, including 'lord', 'Lord', 'master' and 'owner'. It is a positive status term, often defined in terms either of an object over which the κύριος exercises control (e.g. Mark 12.9: 'owner of the vineyard'; 13.35: 'master of the house'; Luke 12.46: 'the master of the slave'), or of a person over whom the κύριος exercises authority (e.g. 1 Pet. 3.6; Matt. 21.29; 27.63). In the vocative it is used by slaves towards their masters (e.g. Matt. 13.27; 25.20, 22, 24; Luke 13.8; 14.22; 19.16, 18, 20, 25), as the connection between δοῦλος and κύριος also suggests (e.g. John 13.16; Matt. 6.24; 10.24f); or towards anyone in a higher status position, and can often most appropriately be translated as 'sir', as in modern Greek (Matt. 25.11; John 12.21; 20.15; Acts 16.30; Rev. 7.14; cf. also LXX Gen. 23.6; 44.18; Epictetus III.23.11, 19; P. Fayyum 106.15 [IIAD]).

Κύριος was also used as a divine title, as a designation either for God, or for the emperor (e.g. Acts 25.26; P.Oxy. 37.6 (AD 49); 246.30, 34 (AD 66)),[22] or for other deities (e.g. 1 Cor. 8.5). Clearly

---

[21] Nolland, *Luke*, vol. I, p. 222. This distinction is widely recognised cf. Marshall, *Luke*, p. 203; Fitzmyer, *Luke*, vol. I, p. 566; Glombitza, 'Die Titel διδάσκαλος und ἐπιστάτης für Jesus bei Lukas'.

[22] See Foerster, *TDNT*, vol. II, pp. 1049–54; Deissmann, *Licht von Osten*, pp. 300–2 (ET, pp. 353–4).

the NT adapts this type of usage and directs it to Jesus in many places (1 Cor. 8.6; 12.3; Phil. 2.9,11; Rom. 10.9; Acts 2.36; John 20.28), perhaps reflecting a 'polemical parallelism between the cult of Christ and the cult of Caesar'.[23]

It now seems unlikely that κύριος translated *yhwh* in pre-Christian versions of the Greek OT. The oldest manuscripts of the Greek OT, and every manuscript of known Jewish milieu, use *yhwh* in Hebrew letters, sometimes in Aramaic, sometimes in palaeo-Hebrew. These include: P. Fouad 266 (II BC); 8HevXIIgr (I BC); 4QLev[b] [uses ΙΑΩ]; the Cairo Geniza fragments of Aquila; Symmachus; and P.Oxy. 1007.[24] This is further supported by statements in the Fathers to the effect that in the most ancient manuscripts the divine name was written in Hebrew script (Origen, *Psalms* II.2; Jerome, *Prol. Galeat.*; cf. Jerome's comment on the misunderstanding of PIPI in *Ep.* 25, *ad Marcellam*). Jellicoe summarises:

> LXX texts, written by Jews for Jews, retained the Divine Name in Hebrew Letters (palaeo-Hebrew or Aramaic) or in the Greek imitative form ΠΙΠΙ, and . . . its replacement by κύριος was a Christian innovation.[25]

This conclusion must, however, be nuanced somewhat because both Philo and Josephus use κύριος and θεός to render the tetragrammaton (e.g. specifically Philo, *De mutatione nominum* 18–24; cf. also Josephus, *Antiquities* XIII.68; XX.90).[26] This suggests that Greek-speaking Jews would have been in the habit of pronouncing κύριος, and writing it in discussions of the text. This would correspond, firstly, to the practice of substituting various other forms for *yhwh* in Jewish literature from Qumran (e.g. *'lh'*, *'l 'lywm, mrh* in 1QapGen),[27] secondly to the testimony of Origen that among the Greeks *Adonai* was pronounced as *kurios* (*Psalms* II.2),

---

[23] Deissmann, *Licht von Osten*, p. 298 (cited from ET, p. 349).

[24] See Howard, 'The Tetragram and the New Testament'; Metzger, *Manuscripts of the Greek Bible*, pp. 33–5; Fitzmyer, 'The Semitic Background of the New Testament Kyrios-Title', pp. 136–8, n. 38; Kahle, *The Cairo Geniza*, p. 222; de Lacey, ' "One Lord" in Pauline Christology'.

[25] Jellicoe, *The Septuagint and Modern Study*, p. 272. Similarly Howard, 'The Tetragram and the New Testament', p. 65.

[26] Fitzmyer, 'The Semitic Background of the New Testament Kyrios-Title', pp. 121–2; Howard, 'The Tetragram and the New Testament', pp. 70–2.

[27] Howard, 'The Tetragram and the New Testament', pp. 66–70. Note that the 'official' targumim continue to use a form of the tetragrammaton, and even to introduce it into new contexts (Chester, *Divine Revelation and Divine Titles in the Pentateuchal Targumim*, pp. 325–51).

and thirdly to other examples of κύριος used to represent the tetragrammaton (in *Ep. Arist.* 155; 2 Kings 23.24Aquila; twenty-seven times in Wis.). The conclusion must be that a connection between *yhwh* and κύριος, while not attributable to the influence of the Septuagint, was nevertheless the common property of Greek-speaking Jews during the first century, and was not a Christian invention.[28] G. Howard's suggestion that NT writers would have used *yhwh* in OT quotations (for which there is absolutely no support in the NT manuscripts) is thus unnecessary; his suggestion that Mark 1.3 originally read Ἑτοιμάσατε τὴν ὁδὸν *yhwh* quite misses Mark's point.[29]

> Hebrew scrolls from Qumran attest the use of *Adonai* in prayers and liturgical contexts (e.g. 1QM 12.8: *qdwš 'dwny*, 18: *'l hšmym 'dwny*; for *'wdkh 'dwny* see 1QH 2.20, 31; 3.19, 37; 4.5; 5.5; 7.6, 34 (*vid*); for *brwk 'th 'dwny* see 1QH 5.20; 10.14; 11.33; 15.6 (*vid*); 16.8). Aramaic texts from Qumran attest the use of *mari* both as address for God (1QapGen: *mry*: 20.12: *'l 'lywm mry*, 15; 22.32: *mry 'lh'*) and for human relations (e.g. 1QapGen 2.9, 13 (husband); 2.24 (father); 20.25 (the king); 22.18 (Abraham)); cf. *mrh*, used exclusively of God: 1QapGen 2.4; 7.7; 12.17; 20.13, 15; 21.2; 22.16, 21.

The breadth of meaning of κύριος is apparent from its use in the NT. The term is used some 717 times (Matt: 80; Mark: 18). It is used *inter alia* of a master, or of a superior, or of God. When used of Jesus it is often difficult to decide which of these, or something else, is intended. In addition, the vocative κύριε stands out as something of a special case, the connotations of which are uncertain. It should be agreed, however, notwithstanding important disputes concerning the origin of the confession of Jesus as κύριος, that every strand of the NT attests this confession.

3.2   Jesus as 'Lord' in Griesbach-Mark

In view of the prominence of the term in his sources it is striking that Griesbach-Mark should have used κύριος of Jesus only seven times (cf. Matt.: twenty-seven times; Luke: forty-one). He uses the vocative κύριε only once, on the lips of the Syrophoenician woman (7.28 // Matt. 15.27). On this occasion Mark follows Matthew, but elsewhere Mark must omit many occurrences of the term from his

---

[28] Metzger, *Manuscripts of the Greek Bible*, p. 35; Fitzmyer, 'The Semitic Background of the New Testament Kyrios-Title', pp. 120–3.
[29] Howard, 'The Tetragram and the New Testament', pp. 76–83.

sources. Several examples, in which both Matthew and Luke use the term but Mark does net, are striking (e.g. 1.40 cf. Matt. 8.2 // Luke 5.12; Mark 10.51: ῥαββουνί cf. Matt. 20.33 // Luke 18.41).[30] Despite the presence of the vocative in his sources Griesbach-Mark uses it only for the Syrophoenician woman, perhaps because he is aware of its Gentile sound; otherwise, as has already been noted, he prefers διδάσκαλε or ῥαββί.

Mark's other uses of κύριος for Jesus appear to parallel his sources, especially Matthew, more closely. Mark 1.3 quotes Isaiah 40.3: Ἑτοιμάσατε τὴν ὁδὸν κυρίου εὐθείας ποιεῖτε τὰς τρίβους αὐτοῦ (cf. Matt. 3.3 // Luke 3.4). Although taken from his sources this is emphasised in Griesbach-Mark by its placement as an introduction to the gospel.[31] This citation already presupposes the identification of Jesus as the Lord,[32] as in Matthew 3.3 and Luke 3.4; especially in view of the pronoun in the following phrase: 'Make straight *his* paths.' This was adjusted to the MT and LXX, 'of our God', in manuscripts of each synoptic gospel (Mark 1.3: D it; Matt. 3.3: it[b] syr[c] Iren.; Luke 3.4: it[r1] syr).

The next use of κύριος in Mark is the saying that the Son of Man is Lord over the sabbath (2.28 // Matt. 12.8 // Luke 6.5). Once again Griesbach-Mark follows the agreement of his sources, although he adds an introductory saying: 'the sabbath was made for man and not man for the sabbath' (2.27). This saying is introduced by καὶ ἔλεγεν αὐτοῖς, which is usually regarded as a link-phrase ('Reihungsformel') indicating an isolated saying (cf. 4.11, 13, 21, 24; 6.10; 7.9; 8.21; 9.1, 31).[33] This addition could plausibly be regarded as clarifying the purpose of the Son of Man's lordly authority in fulfilling God's purposes for humanity and Israel.[34] This suggestion could be further explored in terms of the allusion to Genesis 1–2 in v. 27, and the Adam–true humanity–

---

[30] At Mark 10.51 D and it support κυριε ραββι and 409 reads κυριε but these reflect a harmonising tendency.

[31] Marcus, *The Way of the Lord*, pp. 12–47, esp. pp. 37–41.

[32] So Lane, *Mark*, p. 46; Hooker, *Mark*, pp. 35–6; Gundry, *Mark*, pp. 36 and 42; Pesch, *Markusevangelium*, vol. I, p. 77. In favour of a reference to God is Taylor, *Mark*, p. 153 (but with Messiah in mind); Snodgrass, 'Streams of Tradition emerging from Isaiah 40:1–5 and their adaptation in the New Testament', p. 34 (but this on basis that in Mark κύριος when referring to Jesus is always in vocative; a patently misleading supposition).

[33] Lane, *Mark*, p. 118; Taylor, *Mark*, p. 218; Pesch, *Markusevangelium*, vol. I, p. 184.

[34] See Hooker, *Mark*, p. 105.

Israel complex in Jewish tradition.[35] It is therefore not necessary, on the Griesbach hypothesis, to see the addition of v. 27 as softening the christological impact of the main statement.

In 5.19 Griesbach-Mark alters Luke 8.39 to report that Jesus sends the Gerasene demoniac away to his own people with the command, ἀπάγγειλον αὐτοῖς ὅσα ὁ κύριός σοι πεποίηκεν καὶ ἠλέησέν σε (Luke 8.39 has διηγοῦ ὅσα σοι ἐποίησεν ὁ θεός; not present in Matt.). Since the man goes and begins to proclaim ὅσα ἐποίησεν αὐτῷ ὁ Ἰησοῦς (5.20 // Luke 8.39) it seems likely that Mark intends to suggest the association between Jesus and ὁ κύριος.[36] In 11.3 Mark again includes a statement closely paralleled in both Matthew and Luke. Jesus sent two disciples to fetch a colt and if challenged they were to say: Ὁ κύριος αὐτοῦ χρείαν ἔχει (Luke 19.31 // Matt. 21.3, although Matt. has αὐτῶν). While this is not an absolute lordship (note αὐτοῦ), and it may have related at some point to the claiming of rights over the animal,[37] within the context of Mark's presentation it would clearly be read as a reference to the lordly status of Jesus (particularly on the Griesbach hypothesis).[38]

Another passage taken over from both Matthew and Luke is the question about David's Son and Lord (Mark 12.35–7 // Matt. 22.41–6 // Luke 20.41–4).[39] Despite some differences between the accounts the point in each gospel seems to be that Jesus' messiahship transcended Davidic categories in such a way that he could be called David's Lord. It is important to note that κύριος is not titular here, but relational: David calls him 'Lord' (not 'the Lord'). This acknowledges a status gap between himself (David) and the Messiah (David's Lord), the one greater than David. The text as it stands invites the reader to reflect further on this relationship, and

---

[35] Pesch, *Markusevangelium*, vol. I, p. 184; Wright, *The Climax of the Covenant*, pp. 21–6.

[36] Hooker, *Mark*, p. 146; Gundry, *Mark*, pp. 254–5.

[37] Taylor, *Mark*, p. 455, argued that it referred to the animal's owner; Judge, drawing support from Derrett, argued, on the basis of the Roman powers to requisition transport, that κύριος refers to 'an (unspecified) legitimate claimant' (*NewDocs* 1 (1981) 43; Derrett, 'Law in the New Testament: The Palm Sunday Colt'); similarly Pesch, *Markusevangelium*, vol. II, p. 180.

[38] Gundry, *Mark*, p. 624; Hooker, *Mark*, p. 258; Haenchen, *Der Weg Jesu*, pp. 374–5; Swete, *Mark*, p. 248.

[39] The widespread use of Ps. 110 in the early church (Luke 20.43; Acts 2.34; 1 Cor. 15.25f; Heb. 1.13; 2.8; 10.13) suggests that this passage was the subject of considerable reflection (cf. Hay, *Glory at the Right Hand: Psalm 110 in Early Christianity*).

Griesbach-Mark's addition of the phrase διδάσκων ἐν τῷ ἱερῷ (v. 35) may be an allusion to Malachi 3.1 designed to strengthen this: 'the Lord whom you seek will suddenly come to his temple'.

One of the difficulties facing the Griesbach hypothesis is the contrast between Griesbach-Mark's positive attitude to the use of κύριος with respect to Jesus' status and his non-use of κύριε in his narrative. While individual passages can yield a relatively plausible understanding of Griesbach-Mark's handling of the title this general incongruity remains.

3.3   Jesus as 'Lord' in Matthew

We have already noted Matthew's preference for κύριε in statements of approach to Jesus (section 2.3). In his famous essay, 'Die Sturmstillung im Matthäusevangelium', Bornkamm, noting this preference, suggested that for Matthew κύριε was a 'göttlichen Hoheitsprädikat' or 'divine predicate of majesty'.[40] In a later essay he noted Matthew's treatment of διδάσκαλε and κύριε, arguing that:

> in Matthew's Gospel κύριε is by no means simply an expression of human respect, but is intended as a term of Majesty . . . the title and address of Jesus as κύριος in Matthew have throughout the character of a divine Name of Majesty (*eines göttlichen Hoheitsnamens*).[41]

According to G. N. Stanton, Bornkamm's view has been followed by 'most scholars'; nevertheless, it overstates the case somewhat.[42]

While Bornkamm restricts himself to Matthew's use of the vocative κύριε of Jesus, the relevant evidence is broader. Κύριος occurs seventy-seven times; eighteen refer to God (including one in the vocative), twenty-two are used in Jesus' parables to refer to the master or owner of property (including four in vocative), four are used in Jesus' teaching in general of the same type of master (some of these may refer to Jesus). Of those which refer explicitly to Jesus, twenty-three are in the vocative and seven in other cases (several of

---

[40] Bornkamm, 'Die Sturmstillung im Matthäusevangelium', p. 51 (ET, p. 55), developing an idea suggested by Foerster, *TDNT*, vol. III, p. 1093.
[41] Bornkamm, 'Enderwartung und Kirche im Matthäusevangelium', p. 39 (cited from ET, pp. 42–3).
[42] Stanton, 'The Origin and Purpose of Matthew's Gospel', p. 1923 (e.g. Gundry, *Matthew*, p. 139 and *passim*).

these are Matthean parallels to passages discussed in the previous section: 3.3; 12.8; 21.3; 24.42; 22.43–6ter). The majority of cases where κύριος refers to Jesus are, therefore, in the vocative: κύριε.

Κύριε cannot, however, be regarded as a technical term for Matthew since it is used in many other ways: in references to God (by Jesus, 11.25); to Pilate (by guards, 27.63); in parables to a master (by his servant, 13.27; 25.20, 22, 24); to a father (by his son, 21.30); and to a bridegroom (by the ten maidens, 25.11). Most of these references are in material unique to Matthew (thus 27.63; 13.27; 25.20, 22, 24 (although cf. Luke 19.16, 18, 20); 21.30; 25.11); cf. 11.25 // Luke 10.21. This vocative use is well attested in other sources, and need mean no more than a respectful address. Of course, the term denotes a basic status difference between the speaker and the one addressed (cf. the guards–Pilate, servant–master, son–father examples cited above), but this should not be confused with technicality.

The notable thing about the use of κύριε addressed to Jesus in Matthew is the consistency with which it is deployed. Peter, for example, never uses any other term of approach (14.28, 30; 16.22; 17.4; 18.21), other disciples also use it (8.21, 25; 26.22). It is regularly introduced when Mark has either no term of address (Mark 1.40 // Matt. 8.2; Mark 7.25f // Matt. 15.22, 25; Mark 8.32 // Matt. 16.22; Mark 14.19 // Matt. 26.22) or uses either διδάσκαλε (so Mark 4.38 // Matt. 8.25; Mark 9.17 // Matt. 17.15) or ῥαββί, ῥαββουνί (Mark 9.5 // Matt. 17.4; Mark 10.51 // Matt. 20.33). In the pericope concerning the Syrophoenician woman, the only passage where Mark uses κύριε (7.28), Matthew has the term three times on her lips (15.22, 25, 27).

Related to these passages of approach, although combining both 'Lord' and 'Son of David' terms, are the following passages, involving requests for healing from outsiders, which have a more or less regular form:

> 9.27, two blind men: Ἐλέησον ἡμᾶς, υἱὸς Δαυίδ.
> 15.22, the Canaanite woman: Ἐλέησόν με, κύριε, υἱὸς Δαυίδ
>> cf. v. 25: Κύριε, βοήθει μοι.
> 17.15, the epileptic boy's father: Κύριε, ἐλέησόν μου τὸν υἱόν,
> 20.30, two blind men: Ἐλέησον ἡμᾶς, [κύριε,] υἱὸς Δαυίδ.
>> cf. v.31: Ἐλέησον ἡμᾶς, κύριε, υἱὸς Δαθίδ.

This phrase in Matthew 20.30 has at least five different forms in the textual tradition, and decision on the original is extremely difficult (UBS4 offers a C rating). Since the presence of κύριε is relatively secure in v. 31 (although omitted in 118 209 700 1675 vg^ms sy^pms), and scribes may have omitted it in harmony with 9.27, this passage can function in support of our argument (cf. Metzger, *Textual Commentary*, pp. 53–4).

This plea for mercy echoes biblical models in the Psalms in which petitioners cry out to God for aid in their trouble or sickness.[43] The following examples show clear parallels to Matthew's formulations (cf. also Ps. 9.14; 26.7; 85.3):

> Psalm 6.3: ἐλέησόν με, κύριε, ὅτι ἀσθενής εἰμι, cf. v. 5: σῶσόν με ἕνεκεν τοῦ ἐλέους σου,
> 30.10: ἐλέησόν με, κύριε, ὅτι θλίβομαι,
> 40.5: Κύριε, ἐλέησόν με, ἴασαι τὴν ψυχήν μου, ὅτι ἥμαρτόν σοι. cf. v. 10.
> 108.26: βοήθησόν μοι, κύριε ὁ θεός μου, σῶσόν με κατὰ τὸ ἐλεός σου,
> 122.3: ἐλέησον ἡμᾶς, κύριε, ἐλέησον ἡμᾶς.

We should also note two other passages in which disciples call out to Jesus for help:

> 8.25, disciples in boat during storm: Κύριε, σῶσον, ἀπολλύμεθα.
> 14.30, Peter sinking: Κύριε, σῶσόν με.

These passages also echo the Psalms, for example (LXX):[44]

> Psalm 3.8: ἀνάστα, κύριε, σῶσόν με, ὁ θεός μου,
> 7.1: Κύριε ὁ θεός μου, ἐπὶ σοὶ ἤλπισα, σῶσόν με ἐκ πάντων τῶν διωκόντων με,
> 11.2: Σῶσόν με, κύριε . . .,
> 30.17: σῶσόν με ἐν τῷ ἐλέει σου,
> 105.47: σῶσον ἡμᾶς, κύριε ὁ θεὸς ἡμῶν,
> 117.25: ὦ κύριε, σῶσον δή.

These OT parallels suggest that Matthew is portraying these characters as approaching Jesus as the source of divine aid, specifically in terms of the requests of the Psalms (our investigation of Matt. 14.22–33 in chapter five also drew attention to several

---

[43] Gnilka, *Matthäusevangelium*, vol. II, p. 30; Luz, *Matthäus*, vol. II, p. 434, n. 39.
[44] Cf. also Ps. 6.5 (cited above); 21.22: σῶσόν με ἐκ στόματος λέοντος (cf. κύριε in v. 20); 30.17: σῶσόν με ἐν τῷ ἐλέει σου (cf. κύριε in v. 18); 53.1; 68.1, 15; 70.2; 85.2, 15f; 108.26 (cited above); 118.94, 146.

expressions which were apparently drawn from the Psalms). The use of 'Son of David' in addition to 'Lord' in several of the requests suggests that here, as in other places in Matthew, Jesus as Messiah acts as the agent of divine mercy and salvation. Thus, while it is going beyond the evidence to suggest that Matthew wishes to connote the deity of Jesus every time someone approaches him saying κύριε, there are clear indications that the term plays its part within Matthew's christological purposes.

Matthew does use κύριε twice in the clearly confessional contexts of the judgement scenes of 7.21f and 25.37, 44. In these scenes we find both righteous and unrighteous using the term: there is no indication that the terminology is inappropriate even if, on other grounds, it is insufficient (cf. 7.21f; 25.44). It is noteworthy that in these scenes of judgement, and especially in 25.31–46 (where 'Son of Man' and 'King' are prominent), Matthew uses the vocative κύριε on the lips of those who face Jesus for judgement. For Matthew it is not calling Jesus 'Lord' that is at issue, but living in a way consistent with that confession. Thus, in the first passage, the crucial factor is 'doing the will of my Father in heaven' (7.21), something that in Matthew is inextricably tied up with discipleship (12.50) and acknowledging Jesus (10.32f). The later passage is also, in the Matthean context, concerned with those who have obeyed Jesus by supporting the mission of Jesus' brothers (25.40 cf. 10.42).[45] Thus the fact that even those who receive judgement confess Jesus as κύριε κύριε should not suggest its lack of importance for Matthew: on the contrary, the fact that this term is used within the context of Jesus' exercise of judgement, tradition-ally a divine prerogative (cf. Gen. 18.25; Pss. 50.6; 75.7; 94.2; 96.13; Joel 3.2; Zeph. 1.3), suggests it is, for Matthew, of considerable importance.[46]

Matthew also uses forms of κύριος other than the vocative, and these, while generally following Mark's presentation, cohere with what has been said above. Matthew 3.3 is the formula quotation from Isaiah 40.3: Ἑτοιμάσατε τὴν ὁδὸν κυρίου (// Mark 1.3). In the light of the alteration of the OT text, omitting τοῦ θεοῦ ἡμῶν in favour of αὐτοῦ in v. 3, and the general context of John the Baptist's ministry, κύριος here must refer to Jesus, as it does in

[45] With Stanton, *A Gospel for a New People*, pp. 207–31; for other views see Gray, *The Least of My Brothers, Matthew 25:31–46: A History of Interpretation*.
[46] France, *Matthew: Evangelist and Teacher*, pp. 308–11; Gundry, *The Use of the Old Testament in St Matthew's Gospel*, p. 209.

Mark. In 12.8 (// Mark 2.28) κύριος is used in order to define the Son of Man's relationship to the sabbath (as controller, master etc.). Matthew also follows Mark in Jesus' instruction to the disciples in 21.3 (// Mark 11.3) that if anyone should ask them about the taking of the colt and ass, they should say: Ὁ κύριος αὐτῶν χρείαν ἔχει (see our earlier discussion). Another passage in which the presence of a pronoun indicates that the term is used functionally or relationally is 24.42. The passage about David's Son being David's Lord in Matthew 22.41–6 is quite closely parallel to Mark 12.35–7 and in general the same comments apply, perhaps for Matthew there is more interest in Jesus' relationship to David as 'one greater than David'.

It is noteworthy that in terms of non-vocative uses of the term κύριος Matthew follows Mark very closely. It is in the use of vocative, κύριε, that a new approach is introduced. Matthew uses these vocatives in a fairly consistent manner and in a way that coheres with the other types of usage. This results in a more coherent approach to Matthean redaction on the two-source hypothesis. In particular, the two passages Matthew 3.3 and 22.41–6, in the context of the early Christian confession, 'Jesus is Lord', and the consistent use of κύριε by all the characters who approach Jesus in faith, reflect an important Matthean emphasis. The procedure is also coherent with Matthew's pattern of OT usage and the exploitation of potential ambiguities.

4. Conclusion

In general the material surveyed in this chapter lends its weight to support Markan priority over against the Griesbach hypothesis. In particular the Griesbach hypothesis fails to account for Markan redaction of his sources whereas Matthean redaction of Mark is both coherent and plausible. Markan priority makes good sense of the transition from Mark's interest in Jesus as 'teacher' in the broad sense to Matthew's stricter definition of Jesus' teaching ministry, and the occasionally negative connotations which Matthew gives to the confession of Jesus as 'the teacher' (especially if Matthew is understood in view of a continuing polemic with synagogue teachers).

The Griesbach hypothesis must explain the transition in the reverse direction. Why would a Christian writer, who obviously accepts that Jesus is Lord, and values and even works with the idea, relatively systematically omit the vocative κύριε in favour of other titles, and yet not use a consistent alternative? There does not seem to be any plausible answer to this question. Mark's positive interest in Jesus as teacher could be explained in various ways if it were not at the expense of an interest in Jesus as Lord. Different interests, situations and audiences contribute to the differences between Matthew and Mark but do not seem able to explain Mark as a compilation from Matthew and Luke.

There is no clear tendency in other gospel traditions. Some gospels use κύριος as their basic term of reference for Jesus (e.g. *Gos. Pet.* 2, 3(bis), 6, 8, 10, 19, 21, 24, 50(bis), 59, 60; *Gos. Naz.* 2, 15a, 16, 24, 28, 32, 34; *Gos. Heb.* 2, 5, 7(ter); *Gos. Egypt.* a, c, d, e, f, g, h, i), but others maintain a mix of 'Jesus' and 'Lord' (e.g. *P. Eg. 2*, lines 30, 37: κύριος; lines 17, 50, 65:'Ιησους), and the *Gos. Thom.* uses 'Jesus' as does Tatian, *Diat.* (see Head, 'Tatian's Christology', pp. 135–6). In the textual tradition examples of both the addition and the omission of κύριος can be found (cf. Head, 'Christology and Textual Transmission', pp. 114–15).

Appendix 8.A. Christological titles in the gospels

Christological title	Matthew	Mark	Luke (+ Acts)	John
Son of God	9^1	4^2	$6 (+1)^3$	9^4
the Son, my Son etc.	8^5	3^6	$6 (+1)^7$	20^8
Son of Man	30^9	14^{10}	$25 (+1)^{11}$	13^{12}
Son of David	9^{13}	4^{14}	$4 (+0)^{15}$	0
Christ	16^{16}	7^{17}	$12 (+28)^{18}$	19^{19}
Lord	27^{20}	7^{21}	$41 (+$ many$)^{22}$	44^{23}
Teacher	11^{24}	12^{25}	$14 (+9)^{26}$	6^{27}
Master (ἐπιστάτα)	0	0	6^{28}	0

Note: [1] Matthew 4.3, 6; 8.29; 14.33; 16.16; 26.63; 27.40, 43, 54.
[2] (Mark 3.11; 5.7; 14.61; 15.39 (cf. 1.1 *v.l.*).
[3] Luke 1.35; 4.3, 9, 41; 8.28; 22.70. Acts 9.20.
[4] John 1.34, 49; 3.18; 5.25; 10.36; 11.4, 27; 19.7; 20.31.
[5] Matthew 2.15; 3.17; 11.27 (ter); 17.5; 24.36 (*v.l.* omits); 28.19.
[6] Mark 1.11; 9.7; 13.32.
[7] Luke 1.32; 3.22; 9.35; 10.22 (ter). Acts 13.33.
[8] John 1.18; 3.16, 17, 35, 36(bis); 5.19(bis), 20, 21, 22, 23(bis), 26; 6.40; 8.35, 36; 14.13; 17.1(bis).
[9] Matthew 8.20; 9.6; 10.23; 11.19; 12.8, 32, 40; 13.37, 41; 16.13, 27, 28; 17.9, 12, 22; 19.28; 20.18, 28; 24.27, 30(bis), 37, 39, 44; 25.31; 26.2, 24(bis), 45, 64.
[10] Mark 2.10, 28; 8.31, 38; 9.9, 12, 31; 10.33, 45; 13.26; 14.21(bis), 41, 62.
[11] Luke 5.24; 6.5, 22; 7.34; 9.22, 26, 44, 58; 11.30; 12.8, 10, 40; 17.22, 24, 26, 30; 18.8, 31; 19.10; 21.27, 36; 22.22, 48, 69; 24.7. Acts 7.56.
[12] John 1.51; 3.13, 14; 5.27; 6.27, 53, 62; 8.28; 9.35; 12.23, 34(bis); 13.31.
[13] Matthew 1.1; 9.27; 12.23; 15.22; 20.30, 31; 21.9, 15; 22.45.
[14] Mark 10.47, 48; 12.35, 37.
[15] Luke 18.38, 39; 20.41, 44.
[16] Matthew 1.1 (JC), 16, 17, 18 (JC); 2.4; 11.2; 16.16, 20; 22.42; 23.10; 24.5, 23; 26.63, 68; 27.17, 22.
[17] Mark 1.1 (JC); 8.29; 9.41; 12.35; 13.21; 14.61; 15.32.
[18] Luke 2.11, 26; 3.15; 4.41; 9.20; 20.41; 22.67; 23.2, 35, 39; 24.26, 46.
[19] John 1.17 (JC), 20, 25, 41 (with Messiah); 3.28; 4.25 (with Messiah), 29; 7.26, 27, 31, 41(bis), 42; 9.22; 10.24; 11.27; 12.34; 17.3 (JC); 20.31.
[20] Matthew 3.3; 7.21, 22; 8.2, 6, 8, 21, 25; 9.28; 12.8; 14.28, 30; 15.22, 25, 27; 16.22; 17.4, 15; 18.21; 20.30, 31, 33; 21.3 (?); 22.43, 44, 45; 26.22.
[21] Mark 1.3; 2.28; 5.19 (?); 7.28; 10.51; 11.3 (?); 12.37.
[22] Luke 2.11; 3.4; 5.8, 12; 6.5, 46; 7.6; 9.54, 59, 61; 10.17, 40; 11.1; 12.41; 13.23, 25; 17.37; 18.41; 19.8; 20.42, 44; 22.33, 38, 49. With article: 7.13, 19; 10.1, 39, 41; 11.39; 12.42; 13.15; 17.5, 6; 18.6; 19.8, 31, 34; 22.61; 24.3, 34.
[23] John 1.23; 4.1, 11, 15, 19, 49; 5.7; 6.23, 34, 68; 9.36, 38; 11.2, 3, 12, 21, 27, 32, 34, 39; 13.6, 9, 13, 14, 25, 36, 37; 14.5, 8, 22; 20.2, 13, 15, 18, 20, 25, 28; 21.7, 12, 15, 16, 17, 20, 21.
[24] Matthew 8.19; 9.11; 10.24 (?); 12.38; 17.24; 19.16; 22.16, 24, 36; 23.8; 26.18.
[25] Mark 4.38; 5.35; 9.17, 38; 10.17, 20, 35; 12.14, 19, 32; 13.1; 14.14.
[26] Luke 6.40 (?); 7.40; 8.49; 9.38; 10.25; 11.45; 12.13; 18.18; 19.39; 20.21, 28, 39; 21.7; 22.11.
[27] John 1.38; 3.2; 11.28; 13.13, 14; 20.16.
[28] Luke 5.5; 8.24, 45; 9.33, 49; 17.13.

Appendix 8.B. Vocative titles for approaching Jesus

Mark	Matthew	Luke	Speaker
—	—	ἐπιστάτα (5.5)	Peter
—	—	κύριε (5.8)	Peter
***** (1.40)	κύριε (8.2)	κύριε (5.12)	Leper
—	κύριε (8.6)	*indirect (7.3)	centurion
—	κύριε (8.8)	κύριε (7.6)	centurion
—	—	διδάσκαλε (7.40)	Simon
—	***** (5.31)	ἐπιστάτα (8.45)	Peter
—	διδάσκαλε (8.19)	***** (9.57)	scribe
—	κύριε (8.21)	[κύριε] (9.59)	a disciple
διδάσκαλε (4.38)	κύριε (8.25)	ἐπιστάτα x2 (8.24)	disciples
—	κύριε (9.28)	—	blind men
—	διδάσκαλε (12.38)	—	scribes and Phar
—	κύριε (14.28)	—	Peter
—	κύριε (14.30)	—	Peter
***** (7.25)	κύριε, υἱὸς Δαυίδ (15.22)	—	Can. woman
***** (7.26)	κύριε (15.25)	—	Can. woman
κύριε (7.28)	κύριε (15.27)	—	Can. woman
***** (8.32)	κύριε (16.22)	—	Peter
ῥαββι (9.5)	κύριε (17.4)	ἐπιστάτα (9.33)	Peter
διδάσκαλε (9.17)	κύριε (17.15)	διδάσκαλε (9.38)	father of boy
διδάσκαλε (9.38)	—	ἐπιστάτα (9.49)	John
—	—	κύριε (9.54)	James and John
—	—	κύριε (9.61)	potent. disc.
—	—	κύριε (10.17)	seventy
—	—	κύριε (10.40)	Martha
—	—	κύριε (11.1)	disciples
—	—	διδάσκαλε (11.45)	lawyer
—	—	διδάσκαλε (12.13)	one of crowd
—	—	κύριε (12.41)	Peter
—	—	κύριε (13.23)	a man
—	—	Ἰησοῦ ἐπιστάτα (17.13)	ten lepers
—	—	κύριε (17.37)	disciples
—	κύριε (18.21)	—	Peter
Διδάσκαλε ἀγαθέ (10.17)	διδάσκαλε (19.16)	Διδάσκαλε ἀγαθέ (18.18)	rich yng man
διδάσκαλε (10.20)	***** (19.20)	***** (18.21)	rich yng man
διδάσκαλε (10.35)	***** (20.20)	—	James and John
υἱὲ Δαυίδ Ἰησοῦ (10.47)	[κύριε] υἱὸς Δαυίδ (20.30)	Ἰησοῦ υἱὲ Δαυίδ (18.38)	blind men
υἱὲ Δαυίδ (10.48)	κύριε υἱὸς Δαυίδ (20.31)	υἱὲ Δαυίδ (18.39)	blind men
ῥαββουνί (10.51)	κύριε (20.33)	κύριε (18.41)	blind men

ῥαββί (11.21)	***** (21.20)	—	Peter
—	—	διδάσκαλε (19.39)	Pharisees
διδάσκαλε (12.14)	διδάσκαλε (22.16)	διδάσκαλε (20.21)	Phar and Hers.
διδάσκαλε (12.19)	διδάσκαλε (22.24)	διδάσκαλε (20.28)	Sadducees
—	—	διδάσκαλε (20.39)	scribe
***** (12.29)	διδάσκαλε (22.36)	διδάσκαλε (10.25)	Phar/lwyr
διδάσκαλε (12.32)	—	—	scribe
διδάσκαλε (13.1)	***** (24.1)	***** (21.5)	disciples
***** (13.4)	***** (24.3)	διδάσκαλε (21.7)	they?
***** (14.19)	κύριε (26.22)	—	disciples
—	ῥαββί (26.25)	—	Judas
ῥαββί (14.45)	ῥαββί (26.49)	***** (22.47)	Judas
—	—	κύριε (22.33)	Peter
—	—	κύριε (22.38)	disciples
—	—	κύριε (22.49)	disciples

9

JESUS AS MESSIAH

1. Introduction: Jesus as 'Christ' and 'Son of David'

Both Matthew and Mark begin their gospels by introducing 'Jesus Christ' (Matt. 1.1; Mark 1.1). Like the rest of the NT, albeit with a greater or lesser degree of emphasis, this terminology reflects the conviction that Jesus was the Messiah. The origins of this conviction, and the process by which Jesus' life and ministry were accorded messianic status, cannot be treated here. At the outset it is apparent that all the gospels regard the term 'Christ' as a title. They presuppose that 'Christ' is a known term with a clear denotation which we might define as 'the promised and expected deliverer of Israel'. Hence statements such as that by John the Baptist, 'I am not the Christ' (John 1.20), and the question asked by Herod, 'Where is the Christ to be born?' (Matt. 2.4) are presented as apparently perfectly clear to the reader.

The apparent perspecuity of the term in the NT stands in some degree of tension with the increasingly apparent diversity of messianic expectation in Second-Temple Judaism. Available evidence suggests that in terms of both the interpretation of the promises and the nature of the expected deliverance a great deal of diversity existed in early Judaism concerning the role, status, ministry and identity of the Messiah.[1] One recent survey by K. E. Pomykala concluded that 'there never existed a continuous, widespread, dominant, or uniform expectation for a davidic messiah in early Judaism'.[2] Another survey by J. J. Collins, argues that it was

---

[1] See, e.g., Neusner (ed.), *Judaisms and Their Messiahs at the Turn of the Christian Era*; Charlesworth (ed.), *The Messiah: Developments in Earliest Judaism and Christianity*; cf. earlier Hahn, *Christologische Hoheitstitel*, pp. 133–215 (ET, pp. 136–239); *TDNT*, vol. IX, pp. 493–580.

[2] Pomykala, *The Davidic Dynasty Tradition in Early Judaism: Its History and Significance for Messianism*, p. 271.

precisely the diversity in Jewish messianic thought, albeit around the central Davidic hope, that allowed Christians to emphasise some of the more marginal aspects of the spectrum.[3]

> Two terms are relevant to the messianic expressions of Second-Temple Judaism. 'Messiah' or 'Anointed' (*mšyh* or χριστός) occurs in a range of literature, for example *Pss. Sol.* 17.32; 18.title, 5, 7; 1Q30 1.i.2 (*mšyh hqwdš*); 1Q28a (= Sa) 2.12 (*hmšyh*); 2.14 and 20 (*mšyh yśr'l*); 1QS 9.11 (*mšyhy 'hrn wyśr'l*) CD 12.23f; 14.19; 19.10f; 20.1 (*mšyh 'hrn wyśr'l*); 4Q252 (= PatrBles) 5.3f (*mšyh ḥṣdq ṣmh dwyd*); 4Q521 1.ii.1 (*mšyhw*); 4Q287 10.13 (*mšyhw*); 4Q381 (*mšyhk*); 11QMelch 2.18 (*mšyh hrwh*); 1 Enoch 48.10; 52.4; 4 Ezra 12.32 (cf. 7.28f); 2 Baruch 29.3; 30.1 (cf. 39.7; 40.1; 70.9; 72.2); *T. Reub.* 6.8; see esp. M. de Jonge, 'The Use of the Word "Anointed" in the Time of Jesus'; C. A. Evans, 'Jesus and the Messianic Texts at Qumran' in *Jesus and His Contemporaries*, pp. 83–154 .
> 'Son of David' as a messianic title arose out of the promises in 2 Samuel 7; Isaiah 11; Jeremiah 23.5; Ezekiel 34.23f etc. Second-Temple references include: *Pss. Sol.* 17.21; Sirach 47.22 ('so he gave a remnant to Jacob, and to David a root of his stock'); 3 Enoch 45.5 ('the Messiah the Son of David'); 4Q161 (= pIsa[a]) ([*ṣmḥ*] *dwyd*; contextual citation of Isa: 11.1–3); 4Q174 (= Flor) 1.11f (*ṣmḥ dwyd*; contextual citation of 2 Sam. 7.11–14; Amos 9.11; Ps. 2.1f); 4Q252 (= PatrBles) 5.3f (cited above); 4Q285 5.3 and 4 (*ṣmḥ dwyd*; contextual citation of Isa. 11.1); 4 Ezra 12.32 ('this is the Messiah whom the Most High has kept until the end of days, who will arise from the posterity of David'); see esp. Schneider, 'Zur Vorgeschichte des christologischen Prädikats "Sohn Davids"'; Berger, 'Die königlichen Messiastradition des Neuen Testaments'. For Rabbinic discussions see *y. Ber.* 5a (cf. *Lam. Rab.* 1.51); *b. Sanh.* 97a, 98a. For targumim (esp. to Gen. 49.10–12; Exod. 12.42; 1 Sam. 2.1–10) see Levey, *The Messiah: An Aramaic Interpretation*, and Evans, 'Early Messianic Tradition in the Targums', *Jesus and His Contemporaries*, pp. 155–81. For the designation 'Son of David' outside the synoptic gospels: John 7.42; Romans 1.3f; Acts 2.30f, 13.23, 2 Timothy 2.8; Revelation 5.5; 22.16 (cf. also Ign., *Eph.* 18.2; 20.2).

In this respect, as M. de Jonge observed, it is not so much the terminology as the context, and specifically the scriptural associations and allusions, which are the means by which distinctive themes are communicated.[4] In this chapter, therefore, the investigation of the relationship of Matthew and Mark shall be undertaken with due attention to both context and scriptural echoes, organised in this case around the use of the two christological titles 'Christ' and 'Son of David'.

In some respects the material under investigation in this chapter relates to an early argument for the priority of Matthew on the grounds of Matthew's proximity to the earliest Jewish mission. In

---

[3] Collins, *The Scepter and the Star: The Messiahs of the Dead Sea Scrolls and Other Ancient Literature*, pp. 204–11.
[4] De Jonge, 'The Use of the Word "Anointed" in the Time of Jesus', p. 147.

his *Observations on the Four Gospels* (1764) H. Owen, anticipating somewhat F. C. Baur's *Tendenzkritik*, argued that the situation of the writers 'modified their Histories, and gave them their different colourings'; these modifications influenced the order of the narratives, the selection of material, and its contraction or expansions. The end result of this approach was the assertion that the gospels were each 'modelled . . . to the state, temper, and disposition of the times in which they were written' (p. 16). Specifically Owen argued that Matthew's content, structure and character suited the situation in which the earliest Jewish converts required instruction. This argument was based on external testimony, the persecution background of Matthew, and the apparent desire in Matthew to address 'the passions of the Jews' and lead to the conclusion that Matthew was written around AD 38 in Jerusalem for Jewish converts in Palestine (pp. 16–22). Subsequently Luke wrote for converts from the Gentile mission (AD 58 in Corinth) and Mark wrote at a time 'when the invidious distinctions between Jews and Gentiles had well nigh ceased' (AD 63 in Rome) (pp. 106–108; quotation from p. 107).

Among neo-Griesbachian scholars two similar approaches stand out. O. L. Cope argued that the Jewish interests and exegetical techniques used in Matthew, but obscured, according to his analysis, by Mark, served to prove Matthean priority.[5] Also of interest is W. R. Farmer's recent and specific adoption of the general outlines of Owen's argument, although not the dates.[6] Whether a comparative redactional approach to the messianic interests of the evangelists supports this analysis will be of interest in the following discussion.

2.   Jesus as 'Christ' and 'Son of David' in Griesbach-Mark

Χριστός appears seven times in Mark and 'Son of David' four times (Mark 10.47f; 12.35–7). Griesbach-Mark signals the importance of the concept by introducing it (perhaps on the model of Matt. 1.1) in the opening verse: 'the beginning of the gospel of Jesus Christ' (Mark 1.1). Mark nowhere explains the term 'Christ' to the reader and subsequently it occurs at the pivotal passage in 8.29 where Peter announces 'you are the Christ'. Here Griesbach-Mark follows the agreement of Matthew 16.16 and Luke 9.20 in a

---

[5] Cope, *Matthew: A Scribe Trained for the Kingdom of Heaven*.
[6] Farmer, 'The Two-Gospel Hypothesis', pp. 147–56.

passage that is widely regarded as a significant turning-point. In Mark, in particular, it leads into the 'way' section (8.27–10.45), where the significance of Jesus' death as suffering Son of Man climaxes at 10.45. Throughout this section Jesus' teaching focusses on the necessity that the Son of Man should suffer (8.31; 9.31; 10.33f).[7] In 9.41 Griesbach-Mark adds 'Christ' to Matthew 10.42, as a means of identifying the disciples.

'Son of David' first occurs in the account of the healing of blind Bartimaeus (Mark 10.46–52 parallels). In form this is a call story, focussing on Bartimaeus' faith and discipleship (note especially v. 49b: Θάρσει, ἔγειρε, φωνεῖ).[8] Through his encounter with Jesus, Bartimaeus is transferred from sitting παρὰ τὴν ὁδόν (with the triple tradition) to following Jesus ἐν τῇ ὁδῷ (unique to Mark).[9] Mark's emphasis is not on Bartimaeus' healing, but on his calling as a disciple, hence ἡ πίστις σου σέσωκέν σε, a phrase derived, on the Griesbach hypothesis, from Luke 18.42. Thus the story sums up and concludes the whole 'way' section by describing an individual who enters into the 'way' of Jesus. There is no evidence here that Griesbach-Mark is particularly interested in the title 'Son of David', which is present in both Matthew and Luke.[10] Notably, in Mark, Bartimaeus alone calls Jesus 'Son of David', and this only before his healing; since Mark also explicitly characterises Bartimaues as 'blind' D. O. Via took this as evidence that Mark denigrated such a confession.[11] This is hardly justified by the available evidence; even in this passage, although it can hardly be linked exclusively to the confession 'Son of David', the effect of the crowd's insistence on silence may highlight Bartimaeus' acclamation.[12] Nevertheless, there is little to suggest that Griesbach-Mark

---

[7] E.g. Best, 'Discipleship in Mark: Mark 8:22–10:52'; *Following Jesus*; Head, 'The Self-Offering and Death of Christ as a Sacrifice in the Gospels and the Acts of the Apostles', pp. 111–14.

[8] Steinhauser, 'The Form of the Bartimaeus Narrative (Mark 10.46–52)'; Achtemeier, '"And he followed him": Miracles and Discipleship in Mark 10:46–52', pp. 124–5; Koch, *Die Bedeutung der Wundererzählungen für die Christologie des Markusevangelium*, pp. 129–30; for a different view cf. Gundry, *Mark*, p. 596.

[9] Cf. Hooker, *Mark*, p. 252; Gundry, *Mark*, p. 593.

[10] Pesch, *Markusevangelium*, vol. II, p. 171 argues that the use of the phrase here is more indicative of a 'Jüdische-volkstümliche Sohn-Davids-Erwartung' than a specifically Christian confession.

[11] Via, *The Ethics of Mark's Gospel*, p. 162; cf. also Achtemeier, '"And he followed him": Miracles and Discipleship in Mark 10:46–52'.

[12] Robbins, 'The Healing of Blind Bartimaeus (10:46–52) in the Marcan Theology', pp. 235–6.

in particular was redactionally interested in emphasising Jesus as 'Son of David'. Notably, after the healing Bartimaeus uses 'Rabboni' (Mark 10.51) while both Matthew and Luke use κύριε.

> The tension between the two titles in the story, 'Son of David' and 'Rabboni', has often been noticed (e.g. Bultmann, *Die Geschichte der synoptischen Tradition*, p. 228 (ET, p. 213); Robbins, 'The Healing of Blind Bartimaeus (10:46–52) in the Marcan Theology', p. 231). Robbins argued (with Burger, *Jesus als Davidssohn*, p. 62) that Mark introduced 'Son of David' into the tradition through the contact with healing. This provided a basis for the christianisation of the term, which Matthew subsequently emphasised. There is, however, little evidence of a connection between 'Son of David' and healing in Mark (all the healings except two – 9.14–29; 10.46–52 – take place before 8.27). Against Robbins here see E. S. Johnson, 'Mark 10:46–52: Blind Bartimaeus', pp. 195–7.

The passage in Mark 12.35–7 has been the subject of much discussion.[13] According to the Griesbach hypothesis, Mark follows the common elements of Matthew and Luke. The passage takes the form of a scribal debate: Jesus begins with a Haggadah-question, in which he points to an apparent contradiction between two teachings – that the Messiah is 'Son of David', and yet David calls him Lord in Psalm 110.[14] D. Daube shows from other examples (notably *b. Nid.* 69bff) that in cases where such questions are asked some distinction is usually introduced to the effect that both passages can be upheld: 'each being assigned its proper field of application'.[15] Clearly the passage implies that the conception of a politico-nationalistic Davidic Messiah will have to be modified,[16] and the basis for that modification is the exaltation to Lordship of which Psalm 110 spoke (Griesbach-Mark here simply follows his sources). Evidence for the view that Mark was opposed to regarding Jesus as the 'Son of David' is lacking; although this position is sometimes taken in relation to the pre-gospel traditions upon which the triple tradition was presumably based.[17]

Hitherto we have found no evidence to suggest that Griesbach-Mark has redactionally highlighted the messianic status of Jesus. V. K. Robbins suggested that the switch from 'Son of Man', in Mark 8.27–10.45, to 'Son of David', in 10.46–12.44, was significant,

---

[13] Cf. Schneider, 'Die Davidssohnfrage (Mk 12, 35–37)', for a survey.
[14] Lohse, *TDNT*, vol. VIII, pp. 484–5.
[15] Daube, *The New Testament and Rabbinic Judaism*, pp. 158–63.
[16] Gnilka, 'Die Erwartung des messianischen Hohenpriesters von Qumran und des Neue Testaments', pp. 416–18; Schneider, 'Die Davidssohnfrage (Mk 12, 35–37)', p. 90; Hooker, *Mark*, p. 292.
[17] E.g. Burger, *Jesus als Davidssohn*, pp. 42–71.

as 'Son of Man' does not occur in 10.46–12.44, while 'Son of David' does not occur elsewhere. He argued, assuming Markan priority, that 'for the evangelist, then, this title [i.e. "Son of David"] contains some special relation to Jerusalem'.[18] This view could be supported by Mark's presentation of the entry into Jerusalem (11.9f), which is orientated around the Davidic hope, referring to the Messiah, ὁ ἐρχόμενος ἐν ὀνόματι κυρίου, and the messianic kingdom, ἡ ἐρχομένη βασιλεία τοῦ πατρὸς ἡμῶν Δαυίδ.[19] Nevertheless, there is no straightforward explanation for Griesbach-Mark's redactional procedure at 11.10. Mark focusses on the kingdom, ἡ βασιλεία, while both his sources, Matthew and Luke, focus on the king, ὁ Βασιλεύς (Matt. 21.5, 9; Luke 19.38).

In Mark 13.21 χριστός appears, in agreement with Matthew 24.23, as part of a slogan relating to false-Christs. In 14.61 Mark follows Matthew 26.63 in phrasing the high priest's question: εἰ σὺ εἶ ὁ Χριστὸς ὁ υἱὸς τοῦ εὐλογητοῦ; (this use of 'Blessed One' as a periphrasis for the name of God is unique in the NT, but not uncommon in rabbinic literature e.g. *m. Ber.* 7.3; *b. Ber.* 50a; cf. 1 Enoch 77.2). Although Jesus' answer is more clearly affirmative in Mark, reading ἐγώ εἰμι, than in either Matthew or Luke, in all three gospels the focus moves to his role as 'Son of Man'.

The originality of the variant reading to Mark 14.61 which adds σὺ εἶπας ὅτι (Θ f¹³ 472 543 565 700 1071 geo arm Origen) has been defended, partly on the basis that it explains both Matthew and Luke if Markan priority is assumed (e.g. Streeter, *The Four Gospels*, p. 322; Lohmeyer, *Markus*, p. 328; Taylor, *Mark*, p. 568; Dunn, 'The Messianic Secret in Mark', p. 111). But this solution is unlikely given the prevalence of textual harmonisation to synoptic parallels, the limited extent of manuscript support, the difficulty in accounting for its omission, and the problem that is apparent in early treatments of the differences (e.g. Clement, *Jude*, v. 24; Origen, *Hom. on Matt.*, 110, quoted in Smith, *Ante-Nicene Exegesis of the Gospels*, vol. VI, pp. 19–22; Augustine, *De Consensu*, III.6.20), see in general Kempthorne, 'The Marcan Text of Jesus' Answer to the High Priest'; and for arguments against Taylor see Catchpole, 'The Answer of Jesus to Caiaphas (Matt. XXVI.64)', pp. 220–1.

The term 'Christ' is also used on the lips of the bypassers who mock Jesus in Mark 15.32, where, on the Griesbach hypothesis, Mark follows Luke 23.35 for ὁ χριστός and Matthew 27.42 for βασιλεὺς Ἰσραήλ. In short it is clear that the term, or the concept,

---

[18] Robbins, 'The Healing of Blind Bartimaeus (10:46–52) in the Marcan Theology', p. 241.
[19] Schneider, *TDNT*, vol. II, pp. 669–70. On the allusion to Gen. 49.10 see Blenkinsopp, 'The Oracle of Judah and the Messianic Entry'.

does not play a dominant role in Mark's redactional re-presentation.[20] This is also apparent in view of the positive material in both Matthew and Luke which is not included in Griesbach-Mark.

From the perspective of the Griesbach hypothesis Mark's lack of positive redactional interest in Jesus as Messiah is matched by his omission of six of Matthew's references to 'Son of David'. This cannot be attributed solely to the influence of Luke (who also uses 'Son of David' only four times) since Griesbach-Mark would have been following Matthew in several of the passages concerned: Mark would omit the title from Matthew 1.1; 9.27 (and the whole story as a doublet on 20.29–34); 15.22 (no Lukan parallel); 21.19 (Mark following Matt., see parallels above); 21.15 (where Mark follows Matt. at least up to v. 13). Both these features of Griesbach-Markan redaction might be deemed appropriate and plausible on the basis of a Roman situation for Mark, and a concern to communicate to Gentile readers, except for the fact that Mark exhibits an apparently positive interest in Jesus as Messiah in Mark 1.1 and 8.29. At this point the tendencies of the redaction postulated for Griesbach-Mark fail to cohere with the importance of these structurally significant passages. One possibility would be to adapt T. J. Weeden's theory, that these statements represented the object of Mark's polemic, rather than his positive affirmation.[21] This approach itself, however, suffers from such serious difficulties that it is difficult to regard it as a means by which the Griesbach hypothesis could be made plausible.[22]

3.   Jesus as 'Christ' and 'Son of David' in Matthew

Matthew clearly regards 'Christ' as an adequate identifier for Jesus (not necessarily as a surname); and his interest in this subject is well established in the literature.[23] Jesus is three times identified as Ἰησοῦς ὁ λεγόμενος Χριστός (Matt. 1.16; 27.17 and 22 (by Pilate

---

[20] Lohse, *TDNT*, vol. VIII, p. 485.

[21] Weeden, 'The Heresy that Necessitated Mark's Gospel'; *Mark: Traditions in Conflict*. For an exploration of this possibility from the Griesbach perspective see Dungan, 'Reactionary Trends in the Gospel Producing Activity of the Early Church: Marcion, Tatian, Mark'.

[22] For criticism of Weeden see Schweizer, 'Neuere Markus-Forschung in USA'; Lane, 'Theios Anēr Christology and the Gospel of Mark'; Tannehill, 'The Disciples in Mark: The Function of a Narrative Role'.

[23] Gibbs, 'Purpose and Pattern in Matthew's Use of the Title "Son of David"'; Duling, 'The Therapeutic Son of David: An Element in Matthew's Christological

in order to distinguish Jesus from Barabbas)). In addition 'Jesus Christ' occurs twice (Matt. 1.1, 18). That 'Christ' in these passages has not lost significance for Matthew is apparent from both the structure of Matt 1.1–18 (cf. also 11.2; 23.10).

The introductory triad of 1.1 – 'Jesus Christ, Son of David, Son of Abraham' – is spelt out in reverse order in the genealogy: 'Abraham begat . . .' (1.2); 'David begat . . .' (1.6); 'Jesus who is called Christ' (1.16). The climax of the genealogy is Jesus the Davidic Messiah, as Matthew re-emphasises by repeating the same triad in 1.17: Abraham – David – the Christ.[24] The threefold structure of the genealogy may also be modelled by *gematria* on David's name (since David = ד (= 4) + ו (= 6) + ד (= 4) = 14).[25] It seems obvious that Matthew uses 'Christ' in close connection with 'Son of David' to present Jesus as the Davidic Messiah. That 'Son of David' is not exclusively messianic for Matthew is shown in 1.20 where Joseph is addressed as 'Joseph, Son of David'. Nevertheless even this serves to underscore the Davidic descent of Jesus and the christological theme expressed in the title, since the point of 1.18–25 is arguably to provide the explanation for the inclusion, by adoption, of Jesus into the line of David.[26] Several scholars have argued that 'Son of David' is the most important of Matthew's christological titles (at least for the period of Jesus' ministry).[27]

Matthew 2.1–12 locates the birth of the Messiah in Bethlehem (because of Mic. 5.2). Bethlehem was clearly presented in the OT as the birth place of David (1 Sam. 16.1, 4; 17.12), even as 'his city' (1 Sam. 20.6); this is obviously picked up and related to other

Apologetic'; Chilton, 'Jesus *ben David*: Reflections on the *Davidssohnfrage*'; Kingsbury, 'The Title "Son of David" in Matthew's Gospel'; Suhl, 'Der Davidssohn im Matthäusevangelium'; Burger, *Jesus als Davidssohn*, pp. 72–106.

[24] Tatum, 'The Origin of Jesus Messiah (Matt 1:1, 18a): Matthew's Use of the Infancy Traditions'.

[25] Davies and Allison, *Matthew*, vol. I, p. 163.

[26] Stendahl made a point of approving Schlatter's description of 1.18–25 as 'Die Einpflanzung Jesu in das Geschlecht Davids' (Stendahl, 'Quis et Unde? An Analysis of Mt 1–2', p. 61; Schlatter, *Der Evangelist Matthäus*, p. 7; cf. Vögtle, 'Die Genealogie Mt 1,2–16 und die matthäische Kindheitsgeschichte', pp. 70–3; Suhl, 'Der Davidssohn im Matthäusevangelium', pp. 62–67; Tatum, 'The Origin of Jesus Messiah (Matt 1:1, 18a): Matthew's Use of the Infancy Traditions', p. 531).

[27] Strecker, *Der Weg der Gerechtigkeit*, pp. 118–20; Hummel, *Die Auseinandersetzung zwischen Kirche und Judentum im Matthäusevangelium*, pp. 116–22; Suhl, 'Der Davidssohn im Matthäusevangelium', pp. 68–9 and 81; Davies, 'The Jewish Sources of Matthew's Messianism', p. 500.

aspects of the Davidic expectation in Micah 5. In any case, Matthew's interest is clear, and not least in the final line of the quotation, ὅστις ποιμανεῖ τὸν λαόν μου τὸν Ἰσραήλ, which comes from 2 Samuel 5.2 (= 1 Chron. 11.2) where it is addressed to David.

> Evidence for Jewish expectation that the Davidic Messiah would come from Bethlehem is (in the early period) limited to Christian writings: Matthew 2; John 7.42; *Protevangelium of James* 21.2; Justin, *Dialogue* 78; *Apology* I.34 (these dependent upon the NT). The Messiah's birth in Bethlehem is taught in some later Rabbinic passages (Ginzberg, *The Legends of the Jews*, vol. V, p. 130, cites *y. Ber.* 5a; *Lam. Rab.* 51 (on Lam. 1.16); *Tg. Neb.* Mic. 5.2; *Tg. Ps-J.* Gen. 35.21). Origen argued that Jewish scholars had suppressed this expectation lest they support Christian teaching (*Contra Celsum* I.51).

Matthew obviously goes to some lengths in chapters 1 and 2 to establish that Jesus is the Davidic Messiah, descended from David κατὰ σάρκα, and the fulfilment of Israel's hopes. From this foundation Matthew builds in the following chapters various other considerations (in particular that Jesus is God's obedient Son – chapters 3 and 4, hinted at in 2.15, which will be discussed in the next chapter).

While this introduction suggests that 'Christ' and 'Son of David' are equivalent expressions for Matthew, a number of scholars have noticed an apparent connection between petitioners' use of 'Son of David' and Jesus' healing ministry.[28] In the previous chapter several of these features were noted, in particular the stereotyped way in which the combination of 'Have mercy on us/me, Lord, Son of David' occurs in 9.27; 15.22; 20.30f (and in 17.15 without 'Son of David'). These passages record the opening of blind eyes (9.29f and 20.34) and the healing of the Canaanite woman's daughter (15.28). In addition, Jesus' healing of a blind and dumb demoniac (12.22) provokes amazement from the crowd who ask: Μήτι οὗτός ἐστιν ὁ υἱὸς Δαυίδ; (12.23).

The connection between healing and Davidic messianism is often traced to the intermediate stage of Solomon speculation, whose reputation as possessor of magical healing knowledge was widespread (e.g. Wis. 7.15–22; Josephus, *Antiquties* VIII.45–49; cf. *Bib. ant.* 60.3; 11QpsApᵃ; *T. Sol.* 20.1: 'King Solomon, Son of David, have mercy on me'; *Apoc. Adam* 7.13–16; Origen, *Comm. on Matt.*

---

[28] E.g. Duling, 'The Therapeutic Son of David: An Element in Matthew's Christological Apologetic'; Burger, *Jesus als Davidssohn*, p. 90 regards this as a Matthean innovation.

XXXIII (on Matt. 26.63)).[29] Further support for a Solomonic connection could be drawn from the observation that Jesus was already known to be a descendant of David, and presents himself as 'greater than Solomon' (Matt. 12.42 // Luke 11.31).[30]

However, four factors tell against a strongly Solomonic explanation for the connection between 'Son of David' and Jesus' healing ministry in Matthew. First, in the literature mentioned earlier 'Solomon' is always identified by name, never solely as 'Son of David'.[31] Secondly, in the just mentioned passage in Matthew 12.42 it is Solomon's wisdom rather than his healing or exorcistic reputation that is specified. Thirdly, as already noted, Matthew's introduction clearly identifies 'Son of David' as a messianic title.[32] Fourthly, it is likely that the connection between 'Son of David' and Jesus' healing ministry can be explained along more straightforward lines.

In the previous chapter it was noted that Matthew presents Jesus as the means by which God's aid is given to the petitioner. Since in Matthew's thought Jesus' healing miracles occur in fulfilment of the messianic hopes of Isaiah (e.g. Isa. 35.5f cf. Matt. 11.5; Isa. 53.4 cf. Matt. 8.17; also Isa. 61.1ff cf. Matt. 5.3ff) one could equally suggest that these associations arose out of the Isaianic hope of the coming of the Lord, and lead (along with other factors) to the prominence of κύριος in the passages cited.

Furthermore, although not widespread, there is definite evidence within the OT that the activity of the Davidic Messiah of Ezekiel 34.23f (twice identifying this Davidic Messiah as 'my servant' *'bdy*; cf. Jer. 23.1–6) would include, as part of his role as Shepherd in the restoration of Israel, healing the sick, binding up the injured and strengthening the weak (Ezek. 34.4, 16).[33] In addition, recently published Qumran material attests a connection between messianic shepherding and healing in contexts allusive of Isaiah 61. In 4Q521 the Messiah's shepherding activity is associated with healing the sick and other restorative actions given in Isaiah 61.1–2: 'he will heal the slain, resurrect the dead, and announce glad tidings to the

---

[29] Davies and Allison, *Matthew*, vol. II, pp. 135–6; see further Fisher, ' "Can this be the Son of David?" '; Duling, 'Solomon, Exorcism, and Son of David' and *OTP*, vol. I, pp. 944–51.

[30] Chilton, 'Jesus *ben David*: Reflections on the *Davidssohnfrage*', pp. 95–100.

[31] Ibid., pp. 97–98; cf. Gundry, *Mark*, p. 600.

[32] Chilton, 'Jesus *ben David*: Reflections on the *Davidssohnfrage*', pp. 92–5, 100.

[33] Aune, 'The Problem of the Messianic Secret', pp. 26–30.

poor ... he will lead the holy ones; he will shepherd them ...'
(lines 12 and 13).[34] Although the subject of these verses may be
God, the Lord, mentioned in previous phrases, the parallel with
11QMelchizedek suggests that the Messiah's activity is in view, or,
at the very least, that 'God acts through the agency of a prophetic
messiah.'[35] In 11QMelchizedek 2.18 the one who brings good news
(*hmbśr* of Is 52.7) is identified as the Messiah/Anointed One of the
Spirit (*m]śyḥ* hrw[ḥ]).[36] That this messianic terminology is an
allusion to Isaiah 61.1–2, with *lśbr* functioning as a link-word, is
supported by the numerous allusions to Isaiah 61.1–2 throughout
11QMelch (e.g. lines 4, 6, 9, 13, 18).[37]

These passages form an important backdrop for Matthew's
description of John the Baptist in prison hearing of Jesus' activity.
Matthew describes this activity as τὰ ἔργα τοῦ Χριστοῦ (Matt.
11.2). This clearly functions to identify Jesus as the Messiah,
defined in the following verses in terms drawn from Isaiah 35.5f;
42.18; 61.1 etc. (Matt. 11.5f).

In other passages Matthew supplements Mark's use of 'Christ'
by adding 'Son of God' (notably in 16.16, clarified also in 26.63, see
the next chapter for discussion). This association by collocation
seems characteristic of Matthew, as with 'Lord, Son of David'.
Matthew introduces 'Christ' in 16.20 in the saying concerning the
messianic secret: τότε διεστείλατο τοῖς μαθηταῖς ἵνα μηδενὶ
εἴπωσιν ὅτι αὐτός ἐστιν ὁ Χριστός (cf. Mark 8.30: καὶ ἐπετίμησεν
αὐτοῖς ἵνα μηδενὶ λέγωσιν περὶ αὐτοῦ, while Mark 8.31 follows
with a reference to the Son of Man suffering, Matt. 16.21 uses
indirect speech and a pronoun). Matthew does not reserve 'Christ'
for either his own editorial work, or for the words of the disciples.
He includes it on the lips of Jesus' antagonists (Matt. 2.4: Herod;
26.63: high priest; 26.68: those who struck Jesus; 27.17, 22: Pilate).

---

[34] Wise and Tabor, 'The Messiah at Qumran'; Puech, 'Une apocalypse messianique
(4Q521)'; Collins, 'The Works of the Messiah'.
[35] J. J. Collins, 'The Works of the Messiah', p. 100; also C. A. Evans, 'Jesus and the
Messianic Texts at Qumran' in *Jesus and His Contemporaries*, p. 129. The
distinction may not be that important since the things that God does in the
messianic age are probably not thought of as done independently of the Messiah
(cf. Jub. 23.30 for God healing the sick).
[36] For text see de Jonge and van der Woude, '11Q Melchizedek and the New
Testament'.
[37] Yadin, 'A Note on Melchizedek and Qumran'; de Jonge and van der Woude,
'11Q Melchizedek and the New Testament', pp. 306–7; Miller, 'The Function of
Isa 61.1–2 in 11Q Melchizedek'. Note the similar association of these two verses
in 1QH 18.14f and the collocation of the Messiah and the Spirit in 4Q287.

False-Christs appear in Matthew as in Mark, especially in the statements of Jesus warning the disciples that many would come claiming to be 'the Christ' (Matt. 24.23 // Mark 13.21). An interesting case here is Matthew 24.5 which refers to those who would come and say Ἐγώ εἰμι ὁ Χριστός (// Mark 13.6: Ἐγώ εἰμι); this alteration, however, is not made in connection with any christological emphasis (as the statement is not made by Jesus in reference to himself).

Matthew's version of the entry into Jerusalem (21.1–17) is more explicit than Mark, not only concerning the fulfilment of Zechariah 9.9 (ἰδοὺ ὁ βασιλεύς σου ἔρχεταί σοι . . .), but also concerning the cries of the crowd:

> Ὡσαννὰ τῷ υἱῷ Δαυίδ·
> Εὐλογμένος ὁ ἐρχόμενος ἐν ὀνόματι κυρίου·
> Ὡσαννὰ ἐν τοῖς ὑφίστοις.

(21.9b)

Matthew focusses more narrowly upon the praise of Jesus himself, and specifically as 'Son of David', than does Mark. It is precisely this that is then questioned by the Jewish leaders in 21.15 (although in the context of healings, cf. v. 14). Most important of all is that Matthew brackets the cleansing of the Temple between these two announcements of Jesus as 'Son of David', reinforcing not only the healing idea, but also that Jesus is the Davidic king ('my house', v. 13; cf. v. 16 the quotation of Ps. 8.3 LXX). Finally, Matthew's version of the *Davidssohnfrage* (22.41–6) is very close to Mark's, although it is placed even more specifically in the context of a Haggadah-question.

The christological force of Matthew's treatment of 'Son of David' clearly takes in *both* the messianic fulfilment theme (emphasised in chapters 1 and 2 and by means of the OT citations throughout the gospel) *and* the healing ministry of Jesus. This supplements and fills out the information provided in the first two chapters. Clearly the theme is of great importance for the evangelist. J. D. Kingsbury's oft-repeated attempts to show that Matthew subordinates everything, including his 'Son of David' christology, to a 'Son of God' christology do not really allow for the importance of the introduction (1.1) and genealogy. His attempt to see 1.18–25 and chapter 2 as establishing a higher ranking for 'Son of God' and his analysis of 22.41–6 are far-fetched; in both cases involving the reading of 'Son of God' thinking into passages where it is not clearly present.[38] In this connection, the biggest problem with Kingsbury is his conviction that Matthew has one 'principal christological predication', compared with which all the others are minor and subordinate.[39] There is simply no clear indication that Matthew thought in such terms.[40]

4. Conclusion

That there is a clear emphasis in Matthew upon the presentation of Jesus as Davidic Messiah is evident (as Matt. 1.1 suggests). From the perspective of Markan priority one can observe that Matthew's re-presentation of Markan material is, in this respect, coherent and fairly pervasive. The influence of both OT patterns and contemporary Jewish expectation, the spread of material, and the inclusion of Jesus' miraculous activity within the same category attest to its ubiquity in Matthew. In addition, while we noted Owen's argument for the priority of Matthew based on its Jewishness, there is nothing in the material here discussed which precludes a subsequent reappropriation of Jewish and OT categories in a situation of dialogue or debate with the synagogue down the street. This situational hypothesis is necessary for Matthew's redaction to be regarded as totally plausible.

The Griesbach hypothesis will take Mark as a later version of the tradition, rewritten for Gentile Christian audiences. As a *Sitz im Leben* this may explain Mark's lack of redactional interest in developing the basic Christian confession which he passes on (e.g. Mark 1.1), but it fails to provide a really plausible explanation for the redactional behaviour of Griesbach-Mark.

[38] See, e.g., Kingsbury, 'The Title "Son of David" in Matthew's Gospel'; *Matthew: Structure, Christology, Kingdom*, pp. 99–103.
[39] *Matthew: Structure, Christology, Kingdom*, p. 101.
[40] See especially Hill, 'Son and Servant'.

10

JESUS AS SON OF GOD

1. Introduction

The designation of Jesus as 'Son of God' became characteristic of Christian profession, both within the NT – especially in the writings of Paul, and of John, and in the epistle to the Hebrews – and in other early Christian documents. The title 'Son of God' was also important for the synoptic evangelists, as Appendix 8A suggested (above, p. 171), and as numerous recent studies have highlighted.

> Although not as common in the Pauline corpus as 'Lord' (184 times), 'Son of God' appears in strategic places, *'when he* [i.e. Paul] *is speaking of the close bond between Jesus Christ and God, that is, of his function as the mediator of salvation* between God and man' (Hengel, *Der Sohn Gottes*, p. 23 (cited from ET, p. 10)); see Romans 1.3, 4, 9; 5.10; 8.3, 29, 32; 1 Corinthians 1.9; 2 Corinthians 1.19; Galatians 1.16, 2.20, 4.4, 6; Ephesians 4.13; Colossians 1.13; 1 Thessalonians 1.10. In the Johannine literature note John 1.18 [*v.l.*]; 3.16f; 5.19–26; 20.31; also 1 John 2.22–4; 4.9f, 15; 5.1–12; also cf. Hebrews 1.2, 5 (cf. Ps. 2.7); 3.6; 4.14; 5.8; 6.6; 7.3 etc. For examples of υἱὸς θεοῦ in the early patristic writers see *Barn.* 5.4; 7.9; Ign., *Eph.* 20.2; *Smyrn.* 1.1 (cf. *Rom.* insc: ἐν ὀνόματι Ἰησοῦ Χριστοῦ υἱοῦ πατρός); Justin, *Apology* I.22, 30, 31, 54, 63 etc.; Irenaeus, *Adversus haereses* I.9.3; Origen, *Contra Celsum*, I.49, 57, 66 etc.

As has already been noted, nineteenth-century scholars such as W. M. L. de Wette, H. U. Meijboom and T. Keim (all advocates of the Griesbach hypothesis) regularly took Mark's interest in and emphasis on Jesus as the Son of God as evidence of his posteriority in relation to Matthew and Luke (see chapter one, section 2.3). On the other side of the debate the evangelists' use of the term 'Son of God' has not featured directly in discussions of the synoptic problem. Clearly, the importance of the term for both Matthew and Mark, and its appearance in certain key passages, makes an investigation of evangelical usage desirable in order to broaden the base for comparing the christological presentations of the respective evangelists, and ultimately for comparing the plausibility of the rival synoptic theories.

2. Background considerations

A thorough investigation of the background and usage of terminology of divine sonship is beyond the scope of this study.[1] In a hellenistic milieu the heroes of Greek myths, oriental rulers, famous philosophers, and even all men might be described in terms of divine sonship.[2] Of particular interest is the inscriptional evidence claiming divine sonship for the emperors, for example: 'The Emperor, Caesar, son of a god (θεοῦ υἱὸν), the god Augustus, of every land and sea the overseer' (Pergamum, No. 381); and another describing Nero as 'the son of the greatest of the gods (τὸν υἱὸν τοῦ μεγίστου θεῶν), Tiberius Claudius' (Magnesia, No. 157b).[3] A previous generation of scholars took the hellenistic background as determinative, arguing that within the hellenistic Christianity represented by the evangelists the term 'Son of God' referred to 'divine men' and wonder-workers.[4] Recent investigations, however, suggest both that miracle-workers were never described using (ὁ) υἱὸς (τοῦ) θεοῦ,[5] and that 'divine man' categories have been mistakenly applied to the study of NT christology.[6]

Modern studies, as the discussion in the previous chapter

---

[1] For more detail see Byrne, *'Sons of God' – 'Seeds of Abraham': A Study of the Idea of the Sonship of God of All Christians in Paul against the Jewish Background*, pp. 9–78; Michel and Betz, 'Von Gott gezeugt'; Lohse, *TDNT*, vol. VIII, pp. 353–62; Hengel, *Der Sohn Gottes*, pp. 35–89 (ET, pp. 21–56); Delling, 'Die Bezeichnung »Söhne Gottes« in der jüdischen Literatur der hellenistisch-römischen Zeit'; Descamps, 'Pour une histoire du titre «Fils de Dieu». Les antécédents par rapport à Marc'.

[2] Dunn, *Christology in the Making*, pp. 13–14; Martitz, *TDNT*, vol. VIII, pp. 336–8; Hengel, *Der Sohn Gottes*, pp. 39–67 (ET, pp. 23–41).

[3] Cited by Deissmann, *Licht von Osten*, p. 295 (Abh. 62 and 63) (cited from ET, p. 347 (figs. 53 and 54)); cf. also Deissmann, *Bibelstudien*, pp. 166–7 (ET, pp. 166–7); Martitz, *TDNT*, vol. VIII, p. 337: examples from 27 BC (BGU II.543.3) and 5 BC (IG 12.3 No. 174.2).

[4] Bultmann, *Theologie des Neuen Testaments*, pp. 128–9 (ET, vol. I, pp. 130–1); cf. Bousset, *Kyrios Christos*, pp. 52–7 (ET, pp. 65–70); Dalman, *Die Worte Jesu*, pp. 236–7 (ET, pp. 288–9).

[5] Blackburn, *Theios Anēr and the Markan Miracle Traditions*, p. 95 for the negative conclusion (supported by Martitz, *TDNT*, vol. VIII, pp. 339–40).

[6] Holladay, *Theios Aner in Hellenistic Judaism*; Kingsbury, 'The "Divine Man" as the Key to Mark's Christology – the End of an Era'. For a more positive assessment see Corrington, *The "Divine Man": His Origin and Function in Hellenistic Popular Religion* .

suggests, generally take the Jewish background as determinative for understanding the terminology and concepts of the synoptic gospels. In particular, R. Bultmann's suggestion that the messianic interpretation of Psalm 2 could have given rise to the use of 'Son of God' as a messianic title provides a more appropriate starting-point for understanding the evangelists' usage.[7] This background is particularly important for both Matthew and Mark, since the initial occurrences of sonship terminology applied to Jesus occur in passages apparently quoted from the OT and interpreted in the manner of eschatological fulfilment (Matt. 2.15; Mark 1.11 see below).

Within the OT itself sonship language is used of:

(a) **angels:** Psalms 29.1; 89.7 (*bny 'lym*); Genesis 6.2, 4;[8] Job 1.6; 2.1; 38.7 (*bny h'lhym*); Daniel 3.25 (*br 'lhyn*); Psalm 82.6 (*bny 'lywn*);

(b) **Israel as a whole (using singular terms):** Exodus 4.22f (*bny, bny bkry yśr'l*); Hosea 11.1 (*wmmṣryn qr'ty lbny*); Jeremiah 31.9 (*ky hyyty lyśr'l l'b w'prym bṣry hw'), 20 (hbn yqyr 'prym 'm yld š'šw'ym*);

(c) **Israelites in general (using plural terms):** Deuteronomy 14.1 (*bnym 'tm lyhwh 'lhykm*); 32.5 (*bnyw mwmm*); Hosea 2.1 (*bny 'l hy*); Jeremiah 3.19 (*bbnym*), 22 (*šwbw bnym šwbbym*); cf. also God as father (Deut. 32.6; Jer. 3.4, 19; Isa. 63.16; 64.8; Mal. 2.10) and other parental imagery (Deut. 1.31; 8.5; 32.18; Mal. 3.17; Pss 68.6; 103.13; Isa. 1.2; 30.1; cf. Isa. 66.13); and for Israelites as sons and daughters see Deuteronomy 32.19; Isa. 43.6; 45.11.

(d) **the Davidic king:** 2 Samuel 7.14 (*'ny 'hyh lw l'b whw' yhwh ly lbn*); Psalm 2.7 (*bny 'th 'ny hywm yldtyk*)]; Psalm 89.28 (*'ny bkwr 'tnhw*), cf. v. 27.

It is primarily this final category which gave rise to messianic

---

[7] Bultmann, *Theologie des Neuen Testaments*, p. 51 (ET, vol. I, p. 50).

[8] Gen. 6.1–4 was widely interpreted to refer to angels (LXX^mss; 1 Enoch 6; Jub. 5.1; Josephus, *Antiquities* I.73; Philo, *De gigantibus* 2; cf. Jude 6 and 2 Pet. 2.4), although this view was later opposed by Rabbi Akiba and his followers (for 'sons of the judges/great ones' see *Tg. Neof.* Gen. 6.2, 4; *Tg. Onq.* Gen. 6.2, 4; *Gen. Rab.* 26.5 (R. Simeon b. Yohai) cf. Ginzberg, *Legends of the Jews*, vol. V, pp. 153–6) it nevertheless affected later Rabbinic (and other) traditions: *b. Yoma* 67b (R. Ishmael); *Rab. Deut.* XI.10; *Pirqe R. El.* XXII; *Tg. Ps-J.* Gen. 6.4, *Tg. Neof.* margin at Gen. 6.2, 4; Trypho (acc. Justin, *Dialogue with Trypho.* I. 79). See Alexander, 'The Targumim and Early Exegesis of "Sons of God" in Genesis 6'.

interpretations which led to the use of 'Son of God' as a messianic appellation within Judaism, within the context of the interpretation of these three passages of scripture. Such a conclusion remains controversial and will need to be briefly defended in view of the recent assertion by J. A. Fitzmyer

> 'that neither in pre-Christian Palestinian Judaism nor in that of the Diaspora have we any clear indication that that psalm [i.e. Psalm 2] was being understood 'messianically', i.e. of an expected or coming anointed figure, a Messiah in the strict sense.'[9]

Nevertheless evidence for the messianic appropriation of material listed in group (d) above, including both Psalm 2 and 2 Samuel 7 is extensive, both among definitely pre-Christian Jewish sources and among later targumic and Rabbinic material which in this case arguably reflects a continuous interpretative tradition. We shall survey this material as briefly as possible.

Firstly, 2 Samuel 7.14 itself is presented within its original context as a dynastic prophecy given to David.[10] Targum Jonathan understands the oracle as a 'prophecy', a 'vision for the sons of men' concerning the coming (messianic) age (*Tg. Ps.-J.* 2 Samuel 7.17, 19). Secondly, *Pss. Sol.* 17 (first century BC) expects a Davidic Messiah-King (v 4 refers to 2 Sam. 7; cf. also v. 21) and describes his victory in terms derived from Psalm 2 (particularly v. 9: rod of iron, potter's vessel etc. cf. also v. 23f, 26). Thirdly, both 2 Samuel 7 and Psalm 2 are quoted, with messianic interpretation, in 4Q174 (= *Florilegium*) I.10ff (as also in Acts 13.33–7; Heb. 1.5). Here 2 Samuel 7.11–14 is interpreted as a prophecy of the Branch of David who would come to save Israel, using the clearly messianic title *ṣmḥ dwyd* (cf. Jer. 23.5; 33.15 (Zech. 3.8; 6.12); 4Q161; 4Q252 5.3f; 4Q285 5.3 and 4 – see above, p. 175). Then, within the same context, Psalm 2.1f is quoted and interpreted as a prophecy concerning 'the elect of Israel (*bḥyry yśr'l*) in the last days'. Although it is unclear whether the term 'elect of Israel' should be understood as a reference to the whole eschatological community (with G. J. Brooke and Y. Yadin) or as a messianic title (with J. Allegro and J. Starcky), the generally eschatological orientation is very clear.

---

[9] Fitzmyer, 'The Palestinian Background of "Son of God" as a Title for Jesus', p. 571.

[10] Gordon, *1 and 2 Samuel*, pp. 235–6; McCarter, *II Samuel*, p. 210.

The plural form of (*bḥyry yśr'l*), and the parallels in 1QpHab 10.13; 1QM 12.1, 4, suggest the community itself is in view (cf. Brooke, *Exegesis at Qumran*, p. 158; Yadin, 'A Midrash on 2 Sam. vii and Ps. i–ii (4Q Florilegium)', p. 98). The singular is extant as a messianic title in, for example, *Tg. Isa.* 42.1 (*bḥyry*); 'the Elect One' in 1 Enoch 49.2, 4 and *passim* in 39–62; *Asc. Isa.* 8.7; the closest Qumran text is 4Q534(= Mess ar), which refers to a possibly messianic figure in line 10: 'he is the one chosen by God (*bḥyry 'lh*')' (taken as messianic by Allegro in *DJD* V (1968) 54). Nevertheless the role and function of this figure, although plausibly seen as messianic in view of numerous allusions to Isaiah 11 (so Starcky, 'Un texte messianique araméen de la grotte 4 de Qumrân'; C. A. Evans, 'Jesus and the Messianic Texts from Qumran', *Jesus and His Contemporaries*, pp. 111–13), is sufficiently unclear as to render it problematic as a point of comparison for another unclear text (for a non-messianic interpretation see Fitzmyer, 'The Aramaic "Elect of God" Text from Qumran Cave 4').

Fourthly, Psalm 109.3LXX (with syriac and vulgate support) includes an allusion to Psalm 2.7 in what appears to be a messianic alteration to the MT: ἐκ γαστρὸς πρὸ ἑωσφόρου ἐξεγέννησά σε.

Cooke, noting many parallels between Psalm 110 and Psalm 2, argued that the LXX represents the original text here ('The Israelite King as Son of God', pp. 218–24), but this is neither likely nor necessary for the point made here (cf. Hay, *Glory at the Right Hand: Psalm 110 in Early Christianity*, pp. 21–2). For other messianic interpretations of Psalm 110 see Braude, *The Midrash on Psalms*, vol. II, pp. 206–7; possibly *T. Job* 33.2–9; 1 Enoch 45.1, 3; 51.3; 52.1–7; 55.4; 61.8; 69.27, 29 (cf. 2 Enoch 24.1); other evidence including later Rabbis is cited in Str-B, vol. IV, pp. 453–65, and discussed in Hay, *Glory at the Right Hand*, pp. 21–33. On the relationship between Daniel 7 and Ps 110 see Hengel, 'Psalm 110 und die Erhöhung des Auferstandenen zur Rechten Gottes', pp. 57–66.

Fifthly, 4Q246 (= 4QpsDanA[a]) 2.1 refers to an eschatological figure of whom it is said: '"Son of God" he shall be called, and they will name him "son of the Most High"' (*brh dy 'l yt'mr br 'lywn yqrwnt*).[11] The same document relates the action of this figure to action and attributes traditionally associated with the Messiah; for example, his kingdom as 'an everlasting kingdom' (2.5, 9; cf. Dan. 7.14, 27), 'he shall judge the land with truth' (2.5f; cf. *Tg. Isa.* 11.4; *Pss. Sol.* 17.26–9), and 'all the provinces shall pay him homage' (2.7 cf. 1.8f; cf. *Tg. Isa.* 11.10, 14; *Pss. Sol.* 17.21–5, 30; Ps. 89.27f).[12]

---

[11] For text see Puech, 'Fragment d'une apocalypse en araméen (4Q246 = pseudo-Dan[d]) et le «Royaume de Dieu»', p. 106; ET from Collins, 'The *Son of God* Text from Qumran', p. 66; cf. also Fitzmyer, '4Q246: The "Son of God" Document from Qumran'.

[12] Evans, 'Jesus and the Messianic Texts from Qumran', *Jesus and His Contemporaries*, pp. 108–10.

Puech regards the text as originally messianic, although interpreted at Qumran in terms of Antiochus IV ('Fragment d'une Apocalypse en araméen (4Q246 = pseudo-Dan^d) et le «Royaume de Dieu»', pp. 114–15); J. J. Collins opts for an eschatological figure derived from Daniel 7 with 'messianic overtones' ('The *Son of God* Text from Qumran', p. 81); Kim (citing Stuhlmacher and Betz in support) takes it as straightforwardly messianic ('*The "Son of Man"' as the Son of God*, p. 22, n. 33). More hesitant are Fitzmyer: it refers to a non-messianic future Davidic ruler ('4Q246: The "Son of God" Document from Qumran', pp. 170–4, referring to his earlier arguments); Byrne, '*Sons of God*' – '*Seeds of Abraham*', pp. 61–2; Hengel, *Der Sohn Gottes*, p. 72 (ET, p. 45).

Sixthly, 4Q369, speaking of a prince and ruler, says 'you made him a first-born son to you' (*wtšymhw lkh bn bkwr*, line 6). This statement parallels Psalm 89.28: 'I will make him the firstborn, the highest of the kings of the earth', and suggests that a messianic figure is in view.[13] Seventhly, 1Q28a (= Sa) 2.11ff, in its description of the Messiah presiding over an eschatological banquet, contains a reference to God begetting the Messiah, a concept that would suggest dependence upon Psalm 2.7. This seems the most likely rendering of the damaged text: ('*m ywlyd ['l] '[t] hmšyh 'tm*) (Martinez: 'when [God] begets the Messiah with them'; Vermes: 'when God will have engendered (the Priest-) Messiah; cf. Lohse: 'wenn [Gott] geboren werden läßt d[en] Messias unter ihnen').

Support for this reading includes Barthélemy in *DJD* I (1955) 117; Michel and Betz, 'Von Gott gezeugt', pp. 11–12; Gordis, 'The "Begotten" Messiah in the Qumran Scrolls'; Cross, 'Qumran Cave 1', p. 124, n. 8; Black, 'Messianic Doctrine in the Qumran Scrolls', pp. 448–9 (who appeals in support of a conception of a divine begetting of the Messiah to 1QH3 concerning the birth of a first-born male child in fulfilment of Isa. 9.6); Brownlee, 'Messianic Motifs of Qumran and the New Testament', pp. 23–7; Collins, 'The *Son of God* Text from Qumran', pp. 78–9; Evans, 'Jesus and the Messianic Texts from Qumran', *Jesus and His Contemporaries*, pp. 95–97. Milik restored the text as *ywlyk* 'he will lead forth' instead of *ywlyd* 'he will beget' (*DJD* I (1955) 117, suported by Talman, 'The Concepts of *Masiah* and Messianism in Early Judaism', p. 110, n. 71), other restorations have also been proposed (see Yadin, 'A Crucial Passage in the Dead Sea Scrolls. 1QSa ii.11–17'; Richardson, 'Some Notes on 1QSa', p. 116; Maier, *Die Texte vom Toten Meer*, vol. II, pp. 158–9) but no alternative to *ywlyd* has commanded general assent. Note Vermes' recent comment: 'This reading (*yolid*), which has been queried by many, including myself in the previous editions, seems to be confirmed by computer image enhancement' (*The Dead Sea Scrolls in English*, p. 121).

---

[13] See J. J. Collins, 'The *Son of God* Text from Qumran', p. 79; C. A. Evans, 'A Note on the "First-Born Son" of 4Q369'.

Eighthly, the Messiah is called God's son in some versions of 4 Ezra 7.28f ('my son the Messiah') and 13.32, 37, 52; 14.9 ('my Son'), where dependence upon Psalm 2 is clear in the same context (see, e.g., 13.33f cf. Ps. 2.1f; v. 35f cf. Ps. 2.6).

> The vision of the Messiah in chapter 13 is dependent upon Daniel 7.13f and Isaiah 11 as well as Psalm 2 (cf. Box, *The Ezra-Apocalypse*, pp. lvi–lvii; Charlesworth, 'The Concept of the Messiah in the Pseudepigrapha', p. 202; Knibb and Coggins, *The First and Second Books of Esdras*, p. 169; Collins, 'The *Son of God* Text from Qumran', pp. 76–7) and contains numerous parallels to *Pss. Sol.* 17 (see Box, 'IV Ezra' in *APOT*, pp. 616–17). Stone's argument that the different versions can all be explained on the basis of an original παῖς (reflecting in turn a translation of the Hebrew *'bd*, *Features of the Eschatology of IV Ezra*, pp. 71–7) does not account for the Psalm 2 background (Collins, 'The *Son of God* Text from Qumran', p. 77, notes that παῖς is used of 'son' in Wis. 2.13, 16). Gero suggests an ambiguous original ('"My Son the Messiah": A Note on 4 Esr. 7 28–9').

Ninthly, and finally, Psalm 2 was clearly regarded as messianic by numerous later Rabbis, as attested in *b. Sukk.* 52a, and the *Midr. Pss.* (generally on 2.2 and 2.8; and with specific statements from R. Judah b. Nahmani (on 2.1f), d.339; R. Yudan (on 2.7f), d. *c.*280; R. Huna (on 2.7), d.296; R. Johanan (on 2.8), d.279).

> In addition, *Tg. Ket.* Ps. 80.16 renders 'the son (whom thou hast reared for thyself)' by 'the King Messiah . . .' Levey regards the messianic interpretation as 'clear and unmistakable' (*The Messiah: An Aramaic Interpretation*, pp. 119–20). He takes *b*ᵉ*n* to mean 'branch'.
> Another passage where the Messiah is said to be God's Son is *Exod. Rab.* 19.7 (Exod. 13.1f), in the words of Rabbi Nathan (T4): 'The Holy One, blessed be He, told Moses, "Just as I have made Jacob a firstborn, for it says: *Israel is My son, My firstborn* (Exod. 4.22), so will I make the King Messiah a firstborn, as it says: *I will appoint him firstborn*" (Ps. 89.28).'

It seems from this evidence that the passages describing the Davidic king as God's son (Ps. 2.7; 2 Sam. 7.14; Ps. 89.27f) were understood messianically in the first century and that the terminology of divine sonship could be used in connection with the hoped-for Davidic Messiah. It is quite possible that Christian use of 'Son of God' terminology may have deterred and influenced later Jewish discussions;[14] on the other hand scope for Christian influence on the texts cited above is limited to 4 Ezra. These conclusions are important for understanding the evangelical usage, but the association of 'Son of God' with Israel (categories 2 and 3 above) will also be found relevant.

---

[14] Dalman, *Die Worte Jesu*, p. 223 (ET, pp. 271–2); Lohse, *TDNT*, vol. VIII, p. 362.

A further characteristic of Jewish literature, which has echoes with numerous sayings of Jesus in the synoptic gospels, is that holy or righteous individuals within Israel were sometimes called sons of God (Sir. 4.10; Wis. 2.18; Jub. 1.24f; cf. *Pss. Sol.* 13.8; Wis. 5.5). This could also be applied to specific OT figures: Enoch (1 Enoch 105.2?); Jacob (*Prayer of Joseph* Fr.A. 7); Joseph (*Joseph and Asenath* 6.3, 5; 18.11; 21.4; 23.10); Levi (*T. Levi* 4.2); Moses (Josephus, *Antiquities* II.232; *The Tragedy of Ezekiel* 100); and to charismatic holy men: Hanina ben Dosa (*b. Ber.* 17b: *ḥnyn' bny*; cf. *b. Ta'an* 24b); Eleazer ben Pedath (*b. Ta'an* 25a: *'l'zr bry; 'l'zr bny*; Ishmael ben Elisha (3 Enoch 1:8); cf. also the language of sonship used by Honi the circle drawer (*m. Ta'an* 3.8).

This chapter will follow the pattern of the preceding two chapters in dealing firstly with Mark, assuming the Griesbach hypothesis; and secondly with Matthew, assuming Markan priority. Although some scholars have suggested that terms such as 'Son of God', 'Son', 'my Son' should be dealt with as separate categories, there seems little support for this from the material just surveyed, and if 'Son of God' cannot be regarded as an invariable technical term we should not expect uniformity.[15] In several places 'the Son' is used in connection with 'the Father' (e.g. Mark 13.32; Matt. 11.27), where it should certainly be regarded as a shorthand form of 'Son of God'.[16]

3.   Jesus as 'Son of God' in Griesbach-Mark

With one exception all of Griesbach-Mark's references to Jesus as 'Son of God' or 'Son' are drawn from his sources in Matthew or Luke ('Son of God': 3.11; 5.7; 14.61; 15.39; 'the/my Son': 1.11; 9.7; 13.32; the exception is 3.11 which may be dependent upon Luke 4.41).[17] Some examples of Mark's omission of the term from parallels in Matthew have already been noted (Mark 6.51f cf. Matt.

---

[15] Marshall, 'The Divine Sonship of Jesus', pp. 87–8 against Hahn, *Christologische Hoheitstitel*, pp. 319–32 (ET, pp. 307–16); cf. also Meier, *The Vision of Matthew*, pp. 82–3.

[16] For the opposite view, that it represents 'Son of Man', see Pesch, *Markusevangelium*, vol. I, p. 310 (on Mark 13.32); and Kruijf, *Der Sohn des lebendigen Gottes*, p. 71 (on Matt. 11.25–7).

[17] Note also 'Son of God' as a variant reading at Mark 1.1; on the originality of the shorter reading here see Head, 'A Text-Critical Study of Mark 1.1'; Ehrman, 'The Text of Mark in the Hands of the Orthodox', pp. 149–52; Collins, 'Establishing the Text: Mark 1:1'.

14.33, see above, p. 95; Mark 15.30, 32 cf. Matt. 27.40, 43, see above, p. 139), there are additional passages which will deserve attention here.

Both Matthew and Luke introduce the term in their respective birth/infancy narratives. Matthew develops there a new-Israel theme (2.15 cf. 4.3, 6). Luke links 'Son of God' to Jesus' miraculous conception (1.35), although he also links 'Son' terminology with other messianic categories (e.g. 'Son of David' in 1.32; 'Christ' in 4.41). Griesbach-Mark's omission of the birth/infancy narratives leaves the baptismal pronouncement (Mark 1.11 // Matt. 3.17 // Luke 3.22) to function alone as the initial affirmation of Jesus' divine sonship, whereas both Matthew and Luke, in addition to preceding information in the birth/infancy narratives, provide additional reflection on the nature of this sonship in the temptation story, which follows the baptism.

The narrative structure of Mark 1.9–11 is derived primarily from Matthew; hence: 'from Galilee . . . in the Jordan . . . by John' (Mark 1.9 // Matt. 3.13 and 16; not in Luke). Within this passage Griesbach-Mark departs occasionally from both Matthew and Luke. The minor agreements which result are not necessarily easier to explain on the Griesbach hypothesis than on the two-source hypothesis.[18] For example, Mark uses σχιζομένους rather than ἠνεῴχθησαν // ἀνεῳχθῆναι. The Griesbach hypothesis can thus point to the *inclusio* created between the baptism of Jesus and the tearing of the temple curtain (15.38: Καὶ τὸ καταπέτασμα τοῦ ναοῦ ἐσχίσθη εἰς δύο ἀπ' ἄνωθεν ἕως κάτω) which precedes the climactic announcement of Jesus' sonship in 15.39.[19] On the other hand, since ἀνοίγω is the standard form in revelatory disclosures (Ezek. 1.1; Isa. 24.18; 63.19; 3 Macc. 6.18; Acts 7.56; Rev. 4.1; cf. also Gen. 7.11; Mal. 3.10) it is also understandable that later writers might include it rather than σχίζω.[20]

The baptismal announcement itself, in Mark 1.11, follows Luke in being addressed to Jesus himself: Σὺ εἶ ὁ υἱός μου ὁ ἀγαπητός, ἐν σοὶ εὐδόκησα (Matt. 3.17 has Οὗτος ἐστιν ὁ υἱός μου ὁ ἀγαπητός, ἐν ᾧ εὐδόκησα). The significance and sources of this

---

[18] For a list see Neirynck, *The Minor Agreements*, pp. 58–9.
[19] See, although not advocating the Griesbach hypothesis, Motyer, 'The Rending of the Veil: A Markan Pentecost?'; Jackson, 'The Death of Jesus in Mark', p. 21.
[20] On this use of ἀνοίγω see van Unnik, 'Die "geöffneten Himmel" in der Offenbarungsvision des Apokryphons des Johannes'.

announcement have been much discussed.[21] Jesus is announced as the Son of God in terms derived from Psalm 2.7; the saying thus stands in the messianic tradition outlined above.

Many early Christians noted the allusion to Psalm 2.7 here, e.g. Justin, *Dialogue* 88.8; 103.6; Clement, *Paed.* I.6.25; *Gos. Eb.* 4; NB also the Western variant conforming Luke 3.22 more closely to the LXX of Psalm 2.7 (and therefore unlikely to be original): υἱός μου εἶ σύ, ἐγὼ σήμερον γεγέννηκά σε (D it, also attested in Justin Martyr, Origen, Methodius, Hilary and Augustine; IGNTP, *Luke*, vol. I, p. 68; Ehrman, *The Orthodox Corruption of Scripture*, pp. 62–7 defends its originality to Luke; it is not clear, however, that the many patristic sources he cites actually represent a rendering of Luke, rather than parallel attempts to appropriate the OT passage conceived of prophetically).

Many scholars also accept that the baptismal announcement contains a further allusion to Isaiah 42.1,[22] and this is marginally more likely on the Griesbach hypothesis since the quotation from Isaiah 42.1 in Matthew 12.18 containing both ὁ ἀγαπητός and ἐν σοὶ εὐδόκησα would be known to Mark.[23] The Mark–Luke form is closer to Psalm 2.7 (LXX), υἱός μου εἶ σύ, but the difference is probably best understood as relating to the private nature of the revelation. While Matthew's account of the baptism appears as a public encounter (as we shall see), and Luke's account has some public characteristics ('all the people' in 3.21; the dove which descended εἶδει: 'in visible form'), Mark's account is almost entirely private. Thus Griesbach-Mark omits the people (Luke 3.21), he fronts the singular verb (εἶδεν) to a position dependent upon ἀναβαίνων and thus the whole experience is Jesus' alone; he uses εἰς rather than ἐπι for the descent of the Spirit, thus eliminating any observable element to the account; and the voice from heaven addresses Jesus personally ('You are my son . . . with you I am pleased'). If this assessment is correct then the primary difference between Mark and Matthew at this point is the essentially private nature of the revelation of divine sonship.

The private nature of this knowledge is clear from the other

[21] See Edwards, 'The Baptism of Jesus according to the Gospel of Mark'; Marshall, 'Son of God or Servant of Yahweh? – A Reconsideration of Mark 1.11'.

[22] Jeremias, *TDNT*, vol. V, pp. 701–2 (who argued that an original παῖς μου had been displaced by υἱός μου); Pesch, *Markusevangelium*, vol. I, p. 92; Gundry, *Mark*, pp. 49–50; Marshall, 'Son of God or Servant of Yahweh? – A Reconsideration of Mark 1.11' (*contra*: Hooker, *Jesus and the Servant*, pp. 70–3).

[23] Some scholars also find echoes of Gen. 22.2, 12, 16 and Exod. 4.22f; see Marcus, *The Way of the Lord*, pp. 49–56 and Watts, *The Influence of the Isaianic New Exodus*, pp. 52–8 for discussions and bibliography.

references to 'Son of God' in Mark. As H. L. Jackson observed, Mark presents a widening appreciation of Jesus as Son of God: first heard by Jesus alone (1.11; confirmed by demonic powers in 1.24; 3.11; 5.7); secondly heard by a few disciples (9.7; confirmed by Jesus to them in 13.32); thirdly heard openly by those at the trial (14.61f; cf. 12.6–8); and finally, professed for the first time by a human, by the Gentile centurion in 15.39.[24]

Mark 3.7–12 is a summary passage about Jesus' healing ministry constructed from diverse elements from Matthew 4.25; 12.15f; Luke 6.17f; 4.41.[25] Within this context, Mark presents the unclean spirits as falling before Jesus and crying out: Σὺ εἶ ὁ υἱὸς τοῦ θεοῦ – the syntax, ὅταν with a series of imperfects, suggests a repeated occurrence (BDF, §367). This statement appears to be adapted from Luke 4.41, a passage which Griesbach-Mark used previously in 1.32–4. Specific similarities include the use of κράζω and λέγω and the identically worded statement: Σὺ εἶ ὁ υἱὸς τοῦ θεοῦ.[26] This creates something of a problem for the Griesbach hypothesis, since there is no ready explanation as to why Mark would use the surrounding portions of Luke 4.40f in 1.32–4 (without the 'Son of God' statement), and then return to Luke 4.41 at this point in order to insert one portion of it. Mark 1.34 is particularly notable on the assumption that Mark has adapted Luke 4.41 (ᾔδεισαν τὸν Χριστὸν αὐτὸν εἶναι), since Mark's version refers not to knowledge that Jesus was the Christ but to an undefined, but apparently more absolute, knowledge of him: ᾔδεισαν αὐτόν.

> Most mss harmonise the end of Mark 1.34 to Luke 4.41 in various ways (see UBS4: B אᶜ C L W f¹ f¹³ etc.), but this is to be expected, and the shorter reading given above has good support (א* A (D) it vg etc.).

Thus for Griesbach-Mark, as for Luke, the knowledge of the unclean spirits is true knowledge, reflecting the baptismal proclamation of 1.11. Several other passages in Mark reflect unclean spirits claiming knowledge of Jesus' identity (1.24, 34; 3.11; 5.7).

Although these spirits have knowledge of Jesus, the statements made by them are not identical or in any discernible pattern: 1.24,

---

[24] Jackson, 'The Death of Jesus in Mark', p. 21 (drawing upon Schreiber, Vielhauer, Best, Donahue, Perrin, Kee and Tannehill, his n. 18, p. 35).

[25] Griesbach, 'Demonstration' n. 22 pp. 209–10; de Wette, *Einleitung*, p. 188 (ET, p. 167); Riley, *The Making of Mark*, pp. 36–7.

[26] Commentators on Luke generally accept dependence upon Mark, e.g. Marshall, *Luke*, pp. 196–7; Schürmann, *Lukasevangelium*, vol. I, p. 254; Fitzmyer, *Luke*, vol. I, p. 554; Evans, *Luke*, p. 282.

for example, apparently highlights Jesus as 'the holy one of God' and 1.34 contains no reported statement. In Mark 5.7, the so-called Gerasene demoniac, whose approach to Jesus is described in v. 6 using the verb προσκυνέω (cf. 15.19 and our discussion in chapter 7, section 2), also exhibits knowledge of Jesus' identity in the following terms (following Luke 8.28): Τί ἐμοὶ καὶ σοὶ Ἰησοῦ υἱὲ τοῦ θεοῦ τοῦ ὑψίστου;

It was noted at the outset of this section that Griesbach-Mark omits several passages which contain references to Jesus as 'Son' or 'Son of God'. In addition to the passages noted there he omits, within the context of a large-scale omission of all the material in Matthew 11, the so-called 'Great Thanksgiving', which contains the important statement of Matthew 11.27 // Luke 10.22. Another omission, which occurs within the context of a passage that is taken up in Griesbach-Mark, is the account of Peter's confession in Caesarea Philippi (see Mark 8.29 //Matt. 16.16 and Luke 9.20).

On the whole Mark's version of Peter's confession is closer to Matthew than to Luke. Griesbach-Mark has been following Matthew throughout the preceding two chapters (Mark 6.30–8.21 // Matt. 14.13–16.12 cf. Luke's great omission), adding two new stories in 7.31–7; 8.22–6. Griesbach-Mark remains in closer allegiance to Matthew's order than Luke's in the material that follows the confession, although he follows neither completely; for example, Luke's long travel section, 9.51–18.14, is omitted as are some of Matthew's collections of Jesus' teaching (e.g. chapter 18). In the account itself, Mark 8.27–30, there are several indications of Griesbach-Mark's preference for Matthew (e.g. Mark 8.27 // Matt. 16.13: ten words in common, but not in Luke), supporting Griesbach's assertion: 'In this section he [i.e. Mark] follows chiefly in the footsteps of Matthew, but all the while comparing with Luke.'[27]

The words of the confession of Peter, Σὺ εἶ ὁ Χριστός (Mark 8.29) are exactly parallel with Matthew, although Mark omits the second part of Matthew 16.16: Σὺ εἶ ὁ Χριστὸς ὁ υἱὸς τοῦ θεοῦ τοῦ ζῶντος.[28] As has already been noted, Griesbach-Mark owes little to Luke in this context, so although the shorter form of Peter's confession in Luke (Τὸν Χριστὸν τοῦ θεοῦ) may have influenced

---

[27] Griesbach, 'Demonstration', n. 32, p. 211; also de Wette, *Einleitung*, p. 190 (ET, p. 169); Bleek, *Einleitung*, pp. 254–5 (ET, pp. 271–2); Davidson, *Introduction*, p. 473; Farmer, *The Synoptic Problem*, pp. 245–6.

[28] Several witnesses harmonise Mark's text to that of Matthew by the addition of ὁ υἱὸς τοῦ θεοῦ so ℵ L it^{rl}; or ὁ υἱὸς τοῦ θεοῦ τοῦ ζῶντος so W f¹³ it^b sy^p sa^{mss}.

Mark, omitting Matthew's wording represents a deliberate redactional choice. An explanation for this behaviour might be that Griesbach-Mark must be understood as saving the 'public' confession of Jesus as 'Son of God' until 15.39: a sonship revealed in his death.

This sonship *is* made known during Jesus' ministry, but only in a limited way. In the announcement of Jesus' sonship to the three disciples at the transfiguration (Mark 9.7 // Matt. 17.5; Luke 9.35), Griesbach-Mark's understanding emerges in his additions, which link the event with Jesus' suffering (Mark 9.12b) and resurrection (Mark 9.10), a link already present in Matthew, but not Luke. Griesbach-Mark follows Matthew in recording both the instruction, ἀκούετε αὐτοῦ, and Jesus' command to tell no one about this event until the resurrection (Mark 9.7, 9). While the transfiguration is not to be classified as a misplaced resurrection appearance, it does in some measure anticipate the resurrection.[29]

The parable of the vineyard (Mark 12.1–9, dependent upon both Matt. 21.33–41 and Luke 20.9–16) climaxes with the declaration ἔτι ἕνα εἶχεν, υἱὸν ἀγαπητόν ἀπέστειλεν αὐτὸν ἔσχατον πρὸς αὐτοὺς λέγων ὅτι 'Εντραπήσονται τὸν υἱός μου (Mark 12.6; picking up ἀγαπητόν here from Luke 20.13 in addition to elements of Matthew's account). This reference to 'a beloved son . . . my son' echoes the declarations of God at Jesus' baptism (1.11) and the transfiguration (9.7). This parable is directed to the Jewish leaders (cf. Mark 11.27; 12.1, 12), and the overall point is clearly concerned with the Jewish rejection of Jesus (Mark 12.10f; cf. Matt. 21.43 omitted by Mark), but the christological implication – that as beloved Son Jesus comes to suffer and die – is characteristic of the Markan theology.

The close connection between Jesus' divine sonship and his death reaches its climax in the passion narrative. Mark 14.62, as has already been noted (cf. above, p. 179), provides the most clearly affirmative form of Jesus' answer to the high priest's question: 'Εγώ εἰμι; cf. Matthew 26.64: Σὺ εἶπας, and Luke 22.70, ὑμεῖς λέγετε ὅτι ἐγώ εἰμι. This alteration is clearly explicable on the Greisbach hypothesis. In the following narrative Mark omits Matthean passages where 'Son of God' is used in the mocking of Jesus (Matt. 27.40, 43). Griesbach-Mark primarily follows Matthew's account

---

[29] Stein, 'Is the Transfiguration (Mark 9:2–8) a Misplaced Resurrection Account?' ; Boobyer, *St. Mark and the Transfiguration Story.*

(note especially the close parallels between Mark 15.38 and Matt. 27.51), but he omits the earthquake and the opening of the tombs (Matt. 27.51b–3). In 15.39 Griesbach-Mark makes several alterations to Matthew: he omits mention of those who were with the centurion, thus isolating the centurion: he stands alone before Jesus (ὁ παρεστηκὼς ἐξ ἐναντίας αὐτοῦ). It should be noted that Mark's term here κεντυρίων, a Latin loanword, appears only here and in 15.44, 45 within the NT (cf. *Gos. Pet.* 31f, 38). Mark's characteristic use of Latinisms can be accounted for by Roman provenance or influence even on the Griesbach hypothesis.[30] In Mark it is not the earthquake and surrounding events (as in Matt. 27.54) but the actual death of Jesus ('Ιδὼν . . . ὅτι οὕτως ἐξέπνευσεν) that prompts the 'confession'. Thus the confession that Jesus (οὗτος ὁ ἄνθρωπος) is the Son of God is for Mark tied to the death of Jesus more closely than in his sources.

This connection, which has been recognised by most scholars, is almost certainly the best explanation for Mark's redactional procedure according to the Griesbach hypothesis and provides a measure of coherence to the narrative.[31] We have, however, noted various problems with the detail of Griesbach-Mark's procedure. In addition, Mark's redaction of Matthew and Luke does not cohere with the relatively universal tendency in the scribal traditions to add 'Son of God' to the gospel traditions.[32] Thus the Griesbach hypothesis does not provide a fully compelling explanation of Markan redaction in terms of plausibility *and* coherence. It remains to investigate Matthew's procedure on the two-source hypothesis.

4.   Jesus as 'Son of God' in Matthew

The importance of the title 'Son of God' for Matthew has been widely recognised in recent years. In addition to numerous explicit references (2.15; 3.17; 4.3, 6; 8.29; 11.27; 14.33; 16.16; 17.5; 24.36; 26.63; 27.40, 43, 54; 28.19), R. T. France notes that 'son-language alone gives us only one side of the total picture' – the other side is

---

[30] For the most recent advocacy of Mark's Roman provenance see Gundry, *Mark*, p. 1044.

[31] See Hay, 'The Son-of-God Christology in Mark'; Kingsbury, *The Christology of Mark's Gospel*, pp. 129–33; Gnilka, *Markus*, vol. II, p. 324; and, albeit with slightly different perspectives, Steichele, *Der leidende Sohn Gottes*; and Kazmierski, *Jesus, the Son of God*. For a different view see Gundry, *Mark*, pp. 974–5.

[32] Head, 'A Text-Critical Study of Mark 1.1', p. 627.

the Father-language that is characteristic of Matthew's Jesus (referring to God as 'Father' forty-four times, cf. four in Mark, seventeen in Luke), a relational aspect of divine sonship which D. J. Verseput argued was especially important to Matthew.[33] In particular J. D. Kingsbury has argued not only that Matthew's gospel is 'principally Christological in nature',[34] but that 'Son of God' is the dominant expression of Matthean christology in all its aspects.[35]

Kingsbury's position overstates the evidence and is based on the misguided assumption that there is a single title which is 'superior' or 'pre-eminent' in relation to all the others.[36] Among other things, this position does not allow for the interrelations between titles that seem particularly characteristic of Matthew. Both D. Hill and Verseput, for example, have shown the importance of the Isaianic Servant motif as modifying Matthew's presentation of Jesus as Son of God.[37] H. Geist argues that Matthew constructs a 'christologische Trias' relating 'Son of Man', 'Son of David' and 'Son of God'.[38] These relations and collocations between christological titles occur within a context of Matthew's appropriation of a whole range of OT material.[39] Nevertheless, Kingsbury has highlighted what numerous scholars have agreed on, which is that the term 'Son of God' is of great importance for Matthew.[40] This is supported, on the two-source hypothesis, by the fact that Matthew has included all but one of Mark's uses of 'Son of God' and has additional, and somewhat distinctive, material. The single exception is Mark 3.11; Matthew omits the whole passage (Mark 3.7–12) except for a few phrases which appear in Matthew 4.25 and 12.16.

---

[33] France, *Matthew: Evangelist and Teacher*, p. 294; cf. Verseput, 'The Role and Meaning of the "Son of God" Title in Matthew's Gospel', p. 538.

[34] Kingsbury, *Matthew: Structure, Christology, Kingdom*, p. 36; cf. also 'The Theology of St. Matthew's Gospel according to the Griesbach Hypothesis', pp. 333–4.

[35] Kingsbury, *Matthew: Structure, Christology, Kingdom*, p. 83 and *passim*; 'The Figure of Jesus in Matthew's Story: A Literary-Critical Probe'.

[36] Kingsbury, *Matthew: Structure, Christology, Kingdom*, p. x; cf. pp. 41–2; 'The Figure of Jesus in Matthew's Story: A Literary-Critical Probe', p. 3; cf. 'The Title "Son of God" in Matthew's Gospel', pp. 3–4.

[37] Hill 'Son and Servant' and 'The Figure of Jesus in Matthew's Story'; Verseput, 'The Role and Meaning of the "Son of God" Title in Matthew's Gospel'.

[38] Geist, *Menschensohn und Gemeinde*, p. 438.

[39] Hill's criticisms of Kingsbury are echoed by Stanton, 'The Origin and Purpose of Matthew's Gospel', p. 1924.

[40] Cf. Verseput, 'The Role and Meaning of the "Son of God" Title in Matthew's Gospel'; Gerhardsson, *The Mighty Acts of Jesus*, pp. 88–91; Brown, *The Birth of the Messiah*, pp. 133–37.

The first occurrence, the quotation from Hosea 11.1 in Matthew 2.15 ('Ἐξ Αἰγύπτου ἐκάλεσα τὸν υἱόν μου), signals one of the more important and distinctive elements in Matthew's presentation: a typological association between Jesus as 'Son of God' and Israel. Although some scholars have taken this as an example of Matthew's atomistic and arbitrary appropriation of an OT 'prophecy',[41] several factors suggest that Matthew has typologically connected Jesus and Israel as 'Son of God'.[42] First, Hosea 11.1 functions within its original context as a foundation for future promised salvation from exile in 'Egypt' (11.5, 10). Secondly, it is likely that Matthew's interpretation of Hosea 11.1 was influenced by the Septuagint of Numbers 24.17, which is plainly messianic.[43] Thirdly, the context in Matthew confirms the typological association. Note in particular the two additional references to 'Son of God' in the temptation narrative (Matt. 4.3, 6) which follows Matthew's account of the baptism of Jesus, and clearly functions to interpret the nature of Jesus' sonship announced there (Matt. 3.17).[44] Throughout this context Jesus, as the true Son of God/ Israel retraces the steps of Israel: having passed through the waters, he enters the desert for his time of testing. Jesus is presented as one who has learnt the wilderness lessons (Deut. 8.3; 6.16; 6.13) which Israel (God's first-born son, Exod. 4.22) had failed to learn, and he is obedient Son of God.[45]

It seems likely, if this understanding is correct, that Matthew 1.1–4.16 functions as a prologue or introduction to the gospel.[46]

---

[41] E.g. Rothfuchs, *Die Erfüllungszitate des Matthäus-Evangeliums*, pp. 90–2.

[42] Soares Prabhu, *The Formula Quotations in the Infancy Narrative of Matthew*, p. 296; Tatum, 'The Matthean Infancy Stories', p. 137; Gundry, *Matthew*, p. 34; France, 'The Formula-Quotations of Matthew 2 and the Problem of Communication', pp. 243–4; Davies, *The Setting of the Sermon on the Mount*, p. 78; Kynes, *A Christology of Solidarity*, p. 18.

[43] Lindars, *New Testament Apologetic*, pp. 216–17; cf. also Davies and Allison, *Matthew*, vol. I, p. 262. NB the marginal note in Codex Sinaiticus at Matt. 2.15: ΕΝ ΑΡΙΘΜΟΙΣ.

[44] Gerhardsson, *The Testing of God's Son*, p. 19; Gaechter, *Matthäusevangelium*, p. 116; Przybylski, 'The Role of Mt 3:13–4:11 in the Structure and Theology of the Gospel of Matthew', pp. 223–5; Wilkens, 'Die Versuchung Jesu nach Matthäus', p. 81; Gundry suggests 'since you are God's son . . .' (*Matthew*, p. 55).

[45] Gerhardsson, *The Testing of God's Son*; Kynes, *A Christology of Solidarity*, pp. 28–35; Kruijf, *Der Sohn des lebendigen Gottes*, pp. 55–8.

[46] Lohmeyer, *Matthäus*, p. 1; Stonehouse, *The Witness of Matthew and Mark to Christ*, pp. 129–31; Krentz, 'The Extent of Matthew's Prologue'; Kingsbury, *Matthew: Structure, Christology, Kingdom*, pp. 7–17. Cf. in general Thompson, 'The Structure of Matthew: A Survey of Recent Trends'.

This is also supported by the observation that the use of OT quotations in connection with geographical features extends beyond chapter two to include Matthew 3.3 (John placed in the wilderness) and 4.15 (Jesus comes to the land of Zebulun and Naphtali).[47] This prologue has an important place in the communication of Matthew's christological message. A number of scholars have suggested that the virgin birth provides (for Matthew) the explanation and rationale for Jesus' divine sonship.[48] The evidence appealed to in support of this position is, however, hardly sufficient to establish the point. R. Pesch argued that Matthew's use of ὑπο κυρίου in 1.22; 2.15 suggested a close link to Matthew's 'Son of God Christology'.[49] R. E. Brown argued that 1.20 assumes a divine begetting along the lines of 1QSa 2.11.[50] Against this view Verseput observed: 'Although possessing every opportunity to do so, the First Evangelist actually avoids drawing any direct connection between the miraculous conception and the divine Sonship of Jesus.'[51] Clearer evidence of Matthew's christological interests is found in his alterations and structural reshaping of Markan material, particularly in the story of Jesus' baptism, which has an important place in this 'prologue'.

While it is possible that Q contained a reference to the baptism, there is nothing in either Matthew or Luke that could not be explained as independent variations from Mark.[52] Several of Matthew's alterations suggest that Matthew regarded the revelation as a public event.[53] So, for example, Matthew changes the syntax from Mark's participle, ἀναβαίνων, with εἶδεν, which relates the following events to Jesus alone, into a descriptive statement (εὐθὺς

---

[47] Cf. Stendahl, 'Quis et Unde? An Analysis of Mt 1–2'; extended to Matt. 3 and 4 by Tatum, ' "The Origin of Jesus Messiah" (Matt. 1:1, 18a): Matthew's Use of the Infancy Traditions', p. 532; Brown, *The Birth of the Messiah*, p. 49; Kynes, *A Christology of Solidarity*, pp. 10–11.

[48] Hahn, *Christologische Hoheitstitel*, p. 319 (ET, p. 306); Davies and Allison, *Matthew*, vol. I, p. 212; Dunn, *Christology in the Making*, pp. 49–50.

[49] Pesch, 'Der Gottessohn im matthäischen Evangelienprolog (Mt 1–2)'.

[50] Brown, *The Birth of the Messiah*, pp. 133–8.

[51] Verseput, 'The Role and Meaning of the "Son of God" Title in Matthew's Gospel', p. 532, cf. p. 549 n. 3; see Rothfuchs, *Die Erfüllungszitate des Matthäus-Evangeliums*, pp. 40–1 for alternative explanations of ὑπο κυρίου.

[52] For Q and Jesus' baptism see Streeter, *The Four Gospels*, p. 188; Schürmann, *Lukasevangelium*, vol. I, p. 197; Davies and Allison, *Matthew*, vol. I, p. 328; against see Kloppenborg, *The Formation of Q*, pp. 84–5.

[53] Wink, *John the Baptist in the Gospel Tradition*, p. 37; Webb, *John the Baptizer and Prophet*, p. 57; Hill, *Matthew*, p. 97; Davies and Allison, *Matthew*, vol. I, p. 330; Luz, *Matthäus*, vol. I, p. 156 (ET, vol. I, p. 180).

ἀνέβη . . .) followed by a new phrase introduced by καὶ ἰδού and followed by two co-ordinate aorists (ἠνεῴχθησαν, εἶδεν, Matt. 3.16). These alterations (and the repeated καὶ ἰδού) create a more objective impression, which John (at least) is presumed to have witnessed (cf. also the use of ἐπ' αὐτόν in 3.16; cf. εἰς αὐτόν in Mark 1.10).

This impression is reinforced by the Matthean form of the voice, Οὗτός ἐστιν ὁ υἱός μου . . . (v. 17, as 17.5), which uses an identification formula that is common in Matthew (Οὗτος ἐστιν . . . (18–6–11)). This suggests that Matthew identifies Jesus with an expected messianic figure (Matthew's text thus requires reference to external definitions of terms).[54] The second portion of the saying from heaven is also transferred into the third person. Matthew 12.18 cites Isaiah 42.1 using both ὁ ἀγαπητός μου and the third person form, εἰς ὃν εὐδόκησεν ἡ ψυχή μου. Thus Matthew's version of the baptismal-saying is slightly closer to Isaiah 42.1 than Mark's, and slightly less close to Psalm 2.7.

> The presentation of the baptism as a public event is specifically challenged in some forms of the textual tradition of Matthew, but should probably be regarded as a genuine and important part of the Matthean redactional presentation. Note particularly the addition of πρὸς αὐτόν in 3.17 to introduce the voice from heaven (D it sy[s. c]) and the related use of σὺ εἶ ὁ υἱός μου (D it[a] sy[s. c] Irenaeus). A further, though disputed, example is the addition in many mss of αὐτῷ after ἠνεῴχθησαν in 3.16 (this makes it a private revelation). In my opinion this represents an attempt to harmonise Matthew with Mark. The shorter reading is supported by ℵ* B syr[s.c] cop[sa] lect[3mgs] Irenaeus Hilary Vigilius (with McNeile, *Matthew*, p. 31; Weiss, *Matthäus-Evangelium*, pp. 71–2; Davies and Allison, *Matthew*, vol. I, p. 328 n. 67). *Gos. Eb.* 4 proves that the different traditions in Mark (private) and Matthew (public, at least to John) were recognised in the second century.

The other prominent aspect of Matthew's version of the baptism is the addition of the dialogue between John and Jesus (3.14–15).[55] This could be regarded as a modification due to embarrassment with the Markan report that places Jesus on the same level as those from Jerusalem and all Judea (3.5), who were baptised 'confessing their sins' (3.6). This might also explain Matthew's omission of Mark's description of John's baptism as 'of repentance for forgive-

---

[54] Berger, 'Die königlichen Messiastraditionen des Neuen Testaments', p. 29, n. 108.
[55] Generally regarded as redactional owing to Matthean vocabulary and style (Gundry, *Matthew*, pp. 50–1; Davies and Allison, *Matthew*, vol. I, pp. 323–327; Luz, *Matthäus*, vol. I, pp. 150–1 (ET, vol. I, pp. 173–4)). Strecker regards v. 14 as traditional (*Der Weg der Gerechtigkeit*, pp. 178–9).

ness of sins' (Mark 1.4b). Matthew describes John's baptism as εἰς μετάνοιαν in 3.11, but forgiveness of sins is bestowed by Jesus alone (cf. 26.28).[56]

This embarrassment might also be suggested by later traditions regarding Jesus' baptism. The priority of Mark yields a recognisable tendency in later writers to address the perceived problem of Jesus' baptism by John in different ways.[57] In Luke 3.21 John is not even mentioned, the emphasis is on Jesus as Son of God, cf. also the genealogy which follows, especially 3.38; in John 1.29–34 the baptism itself is not mentioned, the emphasis is again on Jesus as Son of God, especially 1.34. Later in *Gos. Naz.* 2 Jesus is invited by his family to be baptised by John, he responds, 'Wherein have I sinned that I should go and be baptised by him?'[58]

The significance of the passage for Matthew, however, remains disputed;[59] and although John's response to Jesus (v. 14) apparently assumes a submissive (or reverential?) attitude there is perhaps little more that can be said on specifically christological material in these verses.[60]

Matthew includes an abbreviated form of the question of the Gadarene demoniac, τί ἡμῖν καὶ σοί, υἱὲ τοῦ θεοῦ; (Matt. 8.29 // Mark 5.7), omitting 'Jesus' and 'of the most high' from Mark, and removing the adjuration of the demons in favour of a question that expresses an eschatological and christological truth: ἦλθες ὧδε πρὸ καιροῦ βασανίσαι ἡμᾶς;[61] He also omits the discussion (bargaining?) between Jesus and the spirits, which in Mark 5.9 takes place after Jesus' command that they come out. This is explicable in terms of a drastically abbreviated account which concentrates on the christological import of the story.[62]

---

[56] Wink, *John the Baptist in the Gospel Tradition*, p. 36; Webb, *John the Baptizer and Prophet*, p. 57.

[57] Hollenbach, 'The Conversion of Jesus: From Jesus the Baptizer to Jesus the Healer', pp. 198–9 n. 4.

[58] Jerome, *Pelag.* III.2 (cited from *NTA*, vol. I, pp. 146–7).

[59] Davies and Allison, *Matthew*, vol. I, pp. 325–7; note Kynes' solution (*A Christology of Solidarity*, pp. 24–7).

[60] A different argument comes from Keck who argues that the connection between the Spirit and the dove is ambiguous in Mark, and is progressively clarified in Matthew, Luke and later traditions ('The Spirit and the Dove', p. 41).

[61] The question may be constructed under the influence of Mark 1.24 (Held, 'Matthäus als Interpret der Wundergeschichten', p. 163 (ET, p. 173)).

[62] Held, 'Matthäus als Interpret der Wundergeschichten', p. 164 (ET, pp. 174–5); Gnilka, *Matthaüsevangelium*, vol. I, p. 320; Davies and Allison, *Matthew*, vol. II, pp. 76–7.

We have seen the importance of Jesus' sonship in Matthew's opening chapters, where the redactional focus seems to be on Jesus' role as the obedient Son of God, an Israel figure. In Matthew 11.27 the Matthean Jesus announces his sonship in relational terms: 'no one knows the son except the father nor does anyone know the father except the son'. This is clearly an important element in Matthew's christological presentation, occurring as it does within a passage that contains many important Matthean themes. E. P. Blair exaggerated to make the point: 'the Gospel of Matthew as a whole is simply a commentary on the crucially important passage 11:27–30'.[63]

On the two-source hypothesis, Matt. 11.25–7 is probably incorporated relatively unchanged from Q, since it is generally agreed that Luke's form in 10.22 is secondary compared to Matthew.[64] Verse 27 is the climax of the Great Thanksgiving, providing the christological basis for the statement of 11.25 concerning the revelation of ταῦτα to infants. 'These things' probably refers, in Matthew, to the miraculous deeds of Jesus (cf. 11.2, 19, 20f) which testify to the coming of the Kingdom (11.5) which is present in Jesus' ministry (cf. 11.11–15).[65] This is what the cities in vv. 20–4 have failed to understand, and this is what the father has revealed to infants. Verse 27 then explains the basis for that revelation, occurring as it does within the context of the mutual knowledge of Father and Son, and that the Son is the means by which the Father reveals 'these things'.

The conclusion to be drawn is that, for Matthew, Jesus' relational sonship is the basis for his messianic deeds. Thus, as others have noted, 'Son of God' cannot be understood in a 'merely' messianic manner.[66] It is Jesus as unique Son of the Father, Jesus

---

[63] Blair, *Jesus in the Gospel of Matthew*, p. 108; cf. Kinsgbury, *Matthew: Structure, Christology, Kingdom*, p. 64.

[64] Marshall, *Luke*, p. 436; Fitzmyer, *Luke*, p. 874; Nolland, *Luke*, vol. II, p. 573; cf. Deutsch, *Hidden Wisdom and the Easy Yoke*, pp. 47–9.

[65] Carson, 'Matthew', p. 274; Davies and Allison, *Matthew*, vol. II, p. 277; Deutsch, *Hidden Wisdom and the Easy Yoke*, pp. 28–9. Gnilka argues that the ταῦτα of v. 25 is explained in v. 27: that Jesus, the Son, is the revealer of God (*Matthäusevangelium*, vol. I, p. 435). This may have been the meaning if the saying is isolated, but even studies of Q have suggested an eschatological-christological understanding (Hoffmann, *Studien zur Theologie der Logienquelle*, p. 110, cf. pp. 131–3, who takes it to refer to the Son of Man; Boring, *Sayings of the Risen Jesus*, p. 151; Schulz, *Q: Die Spruchquelle der Evangelisten*, pp. 217–18).

[66] Kingsbury, *Matthew: Structure, Christology, Kingdom*, pp. 64–5; cf. Verseput, 'The Role and Meaning of the "Son of God" Title in Matthew's Gospel', p. 543.

as meek and lowly one, Jesus as bestower of eschatological salvation-rest (cf. 4 Ezra 7.36, 38; 8.52; Heb. 4.1–13),[67] who is presented here. G. N. Stanton defends an association between this verse and Matthew's use of Isaiah 42.1–4 in Matthew 12.18–21, suggesting that the invitation of v. 28 is issued by 'Jesus as the humble Servant of God on whom God's Spirit rests'.[68] In support of this note the Isaianic background to Jesus' miraculous ministry in 8.17 and 11.3–6; and the connection between Jesus as Son and Servant which was earlier also found in Matthew 3.17 cf. 17.5 (not, of course, at this point associated with a *suffering* Servant figure). This Jesus calls the weary and heavy-laden into discipleship.[69] This passage thus looks forward to the great commission (28.19f) and clearly does play an important role in Matthew's overall christological presentation.

> In this passage there are numerous other aspects which can only be mentioned here: Jesus' yoke (of discipleship) displaces the yoke of Torah (cf. Jer. 5.5; Sir. 51.23–26; Acts 15.10; 2 Enoch 34.1; 2 Bar. 41.3f; *m. 'Abot* 3.5f; *'Abot R. Nat.* 20); Jesus is identified with Wisdom (Deutsch, *Hidden Wisdom and the Easy Yoke*; Dunn, *Christology in the Making*, p. 210; Suggs, *Wisdom, Christology and Law in Matthew's Gospel*, p. 96), although this is questioned by Stanton, 'Matthew 11.28–30: Comfortable Words?'; Kynes, *A Christology of Solidarity*, pp. 89–91, who prefer to speak either of Matthew's 'use of some Wisdom themes' (Stanton, 'Matthew 11.28–30: Comfortable Words?', p. 6) or of Jesus as 'the fulfillment of Wisdom' (Kynes, *A Christology of Solidarity*, p. 91).

Matthew 14.33 has already been discussed in chapter five (section 2.4). It was there noted that the theophanic elements in the context combine with the worshipful confession of the disciples to suggest a 'more than messianic' use of 'Son of God' on the lips of the disciples.

Matthew's version of the confession at Caesarea Philippi reports the words of Peter as Σὺ εἶ ὁ Χριστὸς ὁ υἱὸς τοῦ θεοῦ τοῦ ζῶντος (Matt. 16.16). This expands the confession in Mark by the addition of 'Son of the living God'. Since the issue at stake in the passage is the identity of Jesus (cf. 16.13f), the expansion of the confession is important for Matthew. Several factors suggest that

---

[67] Bacchiocchi, 'Matthew 11:28–30: Jesus' Rest and the Sabbath', pp. 296–9; Davies and Allison, *Matthew*, vol. II, pp. 288–9.

[68] Stanton, 'Matthew 11.28–30: Comfortable Words?', pp. 371–2, cf. Deutsch, *Hidden Wisdom and the Easy Yoke*, p. 37; and Neyrey, 'The Thematic Use of Isa 42.1–4 in Matthew 12' for the influence of Isa. 42.1–1 on Matt. 12.

[69] Not into sonship (against Kynes, *A Christology of Solidarity*, p. 99).

Matthew's emphasis falls on the confession of Jesus as divine Messiah:[70]

(i)   the previous use of 'sonship' terminology in 11.27 and 14.33;

(ii) Jesus' express commendation: this confession comes by a revelation from the Father (v. 17). This in particular suggests a link with the unique relational sonship of 11.27;

(iii) the implication that this is also the foundation of the church (v. 18f).[71]

Nevertheless, there is no opposition between 'messianic' and 'sonship' categories in Matthew; recall the opening chapters, where 'Son of God' is present in tandem with a strong emphasis on Jesus' Davidic descent and royal status, cf. 1.1, 16f; 2.5f. The only other occurrence of this titular combination is in the chief priest's request in Matthew 26.63 (ἵνα ἡμῖν εἴπῃς εἰ σὺ εἶ ὁ Χριστὸς ὁ υἱὸς τοῦ θεοῦ) where it presumably refers to a messianic category, parallel to 'King of the Jews' (27.37, 42). In addition, Matthew concludes the confession pericope (16.20) with Jesus' command to the disciples that they tell no one that αὐτός ἐστιν ὁ Χριστός, thus placing the emphasis, in a redactional addition, on the 'messianic' nature of the revelation.[72] Matthew's aim is to present Jesus as both unique Son of the Father and as the royal Davidic Messiah. Indeed, Verseput argues that Matthew uses the filial associations of 'Son of God' to christianise the presentation of Jesus as humble, obedient, Davidic Messiah in the face of Israel's rejection.[73] Matthew thus exploits the ambiguity of the title 'Son of God' (cf. the background information discussed earlier).

In addition, the continuation of the narrative clearly reveals that confession of Jesus as 'Son of God' is not sufficient or complete without an appreciation of his necessary suffering (16.21–3). The

---

[70] Lagrange, *Matthieu*, p. 322; Hill, *Matthew*, p. 260; Beare, *Matthew*, p. 352; Kingsbury, *Matthew: Structure, Christology, Kingdom*, p. 67; Davies and Allison, *Matthew*, vol. II, p. 621; Gundry, *Matthew*, pp. 330–1; cf. Bornkamm, 'Enderwartung und Kirche im Matthäusevangelium', pp. 43–4 (ET, pp. 47–8).

[71] Kingsbury, *Matthew: Structure, Christology, Kingdom*, p. 67. At the very least it must be confessing Peter who is the foundation (Kynes, *A Christology of Solidarity*, p. 104); see also Caragounis, *Peter and the Rock* (with a survey of scholarship).

[72] Kynes, *A Christology of Solidarity*, pp. 102–3; Caragounis, *Peter and the Rock*, p. 110.

[73] Verseput, 'The Role and Meaning of the "Son of God" Title in Matthew's Gospel'.

contrast between Peter's confession (v. 16), revealed by the Father
(v. 17); and Peter's rebuke (v. 22), thinking along human lines (v.
23), is stark and indicates clearly that Peter's confession in
Matthew (as in Mark) does not yet reflect a complete understanding. The passage recalls the temptations of 4.1–11.

In a further three passages Matthew takes over sonship terminology from Mark (Matt. 17.5 // Mark 9.7; Matt. 21.37 // Mark
12.6; Matt. 24.36 // Mark 13.32). The last two of these passages we
shall not discuss, as there are few significant differences between
Matthew and Mark at these points (assuming that the text of Matt.
24.36 in NA27 = UBS4 is correct). The parable of the vineyard
(Matt. 21.33–46) has a distinct importance for Matthew, but this is
not closely related to the 'Son' of 21.37. In the transfiguration
narrative as a whole, however, Matthew does make several alterations to Mark's account, and these include, *inter alia*:[74]

   (i)   addition of Jesus' face shining like the sun (17.2);

> This is one of a series of agreements between Matthew and Luke against
> Mark (see Neirynck, 'Minor Agreements Matthew–Luke in the Transfig-
> uration Story'). Some have suggested an additional source in addition to
> Mark (McGuckin, *The Transfiguration of Christ in Scripture and Tradi-
> tion*, pp. 5–14; Schramm, *Der Markus-Stoff bei Lukas*, pp. 136–9), others
> identify this source with Matthew (Gundry, *Matthew*, p. 346); but inde-
> pendent redaction of Mark (often developing Markan themes) seems the
> best option on the two-source hypothesis (Neirynck, 'Minor Agreements
> Matthew-Luke in the Transfiguration Story'; Davies and Allison,
> *Matthew*, vol. II, p. 685; Carson, 'Matthew', p. 383). Luz wavers between
> these two options (*Matthäusevangelium*, vol. II, p. 506).

  (ii)   use of κύριε in Peter's address (v. 4 cf. Mark's ῥαββί);

 (iii)   addition of ἐν ᾧ εὐδόκησα to the voice from the cloud,
        bringing Matthew's form into direct parallel with the
        baptismal voice (this also involves incorporating an allu-
        sion to Isa. 42.1, which is cited in Matt. 12.18: εἰς ὅν
        εὐδόκησεν).[75] B. Przybylski suggests that the transfigura-
        tion is presented as God's answer to the devil's question in
        4.6, thus establishing links between the temptation and
        transfiguration;[76]

---

[74] For fuller listings: Donaldson, *Jesus on the Mountain*, p. 269, n. 77; Gundry,
    Matthew, pp. 342–345.
[75] Davies and Allison, *Matthew*, vol. II, p. 702; Gundry, *The Use of the Old
    Testament in St Matthew's Gospel*, pp. 35–6.
[76] 'The Role of Mt 3:13–4:11 in the Structure and Theology of the Gospel of
    Matthew', pp. 227–8.

(iv)   addition of the disciples' response to this voice (cf. Mark
       9.6): falling on their faces, καὶ ἐφοβήθησαν σφόδρα
       (σφόδρα is Matthean (7–1–1); for ἐφοβήθησαν σφόδρα as
       a response to a revelation of Jesus as 'Son of God' cf.
       Matt. 27.54);
(v)   addition (following the disciples' aweful response) of Jesus'
       approach and statement: Ἐγέρθητε καὶ μὴ φοβεῖσθε. In
       Matthew Jesus three times reassures disciples after a
       moment of revelation with μὴ φοβεῖσθε (14.27; 17.7;
       28.10; cf. Mark 6.50).

Several of these alterations emphasise the theophanic (or perhaps
better 'christophanic') nature of the transfiguration.[77] Commentators have not, however, agreed on the overall intent of the
Matthean redaction: some have emphasised the Moses/Exodus
elements in the passage,[78] others the supposed 'enthronement'
elements,[79] or the eschatological *parousia* setting.[80] It may not be
necessary to select one option; it is clear that many of the elements
of the transfiguration narrative are extremely suggestive, with
manifold associations, echoes and parallels within a first-century
setting, as well as numerous connections between this passage and
others in Matthew (whether by virtue of the mountain setting, the
baptismal echoes, the resurrection narratives, or the context of
16.28). It is not clear that Matthew intends to provide any
interpretative key; as G. B. Caird commented, 'Every detail of the
story is surrounded by so great a wealth of association that
explanations can be multiplied without departing from the bounds
of probability.'[81] Nevertheless, as a redaction of Mark 9.2–10,
Matthew's version does serve to highlight elements of Matthean
interest in a manner that is comparable with Matthew's redaction
of other passages; especially in the allusive use of Isaiah 42.1, and
the general presentation of a divine sonship which transcends
human messianic categories.

---

[77] Grundmann, *Matthäus*, pp. 403–4; Kingsbury, *Matthew: Structure, Christology,
    Kingdom*, p. 68 (building on parallels to 14.22–33).
[78] Gundry entitles the passage: 'Understanding Jesus as the New and Greater
    Moses' (*Matthew*, pp. 342–5); Davies, *The Setting of the Sermon on the Mount*,
    pp. 51–6; Davies and Allison, *Matthew*, vol. II, pp. 685–7.
[79] Donaldson, *Jesus on the Mountain*, pp. 150–1.
[80] Gnilka, *Matthäusevangelium*, vol. II, p. 93; cf. Schweizer, *Matthäus*, p. 227–8
    (ET, p. 349).
[81] Caird, 'The Transfiguration', p. 291.

'Son of God' is used by Matthew in the chief priest's question at the trial (26.63; modifying Mark 14.61: 'Son of the Blessed'). Jesus' response, σὺ εἶπας (Matt. 26.64) is altered from Mark's ἐγώ εἰμι (Mark 14.62) but remains affirmative (cf. Matt. 26.25; 27.11 parallels; John 18.37; as D. R. Catchpole argued, Matt. 27.40 and 43 require the earlier account to involve a positive claim).[82] As with Mark the question is redirected to the coming of the Son of Man. This 'Son of God' is picked up by the bystanders in 27.40b (note the trial context suggested by 27.40a cf. 26.61), and the Jewish leaders in v. 43.[83] Both taunts suggest that Jesus' escape from the cross, involving an allusive reference to the temptation of Jesus (v. 40: εἰ υἱὸς εἶ τοῦ θεοῦ . . . is exactly parallel to 4.3, 6; v. 43 raises the general issue of Jesus' trust in God), and an ironic preparation for the vindication that is to follow.

This sets the scene for Matthew's version of the centurion's statement. When Jesus dies (ἀφῆκεν τὸ πνεῦμα) the temple veil is split (as in Mark), and Matthew adds the enigmatic passage concerning the earthquake and the resurrection of the saints (27.51b–3). Immediately after this the centurion (and those with him – an addition to Mark), as a result of the earthquake (ἰδόντες τὸν σεισμὸν) and the accompanying events (τὰ γενόμενα), experience a revelatory fear (ἐφοβήθησαν σφόδρα) and make their 'confession': Ἀληθῶς θεοῦ υἱὸς ἦ οὗτος. Only the statement itself follows Mark, the rest is added by Matthew.

Clearly the additional material in v. 51b–3, like the tearing of the temple veil, serves to interpret the meaning of Jesus' death. D. P. Senior argues that the tearing of the veil is, for Matthew, a 'symbolic representation of the power of the death of Jesus which brings the Old Testament economy of salvation to a halt *and* opens the way to salvation to all peoples'.[84] The central feature of this section is the raising of the dead 'saints'; the rest is, as Senior notes, either preparatory – the earth shakes, so the rocks split and the tombs open – or consequent – after Jesus' resurrection they depart and come to Jerusalem and appear to many.[85] The events which accompany the raising of the dead are described using traditional imagery of the eschatological coming of Yahweh.

---

[82] Catchpole, 'The Answer of Jesus to Caiaphas (Matt. XXVI.64)', pp. 216–18, p. 226.
[83] Klostermann, *Matthäusevangelium*, p. 233.
[84] Senior, *The Passion Narrative according to Matthew*, p. 311.
[85] Ibid., p. 312.

Earthquakes: Ezekiel 38.19; Joel 2.10; 3.16 (MT 4.16); *As. Mos.* 10.4; 4 Ezra 5.8; 9.3; 2 Baruch 70.8; cf. Mark 13.8; Revelation 6.12; 11.13 (see Bauckham, 'The Eschatological Earthquake in the Apocalypse of John'). Splitting of rocks: Nahum 1.5f. This is clearly also true of resurrection (cf. texts in Str-B, vol. IV, pp. 1175–98; Puech, 'Messianism, Resurrection, and Eschatology at Qumran and in the New Testament').

In particular Matthew seems to be dependent upon an apocalyptic interpretation of Ezekiel 37.1–14.[86] All these 'events' (τὰ γενόμενα) 'form an ensemble of traditional eschatological signs of the last day, the moment of completion of God's salvific activity'.[87] Thus the statement of the centurion and his men serves in Matthew as a confirmation of the identity of Jesus as the 'Son of God' in view of the eschatological significance of his death.[88] Note also that the terms of the 'confession' – ἀληθῶς θεοῦ υἱὸς ἦν οὗτος – is most closely paralleled in the 'confession' of the disciples in Matthew 14.33: ἀληθῶς θεοῦ υἱὸς εἶ.[89]

The so-called Great Commission has been described as Matthew's *'grand finale'*,[90] and as *'the key to the understanding of the whole book'*.[91] In terms of Matthew's christology the passage contains allusions to Daniel 7.13f ('all authority . . .'), to the Emmanuel passage (1.23), and to other elements of Matthean christology (see our earlier discussion, where the key studies were mentioned, p. 141). Our interest, briefly, is in the 'triadic' baptismal formula of v. 19, and the implications of this for Matthew's view of Jesus as 'Son of God'.

We follow here the longer reading of UBS4 = NA27 for Matthew 28.19.

[86] The eschatological interpretation of Ezek. 37 is paralleled in frescos at Dura-Europos (Monasterio, *Exegesis de Mateo, 27,51b–53*, pp. 74–97). See further Senior, 'Matthew's Special Material in the Passion Story', pp. 277–85; Maisch, 'Die österliche Dimension des Todes Jesus. Zur Osterverkündigung in Mt 27,51–54'; Hill, 'Matthew 27,51–53'; de Jonge, 'Matthew 27:51 in Early Christian Exegesis'.

[87] Senior, *The Passion Narrative*, p. 321 (cf. also Senior, 'The Death of Jesus and the Resurrection of the Holy Ones (Matthew 27:51–53'). Cf. Jeremias: 'the shift in the ages has arrived' (*Neutestamentliche Theologie 1*, p. 294 (cited from ET, pp. 309–10)).

[88] 'Confirmation' because, as Senior notes, 'the identity of Jesus as Son of God has been at the forefront throughout the Passion' (*The Passion Narrative*, p. 327).

[89] Lohmeyer, *Matthäus*, p. 397; Mowery, 'Subtle Differences: The Matthean "Son of God" References', p. 196 (who argues that the anarthrous form reflects the confessional langauge of the Matthean community). Other parallels between the accounts (divine manifestation, response of fear, solemn confession of faith) are noted by Senior, *The Passion Narrative*, p. 328.

[90] Stanton, 'Matthew as a Creative Interpreter of the Sayings of Jesus', p. 287, n. 37.

[91] Michel, 'Der Abschluß des Matthäusevangeliums', p. 21 (cited from ET, p. 35).

Eusebius' shorter reading (otherwise unattested): πορευθέντες μαθητεύσατε πάντα τὰ ἔθνη ἐν τῷ ὀνόματι μου, διδάσκοντες . . . (*Demonstratio* 3.6, 7(bis); 9.11; *Hist. eccl.* III.5.2; *Psalms* 65.6; 67.34; 76.20 (59.9 not the same reading); *Isaiah* 18.2; 34.16 (*v.l.*); *Theophania* 4.16; 5.17; 5.46; 5.49; *Oratio* 16.8) is not to be regarded as original (despite Conybeare, 'The Eusebian Form of the Text Matth. 28, 19'; 'Three Early Doctrinal Modifications of the Text of the Gospels', pp. 102–8; *History of New Testament Criticism*, pp. 74–7; Lohmeyer, *Matthäus*, p. 412; Vermes, *Jesus the Jew*, p. 200; H. B. Green, 'The Command to Baptize and Other Matthean Interpolations', pp. 60–6; 'Matthew 28:19, Eusebius, and the *lex orandi*').
The omission of the trinitarian phrase can be explained as due to Eusebius' tendency to abbreviate, as Eusebius elsewhere often cites the longer form (*Contra Marcellum* I.1.9; I.1.36; *Theologia* III. 5.22; *Ep. Caesarea* 3 (Socrates, *Eccl. hist* 1.8); *Psalms* 117.1–4; *Theophania* 4.8). The shorter reading 'in my name' could have been formed as a result of harmonising Luke 24.47 and Mark 16.17 (as seems to occur in *Psalms* 59.9). Note that Eusebius also alludes to this passage without using either 'in my name' or the full clause (*Demonstratio* 1.3, 4, 6; *Psalms* 46.4; 95.3; 144.9; *Isaiah* 41.10; *Theophania* 3.4; *Theologia* III.3). See further Hubbard, *The Matthean Redaction of a Primitive Apostolic Commissioning*, pp. 151–75; Schaberg, *The Father, the Son and the Holy Spirit*, pp. 27–9 (who refer to earlier studies).

In terms of content the triadic 'formula' remains somewhat enigmatic. Kingsbury, in his somewhat overstated attempt to correlate the whole of 28.16–20 around a 'Son of God' theme,[92] has nevertheless pointed out many significant connections with 'Son of God' traditions elsewhere in the gospel: Jesus' baptism included the descent of the Spirit and God's affirmation, 'You are my Son' (cf. the baptismal triad of 28.19); 'all authority has been given to me' echoes 11.27, 'all things have been given to me',[93] and could be taken as a reference to the establishment of Jesus' Davidic rule over all nations (cf. Ps. 2.8).[94] In addition the universal authority of the resurrected Jesus corresponds to the third temptation.[95] This creates a final scene which provided a counterfoil to Matthew's opening, 'Son of David, Son of Abraham', in terms of the lordship of the Davidic Messiah, and the fulfilment of the promise to Abraham that all nations would be blessed. While we should not regard the 'formula' of 28.19 as a witness to a fully developed trinitarian faith, it is nevertheless clear that the association of the

[92] 'The Composition and Christology of Matt. 28:16–20'.
[93] Lange described 28.16–20 as 'einer Neuauflage von Mt 11,27/Lk 10,22' (*Das Erscheinen des Auferstandenen im Evangelien nach Matthäus*, p. 488).
[94] Donaldson, *Jesus on the Mountain*, pp. 181–2.
[95] Przybylski, 'The Role of Mt 3:13–4:11 in the Structure and Theology of the Gospel of Matthew', pp. 228–30; Wilkens, 'Die Versuchung Jesu nach Matthäus', pp. 485–6.

father, the son and the holy spirit with the one name goes somewhat beyond the rest of the gospel in the direction of Christian trinitarianism.

> Gundry argued that Matthew introduced trinitarian ideas at 3.16 and 12.28 (*Matthew*, pp. 52, 235). We might also note the connection between 28.19a and the mission discourse in Matt. 10, where the promise was given that when sent out by Jesus and dragged before the Gentiles for his sake 'the Spirit of your Father [will be] speaking through you' (10.20, cf. vv. 16–18).
> Schaberg argues that the triad is drawn from the triad of Dan 7: the Ancient of Days, the Son of Man and the angels (cf. Matt. 24.36 parallel; 25.31–46; Mark 8.38; 13.36–43; Luke 12.8f, listed in *The Father, the Son and the Holy Spirit: The Triadic Phrase in Matthew 28:19b*, p. 286). While not 'trinitarian', it stands in a line of development which leads or 'impels' (Schaberg's term, p. 336) towards such a conception. There are, of course, comparable statements within the NT, containing an implicit trinitarianism, e.g. 1 Corinthians 12.4–6; 2 Corinthians 13.14; Ephesians 4.4–6; 2 Thessalonians 2.13f; 1 Peter 1.2; Revelation 1.4–6 (Wainwright, *The Trinity in the New Testament*, pp. 241–7 cf. *Didache* 7.1–13; Justin, *Apology* 61).

Matthew has repeatedly suggested that Jesus' divine sonship is of a peculiarly elevated type, and the formula here 'reflects the superior appropriateness of the Sonship category for expressing the relationship of Jesus to God'.[96]

In general, Matthean redaction, assuming Markan priority, is explicable in terms of his use of Markan material and the addition of new material. Matthew's approach includes the use of additional OT background (both in 'Israel/Son of God' material, and an allusive use of Isa. 42 in several places), the 'levelling' of the narrative (in the sense that Jesus is confessed as 'Son of God' in several places whereas in Mark it is held back until 15.39), an increased emphasis on Jesus' relationship as Son to the Father, and the use of similar phrases in different parts of the gospel. Matthew clearly relates Jesus' sonship to his humble obedience to the Father (4.1–11, in contrast to Israel; 17.5; cf. 27.40, 43, ironically);[97] this same attitude of humble obedience is elsewhere in Matthew associated with a presentation of Jesus as the Spirit-endowed Servant of God (3.17; 11.4–6; 12.18–21). Such associations have been seen in our previous chapters and suggest that, although complex, Matthew's redactional procedure can be regarded as coherent and results in a multi-faceted presentation of Jesus as 'the Son of God'.

---

[96] Verseput, 'The Role and Meaning of the "Son of God" Title in Matthew's Gospel', p. 541.
[97] Ibid., pp. 542–7.

5. Conclusion

Once again we have discovered that the Griesbach hypothesis faces some difficulties in explaining Griesbach-Mark's redactional procedures. His behaviour is not particularly consistent, nor is it readily explicable. On the other hand Matthean preferences assuming Markan priority do seem to be generally consistent. It is not so easy to point to additional external features which might render Matthean redaction more plausible. For example, some statements in the epistles are similar to the triadic shape of Matthew 28.19, but these statements are probably earlier than the gospels. Nevertheless, a development could be traced in the later period towards (rather than away from) 'trinitarian' formulations and an emphasis on Jesus as divine Son of God.

> No clear evidence occurs within the first century. Ignatius used trinitarian expressions (e.g. *Eph.* 9.1; *Magn.* 13.1; *Phld.* prol.) and regarded 'Son of God' as a divine title (*Eph.* 7.2; 20; *Smyrn.* 1.1). But his distance from synoptic christology is evident in his use of θεός of Jesus (*Eph.* prol.; 18.2; *Rom.* prol.; 3.3; *Smyrn.* 1.1; *Pol.* 8.2).

In both of these areas Matthew's redaction of Mark 'fits' the expected pattern more than the other alternative. One could also argue that Matthew, to a greater extent than Mark, brings a breadth of gospel traditions into alignment with the christology exhibited in the epistles. Scribal preference for inclusion of 'Son of God', although based on only a few passages, also fits with Matthew's inclusion of additional references (on the two-source hypothesis) rather than Mark's omission of them (on the Griesbach hypothesis).

Matthew's procedure, on the two-source hypothesis, might be compared with that of Luke, who follows all of the occurrences of 'Son of God' in Mark and Q with two exceptions and two additions. The two exceptions are Mark 13.32 (a passage not reproduced by Luke) and Mark 15.39 which Luke 23.47 renders ὄντως ὁ ἄνθρωπος οὗτος δίκαιος ἦν (in accord with a broader thematic interest in the innocence of Jesus, cf. 23.4, 14f, 22, 34, 41).[98] The additional references occur in relation to the birth of Jesus: Jesus will be called 'the Son of God' as a consequence of the Spirit's operation at conception (Luke 1.35; cf. v. 32); and the genealogy is traced back to God (3.38, cf. v. 23); a further two

---

[98] Schmidt, 'Luke's "Innocent" Jesus: A Scriptural Apologetic'.

references in Acts 9.20 and 13.33 (in Paul's speeches) suggest that this title was not the most important in Luke's repertoire. Luke's procedure is explicable, and supplies a parallel model to Matthew's use of additional references to further his own particular interests. Luke, like Matthew, reflects a shift in emphasis from Mark (not as a reaction, but as a plausible development) and represents a further 'Christianising' of the traditions.

11

JESUS AS 'THE SON OF MAN'

1. Introduction

Ὁ υἱὸς τοῦ ἀνθρώπου is the most prolific christological title in the canonical gospels; where, whatever may be said about its origins and Aramaic background, it clearly functions in a titular manner.[1] Ὁ υἱὸς τοῦ ἀνθρώπου has also emerged as one of the most interesting and difficult problems in NT scholarship; B. Lindars, for example, described it as 'the great centre of debate in New Testament studies in the twentieth century'.[2] The sayings of Jesus which include reference to ὁ υἱὸς τοῦ ἀνθρώπου were divided by R. Bultmann into three groups, 'which speak of the Son of Man (1) as coming, (2) as suffering death and rising again, and (3) as now at work'.[3] This division has been widely, although not universally, accepted and C. Caragounis provides a helpful table listing the total number of sayings in each of the three categories:[4]

	Earthly life	Sufferings	Exaltation	Total
Matt.	7	10	13	30
Mark	2	9	3	14
Luke	7	8	10	25
	16	27	26	69

---

[1] Dunn, *Christology in the Making*, p. 66; Geist, *Menschensohn und Gemeinde*, p. 71.

[2] Lindars, *Jesus Son of Man*, p. 1. See: Higgins, 'Son of Man-*Forschung* since "The Teaching of Jesus"' (1959); Vermes, 'The Present State of the "Son of Man" Debate' (1978); Walker, 'The Son of Man: Some Recent Developments' (1983); Donahue, 'Recent Studies on the Origin of "Son of Man" in the Gospels' (1986); Burkett, 'The Nontitular Son of Man: A History and Critique' (1994).

[3] Bultmann, *Theologie des Neuen Testaments*, p. 31 (cited from ET, vol. I, p. 30), cf. earlier Foakes-Jackson and Lake, *The Beginnings of Christianity*, vol. I, pp. 375–6.

[4] Caragounis, *The Son of Man. Vision and Interpretation*, p. 146. For questions about the appropriateness of these divisions see Hooker, *The Son of Man in Mark*,

It is obvious from this evidence that Mark has a majority of sayings which relate to the Son of Man's suffering, amounting to two-thirds of his sayings, compared to about one-third of those in Matthew and Luke. By way of contrast, both Matthew and Luke have approximately equal numbers of sayings in each of the three groups. These and other considerations suggest that different views concerning the origin and development of the Son of Man sayings can affect conclusions drawn about the growth of the synoptic tradition and the resolution of the synoptic problem.

A recent example of this is W. O. Walker's claim that the Son of Man phenomenon supports the Griesbach hypothesis over the two-source hypothesis ('The Son of Man Question and the Synoptic Problem', p. 379). Following N. Perrin, Walker locates the origin of the Son of Man title and concept in Christian reflection on Daniel 7.13 within the Greek-speaking church.[5] He argues that the earliest sayings are those with an eschatological focus; the other types, dealing with both the earthly life and suffering of Jesus, are secondary and derivative, and the concept never became widely established within early Christianity (pp. 375–6). This movement from eschatology to suffering is, considering the higher proportion of suffering sayings in Mark, best reflected in Mark's use of Matthew and Luke (pp. 378–9).

Walker argues that none of the Son of Man sayings are authentic (p. 376), but his conclusions do not depend on this.[6] A similar argument could be based on Bultmann's view that some of the future sayings (Mark 8.38; Luke 12.8f; 17.23f, 30; Matt. 24.27 parallel; 24.37–9 parallel; 24.43f parallel) went back to Jesus, who expected a future coming of the Son of Man as someone other than himself, since Bultmann also argued that the passion and present sayings developed later.[7] Within such a context the preponderance

---

p. 80; 'Is the Son of Man Problem Really Insoluble?', pp. 159–60; Maddox, 'The Function of the Son of Man according to the Synoptic Gospels', pp. 73–4.

[5] Perrin, 'Mark XIV.62: The End Product of a Christian Pesher Tradition?'; 'The Son of Man in Ancient Judiasm and Primitive Christianity: A Suggestion'; 'The Creative Use of the Son of Man Traditions by Mark'; 'The Son of Man in the Synoptic Tradition'; cf. Walker, 'The Origin of the Son of Man Concept as applied to Jesus'; 'The Son of Man: Some Recent Developments'.

[6] Cf. Walker, 'The Son of Man: Some Recent Developments', pp. 589–95 following *inter alia* Vielhauer, 'Gottesreich und Menschensohn in der Verkündigung Jesu'; 'Jesus und der Menschensohn'; 'Ein Weg der neutestamentlichen Theologie?', pp. 26–8.

[7] Bultmann, *Theologie des Neuen Testaments*, pp. 29–31 (ET, vol. I, pp. 29–30); cf. *Die Geschichte der synoptischen Tradition*, p. 163 (ET, pp. 151–2).

of future sayings in Matthew and Luke, over against the preponderance of suffering sayings in Mark, could support the contention that Matthew and Luke were earlier than Mark. Bultmann himself did not, of course, make this argument; he regarded the development as having already taken place before the composition of the gospels.

From a different perspective some scholars have regarded the 'present' sayings (with possibly some of those concerning the suffering of Jesus) as the earliest and only authentic group.[8] This view regards the influence of Daniel 7.13 and the apocalyptic associations as secondary developments in the tradition. Markan priority would be the most plausible explanation for the phenomenon on this understanding, since Matthew and Luke have a much higher proportion of 'future' sayings, and clearer associations with Daniel 7.13.[9]

2. Background considerations

Since it is apparent that different perspectives on the origin and background of the term Son of Man lead to different analyses of the synoptic problem some attempt must here be made, albeit briefly, to address two key issues: the use of *br nš* and related terms in Aramaic literature, and the use of Daniel 7.13 within first-century Judaism.

Up until 1967 it had been customary to accept that 'Son of Man' was a known messianic title within apocalyptic Judaism influenced by Daniel 7.13f.[10] In 1967 G. Vermes concluded that no trace could be found of the use of the terms *br nš* and/or *br nš'* (indefinite/definite) as a messianic designation ('The Use of בר נש / בר נשא in Jewish Aramaic', p. 327).[11] In Jewish Aramaic sources, he argued,

---

[8] Thus Lindars, *Jesus Son of Man*, and *mutatis mutandis* Vermes, *Jesus the Jew*, pp. 160–91; 'The Use of בר נש / בר נשא in Jewish Aramaic'; 'The Present State of the "Son of Man" Debate'; Casey, *The Son of Man: The Interpretation and Influence of Daniel 7*; 'General, Generic and Indefinite: The Use of the Term "Son of Man" in Aramaic Sources and in the Teaching of Jesus'.

[9] See Hooker, 'The Son of Man and the Synoptic Problem', pp. 193–4, in response to Walker (although Hooker does not adopt the Vermes–Lindars position).

[10] See, for example, Cullmann, *Die Christologie des Neuen Testaments*, p. 153 (ET, p. 150); Tödt, *Der Menschensohn in der synoptischen Überlieferung*, p. 19 (ET, p. 22); Hahn, *Christologische Hoheitstitel*, p. 22 (ET, p. 20). Leivestad ('Der Apokalyptische Menschensohn ein theologische Phantom') and Hooker (*The Son of Man in Mark*) both concurrently rejected the notion of an apocalyptic Son of Man figure. For earlier nontitular approaches see Burkett, 'The Nontitular Son of Man: A History and Critique'.

[11] Cf. also Fitzmyer: 'I could not agree more' ('The New Testament Title "Son of Man" Philologically Considered', p. 153); Lindars, *Jesus Son of Man*, p. 8.

three interchangeable types of usage could be found: perhaps the most common, certainly in the Targums, is of 'a human being'. Secondly, it could be used as an indefinite pronoun signifying 'everyone', 'anyone', 'someone', 'some people', or 'a certain man'. The third category advocated by Vermes is that of a circumlocution for 'I', and he offered eleven examples (pp. 321–6):

> *Gen. Rab.* 7.2; *Num. Rab.* 19.3; *y. Ber.* 5c (twice: lines 24ff
> from bottom and lines 29ff); *Frg. Tg.* Gen. 4.14; *y. Ber.* 5b
> (lines 5ff from bottom); *y. Ketub.* 35a (lines 9ff); *Gen. Rab.*
> 38.13; *y. Ber.* 3b (esp cf. *y. Šabb.* 3a); *y. Šebu.* 38d (lines
> 24ff) // *Gen. Rab.* 79.6.

Vermes' investigation has been extremely influential, setting the agenda for numerous other studies. The circumlocutionary use has been the most disputed: J. A. Fitzmyer argued that none of Vermes' examples could be dated with any certainty to the first century;[12] while P. M. Casey argued that the supposed circumlocutionary idiom is really a type of general statement.[13] B. Lindars divided the circumlocutionary uses of *bar enash(a)* into three ways of referring to oneself: the one which is most characteristic of Jesus is 'an idiomatic use of the generic article, in which the speaker refers to a class of persons, with whom he identifies himself'.[14] The importance of the other categories, doubtless well attested in Aramaic, for the study of Jesus and the gospels remains disputed.[15] Several recent studies have returned to the question of the messianic associations of Daniel 7.13.

Vermes himself had recognised that 'mainstream Jewish interpretative tradition recognised Daniel 7:9–14 from the second century AD at least, but almost certainly even earlier, as a Messianic text'.[16]

The relevant texts include *b. Sanh.* 38b (// *b. Hag.* 14a, Akiba, d. AD 132); *b. Sanh.* 98a (R. Joshua (AD III)); *Midr. Num.* 13.14 (on Num. 7.13);

---

[12] Fitzmyer, 'Book Review: Matthew Black, *An Aramaic Approach to the Gospels and Acts*', pp. 426–7; 'The New Testament Title "Son of Man" Philologically Considered', pp. 149–52; for Vermes' response see *Jesus the Jew*, pp. 190–1; 'The Present State of the "Son of Man" Debate', pp. 127–30.

[13] Casey, *The Son of Man*, pp. 224–8; 'General, Generic and Indefinite'.

[14] Lindars, *Jesus Son of Man*, p. 24.

[15] Fitzmyer identified further examples of both categories in Qumran ('The New Testament Title "Son of Man" Philologically Considered', p. 148): 1QapGen 21.13; 11QtgJob 26.3; 9.9 (all these take the form *br 'nš* or *br 'nwš*, that is, with an initial *aleph*). Burkett argues that the whole nontitular line of research is a dead end, 'The Nontitular Son of Man: A History and Critique'.

[16] Vermes, *Jesus the Jew*, p. 172.

Midr. Ps. 21.5 (R. Samuel (*c.* 260)); *'Ag. Ber.* 14.3; 23.1; *Midr. HG.* Gen.
49.10; see Str-B, vol. I, pp. 956–7; Moore, *Judaism*, vol. II, pp. 336–7;
Horbury, 'The Messianic Associations of "The Son of Man"', pp. 45–6;
Casey, *The Son of Man*, pp. 86–90. Christian writers claim knowledge of
Jewish messianic exegesis of Dan. 7.13f: Justin, *Dial.* 32 (challenged by
Higgins, 'Jewish Messianic Beliefs in Justin Martyr's *Dialogue with
Trypho*', pp. 301–2); Lactantius, *Div. inst.* IV.12.12; Eusebius, *Demon-
stratio* 9.17.4–7; Jerome, *Daniel, passim* (Casey, *The Son of Man*, p. 84).

Even earlier evidence has recently been surveyed by W. Horbury,
who argues that Daniel 7.13f, with its reference to 'one like a Son
of Man', had 'established messianic associations' in the first
century.[17] While this cannot be discussed at length, the two major
pieces of evidence are worth noting here.

1 Enoch 37–71 (pre AD 100, see below) alludes to Daniel 7 in
connection with a figure called 'that Son of Man' (1 Enoch 46.1–5;
48.2; 62.5–9, 14; 63.11; 69.27–9; 70.1; 71.17).[18] He is an individual
figure, characterised by righteousness and victory, is often seen
seated on the throne of glory (62.5; 69.29), and is associated with
the Lord of the Spirits (69.29). The *Similitudes* apparently identify
this figure with 'the Elect One' (also characterised by righteousness,
39.6; 53.6; on the throne of glory, 45.3; 49.4; 51.3; 55.4; with the
Lord of the Spirits, 49.2, 4; 52.9; and judge of the people of God,
55.4; 61.8,9) and the 'Messiah' (associated with the Lord of the
Spirits, 48.10; who had authority on earth, 52.4).[19] The basic
function of the Son of Man figure (that of eschatological judge)
arises from a twofold OT background: (a) 'no idle word shall be
spoken before him' (1 Enoch 49.4; 62.3) comes from an Isaianic
background (Isa. 11.1ff); and (b) 'he sits on the throne of glory'
(1 Enoch 45.3 etc.) comes from Psalm 110.[20]

> Although the date is uncertain, partly owing to the absence of any
> fragments of this section from Qumran (eleven separate manuscripts,
> Milik, *The Books of Enoch*, p. 6; but only amounting to 5 per cent of total
> document, Ullendorf and Knibb, 'Review of Milik, *The Books of Enoch*',

[17] Horbury, 'The Messianic Associations of "The Son of Man"', p. 36; cf. also
Collins, 'The "Son of Man" in First Century Judaism'.

[18] Beale, *The Use of Daniel in Jewish Apocalyptic Literature*, pp. 97–100; Theisohn,
Der auserwählte Richter, pp. 14–23. The Ethiopic expressions for Son of Man
vary, probably as a result of non-rigorous translation (Charles, *The Book of
Enoch or 1 Enoch*, pp. 86–7; Caragounis, *The Son of Man*, p. 106, n. 115; Black,
'Aramaic Barnasha and the "Son of Man"', pp. 201–2).

[19] Theisohn, *Der auserwählte Richter*, pp. 31–5; Vanderkam, 'Righteous One,
Messiah, Chosen One, and Son of Man in 1 Enoch 37–71'. 'Righteous One' is a
similar title (used in 38.2, 3(?); 53.6); he is identified with the Elect One (in 53.6;
39.6) and the Son of Man (46.3).

[20] Theisohn, *Der auserwählte Richter*, pp. 53–68; 94–9.

pp. 601–2), it is unlikely to have been effected by Christian influence (Collins, 'The "Son of Man" in First Century Judaism', pp. 451–2; cf. Bamptfylde, 'The Similitudes of Enoch: Historical Allusions' (AD 6); Greenfield and Stone, 'The Enochic Pentateuch and the Date of the Similitudes' (early first century); Mearns, 'Dating the Similitudes of Enoch' (AD 40s); Knibb, 'The Date of the Parables of Enoch: A Critical Review' (late first century); against Milik, *The Books of Enoch*, pp. 91–6 (AD 270)). 1 Enoch 37–71 was known by the author of 4 Ezra (e.g. 4 Ezra 6.49–52//1 Enoch 60.7–9; 4 Ezra 7.32//1 Enoch 51.1; 4 Ezra 7.33//1 Enoch 51.3; 4 Ezra 7.37//1 Enoch 62.1; 4 Ezra 7.125//1 Enoch 62.10; 4 Ezra 13.26//1 Enoch 48.6).

In 4 Ezra 13 (*c.* AD 100[21]) there is a vision dependent upon Daniel 7 in which 'something like the figure of a man' came up out of the sea and 'flew with the clouds of heaven . . .' (4 Ezra 13.3).[22] This figure is the Messiah (13.26 // 12.32), God's Son (13.32, 37, 52), the agent of God's judgement who 'will stand on the top of Mount Zion' (13.35 cf. Ps. 2.6).

Additional, if controversial, evidence of the messianic interpretation of Daniel 7.13f has also been detected in the *Sib. Or.* V.414–33 (reflecting the influence of Dan. 7.13, 14, 22; Num. 24.17ff; Ps. 2.9; Isa. 11.4; 2 Sam. 7.10ff; etc.);[23] the *Tragedy of Ezekiel* 68–89;[24] 4Q246 (an apocalyptic reapplication of Dan. 7);[25] *Tg. Ket.* Psalm 80.16–18 (has a parallelism between 'King Messiah' and 'Son of Man' in Aramaic);[26] Daniel 7.13f LXX (the Son of Man comes as the Ancient of Days);[27] and in targumic additions to Exodus 12.42 (the King Messiah leads the way on top of a cloud).[28]

---

[21] Normally deduced from 1.1 (Metzger, *OTP*, vol. I, p. 520); Stone opts for an earlier date, under Domitian (*Fourth Ezra*, p. 10).

[22] For 4 Ezra's dependence upon Dan. 7 see Myers, *I and II Esdras*, pp. 307–8, 316; Stone, *Fourth Ezra*, pp. 383–4; Lacocque, 'The Vision of the Eagle in 4Esdras, a Rereading of Daniel 7 in the First Century CE'; Collins, 'The "Son of Man" in First Century Judaism', pp. 459–464.

[23] Horbury, 'The Messianic Associations of "The Son of Man"', pp. 44–5.

[24] Robertson, *OTP*, vol. II, p. 811, n. z; van der Horst, 'Moses' Throne Vision in Ezekiel the Dramatist', p. 24; Horbury, 'The Messianic Associations of "The Son of Man"', pp. 42–3.

[25] Collins, 'The *Son of God* Text from Qumran', pp. 69–73; Kim, *'The "Son of Man"' as the Son of God*, pp. 20–2.

[26] McNeil, 'The Son of Man and the Messiah: A Footnote'; Bittner, 'Gott–Menschensohn–Davidssohn: Eine Untersuchung zur Traditionsgeschichte von Daniel 7, 13f', p. 368.

[27] Lust, 'Dan 7.13 and the Septuagint'; Bittner, 'Gott – Menschensohn – Davidssohn', pp. 344–5; Bruce, 'The Oldest Greek Versions of Daniel', pp. 25–6; Rowland, *The Open Heaven*, pp. 98, 101; cf. Stuckenbruck, '"One like a Son of Man as the Ancient of Days" in the Old Greek Recension of Daniel 7, 13'.

[28] Levey, *The Messiah: An Aramaic Interpretation*, pp. 12–13; denied by Casey, *The Son of Man*, p. 90.

Characteristic of both the sure examples and a number of the other texts is the exegetical association between the Son of Man text in Daniel 7.13f and other clearly messianic texts such as Isaiah 11.2–4; Psalms 2 and 110; Numbers 24.17ff. This material suggests that while we should not speak of an independent heavenly 'Son of Man' expectation within apocalyptic Judaism, Daniel 7 *was* related to other OT texts concerning the Messiah within a broad spectrum of early Judaism.[29] 'Son of Man' does not appear anywhere to have functioned as a definitive title on its own, although 'the Son of Man' could function to direct attention back to the vision of Daniel 7 within the context of other messianic passages (particularly Ps. 110, and Ps. 2; Isa. 11; Gen. 49.10; Num. 24.17). Such exegetical combinations should not, therefore (against Walker and Perrin as well as Casey), be regarded as proof of distinctively Christian reflection.[30]

3. 'The Son of Man' in the gospels

It follows from this conclusion that the circumlocutional usage should not be set up in contrast to using 'the Son of Man' as a messianic designation, but might be shown to be consistent with it. The circumlocutional nature of the phrase ὁ υἱὸς τοῦ ἀνθρώπου is clearly apparent in the gospels. First, in terms of the contents of the passages themselves sayings concerning Jesus' earthly life and sufferings are evidently self-referential (most clearly in e.g. Matt. 8.20 // Luke 9.58; Matt. 11.19 // Luke 7.34), and the future sayings are no less so for the evangelists. Secondly, the evidence of parallel passages supports the same conclusion. In several places Matthew uses 'I' or 'me' where Luke has 'Son of Man' (Matt. 5.11 // Luke 6.22; Matt. 10.32 // Luke 12.8). Matthew uses an indirect form αὐτόν (referring to Jesus) when the parallels in both Mark and Luke use the direct form with 'Son of Man' (Matt. 16.21 // Mark 8.31 // Luke 9.22). Matthew also does this in reverse: where Mark and Luke have 'me', Matthew has 'Son of Man' (Matt. 16.13 // Mark 8.27// Luke 9.18). This last is clear evidence of Matthew's understanding of the phrase on any account, since the question is

---

[29] Horbury, 'The Messianic Associations of "The Son of Man"'', p. 36; cf. Hooker, 'Is the Son of Man Problem Really Insoluble?', p. 156.

[30] Casey, *The Son of Man*, pp. 213–17; cf. n. 5 for Walker and Perrin.

repeated and focussed on the disciples in 16.15 with 'me': Ὑμεῖς δὲ τίνα με λέγετε εἶναι; The flexibility of Matthew's usage suggests that the title itself could be added and subtracted from various sayings, without implying that the saying was necessarily invented (something that few studies take adequately into account).

It seems clear that, in the gospels, ὁ υἱὸς τοῦ ἀνθρώπου does not always function as a messianic designation, except in the sense that it always designates Jesus, who is Messiah. It never fits into a 'predication formula'.[31] In other words, no one says to Jesus: 'You are the Son of Man.' It is however, exclusive, in the sense that no one other than Jesus is referred to by the term, and arguably demonstrative, referring the reader to 'that Son of Man', i.e. the Danielic Son of Man, as C. F. D. Moule has suggested.[32] Its inherent ambiguity – 'Son of Man' does not seem to have been clear enough to function as 'a messianic title' without associations – combined with its ability to be both self-referential *and* messianic, means that it is impossible to rule out the authenticity of any particular group of Son of Man sayings. Ultimately of course it is not the presence or absence of 'Son of Man' in a saying which will determine the (in?)authenticity of any particular saying, but a host of factors: theological, historical and critical. Our concern is simply to suggest firstly that no group of sayings be ruled out, and secondly that authentic sayings are probably to be found in all three groups.[33] The features noted above would appear to render the term an ideal vehicle for veiled 'messianic' claims.[34]

[31] For this term see Kingsbury, *Matthew as Story*, p. 96.

[32] Manson, *Studies in the Gospels and Epistles*, pp. 130–1; Moule, 'Neglected Features in the Problem of "the Son of Man" ', reiterated in ' "The Son of Man": Some of the Facts'; Luz, 'The Son of Man in Matthew: Heavenly Judge or Human Christ?', p. 3. This is granted at the level of the gospels by Lindars, *Jesus Son of Man*, p. 11.

[33] With *inter alia* Taylor, *The Names of Jesus*, pp. 25–35; Cranfield, *Mark*, pp. 272–7; Marshall, 'The Synoptic Son of Man Sayings in Recent Discussion'; 'The Son of Man in Contemporary Debate'; 'The Synoptic "Son of Man" Sayings in the Light of Linguistic Study'; Hooker, *The Son of Man in Mark*; 'Is the Son of Man Problem Really Insoluble?'; Moule, *The Origin of Christology*, p. 19; A. Y. Collins, 'The Apocalyptic Son of Man Sayings', pp. 227–8.

[34] Horbury, 'The Messianic Associations of "The Son of Man" ', p. 53; cf. Black, *An Aramaic Approach to the Gospels and Acts*, pp. 328–9; Longenecker, *The Christology of Early Jewish Christianity*, pp. 85–6; Marshall, 'The Son of Man in Contemporary Debate'.

4. 'The Son of Man' in Griesbach-Mark

Attempts to find a common theme in Mark's Son of Man sayings have focussed on the idea of authority.[35] According to M. D. Hooker all the Markan Son of Man sayings are expressions of authority – 'whether it is an authority which is exercised now, which is denied and so leads to suffering, or which will be acknowledged and vindicated in the future' (*The Son of Man in Mark*, p. 180). This theme binds the sayings in the three groups together as the link between suffering and vindication, the authority of the Son of Man 'is in turn proclaimed, denied and vindicated' (p. 181). A further bond is that each saying in Mark 'implies, to a greater or lesser degree, a corporate significance for the term "Son of man"'; in other words, 'the consequences of the Son of man's authority always extend to others' (p. 181).

The high proportion of Son of Man sayings concerned with the passion of Jesus in Mark has already been noted. On the Griesbach hypothesis this emphasis is obtained primarily by the omission of sayings in the other two categories from Matthew and Luke. The importance of the 'passion' sayings for Mark is apparent, particularly the three predictions which link the 'way' section in the middle of Mark (8.31; 9.31; 10.33, cf. our discussion earlier on p. 177). Indeed, most of Mark's suffering Son of Man sayings occur in this section of the gospel (8.31; 9.9, 12, 31; 10.33, 45; exceptions are 14.21(bis), 41). These sayings, although generally labelled 'suffering', often include a reference to the resurrection/vindication which will follow the suffering (8.31; 9.9, 31; 10.33). Two of the exceptions to this rule relate the sufferings to the scriptures (9.12; 14.21), and one of the others focusses on the salvific function of the suffering (10.45). Thus the distinction between this group of sayings and those which relate to a future vindication should not be overdrawn (Hooker, p. 181).

Broadly speaking Mark moves from earthly sayings (2.10, 28), which are given no compositional prominence by Mark,[36] to suffering (as noted above), and from there to the future-orientated sayings (8.38; 13.26; 14.62). These last three sayings have common

---

[35] Hooker, *The Son of Man in Mark: A Study of the Background of the Term 'Son of Man' and its use in St Mark's Gospel*, pp. 178–182; Tödt, *Der Menschensohn in der synoptischen Überlieferung*, pp. 253–4 (ET, pp. 279–80); Coppens, 'Les logia du Fils de l'Homme dans l'evangile de Marc', p. 487.

[36] Tödt, *Der Menschensohn in der synoptischen Überlieferung*, p. 254 (ET, p. 280).

elements, but are not of identical form; they all refer to the Son of Man 'coming'; 8.38: with glory and angels; 13.26: with clouds, power, glory and angels (v. 27); 14.62: power, with clouds. Inasmuch as they refer to a future event (for Mark), it appears to combine elements of vindication (esp. 14.62; but perhaps implicit in the others) with judgement (implied in 8.38 and 13.26). It is in these sayings in particular that the Danielic background to the Markan Son of Man sayings emerges (NB. Dan. 7.13: Son of Man coming with clouds; 7.14: glory, dominion). It is noteworthy, however, that Griesbach-Mark nowhere strengthens the allusion to Daniel 7.13f in 8.38 or 14.62. In Mark 13.26, despite following Matthew 24.29–31 quite closely in the surrounding context, Griesbach-Mark omits the first mention of the Son of Man in Matthew 24.30a and then alters Matthew's clear allusion to Daniel 7.13, τὸν υἱὸν τοῦ ἀνθρώπου ἐρχόμενον ἐπὶ τῶν νεφελῶν τοῦ οὐρανοῦ (= Dan. 7.13LXX), following Luke 21.27 in giving a less allusive version: τὸν υἱὸν τοῦ ἀνθρώπου ἐρχόμενον ἐν νεφέλαις (Mark 13.26; note D and syr[s], presumably under the harmonising influence of Matthew, attest a text closer to Dan 7.13: ἐπὶ τῶν νεφελῶν).

Many of the Son of Man sayings omitted by Mark, assuming the Griesbach hypothesis, are common to both Matthew and Luke and occur within the context of a whole passage omitted by Griesbach-Mark (so, for example, Matt. 8.20 // Luke 9.58; Matt. 11.19 // Luke 7.34; Matt. 12.32 // Luke 12.10; Matt. 12.40 // Luke 11.30; Matt. 24.27, 37, 39 // Luke 17.24, 26, 30; Matt. 24.44 // Luke 12.40). The omission of Son of Man sayings within large-scale omissions also applies to material unique to either Matthew (e.g. 10.23; 13.37, 41; 19.28; 25.31) or Luke (e.g. 17.22; 21.36; 18.8). Although this does affect the overall nature of Mark's use of Son of Man terminology in terms of Markan redaction it is necessary to focus on passages held in common in order to discover any distinctive redactional interests in detail.

Mark 8.27, for example, follows Luke 9.18 in using με rather than Son of Man (as Matt. 16.13), although the rest of Jesus' question, 'Who do men say that I am?', is closer to Matthew. Mark 8.31, on the other hand, follows Luke 9.22 in including Son of Man (rather than Matt. 16.21 indirect). Although the immediate phrases are closer to Luke, the broader context shows Griesbach-Mark's dependence upon Matthew (esp. Mark 8.32f // Matt. 16.22f).[37]

---

[37] De Wette, *Einleitung*, p. 190 (ET, p. 169); Farmer, *The Synoptic Problem*, p. 245.

This procedure might be explained not only as a preference for Luke's wording at these points, but as an attempt to link Jesus' suffering with the Son of Man terminology. Mark 8.38 and 9.31 are additional examples of allegiance to Luke 9.26f for the basic structure of the sentences (although the influence of Matthew's wording is also clear, cf. Matt. 16.27f). The alterations are describable, but it is difficult to find compelling explanations for Griesbach-Mark's preferences in these passages.

Thus at Mark 8.38 one can describe the alterations that Griesbach-Mark must have made to his sources:

   (i)   the basic framework is derived from Luke 9.26 (close parallels in the first part of the verse);
   (ii) he adds ἐν τῇ γενεᾷ ταύτῃ τῇ μοιχαλίδι καὶ ἁμαρτωλῷ (similar to Matt. 12.39; 16.4 with ἁμαρτωλός added (5–6–17));
   (iii) he follows Luke for ὁ υἱὸς τοῦ ἀνθρώπου ἐπαισχυνθήσεται . . . ὅταν ἔλθῃ . . ., but
   (iv) follows Matthew in describing the glory as τοῦ πατρὸς αὐτοῦ and for the phrase μετὰ τῶν ἀγγέλων, before
   (v)   returning to Luke for ἁγίων (a parallel for the omission of Matthew's αὐτοῦ re angels is Mark 13.27 (B D L W it etc.)).

Nevertheless, it is difficult to account for all these alterations on the basis of either vocabulary preferences or theological intentions, since, for example, in 10.37 Mark does follow Matthew in referring to 'your glory'. In general Griesbach-Mark's emphasis on the suffering of the Son of Man is not reflected in his redaction of individual sayings, although it does cohere with other elements of the Markan presentation, as we saw in relation to 'Son of God' in the previous chapter. In addition, if Mark is not opposed to the idea of the Son of Man in a judging role, it is difficult to account for the careful omission of Matthean features from Mark 13 (// Matt. 24). These features are a distinctive element of the Matthean presentation, which is the subject of the next section.

5.   'The Son of Man' in Matthew

Matthew has all the Son of Man sayings of Mark plus two more in the 'suffering' group (Matt. 12.40 and 26.2 – Matthew has no Son of Man in 16.21 // Mark 8.31 although the content of the saying is recorded); five more in the 'earthly' group (Matt. 8.20; 11.19; 12.32; 13.37; 16.13: the first three of these are paralleled in Luke); and ten more in the 'future' group (Matt. 10.23; 13.41; 16.28; 19.28; 24.27, 30 (1st), 37, 39, 44; 25.31). Compared with Mark, Matthew appears more interested in the sayings about the future of the Son of Man (Matthew: thirteen; Mark: three). In addition, Matthew's structure does not emphasise the passion predictions in the way that Mark does, and Matthew omits 'Son of Man' from the first prediction. Two recent studies have suggested that Matthew focusses on the representative and exemplary function of the Son of Man (so M. Pamment), or on the ecclesiological dimension, so H. Geist who argues that the Matthean community understands itself 'als ἐκκλησία des Menschensohnes' ('as the church of the Son of Man').[38] It is not clear that either scholar clarifies the major differences between Matthew and Mark. U. Luz argues that Matthew's special interest is in presenting Jesus, the Son of Man, as judge; this is clearly seen in his redaction of Markan material.[39]

Matthew has important differences from Mark in the three future sayings which they share. In 16.27 (// Mark 8.38) Matthew has a different context for the saying about the Son of Man coming. While in Mark it follows and completes the sentence about being ashamed of Jesus, in Matthew it follows the saying about losing one's life/soul. In Mark the context may imply that the Son of Man will function as judge when he comes, but in Matthew this becomes explicit: καὶ τότε ἀποδώσει ἑκάστῳ κατὰ τὴν πρᾶξιν αὐτοῦ, a phrase which echoes several passages in the OT where Yahweh is said to render to men according to their deeds (Ps. 62.12 (LXX 61.13); Prov. 24.12; Sir. 35.24 (LXX one text)). The appropriation of OT passages which refer to Yahweh's judging is notable: Matthew's Son of Man assumes himself the presidency of the eschatological tribunal.[40]

The situation in Matthew 24.30 (// Mark 13.26) is different from Mark in that the whole context in Matthew 24 has been charged with Son of Man sayings (24.27, 30, 37, 39, 44), introduced by the different wording of 24.3: καὶ τί τὸ σημεῖον τῆς σῆς παρουσίας καὶ συντελείας τοῦ αἰῶνος. The saying of v. 30 has additional elements in Matthew – the sign of the Son of Man, and the loud trumpet –

---

[38] Pamment, 'The Son of Man in the First Gospel'; Geist, *Menschensohn und Gemeinde*, quotation from p. 432.
[39] Luz, 'The Son of Man in Matthew: Heavenly Judge or Human Christ?'
[40] Marguerat, *Le jugement dans l'evangile de Matthieu*, p. 93.

and includes an allusion to Zech. 12.10, producing the neat word play: καὶ τότε κόψονται . . . καὶ ὄψονται . . . This 'sign of the Son of Man' is directly and, by means of assimilating Mark 13.26 to Daniel 7.13, clearly associated with the Danielic coming of the Son of Man,[41] suggesting that the genitive is best taken as epexegetical: the sign is the Son of Man.[42] Elsewhere in this chapter Matthew refers three times to the παρουσία of the Son of Man (Matt. 24.27, 37, 39). Παρουσία is something of a technical term in eschatological contexts, used to refer to Christ and 'his Messianic Advent in glory to judge the world at the end of this age' (BAGD, p. 630). The whole context of the discourse in Matthew 24 supports the contention that Matthew's use of παρουσία includes the idea of Jesus as judge, inasmuch as it appears that the day of Yahweh has been replaced by 'the *parousia* of the Son of Man' (cf. Luke 17.24, 30 which refers to 'the day of the Son of Man').[43]

The third passage is Matthew 26.64 (// Mark 14.62). The content is similar, although the wording of the Daniel citation differs slightly (Matt. with ἐπὶ τῶν νεφελῶν τοῦ οὐρανοῦ follows the LXX; Mark with μετὰ τῶν νεφελῶν τοῦ οὐρανοῦ follows the MT and Theodotion, although note G f¹ 33 itᵃ syrˢ·ᵖ copˢᵃʰ provide a text of Mark harmonised to Matt.). As we discussed previously, Matthew's use of σὺ εἶπας rather than Mark's more direct ἐγώ εἰμι is not meant to obscure the fact that Jesus accepted the ascription 'Son of God', but it does serve to contrast this with Jesus' preference for Son of Man. The most significant difference is Matthew's ἀπ' ἄρτι: '*from now* you will see the Son of Man seated . . .' (cf. Ps. 110.1). Matthew uses the same phrase ἀπ' ἄρτι redactionally in 23.39 and 26.29.[44] Matthew's text implies an immediate vindication, a fulfilment of Daniel 7.13, but also seems to allow for a dual fulfilment.

Similar emphases can be found in the passages unique to Matthew. Matthew 25.31, for example, is obviously to be understood as a coming in judgement at the End. The references to the Son of Man's 'coming', in connection with 'his glory', and 'the throne' clearly allude to Daniel 7. In addition, the allusion to Zechariah 14.5 (LXX 13.13b: καὶ ἥξει κύριος ὁ θεός μου καὶ πάντες οἱ ἅγιοι μετ' αὐτοῦ) is strong, and provides further evidence

---

[41] Geist, *Menschensohn und Gemeinde*, pp. 180–1.
[42] Gnilka, *Matthäusevangelium*, vol. II, p. 329.
[43] Gundry, *Matthew*, p. 486.
[44] Cf. Geist, *Menschensohn und Gemeinde*, p. 334.

that language and themes from the day of Yahweh are applied by Matthew to the coming of the Son of Man. As far as this passage is concerned, the final coming of Jesus is to be understood as a Danielic coming.

The idea of judgement is also present, albeit in a different form, in Matthew 19.28 (which has many parallels with 25.31, including the reference to a glorious throne which also appears in 16.27; cf. 1 Enoch 45.3; 49.4; 51.3; 55.4 'the Elect One'; and 62.5; 69.29 'the Son of Man'). Judgement is exercised by the twelve ἐν τῇ παλιγγενεσίᾳ. If Daniel 7.26f is in view, then this passage probably refers to the disciples as 'governing' in a renewed Israel (cf. BAGD, p. 452, citing 2 Kings 15.5; Ps. 2.10; 1 Macc. 9.73; *Pss. Sol.* 17.29 for this rendering of κρίνω).[45]

Another important passage, already mentioned once, is Matthew 16.27f. Where Mark 9.1 refers to the coming of the Kingdom of God in power, Matthew refers to 'the Son of Man coming in his Kingdom'. Matthew elsewhere equates the Kingdom of God with the Kingdom of the Son of Man. This is most clear in Matthew 13.41, where (in the interpretation of the parable of the weeds, vv. 24–30) that which was introduced as the Kingdom of God (or 'heaven') is identified as the kingdom belonging to the Son of Man (v. 41: 'his kingdom'). In this parable, the Kingdom of the Son of Man is assumed to be in existence even before the coming of the Son of Man in judgement.

It appears, then, that in Matthew the language of Daniel and the coming of the Son of Man can be applied to more than one point of time. In the same way that the Kingdom of God comes and grows gradually and even in fits and starts (6.10; 12.28), so the coming of the Son of Man can be related to various times. The final allusion to Daniel 7.13f, in Matthew 28.18, relates the granting of authority to Jesus after the resurrection, but other passages seem more closely related to the fall of Jerusalem, and others yet to the *parousia* of the Son of Man. It seems that Matthew expects a kind of differentiated fulfilment of Daniel 7.[46]

In general, assuming Markan priority, Matthew has maintained Mark's Son of Man material and added new Son of Man sayings which almost exclusively concern the future and judging role of the Son of Man. Matthew has apparently developed a more sophisti-

---

[45] Gundry, *Matthew*, pp 392–3; cf. Gnilka, *Matthäusevangelium*, vol. II, pp. 171–2.
[46] Davies and Allison, *Matthew*, vol. II, p. 679; cf. Meier, *Matthew*, p. 188.

cated understanding of the relationship between the Kingdom of God and the Son of Man, concepts not specifically related in Mark, focussing on the idea of Jesus as judge.[47] In addition Matthew has related the eschatological judgement of Jesus the Son of Man to the OT language and imagery of the day of Yahweh. Both of these ideas are present (at least implicitly) in Mark, but receive much fuller treatment in Matthew. This second theme is characterised by Matthew's use of various OT passages relating to Yahweh in connection with Jesus the Son of Man (Ps. 62; Zech. 14 etc.).

On these accounts Matthew's redaction of Mark is coherent, in that the additions reflect a broad pattern of Matthean thinking and his unique material shares ideas with his alterations of Markan sayings. In addition, the OT has been shown repeatedly to be basic to Matthew's redactional activity. Matthew's redactional activity might also be rendered plausible by several considerations. At a general level the use of additional apocalyptic language and imagery in the redaction of gospel traditions is also attested in *Gos. Pet.*, and this coheres with the tendency observed in Matthew.[48] On a more specific level Matthean redaction of Mark, with his interest in the judging role of the Son of Man, is reflected quite closely in the movement of thought from Daniel to 1 Enoch, which also emphasises the kingly authority and judging activity of the Son of Man.[49]

6. Conclusion

If Matthew's activity (assuming Markan priority) can be understood as both coherent and plausible, it is not the case with the Griesbach hypothesis. Mark would have abbreviated the presentation of his sources in every area except that of the suffering Son of Man. This Markan emphasis on the way of the cross provides a plausible explanation for some of the redactional characteristics of Griesbach-Mark. Difficulties involved in, for example, his omission of allusions to the OT might be explained as a general tendency in

[47] Luz, 'The Son of Man in Matthew: Heavenly Judge or Human Christ?', p. 7; Davies and Allison, *Matthew*, vol. II, p. 51.

[48] Hooker noted the tendency towards emphasising the apocalyptic and eschatological element in the sayings in Hooker, *The Son of Man in Mark*, pp. 186, 195–6; cf. also 'Is the Son of Man Problem Really Insoluble?', pp. 161–2.

[49] Cf. also Hooker, 'The Son of Man and the Synoptic Problem', p. 199. Theisohn, of course, argued that Matthew was directly influenced by 1 Enoch (*Der auserwählte Richter*, pp. 158–201).

view of a Gentile audience. In view of the fact, however, that Mark moves from suffering sayings to future sayings in the later chapters it is difficult to explain his redaction of the Matthean material, especially since the redaction apparently involves omitting information on the judging role of 'Son of Man' and replacing it with less specific teaching (Mark 8.38 and chapter 13).

Throughout the last four chapters the inability of the Griesbach hypothesis to provide a coherent and plausible account of the redactional activity of Griesbach-Mark has been regularly observed. This is particularly emphasised in comparison with the view of Matthean redaction implied when Markan priority is assumed. This current chapter is no exception and concludes our discussion of christological titles. The conclusion awaits, and will probably not surprise anyone who has read thus far. Nevertheless an important topic must still be tackled, one which could yet provide the Griesbach hypothesis with the rationale it needs to explain Markan redaction. That is the general topic of the messianic secret.

12

THE MESSIANIC SECRET

1. Introduction

The importance of the secrecy motif in Markan christology and the suggestion referred to previously that such a motif might explain the redactional perspective taken by Griesbach-Mark require an investigation of this topic here. In this connection it is noteworthy that W. Wrede himself, looking back on his investigation of Mark's secrecy material, could write: 'those who find essentially convincing the view of Mark here expounded will probably be easily led to doubt the priority of Mark in relation to Matthew and Luke'. He went on to comment that it would be 'most highly desirable' if such a gospel as Mark were not the oldest gospel ('Wünschenswert wäre es in der That im höchsten Grade . . .').[1]

W. R. Farmer suggested that Wrede, by virtue of an uncritical assumption of Markan priority, had therefore missed the very opportunity to which his study of Mark had led – Markan posteriority.[2] Farmer's point, however, is clearly invalid: notwithstanding the comment cited above and Wrede's dependence upon Griesbachian scholars, Wrede gives no impression of an *uncritical* acceptance of Markan priority: 'Certain supports for according priority to Mark . . . have shown themselves unsound. But even if these collapse sufficient props of better timber remain.'[3] In support of Markan priority Wrede appealed to the narrative order of Mark as foundational for both Matthew and Luke; he also believed that his discussion of Matthew's treatment of the secrecy material, involving as it did an examination of Matthean redaction of the

---

[1] Wrede, *Das Messiasgeheimnis in den Evangelien*, p. 148 (ET, p. 148).
[2] Farmer, 'The Two-Document Hypothesis as a Methodological Criterion in Synoptic Research', pp. 389–90.
[3] Wrede, *Das Messiasgeheimnis in den Evangelien*, p. 148 (cited from ET, p. 148).

Markan material, supported the general principle of Markan priority.[4]

In this respect secrecy scholarship since Wrede has followed his own source-critical assumptions rather than his 'wishful thinking'. The major studies have all either assumed Markan priority,[5] or, with M. E. Glaswell, have argued that the secrecy motif provided an additional argument in support of Markan priority.[6] It is noteworthy in this connection that the neo-Griesbachians have placed no emphasis on the secrecy phenomena. Neither Farmer, despite his comments cited above, nor T. R. W. Longstaff, despite his concentration on Markan christology in 'Crisis and Christology: The Theology of Mark', discusses the secrecy motif. C. S. Mann attributes the Markan emphasis to the historical Jesus without ever addressing Mark's redactional purposes.[7] N. Elliott investigates the secrecy motifs in the three gospels but despite his sympathy with the Griesbach hypothesis does not attempt a redaction-critical approach to Griesbach-Mark's activity.[8]

Nevertheless the question posed by Wrede's comments remains: could a combination of Matthew and Luke provide the kind of source material that Wrede envisaged behind Mark? Or, to what extent is the secrecy material of the synoptic gospels compatible with the Griesbach hypothesis? Does the Griesbach hypothesis provide a coherent and plausible account for the redactional behaviour of Griesbach-Mark in this area? Or are these phenomena either more explicable or only explicable on the assumption of Markan priority?

In order to answer these questions the 'messianic secret' must be adequately defined, and the areas to be discussed clearly delimited. In the first connection it is clear that by 'Messiasgeheimnis', or 'messianic secret', Wrede meant to refer to the whole gamut of christological information concerning the identity of

---

[4] Ibid., pp. 148–9 (ET, pp. 148–9); cf. p. 150 (ET, p. 151) for his general comments in favour of the two-source hypothesis.

[5] Surveys in Blevins, *The Messianic Secret in Markan Research, 1901–1976*; Tuckett, 'Introduction: The Problem of the Messianic Secret'; Räisänen, *Das 'Messiasgeheimnis' im Markusevangelium*, pp. 18–49 (ET, pp. 38–75).

[6] Glaswell, 'The Concealed Messiahship in the Synoptic Gospels', p. 66, cf. pp. 289–90; Powley, 'The "Messianic" Secret in Mark's Gospel: An Historical Survey', pp. 46–7.

[7] Mann, *Mark*, p. 216.

[8] Elliott, 'The Silence of the Messiah: The Function of the "Messianic Secret" Motifs Across the Synoptics'.

Jesus. So, for example, he discusses a range of christological material including the Son of Man and demonic knowledge of Jesus' sonship. According to Wrede, 'Messiah' or 'Christ' are for Mark 'no less a description of the supernatural nature of Jesus than the title Son of God'.[9] Hence numerous other scholars have dubbed the motif *Sohnesgeheimnis*.[10] What is not so clear is the extent of Markan material which should be regarded as related to the secrecy motif.

Wrede argued that the messianic secret was a relatively well-integrated motif consisting of four major elements: Jesus' commands to silence, his intentional avoidance of publicity, the 'parable theory' and the disciples' lack of understanding. Several recent scholars have urged a distinction between these aspects of Mark's presentation.[11] For example, Wrede's argument for integrating the so-called 'parable theory' into the messianic secret depended upon his assumption that Mark 4.11f referred to a revelation understood only after the resurrection.[12] But this particular assumption cannot be sustained, since Mark is concerned rather with something 'given' to the disciples which distinguishes them from those outside during Jesus' ministry; thus, as R. Pesch noted, the Markan parable theory has nothing to do with the so-called messianic secret.[13]

If it is thus possible to distinguish between the diverse elements which make up the complex whole of Mark's messianic-secrecy motif, it is reasonable for our purposes – which do not include the proposition of a theory to explain this motif – to focus on particular

---

[9] For 'Son of Man' as meaning Messiah see Wrede, *Das Messiasgeheimnis in den Evangelien*, p. 16 (ET, p. 18); for demonic knowledge of Jesus' sonship as 'knowledge of the Messiah' p. 23–4 (ET, pp. 24–5); for citation see p. 76 (cited from ET, p. 77) and cf. pp. 58, 80, 114, 125 (ET, pp. 60, 80, 113–14, 126).

[10] Cranfield, *Mark*, p. 79; Bieneck, *Sohn Gottes als Christusbezeichnung der Synoptiker*, p. 51; Kingsbury, *The Christology of Mark's Gospel*, pp. 14–15 cf. other scholars listed in n. 52; Räisänen, *Das 'Messiasgeheimnis' im Markusevangelium*, p. 27 (and scholars listed in n. 44) (ET, p. 48); cf. Johnson, *The Griesbach Hypothesis and Redaction Criticism*, p. 103.

[11] Moule, 'On Defining the Messianic Secret in Mark'; Luz, 'Das Geheimnismotiv und die Markinische Christologie'; Räisänen, *Das 'Messiasgeheimnis' im Markusevangelium* (on internal grounds); Dunn, 'The Messianic Secret in Mark' (on historical grounds).

[12] Wrede, *Das Messiasgeheimnis in den Evangelien*, p. 70 (ET, p. 71).

[13] Pesch, *Markusevangelium*, vol. I, p. 240; S. Brown, ' "The Secret of the Kingdom of God" (Mark 4.11)' (noting differences between the mystery of the Kingdom of God and the messianic secret); Taylor, *Mark*, p. 255; Lane, *Mark*, pp. 157–8; Guelich, *Mark*, vol. I, p. 206.

aspects within Mark's treatment.[14] In the first place, the passages which contain christological confessions or information – Jesus' silencing of demons (Mark 1.24f, 34; 3.11f) and his disciples (Mark 8.30; 9.9) – are clearly the basis of Mark's christological secrecy motif and 'must be interpreted as special cases'.[15] They can be distinguished from the silence commands in the healing miracles (1.43f; 5.19, 43; 7.36; cf. 8.26) on various grounds:

   (i)   the silencing of demons and disciples relates to explicit christological information possessed by them; this is not so in healing accounts where the information remains implicit at best;
   (ii) the silence commands in the healing miracles are not always obeyed (see esp. 1.45; 5.20; 7.36f); this is not the case for demons and disciples;
   (iii) all the silence commands in the healing miracles appear to function, within the narrative as a whole, as a foil to emphasise the impact of Jesus (this is true of only some episodes concerning demons).

Two further points on this subject deserve mention. First, on the subject of silence commands functioning as a foil to emphasise Jesus' impact, H. J. Ebeling, drawing some support from Wrede, attempted to interpret the Markan secrecy theme *in toto* and specifically including the *Dämonengeschichten* as a foil for the revelation of Jesus' identity rather than for concealment: 'With [the secrecy] motif Mark proclaims the ephiphany of the Son of God, not his temporary concealment.'[16] But U. Luz has shown, on the basis of 1.44; 7.24, 36 (especially), and even 10.47f (where the

---

[14] A unified theory continues to evade a scholarly consensus (Tuckett, 'Introduction: The Problem of the Messianic Secret'; Powley, 'The "Messianic" Secret in Mark's Gospel: An Historical Survey', pp. 230–2).

[15] Luz, 'Das Geheimnismotiv und die Markinische Christologie', p. 19 (ET, p. 81); this general distinction is also supported by Räisänen who notes in particular the similarities between 3.11f and 8.30 (see *Das 'Messiasgeheimnis' im Markusevangelium*, p. 118 and pp. 159–60 (ET, p. 192 and pp. 242–3)). In Mark 5.6f a similar demonic statement is not silenced (cf. v. 16 which suggests this was public knowledge); in 9.20 a demon apparently displays knowledge of Jesus without any confession.

[16] Ebeling, *Das Messiasgeheimnis und die Botschaft des Marcus-Evangelisten*, p. 125 ('So predigt Mc die Epiphanie des Gottessohnes, nicht seine einstweilige Verhüllung mit unserem Motiv'); Wrede, *Das Messiasgeheimnis in den Evangelien*, p. 127 (ET, pp. 127–8); cf. also Theissen, *Urchristliche Wundergeschichten*, pp. 220–1 (ET, p. 221).

crowds urge silence with similar results) that within the Markan context this is universally true only of the silence commands in the healing stories. Luz draws particular attention to the positive connotations of κηρύσσειν in 1.45 and 7.36 (used twelve times in Mark – always redactional according to Luz).[17] Some epiphanic/ revelatory elements are present in some of the *Dämonengeschichten* (esp. Mark 1.27f), but it is not characteristic of all the Markan passages, as shall be shown in what follows.[18]

Secondly, M. D. Hooker has suggested that the commands to secrecy in the healing miracles, occurring as they do in miracles of resurrection (Mark 5.43), restoration of hearing (7.36) and restoration of sight (8.26), might be integrated at the Markan level with the other secrecy commands because seeing and hearing function as symbols of understanding and belief (e.g. Mark 4.3, 9, 12, 15ff, 23f, 33; 6.11; 7.14; 8.18; 9.7; 12.29, 37; 14.40; 15.39), while lack of sight and inability to hear represent misunderstanding and rejection of Jesus.[19] Nevertheless the differences remain substantial, and the material will be treated separately here.

Another important group of passages relates to Mark's emphasis on the impact of Jesus upon the crowds, in which both crowds and individuals exhibit knowledge of Jesus' activity and identity. These passages will be the subject of the final section of this chapter. This chapter will therefore treat the secrecy motif under three topics: Jesus' silencing of the demons; Jesus' silencing of the disciples; and public awareness of Jesus' activity and identity. The particular interest of this chapter is in the plausibility of the Griesbach hypothesis; the perspective of Markan priority and the two-source hypothesis perspective will be noted only briefly. Since the secrecy motif appears to be an important element in Mark it is clearly important for the Griesbach hypothesis that it can explain the phenomenon. This must be the case even if aspects of the messianic

---

[17] Luz, 'Das Geheimnismotiv und die Markinische Christologie', pp. 15–17 (ET, pp. 78–80), note 23 on κηρύσσειν.

[18] For further critical discussions of Ebeling see Räisänen, *Das 'Messiasgeheimnis' im Markusevangelium*, pp. 36–8 (ET, pp. 60–2) and Tuckett, 'Introduction: The Problem of the Messianic Secret', pp. 13–15.

[19] Hooker, *Mark*, pp. 67–8; cf. Beavis on Mark 4.10–12 in *Mark's Audience: The Literary and Social Setting of Mark 4.11–12*, pp. 87–130; cf. C. D. Marshall, *Faith as a Theme in Mark's Narrative*, p. 131; Donahue, 'Jesus as the Parable of God in the Gospel of Mark' and 'A Neglected Factor in the Theology of Mark', p. 593, n. 107.

secret can be traced to the historical Jesus;[20] the Markan presentation – in our case via the Griesbach-Markan redaction – remains to be understood on its own terms.[21]

2. Silencing the demons

2.1 The Griesbach hypothesis evaluated

We shall begin therefore where Wrede did with the 'Messiaserkenntnis der Dämonen': the demons' recognition of the Messiah (Mark 1.23–5, 34; 3.11f; 5.6f; 9.20).[22] Mark 1.23–8 // Luke 4.33–7 reflects the relatively simple scenario of Griesbach-Mark's alterations to Luke, as there is no parallel story in Matthew (although on the Griesbach hypothesis Mark 1.22 is drawn from Matt. 7.29). Mark's introduction is slightly altered, adding εὐθύς and αὐτῶν,[23] and he simplifies Luke's unusual form, ἄνθρωπος ἔχων πνεῦμα δαιμονίου ἀκαθάρτου (unparalleled in the NT), into ἐν πνεύματι ἀκαθάρτῳ (cf. Mark 5.2). The pronoun αὐτῶν is an unusual addition given the number of occasions on which Griesbach-Mark elsewhere omits such a pronoun from Matthew (e.g. Mark 3.1 cf. Matt. 12.9; Mark 6.2 cf. Matt. 13.54; cf. also Mark 1.21, 29; 3.6; 12.39; 13.9); the only similar case is in Mark 1.39. It is not a necessary addition, although it could be said to make explicit, with εὐθύς understood in its proper sense, the link between the teaching and response (of vv. 21f) and the following incident: on the same day and in the same synagogue. This explanation would fit with the impression that Mark has created a 'Day in the Life' in 1.21–39. Mark also uses τὸ πνεῦμα τὸ ἀκάθαρτον (1.26) instead of Luke's τὸ δαιμόνιον (4.35). Although the 'unclean spirit' terminology is characteristic of Mark,[24] this type of alteration is not carried through in a consistent manner. Mark often uses δαιμόνιον, especially, but not exclusively, in redactional summary statements:

---

[20] With Taylor, *Mark*, pp. 122–4; Cranfield, *Mark*, pp. 78–9; O'Neill, 'The Silence of Jesus'; Dunn, 'The Messianic Secret in Mark'; Aune, 'The Problem of the Messianic Secret'; Longenecker, 'The Messianic Secret in the Light of Recent Discoveries'.

[21] Cf. Räisänen, *Das 'Messiasgeheimnis' im Markusevangelium*, p. 32 (ET, p. 54); Tuckett, 'Introduction: The Problem of the Messianic Secret'.

[22] Wrede, *Das Messiasgeheimnis in den Evangelien*, p. 23 (ET, p. 24).

[23] Note that both of these words are omitted in some manuscripts, presumably under the harmonising influence of Luke's version (cf. Aland, *Synopsis*, p. 53).

[24] Pimental, 'The "unclean spirits" of St Mark's Gospel'.

Griesbach-hypothesis redactional in 1.34 (bis), 39; 3.15 (disciples); 6.13 (from Matt. 10.8 but redactionally placed); 7.29f (other occurrences in 3.22 parallels; 7.26 parallel; 9.38 parallel). Thus this cannot be regarded as consistent Griesbach-Markan practice.

Griesbach-Mark also omits the reference to 'a loud voice' from the introduction, and from then follows Luke for twenty-six identical words (Mark 1.24f // Luke 4.34f). This includes the statement of the unclean spirit, in which Mark follows Luke in using a plural form (cf. 1.34, 39; 3.11f; for plural references to demons; cf. also 5.7, 9), which claims knowledge of Jesus' identity and identifies him as ὁ ἅγιος τοῦ θεοῦ, and the command to silence: Φιμώθητι καὶ ἔξελθε ἐξ αὐτοῦ. Griesbach-Mark transfers the loud cry to the account of the actual exorcism (v. 26), where he uses σπαράσσω ('convulse', cf. 9.20 v.l., 26) instead of Luke's ῥίπτω (not used elsewhere in the NT in this sense, BAGD, p. 736).

The astonished response of those who witnessed the event is described by Mark using different terminology than Luke, but with similar effect. All those present (ἅπαντες) were astonished (here Mark uses θαμβέομαι, as in 10.24, 32; Luke uses θάμβος, as in 5.9; Acts 3.10; in both cases these are the only occurrences in the NT), and remarked on the significance of Jesus' authority, although Mark alone relates this in turn to Jesus' teaching. Griesbach-Mark also adds the statement concerning the unclean spirits' obedience: καὶ ὑπακούουσιν αὐτῷ (cf. Mark 4.41 where a similar phrase also occurs in Matt. 8.27 // Luke 8.25). The result is that the knowledge of Jesus' activity (ἡ ἀκοὴ αὐτοῦ) spread into all the region; here Mark's construction is different from Luke, noting Galilee in particular, but it cannot be said to intensify the response. In both accounts the silence motif is limited to the exorcistic command, the overall force of the account is to intensify the public nature of the activity and attention is explicitly drawn to the positive response of all those who witnessed it.[25]

The second silence command in Mark 1.34 must have been composed by Griesbach-Mark from the similar account in Luke 4.41 with some influence from Matthew 8.16f.[26] Evidence for the influence of Matthew is clear in Mark 1.32 (a classic text for conflation of Matt. and Luke by Griesbach-Mark), but also extends

---

[25] Cf. Gundry, *Mark*, pp. 78, 84–5.
[26] Griesbach, 'Demonstration', p. 108 (Mark follows Luke); Farmer, *The Synoptic Problem*, pp. 237–8; others suggest a conflation of both Matthew and Luke (de Wette, *Einleitung*, p. 187 (ET, p. 166); Riley, *The Making of Mark*, p. 15).

to words in Mark 1.34 (e.g. ἐθεράπευσεν . . . κακῶς ἔχοντας . . . ἐξέβαλεν, cf. Matt. 8.16). Of particular interest is Griesbach-Mark's omission of Luke's record of what the demons said: κρ[αυγ]άζοντα καὶ λέγοντα ὅτι Σὺ εἶ ὁ υἱὸς τοῦ θεοῦ (Luke 4.41). Given, however, that Mark later uses this statement in 3.11, it is difficult to understand why he omits it at this point, if it was present in his source. This is particularly puzzling given Griesbach-Mark's alteration of the next phrase of Luke (from 'because they knew that he was the Christ' to 'because they knew him'), an alteration which points to the demons having genuine knowledge of Jesus' identity.

On the general point of the secrecy motif in Mark it is clear that the presence of Jesus in the house functions to highlight the number of those who come to Jesus. Mark adds 1.34: 'the whole city (ὅλη ἡ πόλις) was gathered at the door'. The terms used in Mark's statement of Jesus' activity emphasise this influence (πολλοὺς . . . ποικίλαις . . . πολλά), as does the following story (cf. Mark 1.37, Πάντες ζητοῦσίν σε, differently in Luke 4.42). It is worth noting that Jesus' command to the healed leper (Mark 1.43f) also serves, by way of contrast, as a means of highlighting the response of those who heard about it: καὶ ἤρχοντο πρὸς αὐτὸν πάντοθεν (1.45, although other aspects of 1.45 miss the opportunities present in Luke 5.15: 'great multitudes gathered to hear and to be healed of their infirmities'). In Mark the inability of Jesus to enter a town without publicity, and the positive response of the people, provide a clear link with the following passage (cf. Mark 2.1f).

The third secrecy command occurs in the transitional passage, Mark 3.7–12. Hitherto Griesbach-Mark has been following Luke's controversy stories (Mark 2.1–3.6 // Luke 5.17–6.11), while the influence of Matthew can be seen at various points (esp. Mark 3.6 // Matt. 12.14). At this point Griesbach-Mark has undertaken a relatively complex combination of elements from Matthew 4.24f; 12.15f; Luke 6.17–19; 4.41. Note Griesbach's description:

> Mark 3:7–12 expresses more fully and expansively Matt. 12:15–21, but in such a way that Mark (1) deliberately omitted the prophecy cited in 12: 17–21, (2) simultaneously matched Luke 6: 17–19, and (3) added certain details of his own, 3:9.[27]

---

[27] Griesbach, 'Demonstration', n. 20 p. 210 to p. 109; cf. also Farmer, *The Synoptic Problem*, p. 236; de Wette, *Einleitung*, p. 188 (ET, p. 167); Riley, *The Making of Mark*, pp. 35–7.

Griesbach-Mark emphasises the numbers of people who come to Jesus by gathering place names from both Matthew and Luke (although notably failing to utilise 'the Decapolis' which stands in Matt. 4.25 despite his redactional interest in this area in 5.20 and 7.31), and explains in v. 8b that πλῆθος πολύ, ἀκούοντες ὅσα ἐποίει ἦλθον πρὸς αὐτόν. Here he repeats πλῆθος πολύ (cf. v. 7), he specifies that they came because they had heard reports of his acts (cf. 1.45; 2.11) and emphasises that they came πρὸς αὐτόν – this last makes clear that he is not intending a negative comment on this response of the multitudes.[28]

Mark provides a physical reason for Jesus to have an escape route (vv. 9f), but it is only the unclean spirits who are silenced. According to the Griesbach hypothesis the knowledge of the demons, Σὺ εἶ ὁ υἱὸς τοῦ θεοῦ, comes from Luke 4.41 while the command to silence, καὶ πολλὰ ἐπετίμα αὐτοῖς ἵνα μὴ αὐτὸν φανερὸν ποιήσωσιν, comes from Matthew 12.16 (parallel words underlined). The tone of the command is strengthened by the characteristic addition of πολλά (used adverbially in Mark 5.10, 23, 38; 6.20; 9.26a; 15.3; cf. 1.45, see BAGD, p. 688). Nevertheless, this is a somewhat unusual procedure for Griesbach-Mark. Griesbach-Mark has also added other individual touches, describing the response of the unclean spirits, who, having seen Jesus, fall down before him (cf. Mark 9.20 for the response at the sight of Jesus and 5.6 for falling down before Jesus). This activity clearly suggests that for Mark the unclean spirits had a 'supernatural' knowledge of Jesus' identity;[29] and that Jesus' silencing of the demons has to do with this special knowledge.

From the perspective of the Griesbach hypothesis we can deal with the two other episodes (Mark 5.6f; 9.20) fairly briefly. In the first of these Griesbach-Mark offers a generally expanded version of the story, dependent primarily upon Luke 8.26–39 and secondarily upon Matthew 8.28–34.[30] Griesbach argued that Mark was here dependent upon Luke alone and not Matthew; but this is unlikely in view of Mark 5.1f // Matthew 8.28 (nine words in common, but not in Luke); Mark 5.12–14 // Matthew 8.30–2 (seven

---

[28] Cf. mention of crowds coming πρὸς αὐτόν in 1.45; 2.13; 4.1; 10.1 (also the disciples in 3.13). On Jesus' magnetism see Gundry, *Mark*, p. 157.

[29] Wrede, *Das Messiasgeheimnis in den Evangelien*, p. 24 (ET, p. 25).

[30] De Wette, *Einleitung*, p. 189 (ET, p. 168); Farmer, *The Synoptic Problem*, pp. 240–1.

words in common, but not in Luke).[31] The approach of the demoniac is described very fully in Mark – seeing, running, worshipping and crying out (following Luke 8.28 except that Mark has altered Luke's δέομαί σου to ὁρκίζω σε τὸν θεόν) – Τί ἐμοὶ καὶ σοί,'Ιησοῦ υἱὲ τοῦ θεοῦ τοῦ ὑψίστου; ὁρκίζω σε τὸν θεόν, μή με βασανίσῃς. At this point, however, there is no silence command despite the presence of witnesses (Mark 5.16) and Jesus commands the man to go and tell ὅσα ὁ κύριός σοι πεποίηκεν καὶ ἠλέησέν σε. In the second passage the spirit responds to Jesus' presence (Mark 9.20), but says nothing – as it is specifically identified as a dumb spirit – and there is no silence command although the spirit is rebuked in the exorcistic command (9.25). Within the context of Mark this takes place in the presence of a large crowd (9.14 // Luke 9.37 and Mark 9.25f; cf. v. 28).

It is clear that although Griesbach-Mark gathers the elements of his secrecy motif from his sources, especially Luke, he has not really stamped them with a clear redactional emphasis. It might be suggested that the Griesbach hypothesis lends support to Ebeling's contention that Mark's interest is in the public awareness of Jesus which often arises in the wake of the secrecy commands (as in 1.27f, 37), but this hardly accounts for the Markan redaction of the other accounts and in any case has more general difficulties: firstly that the public do not appear in Mark to have a clear appreciation of the identity of Jesus; and secondly that there were particular difficulties in explaining the motives and procedure controlling the Markan redaction. Thus it remains difficult to understand why Mark would have proceeded in the manner which the Griesbach hypothesis suggests (and demands).

2.2   *Markan priority evaluated*

The most notable aspect of Matthew's secrecy motif in relation to Markan priority is that Matthew never reproduces Jesus' commands silencing the demons (Mark 1.25, 34b; 3.12). Matthew omits the whole pericope containing the first command, and transforms the other two passages in similar and striking ways. Matthew 8.16f (// Mark 1.32–4) abbreviates Mark's account, focussing on the twofold activity of Jesus in casting out the spirits and healing all who were ill, and omitting the command to keep silent. Matthew

---

[31] Cf. Griesbach, 'Demonstration', n. 29 p. 211 to p. 109.

emphasises the powerful effect of Jesus (who casts out with a word, cf. 8.8) by changing Mark's 'many' to 'all' (cf. below, section 4.1) and introduces a fulfilment citation from Isaiah 53.4, which here relates to Jesus' healing ministry.[32]

In Matthew 12.15–21 (// Mark 3.10–12) we find a similar abbreviation of the Markan report, and a similar use of πάντας to describe the scope of Jesus' healing activity. Matthew omits all mention of the unclean spirits and their statements; thus the statement in Matthew 12.16, καὶ ἐπετίμησεν αὐτοῖς ἵνα μή φανερὸν αὐτὸν ποιήσωσιν, although formally very close to Mark 3.12, has a different antecedent for αὐτοῖς, that is, those who were healed rather than the demons. For Matthew this becomes a command silencing those who followed Jesus and were healed, although Jesus' identity remains the focus of attention. The reason for the silencing is provided in an extended citation from Isaiah 42.1–4, with numerous contextual connections,[33] which includes the statement that 'he will not wrangle or cry aloud, nor will any one hear his voice in the streets . . . till he brings justice to victory'. Thus Matthew associates the public reticence of Jesus with his fulfilling of the scriptures, specifically those concerning the Lord's Servant. He also introduces a chronological element, partially supporting R. N. Longenecker's argument connecting the secrecy motif with the expectation that Messiah's task must be complete before his identity can be acknowledged.[34]

Many commentators take these two passages as evidence that Matthew thought in terms of a Servant figure or role to which Jesus could be related, as B. Gerhardsson said, 'The prophetic words seem to be usable because Jesus is considered as "the Servant of the Lord".'[35] Even if such a figure or role cannot be assumed it is enough for our purposes to point out that Matthew's redaction of

---

[32] Cf. Stendahl, *The School of St Matthew*, pp. 106–7; Gundry, *The Use of the Old Testament in St Matthew's Gospel*, pp. 229–301; Gerhardsson, *The Mighty Acts of Jesus*, p. 25; Davies and Allison, *Matthew*, vol. II, pp. 37–8.

[33] See Stendahl, *The School of St. Matthew*, pp. 107–15; Gundry, *The Use of the Old Testament in St. Matthew's Gospel*, pp. 110–16; Davies and Allison, *Matthew*, vol. II, pp. 323–7; Gerhardsson, *The Mighty Acts of Jesus*, pp. 25–7; cf. also Neyrey, 'The Thematic Use of Isa 42.1–4 in Matthew 12'.

[34] Longenecker, 'The Messianic Secret in the Light of Recent Discoveries' (building on Flusser, 'Two Notes on the Midrash on 2 Sam. vii').

[35] Gerhardsson, *The Mighty Acts of Jesus*, p. 25; cf. also Davies and Allison, *Matthew*, vol. II, p. 37; cf. pp. 323–4; France, *Matthew: Evangelist and Teacher*, pp. 300–2; Hill, 'Son and Servant', pp. 9–12. This is denied by Hooker, *Jesus and the Servant*, p. 149 (although cf. p. 84).

Mark, in these two places, is consistent with other passages where Matthew adds OT citations or allusions and the use of servant-passages from Isaiah 40–55 which have been observed previously.[36]

While either the general explanation that Matthew wished to emphasise the OT background to Jesus' career, or the more specific one that he correlated Jesus with the servant of Isaiah 40–55, might serve to provide plausible explanations for much of Matthew's redactional behaviour, some scholars have added another explanation. They have suggested that Matthew's remodelling of these passages about Jesus silencing demons was connected with Jewish accusations that Jesus was involved in magical practices.[37] In other words, Matthew removes material that was potentially embarrassing or open to polemical use by his Jewish opponents.[38] Celsus, for example, alleged that 'it was by means of sorcery that he [Jesus] was able to accomplish the wonders which he performed'.[39]

This argument, although possible, is not firmly based. In the first place, there is no clear evidence that silence commands, a standard feature of exorcisms, would have had particularly magical overtones within a first-century Jewish milieu. H. C. Kee, in particular, insists on a sharp distinction between first-century attitudes in a Jewish milieu and 'the coercive, manipulating mood of the second and third centuries when magic was flourishing'.[40] In the second

---

[36] Cf. pp. 183–4 above for further discussion concerning Matthew's use of servant passages.

[37] Hull, *Hellenistic Magic and the Synoptic Tradition*, pp. 128–33; Davies and Allison, *Matthew*, vol. II, pp. 14–15. For similar suggestions in relation to Mark and Luke (respectively) see Smith, 'Good News is No News: Aretalogy and Gospel', esp. pp. 24–5 and Garrett, *The Demise of the Devil: Magic and the Demonic in Luke's Writings*.

[38] For a similar suggestion relating to the accusation that Jesus cast out demons 'by the prince of demons' (Matt. 9.34; 10.25; 12.24, 27) see Stanton, 'Matthew's Christology and the Parting of the Ways', pp. 101–8 (= *A Gospel for a New People*, pp. 171–80).

[39] Origen, *Contra Celsum* I.6; cf. also I.28; II.48f; VI.39; for Jewish accusations see Justin, *Dialogue with Trypho* 69 (cf. *Apology* I.30); *b. Sanh.* 43a (cf. Str-B, vol. I, pp. 38–9, 631) and possibly *b. Šabb.* 104b and *b. Sanh.* 67a: if ben Stada (= ben Pandira), is a code for Jesus (this is considered unlikely by the editors of the Soncino edition, see note b(5) to *b. Sanh.* 67a; but is beyond reasonable doubt according to Herford, *Christianity in Talmud and Midrash*, pp. 35–41). For discussion see Herford, *Christianity in Talmud and Midrash*, pp. 54–6; Klausner, *Jesus of Nazareth*, pp. 18–47; van der Loos, *The Miracles of Jesus*, pp. 156–75; Smith, *Jesus the Magician*, esp. pp. 45–67.

[40] Kee, *Medicine, Miracle and Magic in New Testament Times*, pp. 112–15, citation from p. 114 (following Brown, 'Sorcery, Demons and the Rise of Christianity from Late Antiquity into the Middle Ages') against Hull, *Hellenistic Magic and*

place, a less specific explanation can be given for Matthew's redactional behaviour. In the two other places in Mark where demons exhibit knowledge of Jesus within an exorcistic context (Mark 5.1–20, esp. v. 7; 9.17–29, esp. v. 20), Matthew's parallel accounts (Matt. 8.28–34; 17.14–20) are severely abbreviated, lacking both the dialogue with the father and some of the exorcistic details. The general effect of the changes is to emphasise the authority of Jesus.

For example, in Matthew 8.32 he tells the demons to go, whereas in Mark 5.13 he merely allows them do what they have suggested. J. Gnilka described this procedure in terms of 'die christologische Konzentration' of the Matthean redaction, which reinforces (*vertiefen*) the christological orientation of the Markan pericope.[41] Similarly in Matthew 17.18 the demon comes out of the boy and he is instantly cured whereas in Mark 9.26 the demon leaves with a great convulsion and the boy needs a subsequent touch from Jesus (an analogous abbreviation resulting in a concentration on Jesus' authority and healing power is evident in Luke 9.42).[42] These alterations are analogous to those which Matthew makes to other miracle stories: abbreviating and highlighting Jesus' authority. If this is accepted, there seems little need to postulate a reaction against accusations of sorcery. In any case there is no difficulty in describing Matthew's redaction as both plausible and coherent.

3. Silencing the disciples

3.1 The Griesbach hypothesis evaluated

In Mark Jesus twice silences his disciples (8.30; 9.9f). In the first of these passages (8.27–30) Griesbach-Mark must draw upon both Matthew and Luke: 'he chiefly follows the footsteps of Matthew, but all the while comparing with Luke'.[43] In view of Mark 1.1 there

---

the *Synoptic Tradition*. For a different view see Crossan, *The Historical Jesus*, pp. 304–10.

[41] Gnilka, *Matthäusevangelium*, vol. I, p. 320; cf. Davies and Allison, *Matthew*, vol. II, p. 84.

[42] Davies and Allison, *Matthew*, vol. II, p. 725 (although noting elsewhere the importance of discipleship in the Matthean redaction, p. 728); cf. Marshall, *Luke*, p. 392.

[43] Griesbach, 'Demonstration', n. 32 p. 211 to p. 109; cf. also de Wette, *Einleitung*, p. 190 (ET, p. 169); Farmer, *The Synoptic Problem*, p. 245; Riley, *The Making of Mark*, pp. 96–7.

can be little doubt that Peter's confession is understood as appropriate, even if incomplete (cf. 8.31–3). The terms of the command to silence, καὶ ἐπετίμησεν αὐτοῖς ἵνα μηδενὶ λέγωσιν περὶ αὐτοῦ (8.30), while resembling both Luke 9.21 and Matthew 16.20, suggest a distinctive slant. Luke's version, παρήγγειλεν μηδενὶ λέγειν τοῦτο, refers specifically to Peter's confession,[44] as does Matthew's, ἵνα μηδενὶ εἴπωσιν ὅτι αὐτός ἐστιν ὁ Χριστός; but Mark's version is more absolute: they are not to speak to anyone 'about him' (περὶ αὐτοῦ).[45] No doubt in view of the context this statement must relate to the preceding confession,[46] but the link is much less strong than in either Matthew or Luke and as an intentional alteration this is difficult to explain. In Mark as in the other two gospels the following account serves to redefine the Messiahship of Jesus by means of the first passion prediction (8.31). Peter's rebuke of Jesus and Jesus' response (neither of which is in Luke) serve to highlight the inadequacies of Peter's understanding. The necessity of transformed understanding makes Matthew 16.20 and Luke 9.21 readily explicable as alterations to Mark – the secret relates to a confession of Messiahship which is not totally adequate until filled out by the suffering of Jesus – but leaves Griesbach-Mark once again without a clear rationale for his redactional activity.

The second silence command follows the transfiguration (Mark 9.9f // Matt. 17.9 cf. Luke 9.36b which reports the silence without a command). Jesus instructs the disciples to tell no one what they had seen, until the resurrection. Griesbach-Mark is clearly indebted to Matthew's wording (fourteen words in common). Some alterations are explicable, on the Griesbach hypothesis, in terms of Markan vocabulary preferences:

(i)   Mark prefers διαστέλλομαι (1–5–0; used in 'miracle secrecy' commands in Mark 5.43; 7.36) over ἐντέλλομαι (5–2–1);

(ii) he uses διηγέομαι (0–2–2; cf. Mark 5.16; Matt.'s τὸ ὅραμα is a synoptic hapax);

(iii) he prefers ἀνίστημι when speaking of the resurrection (cf.

---

[44] Marshall, Luke, p. 369; Bovon, Lukas, p. 479; Evans, Luke, p. 406.
[45] This statement is grammatically similar to Mark 3.12, utilising ἐπιτιμάω (6–9–12), αὐτοῖς, and a ἵνα-clause which focuses on Jesus himself (μὴ αὐτὸν φανερὸν ποιήσωσιν). For περὶ αὐτοῦ cf. Mark 7.25; 14.21.
[46] Against Lohmeyer, Markus, p. 165.

8.31; 9.9, 10, 27, 31; 10.34; 12.23, 25; Matt. uses it only once, 12.41, and never of Jesus' resurrection (but cf. 17.9 v.l. ; 17.23 v.l. ; 20.19 v.l.)).[47]

Mark adds a further (and difficult) remark: καὶ τὸν λόγον ἐκράτησαν πρὸς ἑαυτοὺς συζητοῦντες τί ἐστιν τὸ ἐκ νεκρῶν ἀναστῆναι (9.10). It seems likely that we should understand the first clause to mean 'they seized on this saying' (i.e. they kept or obeyed it; cf. 7.3) and link πρὸς ἑαυτοὺς with the verb, 'discussing among themselves',[48] rather than punctuate the verse differently: 'they kept this matter to themselves, questioning . . .'[49] Several scholars have argued that the variant reading: 'questioning what "when he rises from the dead" meant', is original to Mark (reading ὅταν ἐκ νεκρῶν ἀναστῇ with D W f¹ f¹³ OL Vg syrˢ·ᵖ geo Tatian).[50] This reading removes the difficulty that the disciples might not understand about the general resurrection (which is unlikely), but for this reason it seems more likely to be a secondary alteration. Taking the definite article as anaphoric with reference to verse 9 removes the difficulty[51] – clearly in Mark's intention it is not the general resurrection that is in view but the resurrection of Jesus the Son of Man (cf. 9.32) – and this explains how the discussion can move to Elijah (9.11–13). The variant reading makes Mark's meaning explicit.

Mark's misunderstanding theme (cf. previously 6.52; 8.17–21) focusses on the necessity of the passion throughout chapters 8–10 (8.31 3; 9.12, 30 2; 10.33f, 45). The point appears to be that Jesus' identity and mission can only be properly understood at the point of his death (cf. 15.39 and our comments in the previous chapter). This understanding was to be communicated, and further understood, after the resurrection (cf. also 16.6). This observation is not dependent upon the Griesbach hypothesis, in fact Griesbach-Markan redaction does not emphasise this thought to any great

---

[47] Although these phenomena are coherent on the Griesbach hypothesis, the reverse is also true and would explain Matthean redaction of Mark's vocabulary (Gundry, *Matthew*, p. 346; Davies and Allison, *Matthew*, vol. II, pp. 712–13).

[48] Hooker, *Mark*, p. 219; Taylor, *Mark*, p. 394 (he compares 9.14, 16); Gnilka, *Markus*, vol. II, p. 39; Lane, *Mark*, p. 322; Gundry, *Mark*, p. 483.

[49] RSV. Pesch supports this reading in his translation, but suggests that it does not make a difference to the meaning (*Markusevangelium*, vol. II, p. 78).

[50] Lagrange, *Marc*, p. 234; Taylor, *Mark*, p. 394; Cranfield, *Mark*, p. 297; Lane, *Mark*, p. 322.

[51] Robertson, *A Grammar of the Greek New Testament*, p. 1065; Gundry, *Mark*, p. 463.

extent. In general, although the Griesbach hypothesis can explain some of Mark's redactional alterations in terms of vocabulary preferences, it fails to explicate Mark's theological concerns in any clear manner. In terms of our reorientation of Wrede's question, whether in fact Mark might be explained as dependent upon both Matthew and Luke, the answer must be negative: there is no clear evidence that this hypothesis explains the various secrecy phenomena in a coherent and plausible manner.

3.2   Markan priority evaluated

The two-source hypothesis, unlike the Griesbach hypothesis, does provide a relatively clear and consistent picture of Matthean redaction in these passages. It was noted above that in addition to omitting two references to silencing demons Matthew transformed the third (Mark 3.10–12) from a command silencing demons to one silencing those who were healed. Matthew 16.20 (// Mark 8.30) has already been discussed (in chapters nine and ten) and shall be dealt with only briefly at this point (cf. above. pp. 184 and 207). In the preceding verses Matthew emphasises the fundamentally 'correct' nature of Peter's confession, regarding it as the result of divine revelation (16.17). Matthew 16.20b reads ἵνα μηδενὶ εἴπωσιν ὅτι αὐτός ἐστιν ὁ Χριστός. This modification, as already suggested, makes good sense: the secret relates to the Messiahship of Jesus (Mark's περὶ αὐτοῦ would have Peter as its antecedent; cf. vv. 17–19). The absence of ὁ υἱὸς τοῦ θεοῦ τοῦ ζῶντος (cf. v. 16) might also suggest that Matthew's source read only ὁ χριστός (as Mark 8.29). The general thrust of the passage is not dissimilar to that in Mark.

This is also the case with the third passage (Matt. 17.9 // Mark 9.9) where Jesus commands those who had seen the transfiguration (τὸ ὅραμα) not to tell anyone until after the resurrection of the Son of Man. Matthew has omitted Mark 9.10 which refers to misunderstanding on the part of the disciples. If anything Matthew is interested in suggesting that the information to be kept secret is something understood by the disciples (cf. also 14.33),[52] rather than, as Mark suggests, something that cannot be properly under-

---

[52] So also Wrede, following Ritschl, in *Das Messiasgeheimnis in den Evangelien*, p. 11 (ET, p. 13) noticing also the 'Son of David' statements of others (see 9.27; 12.23; 15.22).

stood until the death–resurrection of Jesus. A common feature of these two episodes in Matthew is that they both concern Jesus as 'Son of God'. That is, Peter's confession is that Jesus is 'the Christ, the Son of the Living God' (Matt. 16.16), and the revelation on the mountain is that Jesus is 'my beloved Son' (17.5, cf. 3.17). Nevertheless it is not Jesus' sonship which is a special focus of the silence commands. In short, while these passages can be understood as Matthean redaction of Mark (especially in terms of vocabulary preferences[53]), it seems likely that 'the idea of the messianic secret no longer has the importance for Matthew that it has for Mark'.[54]

4. Public awareness of Jesus' activity and identity

In a previous section the differences between the account of the baptism of Jesus in Matthew and Mark were noted (pp. 195–6). While Mark's account is essentially a private disclosure, Matthew's takes on an objective and public side. This is an example of the issue before us: to what extent is the identity of Jesus publicly recognised throughout the story? This will concern the crowds – how do they respond to Jesus? – and individuals – how do they approach Jesus?

4.1 The crowds and Jesus

Prominent in Mark are the accounts of people and crowds hearing reports of Jesus' activity and coming to him. Many of these do not occur in the other gospels and so function (on the Griesbach hypothesis) as relatively good expressions of Markan interest. U. Luz argues much the same from the perspective of Markan priority: Markan redaction stresses the public significance of the healing miracles and summary statements.[55] Relevant passages include:

---

[53] For discussion of vocabulary preferences here see the previous section (for Matt. 17.9 cf. Mark 9.9f; also earlier in chapter ten, pp. 209–10; Gundry, *Matthew*, pp. 346–7) and, for 16.20 see Gundry, *Matthew*, pp. 336–7.

[54] Wrede, *Das Messiasgeheimnis in den Evangelien*, p. 153 (ET, p. 154); cf. Glasswell who argued that the elimination of Mark's secrecy motif 'is a major part of Matthew's rewriting of Mark' ('The Concealed Messiahship in the Synoptic Gospels', p. 295). Cf. also Davies and Allison: 'the difficulty modern scholars have had in sorting out Mark's commands to secrecy . . . was evidently shared by our evangelist' (*Matthew*, vol. II, p. 14).

[55] Luz, 'Das Geheimnismotiv und die Markinische Christologie', p. 14 (ET, p. 77–8).

1.28 (Jesus' fame spreads throughout Galilee; from Luke 4.37, slightly modified);

1.32f (whole city comes to Jesus; summary statement, v. 33 not paralleled);

1.45 (people come to Jesus from everywhere, substantial parallel in Luke 5.15f);

2.2 (many crowd at the door, partial parallel in Luke 5.17);

2.13 (crowd gathers for teaching, no parallel);

3.8 (great multitudes come to Jesus, parallels with Matt. 4.25 and Luke 6.18);

3.20 (the crowd gathers again, no parallel);

4.1 (a large crowd gathers, parallel in Matt. 13.2; Luke 8.4);

5.21 (a large crowd gathers to Jesus, partial parallel with Luke 8.40);

5.24 (a large crowd follows Jesus, parallel with Luke 8.42);

6.31 (many coming and going, no parallel);

6.54–6 (people recognise Jesus, bring sick to him etc.; partial parallel Matt. 14.35f);

8.1 (a great crowd gathers, no parallel in Matt. 15.32);

9.14f (a large crowd runs and greets Jesus, partial parallels in Matt. 17.14; Luke 9.37);

10.1 (crowds come to Jesus, partial parallel in Matt. 19.2);

10.46 (crowd with disciples, parallel Matt. 20.29);

11.8 (many acknowledge Jesus, parallel Matt. 21.8);

11.18b (the crowd astonished at Jesus' teaching, different Luke 19.48b).

Granted that a tendency to increase the impact of Jesus upon crowds is attested in the early variants introduced to the manuscript tradition of the gospels (notably by the addition of forms of πᾶς and/or πολύς to narrative descriptions of Jesus' activity or the crowds' response[56]), it might be suggested that this provides a plausible rationale for Griesbach-Mark's redaction of Matthew and Luke in the passages listed. There remain, however, several problems with this argument. First, it is clear that Mark does not use all the material available to him, that is he does not include material concerning the positive response of crowds from both Matthew and Luke (including passages that Mark clearly

---

[56] In variants to Matt. 4.24; 7.28; 8.18; 9.35; 15.30; Mark 1.34; Luke 4.32, 36; 5.17 (Head, 'Christology and Textual Transmission', pp. 119–20).

knows).[57] Secondly, the passages in Mark do not habitually intensify the nature of the response exhibited by the crowds in his sources, nor does Mark use any regular forms in these redactional contexts. Thirdly, the crowds in Mark exhibit little awareness of the identity of Jesus; indeed those passages in Matthew and Luke which state the response of the crowd in positive terms are not reproduced in Mark (e.g. Matt. 9.33: 'Never was anything like this seen in Israel'; 15.31: they glorified the God of Israel; Luke 9.43: all were astonished at the majesty of God). One example, where the response is voiced by the crowds, is worth fuller discussion:

Matt. 9.8	Mark 2.12b	Luke 5.26
ἰδόντες δὲ οἱ ὄχλοι ἐφοβήθησαν	ὥστε ἐξίστασθαι πάντας	καὶ ἔκστασις ἔλαβεν ἅπαντας
καὶ ἐδόξασαν τὸν θεὸν τὸν	καὶ δοξάζειν τὸν θεὸν	καὶ ἐδόξαζον τὸν θεόν, καὶ
δόντα ἐξουσίαν τοιαύτην τοῖς	λέγοντας ὅτι	ἐπλήσθησαν φόβου λέγοντες ὅτι
ἀνθρώποις.	Οὕτως οὐδέποτε εἴδομεν.	Εἴδομεν παράδοξα σήμερον.

Griesbach-Mark here prefers ἐξίστημι (1–4–3) to the φοβ-terminology of his sources (φόβος 3–1–7; φοβέομαι 17–12–22). This seems consistent with his vocabulary preferences, except for the observation that elsewhere in Mark ἐξίστημι is used only in the contexts of neutral (5.42) or negative (3.21) or uncomprehending (6.51) responses to Jesus. The positive connotations of the present context are described elsewhere in Mark using φοβ- terminology, as for example those passages which portray a reaction to Jesus of fear at the manifestation of the divine (e.g. 4.41; 5.15, 33; 10.32; 16.8).[58] Thus the reason for Mark's alteration of the terminology is unclear. On the other hand Matthean redaction of Mark is readily explicable, emphasising the authority of Jesus, and perhaps, by virtue of the plural τοῖς ἀνθρώποις, the authority that he passed on

---

[57] Cf. (Mk = Markan knowledge of context) Matt. 8.1 (Mk), 34 (Mk); 9.31 (Mk), 33 (Mk), 35f (Mk); 12.15 (Mk); 14.13f (Mk); Luke 4.15 (Mk); 5.1; 7.17, 29; 9.11, 43 (Mk); (11.14, 29; 12.1; 13.17; 14.25); 21.38. NB also Matt. 9.33 // Luke 11.14; Matt. 12.15 // Luke 6.17; Matt. 14.13 // Luke 9.11.

[58] With, e.g., Catchpole, 'The Fearful Silence of the Women at the Tomb'. For the opposite view, that fear is generally understood negatively in Mark, see J. M. Robinson, *The Problem of History in Mark*, pp. 68–73; Lincoln, 'The Promise and the Failure: Mark 16:7, 8', pp. 286–7.

to others.[59] And Lukan redaction also conforms to Lukan vocabulary and themes: although παράδοξος is a NT *hapax*, other terms are Lukan, e.g. ἔκστασις: Acts 3.10; 10.10; 11.5; 22.17; σήμερον: (8–1–12 + 9–0, note especially 4.21).[60]

Fourthly, the only passages which *unambiguously* fit the tendency observed among the scribes (that is to introduce πᾶς and/or πολύς terminology) suggest Markan rather than Matthean priority.[61] In Mark 1.32–4 there seems to be a decline from the emphasis on all those who were brought to Jesus (v. 32: πάντας . . .; v. 33: ὅλη ἡ πόλις . . .) to the many of those who were healed (v. 34: ἐθεράπευσεν πολλοὺς κακῶς ἔχοντας ποικίλαις νόσοις, καὶ δαιμόνια πολλὰ ἐξέβαλεν). The parallel in Matthew 8.16, by contrast, begins with 'many' (πολλούς) brought to Jesus, implies that all the spirits were cast out, and states clearly πάντας τοὺς κακῶς ἔχοντας ἐθεράπευσεν. Luke 4.40 makes a similar point (in a different way to Matthew) by adding: ὁ δὲ ἑνὶ ἑκάστῳ αὐτῶν τὰς χεῖρας ἐπιτιθεὶς ἐθεράπευεν αὐτούς. Another example is found at Mark 3.10, πολλοὺς γὰρ ἐθεράπευσεν, when compared with Matthew 12.15: καὶ ἐθεράπευσεν αὐτοὺς πάντας (cf. also Luke 6.10b: ὅτι δύναμις παρ' αὐτοῦ ἐξήρχετο καὶ ἰᾶτο πάντας). A somewhat similar situation pertains to details in the feeding miracles concerning the number of those fed by Jesus: where Mark 6.44 has καὶ ἦσαν οἱ φαγόντες [τοὺς ἄρτους] πεντακισχίλιοι ἄνδρες, Matthew 14.21 has οἱ δὲ ἐσθίοντες ἦσαν ἄνδρες ὡσεὶ πεντακισχίλιοι χωρὶς γυναικῶν καὶ παιδίων. In the other account Mark has ἦσαν δὲ ὡς τετρακισχίλιοι (Mark 8.9), while Matthew 15.38 reads: οἱ δὲ ἐσθίοντες ἦσαν τετρακισχίλιοι ἄνδρες χωρὶς γυναικῶν καὶ παιδίων. Both of these, particularly the second, function to emphasise the numbers, although Matthew may also be alluding 'to the way the people in the wilderness were counted' (cf. Exod. 12.37).[62]

While these four considerations militate against using this material in support of the Griesbach hypothesis, it is not clear that Davies and Allison are on particularly strong ground in using this material as a definite proof of Markan priority. Two passages alone

---

[59] Held, 'Matthäus als Interpret der Wundergeschichten', pp. 260–1 (ET, pp. 273–4); Bultmann, *Die Geschichte der synoptischen Tradition*, pp. 13–14 (ET, pp. 15–16); Schlatter, *Der Evangelist Matthäus*, p. 301.
[60] Marshall, *Luke*, pp. 216–17; Fitzmyer, *Luke*, p. 586.
[61] Davies and Allison (*Matthew*, vol. I, p. 105) refer to these in support of Markan priority.
[62] Davies and Allison, *Matthew*, vol. II, p. 493.

are not a very broad base and when we investigate the other aspect of the textual tendency – the crowds – it is notable that there are very many places in which Matthew shows no interest in Mark's reports of crowds following Jesus – not including them in his version (Mark 2.2, 15; 3.8; 5.21, 24; 6.2; 8.1; 9.14; 12.37) – and many other places in which Matthew's version is basically the same as Mark's (Mark 2.15a//Matt. 9.10; Mark 3.7//Matt. 4.25; Mark 6.34//Matt. 14.14). Matthew's tendency to include additional parti-cipants in various accounts (Matt. 8.28 cf. Mark 5.2; Matt. 9.27 and 20.30 cf. Mark 10.46; Matt. 27.49 cf. Mark 15.36; Matt. 27.54 cf. Mark 15.39; also Matt. 21.2,7) might be thought to be an aspect of a similar tendency, although perhaps the influence of a two-witness tradition, from Numbers 35.30; Deuteronomy 17.6; 19.15, might explain at least some of these alterations, e.g., Matthew 26.60 // Mark 15.57.[63]

It seems clear that the narrative descriptions of the responses of crowds to Jesus cannot provide a conclusive argument for one or other of the two hypotheses. One of the reasons for this is that in many cases it is merely the fact of a response that is reported, rather than the nature of that response. What we do find, in both Matthew and Luke, are indications of faith in the approach of individuals to Jesus and further indications in the responses of individuals and the disciples to Jesus in the wake of his miraculous activity.

4.2   Individuals approach Jesus

It may not be too much to say that in Mark when individuals approach Jesus with faith, this faith is never expressed in confes-sional or christological terms. Consider the following examples:

(i)   the leper approaches Jesus: 'if you will you can make me clean', 1.40;

(ii)   those who carried paralytic: 'Jesus saw their faith', 2.5;

(iii)   Jairus beseeches Jesus: 'come and lay your hands on her, so that she may be made well, and live', 5.23;

(iv)   woman with flow of blood: 'if I touch even his garments, I shall be made well', 5.28, cf. v. 34: 'your faith has made you well';

---

[63] For a survey of opinion see Braumann, 'Die Zweizahl und Verdoppelungen im Matthäusevangelium' and Davies and Allison, *Matthew*, vol. II, p. 80.

(v)   Syrophoenician woman begs Jesus to cast the demon out of her daughter, 7.26;
(vi)   others bring blind man to Jesus and beg him to touch him, 8.22;
(vii) man brings son to Jesus, 9.17f: 'teacher, I brought my son to you, for he has a dumb spirit'.

The single exception to this is the healing of blind Bartimaeus who cries out 'Jesus, Son of David, have mercy on me!' and will not be silenced (10.47ff).

By way of contrast, in both Matthew and Luke several of these accounts introduce a confessional element into the approach of the person to Jesus:

(i)   Matthew 8.2 // Luke 5.12: 'Lord, if you will you can make me clean' (cf. Mark 1.40);
(ii)   Matthew 15.25: 'Lord, help me (cf. Mark 7.26);
(iii) Matthew 17.15: 'Lord, have mercy upon my son' (cf. Mark 9.17 // Luke 9.38: 'teacher').

Many of these passages and the significance of the christological terminology have been discussed already. In terms of the specific interests of this chapter the question to be faced is whether and how Griesbach-Mark's omission of these vocatives might be explained, especially in view of his obvious interest in presenting petitioners approaching Jesus in faith. In Griesbach-Mark, considered as a redaction of Matthew and Luke, faith appears to have no content, although it does have a direction: it is directed towards Jesus' ability to help or heal. Furthermore Griesbach-Mark does not alter his sources consistently whereas, on the two-source hypothesis, Matthew can be shown regularly to introduce distinctive terminology.

For example, among other differences between the accounts of the Syrophoenician/Canaanite woman (Matt. 15.21–8; Mark 7.24–30) Matthew has the woman approach Jesus, saying, 'Have mercy upon me, Lord, Son of David' (Matt. 15.22). This is a characteristic Matthean statement of faithful approach to Jesus (cf. 9.27; 20.30 and on 17.15 see below), and is another example of an addition, assuming Markan priority, which fits Matthean preferences. A further example is the man who brings his son to Jesus. In Matthew 17.15 he approaches Jesus, saying, 'Lord, have mercy on my son' (cf. Mark 9.17 quoted above, parallel Luke 9.38). The main grounds for regarding these as Matthean redaction of Mark are the consistent use of Matthean vocabulary and themes. In other words, on the two-source hypothesis Matthew alters his source in order to emphasise and communicate particular themes. Griesbach-Mark edits and alters with no clear purpose.

5. Conclusion

In view of the evidence discussed in this chapter it is not perhaps surprising that Wrede's expectation (discussed in the introduction) has not been fulfilled. Griesbach-Mark offers no clearer perspective on the secrecy motif and his redactional alterations to Matthew and Luke do not contribute strongly to a development of this theme. While individual alterations can be explained, sometimes quite plausibly, there is little or no evidence of a consistent theological motivation for the changes that Mark must have made to his sources. On the other hand, from the perspective of Markan priority (there are no Q sayings which bear directly on the secrecy motif), Matthew's use of Mark coheres with tendencies observed elsewhere in Matthew (especially the importance of the OT), with vocabulary preferences and with the omission of material in order to highlight the christological features of a narrative.

13

CONCLUSION

1. Summary

The primary purpose of this study has been to investigate and assess the christological argument for Markan priority. In chapter one it was shown that this argument was developed primarily within British scholarship as a means of defending Markan priority and explaining Matthean alterations of Mark. Although this particular argument played a relatively small role in supporting the structure of the two-source hypothesis, several factors suggested its contemporary importance and the need for a critical assessment. The most important of these factors is the revival of the Griesbach hypothesis, which has involved criticisms of the arguments used to support Markan priority within the overall framework of the two-source hypothesis. These criticisms have, in turn, prompted from Markan priorists a re-assessment of the arguments from wording, order and content. Within this context it seemed appropriate and necessary to reassess arguments from christological development, a notion that was also appealed to by nineteenth-century defenders of the Griesbach hypothesis.

In chapter two, after a survey of proposed criteria for determining literary priority, we argued that a method which focussed on redactional plausibility and coherence was both appropriate to the christological material in view and able to treat the two major hypotheses in a relatively even-handed manner. Thus the discussions of the texts would involve a comparison between the plausibility of Markan redaction, assuming the Griesbach hypothesis, and the plausibility of Matthean redaction, assuming Markan priority. Any alternative method would involve the assumption of a particular pattern of christological development within the early period. Our method, however, focusses on the texts we do have, rather than on the pattern of development which we do not. It also allows both hypotheses to be tested in relation to their treatment of christologically loaded material. It allows this study to test whether the traditional argument should be regarded as a strong support for Markan priority, or whether the Griesbach hypothesis might be able to give a more plausible picture of redactional behaviour.

The investigation proper took as its starting-point two passages which were at the heart of the historical christological argument (described in chapter one). We suggested in chapter three that the significance of Matthew 19.17 // Mark 10.18 as a proof of Markan priority had been exaggerated by many scholars. In the first place Matthew's redactional emphasis has primarily to do with the importance of the law, so that, even when Markan priority is assumed, christological embarrassment cannot be proved to have been operative. On the other hand, the Griesbach hypothesis could explain Mark's redaction of Matthew and Luke in a relatively straightforward manner. No firm conclusions concerning the choice between Griesbach hypothesis and Markan priority could be drawn from this passage. Our investigation of the passage concerning the rejection at Nazareth (chapter four) concluded that here also the presence of 'christological embarrassment' could not be established. In this case, however, Markan priority and the two-source hypothesis emerged as superior to the Griesbach hypothesis in their ability to explain Matthean redactional interests (even without appeal to 'christological embarrassment' or the like). On the other hand, although the Griesbach hypothesis could explain *some* aspects of Markan redaction there were several difficulties noted.

In chapter five we investigated the episode recounting Jesus' walking on the water. This passage exhibits positive christological interests in both accounts and our investigation yielded more firm conclusions concerning the plausibility of the two-source hypothesis over against the Griesbach hypothesis. In this case Matthean redaction highlights christological themes prominent elsewhere in Matthew using characteristic vocabulary and OT allusions. On the other hand the redactional procedure predicated for Griesbach-Mark is less clear, less coherent and therefore less plausible.

In chapter six we investigated several key areas of the traditional christological argument for Markan priority (as outlined in chapter one): Jesus' emotions, questions and 'inability', all of which involve (for the two-source hypothesis) Matthean omission of Markan details. We suggested that these features of the 'traditional' argument were not compelling. Arguments based on the motivation for a redactor's omissions are difficult to control and in any case, other explanations were often indicated in the texts themselves. Thus, although the material could support the two-source hypothesis, this was not in virtue of the christological argument.

In chapter seven we investigated other general areas where scholars have highlighted the christological nature of Matthew's redactional interests, in the terminology of 'worshipping' and 'approaching' Jesus and in the passion narrative. We concluded that although Matthean redaction of Mark in these areas was coherent and plausible and in many ways preferable to the Griesbach hypothesis this was not due to specific or technical christological issues introduced by Matthew.

By this point in the study it becomes clear that a significant weakness in the 'traditional' christological argument for Markan priority is the generally negative cast of its formulations, based more on Matthew's difficulties with Markan material than on the positive christological emphases of Matthew. We thus attempted in the following chapters to compare the evangelists' treatment of major christological themes, using the christological titles as convenient *loci* for study.

In chapter eight we argued that the two-source hypothesis makes much better sense of the treatments of Jesus as teacher and as Lord than does the Griesbach hypothesis. Matthean redaction of Mark (assuming Markan priority) can be described as both coherent and plausible on several levels, especially in relation to the OT, in a way that could not be said of Griesbach-Mark. In chapter nine we again concluded, concerning the presentation of Jesus as Messiah, that the redactional activity of Matthew envisaged by the two-source hypothesis was both coherent and pervasive and plausibly understood as a reappropriation of Jewish and OT categories for Matthew's situation.

In chapter ten we investigated the treatment of Jesus as the Son of God. In this case several specific problems were noted in relation to the redactional procedure of Griesbach-Mark which were not present in Matthew's redaction of Mark. A similar conclusion was drawn from the Son of Man material (chapter eleven). In both cases Matthew's redaction of Mark involves an increased appropriation of OT allusions in service of the tradition.

These chapters form the basis, therefore, for a renewed christological argument for Markan priority, based not on what Matthew omitted from Mark, but on the coherent, plausible, pervasive and positive redactional alterations made by Matthew in his representation of the Markan traditions. In several places, however, the redactional activity envisaged for Griesbach-Mark could have been construed in terms of a developed but previously misconstrued secrecy motif. It therefore proved necessary to investigate the secrecy material with a view to assessing whether this material could be more plausibly explained by the Griesbach hypothesis. We concluded, however, that this material did not offer a key which would explain Griesbach-Mark; on the other hand Markan priority generally offered a reasonable and coherent picture of Matthean redaction activity in this area.

2. Conclusions

Our first and perhaps most obvious conclusion is that *the 'traditional' christological argument for Markan priority is fatally flawed and unable to support on its own the priority of Mark in relation to Matthew.* The traditional argument, as we showed in chapter one, focussed on passages in Mark which Matthew is said to have omitted or altered in order to safeguard his own christological position. But the passages chosen and the topics discussed in this connection were themselves the product of the then topical kenotic movement. Evidence that Matthew was intrinsically concerned with avoiding evidence of Jesus' human limitations does not arise from the study of Matthew's redactional procedure on its own terms. In addition, there is no evidence from later material that gospel traditions developed along a traditio-historical trajectory involving a reaction against Jesus' humanity, defined in terms of his emotional activity, limitations, ignorance etc. Indeed one of the great difficulties in this form of the christological argument is its fundamentally negative orientation. Such negative arguments are practically impossible to establish with probative force, especially when the argument depends on omitted material, for which any number of reasons might be plausibly advanced. If the preferred method is to be an assessment of the plausibility and coherence of the redactional procedures envisaged by the various theories, as outlined in chapter two, then the christological argument must be transformed.

In other words, the great weakness in the 'negative' orientation of the argument is that it focusses on aspects of Matthean christology that are only recognised when Markan priority is assumed.

If we did not have Mark we would hardly be led to suggest that Matthew's concerns were with correcting christological difficulties in his source(s). Thus the traditional formulation of the christological argument for Markan priority depends on both: (a) presupposing Markan priority; and (b) anachronistic concerns informed more by nineteenth- and twentieth-century christology than by known concerns of the first (or even second) century.

A second negative conclusion which must also be drawn from the investigation is that *the data we have surveyed provide little encouragement for modern defenders of the Griesbach hypothesis.* To be sure we have had occasion to point to aspects of the Griesbach-Markan redaction which were of interest or which offered an explanation for some of his projected behaviour. Such examples, combined with a generally negative verdict on the christological argument for Markan priority as customarily framed, should not, however, be taken as indications of support for the Griesbach hypothesis. In no single passage or aspect of our investigation did the Griesbach hypothesis emerge as preferable to the two-source hypothesis in terms of the coherence and plausibility of the redactional activity which the hypothesis requires. Such a negative judgement does not rest upon the christological argument in the first instance (except perhaps in prescribing the selection of material for investigation) but on the method agreed by recent defenders of the Griesbach hypothesis. In this sense our conclusion re-echoes the criticisms made by previous scholars to the effect that the redactional convictions of Griesbach-Mark do not form a coherent enough package to make the basic hypothesis believable.

> Two nineteenth-century critics of the Griesbach hypothesis may be cited here: K. Lachmann described Griesbach-Mark 'as a bungling dilettante, unsure of his way, borne hither and thither between Matthew's and Luke's gospels by boredom, desire, carelessness, folly or design' (ET from Palmer, 'Lachmann's Argument', p. 372). C. G. Wilke went even further, saying that Griesbach-Mark 'was not an abbreviator, nor an epitomator, nor even an excerpter, but was rather a castrator of the sources, how else could one designate the mutilator of secure sentences and the confusion of that which is mutilated?'[1] These were reinforced by C. M. Tuckett's conclusions (and closing exhortation) in *The Revival of the Griesbach Hypothesis*, pp. 186–7.

---

[1] Wilke, *Urevangelist*, p. 443: 'wäre nicht Abbreviator, auch nicht Epitomator, nicht Exzerptor, sondern – Kastrator der Nebentexte, oder wie sollte man den Verstümmler der geborgten Sätze und den Menger des Verstümmelten sonst nennen?' (cf. also pp. 438–9).

This then is the third conclusion to be drawn from our investigation: *the christological argument, if transformed in such a way as to focus on the positive redactional interests of the evangelists, provides powerful support for Markan priority.* It is notable that the most positive indications of support for Markan priority (in terms of the plausibility of the Matthean redaction) came from our investigations of the christological topics in chapters eight to eleven, the passage discussed in chapter five, and, to a lesser degree, the issues addressed in chapter seven. The support for Markan priority in these chapters was so strong as to render this reformulated argument a strong strand of support for Markan priority over against the revived Griesbach hypothesis. Such a reformulation will do for the christological argument what other reformulations have done for the arguments from order, wording and content, that is, place the argument within the broader context of the plausibility of the redactional procedures envisaged and demanded by the competing hypotheses.

In a very real sense, of course, all of these conclusions are more or less direct by-products of the methodological decisions made in chapter two. Once it was decided, for example, that a comparative-redactional approach should be taken, then our first conclusion, that negative arguments are difficult to assess and establish, comes as no surprise, since there is no real mechanism in the method to aid the detection of negative or reactionary redactional interests. Something similar could be said about our third conclusion, that a positive comparative-redactional approach favours Markan priority over the Griesbach hypothesis in relation to the material studied. This, however, is not a weakness of our study but a strength, especially inasmuch as the method was advocated by scholars from divergent viewpoints.

Nevertheless, scholars favouring the Griesbach hypothesis could dispute our negative assessment of the plausibility of this hypothesis in (at least) two ways. The first way to dispute this negative assessment would be to accept the basic principles of the method and argue that Griesbach-Mark was a competent author with a describable purpose to his redactional activity, and to provide an explanation for his activity in the form that has often been requested: a redaction-critical commentary. Our discussion suggests that this is unlikely to be a success, although it remains possible either that some as yet unknown controlling assumptions with compelling explanatory power can be attributed to Griesbach-

Mark or that a longer-term study within the context of a community or group already persuaded of the truth of the Griesbach hypothesis might find individually compelling, or plausible, or at least possible, explanations for the redaction of various passages. It seems likely that research of this type will be published and it remains a challenge to the neo-Griesbachians to produce arguments and approaches that render the redactional activity of Griesbach-Mark plausible to the scholarly community.

The second way to dispute the conclusion would be to dispute the principle upon which it is based. Did not Griesbach himself conclude his famous essay or Demonstration, by saying: 'Those who argue that Mark wrote under the influence of divine inspiration must surely regard it as being a pretty meagre one!'?[2] Perhaps one could be driven to accept the Griesbach hypothesis on other grounds and thus not really care that the activities of Griesbach-Mark are implausible. Is it necessary to assume that Griesbach-Mark was a competent author? Generally speaking this position has not been regarded as a particularly attractive one and although theoretically possible it is not commonly held. First, there is no external evidence which compels acceptance of the Griesbach hypothesis.[3] Secondly, this is almost certainly not what Griesbach meant by his comment cited above, since the course of his argument seeks to provide plausible reasons for Griesbach-Markan redactional activity. Griesbach's comment should be taken as a theological statement rather than a literary-critical one. He had previously published an attack on the orthodox conception of the inspiration (*theopneustia*, the word used above) of the scriptures.[4] Thirdly, in similar debates in both the nineteenth and twentieth centuries, Griesbachian scholars have continually sought to evade the assertion that the redactional activity of Griesbach-Mark is implausible.[5] For our purposes the general principles of the method focussing on redactional plausibility must be upheld. Not least because the principles upon which our discussion and our conclusion is based were 'agreed by all' (see chapter two).

---

[2] Griesbach, 'Demonstration', p. 135 (no exclamation in the Latin original).
[3] Although Matthean priority was widely taught by Fathers and popes, Clement's comment that the gospels with genealogies were written first (Eusebius, *Eccl. hist.* VI.14.6f) is something of an anomaly.
[4] See Delling, 'Johann Jakob Griesbach: His Life, Work and Times', p. 11; cf. Griesbach, *Theopneustia*.
[5] See our brief discussion in chapter 1 section 2.3 and chapter 2 section 2.

BIBLIOGRAPHY

1. Biblical texts and translations

Biblia Hebraica Stuttgartensia (eds. K. Elliger and W. Rudolph; Stuttgart: Deutsche Bibelgesellschaft, 1977).

Euangelium secundum Marcum. Novum Testamentum Graece secundum textum Westcotto-Hortianum (ed. S. C. E. Legg; Oxford: Clarendon, 1935).

Euangelium secundum Matthaeum. Novum Testamentum Graece secundum textum Westcotto-Hortianum (ed. S. C. E. Legg; Oxford: Clarendon, 1940).

The Gospel According to St Luke; Part One: Chapters 1–12; Part Two: Chapters 13–24 (International Greek New Testament Project (American and British Committees); The New Testament in Greek III; Oxford: Clarendon Press, 1984, 1987).

Η ΚΑΙΝΗ ΔΙΑΘΗΚΗ Novum Testamentum Graecum, editionis receptae cum lectionibus variantibus. Codicum MSS, Editionum aliarum, Versionum et Patrum. Nec non commentario pleniore. Ex Scriptoribus veteribus Hebraeis, Graecis et latinis Historiam et vim verborum illustrante. Opera et Studio Joannis Jacobi Wetstenii (Amsterdam: Dommeriana, 1751,2).

Novum Testamentum Graece. ad antiquissimos testes denuo recensuit apparatum criticum omni studio perfectum apposuit Commentationem Isagogicam praetexuit Constantinus Tischendorf (Editio octava critica maior; Vol. I: Matt., Mark, Luke, John; Lipsiae: Giesecke and Devrient, 1869[8]).

The New Testament in the Original Greek (eds. F. J. A. Hort and B. F. Westcott; Volume II; London: Macmillan, 1896[2] – first 1881).

The Greek New Testament. Fourth Revised Edition (eds. B. and K. Aland et al. ; Stuttgart: Deutsche Bibelgesellschaft, 1993; cf 1966[1], 1968[2], 1975[3]).

Novum Testamentum Graece (eds. B. and K. Aland et al. (E. Nestle); Stuttgart: Deutsche Bibelgesellschaft, 1993[27], cf. 1898[1], 1979[26]).

Septuaginta (ed. A. Rahlfs; Stuttgart: Deutsche Bibelstiftung, 1935[9]; 2 vols.).

Septuaginta. Vetus Testamentum Graecum Auctoritate Societatis Litterarum Göttingensis editum (eds. W. Kappler, R. Hanhart, A. Rahlfs and J. Ziegler; Göttingen: Vandenhoeck and Ruprecht, 1931–).

Synopsis Evangeliorum Matthaei Marci et Lucae una cum iis Joannis pericopis quae omnino cum caeterorum Evangelistarum narrationibus conferendae sunt. Textum recensuit et selectam lectionis varietatem adjecit J. J. Griesbach (Halle, 1776; 1797²; 1809³, 1822⁴).

Synopse des quatre évangiles en français: avec parallèles des apocryphes et des pères (eds. M. -E. Boismard and P. Benoit; 3 vols.; Paris: Editions du Cerf, 1965–77).

Synopsis Quattor Evangeliorum. Locis parallelis evangeliorum apocryphorum et patrum adhibitis (ed. K. Aland; Stuttgart: Deutsche Bibelstiftung, 1978, ©1963).

Synopse der drei ersten Evangelien mit Beigabe der johanneischen Parallelstellen (ed. H. Greeven (A. Huck); Tübingen: J. C. B. Mohr, 1981¹³).

Synopsis. of the Four Gospels in Greek Arranged According to the Two-Gospel Hypothesis (ed. J. B. Orchard; Edinburgh: T. & T. Clark, 1983).

The Holy Bible containing the Old and New Testaments. Revised Standard Version (New York and Glasgow: Collins, 1971. OT = © 1952¹; NT = ©1971²).

The Oxford Annotated Apocrypha: The Apocrypha of the Old Testament. RSV Expanded Edition containing the Third and Fourth books of the Maccabees and Psalm 151 (ed. B. M. Metzger; New York: Oxford University Press, 1977, ©1965, 1977).

The Revised English Bible (Oxford and Cambridge: Oxford University Press and Cambridge University Press, 1989).

2.   Other primary sources

Agrapha: aussercanonische Schriftfragmente (ed. A. Resch; TU 15/3–4; Leipzig: J. C. Hinrichs, 1906²; reprinted Darmstadt: Wissenschaftliche Buchgesellschaft, 1974).

Alexandrian Christianity. Selected Translations of Clement and Origen with Introductions and Notes (eds. J. E. L. Oulton and H. Chadwick; LCC 2; London: SCM, 1954).

Ante-Nicene Christian Library. Translations of the Writings of the Fathers down to AD 325 (eds. A. Roberts and J. Donaldson; 24 vols.; Edinburgh: T. & T. Clark, 1867–72).

A Select Library of the Nicene and Post Nicene Fathers of the Christian Church (eds. P. Schaff and H. Wace; Series 1 and 2; Edinburgh: T. & T. Clark, various dates c. 1890).

Ante-Nicene Exegesis of the Gospels (ed. H. Smith; TCL VI; London: SPCK, 1925–9; 6 vols.).

Apocrypha I, II, III (ed. E. Klostermann; Kleine Texte für theologische und philologische Vorlesungen und Übungen 3, 8 and 11; Bonn: A. Marcus & E. Weber's Verlag, 1903, 1904, 1904).

New Testament Apocrypha (eds. E. Hennecke and W. Schneemelcher; ET ed. R. McL. Wilson; Philadelphia: Westminster Press, 2 vols., 1963 and 1965).

The Apocryphal New Testament. Being the Apocryphal Gospels, Acts, Epistles, and Apocalypses with other narratives and fragments (ed. M. R. James; Oxford: Clarendon Press, 1983 reprint, © 1924¹).

The *Apostolic Fathers, Part I. S. Clement of Rome* (ed. J. B. Lightfoot; 2 vols.; Macmillan & Co., 1890) and *Part II. S. Ignatius, S. Polycarp* (3 vols.; Macmillan & Co., 1889, 2nd edn). Cf. also J. B. Lightfoot and J. R. Harmer (eds.), *The Apostolic Fathers. Revised Greek Texts with Introductions and English Translations* (Grand Rapids: Baker Book House, 1987, reprint from London: Macmillan, 1891).

Clemens Alexandrinus (O. Stählin (ed.); 3 vols.; GCS 12, 15, 17; Leipzig: J. C. Hinrichs, 1905, 1906, 1909).

Codex Sinaiticus Petropolitanus. The New Testament, the Epistle of Barnabas and the Shepherd of Hermas. Preserved in the Imperial Library of St Petersburg now reproduced in facsimile from photographs (eds. H. and K. Lake; Oxford: Clarendon, 1911).

A Concordance to the Greek Testament According to the Texts of Westcott and Hort, Tischendorf and the English Revisers (eds. W. F. Moulton, A. S. Geden and H. K. Moulton; Edinburgh: T. & T. Clark, 1980 reprint of 1978[5], cf 1897[1]).

The Dead Sea Scrolls in English. Revised and Extended Fourth Edition (ed. G. Vermes; Sheffield: Sheffield Academic, 1995).

Die Texte aus Qumran Hebräisch und deutsch mit masoretischer Punktation Übersetzung, Einführung und Anmerkungen (ed. E. Lohse; Munich: Kösel, 1964).

Die Texte vom Toten Meer (ed. J. Maier; Munich and Basel: Reinhardt, 1960; 2 vols.).

Discoveries in the Judean Desert (Oxford: Clarendon, 1955–):
  vol. I (1955) eds. D. Barthélemy and J. T. Milik
  vol. III (1962) eds. M. Baillet, J. T. Milik and R. de Vaux
  vol. V (1968) ed. J. M. Allegro (with A. A. Anderson)
  vol. VI (1977) eds. R. de Vaux and J. T. Milik
  vol. VII (1982) ed. M. Baillet

Konkordanz zu den Qumrantexten (ed. K. G. Kuhn; Göttingen: Vandehoeck and Ruprecht, 1960). Supplements in *RevQ* 1 (1958f) 163–87 (1QapGen); *RevQ* 4 (1963f) 163–234.

Dio Chrysostom (ed. and trans J. W. Cohoon; Loeb Classical Library; 5 vols.; London: W. Heinemann; Cambridge, MA: Harvard University Press, 1971 reprint).

ΔΙΟΝΥΣΙΟΥ ΛΕΙΨΑΝΑ. *The Letters and Other Remains of Dionysius of Alexandria* (ed. C. L. Feltoe; Cambridge: Cambridge University Press, 1904).

Early Christian Fathers (ed. C. C. Richardson; LCC 1; London: SCM, 1953).

Epictetus: The Discourses as Reported by Arrian, the Manual and Fragments (ed. W. A. Oldfather; LCL; London: W. Heinemann; 2 vols.; 1925 and 1928).

Epiphanius, *Ancoratus, Panarion and De fide* (3 vols.; ed. K. Holl; Leipzig: J. C. Hinrich; GCS 25: *Ancoratus and Panarion 1–33*, 1915; GCS 31: *Panarion 34–64*, 1922; GCS 37: *Panarion 65–80 and De fide*, 1933).

Eusebius Werke: I: Über das Lebens Constantins (ed. I. A. Heikel; GCS 1; Leipzig: J. C. Hinrichs, 1902); *II. 1,2,3: Historia Ecclesiastica* (ed. E. Schwarz (and T. Mommsen); GCS 2; Leipzig: J. C. Hinrichs,

1903–8); *III. 2: Die Theophanie* (ed. H. Gressmann; GCS 3; Leipzig: J. C. Hinrichs, 1904); *IV: Gegen Marcell* (ed. E. Klostermann; GCS 4; Leipzig: J. C. Hinrichs, 1906); *VI: Die Demonstratio Evangelica* (ed. I. A. Keikel; GCS 23; Leipzig: J. C. Hinrich, 1913).

Eusebius, *Historia Ecclesiastica. The Ecclesiastical History* (2 vols.; LCL; trans K. Lake (vol. I) and J. E. L. Oulton (vol. II); London: W. Heinemann, 1980).

The Exagoge *of Ezekiel* (ed. H. Jacobson; Cambridge: Cambridge University Press, 1983).

Gnosis. A Selection of Gnostic Texts (ed. W. Foerster; trans. R. McL. Wilson; 2 vols.; Oxford: Clarendon, 1972, 1974).

Sancti Irenaei Episcopi Lugdunensis Libros quinque adversus Haereses (ed. W. W. Harvey; Cambridge: Typis Academicis, 1857, 2 vols.).

Josephus (ed. and trans H. St. J. Thackeray, R. Marcus; LCL; 9 vols.; Cambridge, MA: Harvard University Press; London: W. Heinemann, 1979).

Iustini philosophi et martyris Opera (ed. J. C. T. Otto; vol. I; Jena: Dufft, 1875).

The Works now extant of S. Justin the Martyr (ed. G. J. Davis; Oxford: Parker, 1861).

Memar Marqah. The Teaching of Marqah Edited and Translated (ed. J. MacDonald; BZAW 84; Berlin: A. Töpelmann, 1963, 2 vols.).

Midrasch Tanchuma. Ein agadischer Commentar zum Pentateuch von Rabbi Tanchuma ben Rabbi Abba (ed. S. Buber; Wilna: W. & G. Romm, 1885).

Midrash Rabbah (eds. H. Freedman and M. Simon; 10 vols.; London: Soncino, 1961 third impression).

The Midrash on Psalms (ed. W. G. Braude; Yale Judaica Series vol. XIII; 2 vols.; New Haven: Yale University Press, 1959).

Mishnayoth (ed. P. Blackman; 7 vols.; New York: The Judaica Press, 1964, second edition).

The Mishnah. Translated from the Hebrew with Introduction and Brief Explanatory Notes (ed. H. Danby; Oxford: Oxford University Press, 1983 reprint of 1933[1]).

The Nag Hammadi Library in English. Translated by Members of the Coptic Gnostic Library Project of the Institute for Antiquity and Christianity (ed. J. M. Robinson; Leiden: E. J. Brill, 1984[2]).

New Documents Illustrating Early Christianity (multi-volume; ed. G. H. R. Horsley and S. R. Llewelyn; Macquarie University: Ancient History Documentary Research Centre, 1981–).

The Old Testament Pseudepigrapha (ed. J. H. Charlesworth; 2 vols.; *Volume One: Apocalyptic Literature and Testaments*, London: Darton, Longman and Todd, 1983; *Volume Two: Expansions of the 'Old Testament' and Legends, Wisdom and Philosophical Literature, Prayers, Psalms, and Odes, Fragments of Lost Judeo-Hellenistic Works*, New York: Doubleday and Co., 1985).

Concordance grecque des pseudépigraphes d'Ancien Testament: concordance, corpus des textes, indices (ed. A.-M. Denis; Louvain-la-Neuve: Université Catholique de Louvain, Institut Orientaliste, 1987).

Origenes Werke I and II (ed. P. Koetschau; GCS Origenes 1&2; Leipzig: J. C. Hinrichs, 1899); *Origenes Werke. IX* (ed. M. Rauer; GCS Origenes 9; Berlin: Akademie-Verlag, 1959); *Origenes Werke XII* (eds. E. Klostermann and E. Benz; GCS 38; Berlin: Akademie, 1976², 1933).

The Oxyrhynchus Papyri (eds. B. P Grenfell, A. S. Hunt *et al.*; London: Egypt Exploration Fund, 51 vols.; 1898–). Manuscripts cited by number, e. g., P. Oxy. 1081.

Papyri Graecae Magicae. Die Griechischen Zauberpapyri (ed. K. Preisendanz; 2 vols.; Stuttgart: Teubner, 1973–74²).

The Greek Magical Papyri in Translation, including the Demotic Spells (ed. H. D. Betz; Chicago: University Chicago Press, 1986).

Patrologia Graeca (ed. J. P. Migne; 162 vols.; Paris, 1857–66).

Patrologia Latina (ed. J. P. Migne; 221 vols.; Paris, 1844–64).

Philo (eds. F. H. Colson and G. H. Whitaker *et al.*; LCL; 12 vols.; London: W. Heinemann, 1929–53).

Philostratus, *The Life of Apollonius of Tyana* (2 vols.; LCL; ed. and trans F. C. Conybeare; London: W. Heinemann, 1912).

Pirkē de Rabbi Eliezer (The Chapters of Rabbi Eliezer the Great) According to the Text of the Manuscript belonging to Abraham Epstein of Vienna. Translated and Annotated with Introduction and Notes (ed. G. Friedlander; London: Kegan Paul, Trench and Trubner & Co., 1916).

Pliny Letters (eds. W. Melmoth and W. M. L. Hutchinson; LCL; 2 vols.; London: W. Heinemann, 1915).

Psalterium Chaldaicum ex Lagardiana Recensione (ed. E. Nestle; Tübingen: Fues, 1879).

Second-Century Christianity. A Collection of Fragments (ed. R. M. Grant; London: SPCK, 1946).

Hebrew–English Edition of the Babylonian Talmud (ed. I. Epstein; 20 vols.; London: Soncino, 1969).

Le Talmud de Jérusalem (ed. M. Schwab; 6 vols.; Paris: Maisonneuve, 1960).

The Talmud of the Land of Israel (ed. J. Neusner; Chicago: University of Chicago Press, 1982–).

The Bible in Aramaic. Based on Old Manuscripts and printed Texts. (ed. A. Sperber; 5 vols.; Leiden: Brill, 1959–73): *Volume One. The Pentateuch according to Targum Onkelos* (1959); *Volume Two. The Former Prophets according to Targum Jonanthon* (1959); *Volume Three. The Latter Prophets according to Targum Jonathan* (1962); *Volume Four A. The Hagiographa* (1968); *Volume Four B. The Targum and the Hebrew Bible* (1973).

Biblia Polyglotta Matritensia. Series IV. Targum Palaestinense in Pentateuchum Additur Targum Pseudojonatan ejusque hispanica versio L. 2 Exodus (ed. A. Diez Macho; Madrid: CSIC, 1980).

Neophyti 1 Targum Palestinense MS de la Biblioteca Vaticana. Tomo II Exodo (ed. A. Diez Macho; Madrid: CSIC, 1970).

Targum de Salmos. Edición príncipe del Ms. Villa-Amil n. 5 de Alfonso de Zamora (ed. L. Diez Merino; Bibliotheca Hispana Biblica 6; Madrid: CSIC, 1982).

The Fragment-Targums of the Pentateuch According to their Extant Sources (ed. M. L. Klein; AnBib 76; 2 vols.; Rome: BIP, 1980).

The Aramaic Bible. The Targums (eds. M. McNamara, K. Cathcart and M. Maher; The Aramaic Bible No.; Edinburgh: T. & T. Clark, various dates 1980–, many volumes). Volumes cited include: M. McNamara, *Targum Neofiti 1: Genesis* (1A, 1992); M. Maher, *Targum Pseudo-Jonathan: Genesis* (1B, 1992); B. Grossfeld, *The Targum Onqelos to Genesis* (6, 1988); D. J. Harrington and A. J. Saldarini, *Targum Jonathan of the Former Prophets* (10, 1987); B. D. Chilton, *The Isaiah Targum* (11, 1987); R. Hayward, *The Targum of Jeremiah* (12, 1987); S. H. Levey, *The Targum of Ezekiel* (13, 1987).

Tertullian: Adversus Marcionem (ed. E. Evans; 2 vols.; Oxford: Clarendon, 1972).

The Testaments of the Twelve Patriarchs. A Critical Edition of the Greek Text (ed. M. de Jonge; PsVTGr I,2; Leiden: E. J. Brill, 1978).

The Gospel According to Thomas, Coptic Text Established and Translated (eds. A. Guillamont, H. -C. Puech, G. Quispel, W. Till and Yassah 'Abd al Masîh; Leiden: Brill and London: Collins, 1959).

3. Other literature

Abbott, E. A., 'Gospels' *Encyclopedia Britannica. Ninth Edition* (Edinburgh: A. & C. Black, 1879) vol X. 789–843.

Achtemeier, P. J., '"And he followed him": Miracles and Discipleship in Mark 10:46–52' *Semeia* 11 (1978) 115–145.

'"He Taught Them Many Things": Reflections on Marcan Christology' *CBQ* 42 (1980) 465–81.

Albright, W. F. and Mann, C. S., *Matthew: Introduction, Translation, and Notes* (AB; New York: Doubleday & Co., 1971).

Alexander, P. S., 'The Targumim and Early Exegesis of "Sons of God" in Genesis 6' *JJS* 23 (1972) 60–71.

Allen, W. C., 'Modern Criticism and the New Testament' *Contentio Veritatis: Essays by Six Oxford Tutors* (New York: E. P. Dutton, 1902) 206–242.

A Critical and Exegetical Commentary on the Gospel According to S. Matthew (ICC: Edinburgh: T. & T. Clark, 1912[3], © 1907).

Aune, D. E., 'The Problem of the Messianic Secret' *NovT* 11 (1969) 1–31.

Bacchiocchi, S., 'Matthew 11:28–30: Jesus' Rest and the Sabbath' *AUSS* 22 (1984) 289–316.

Bacon, B. W., *Studies in Matthew* (London: Constable, 1930).

Baird, W., *History of New Testament Research. Volume One: From Deism to Tübingen* (Minneapolis: Fortress, 1992).

Balz, H. R., *Methodische Probleme der neutestamentlichen Christologie* (WMANT 25; Neukirchen-Vluyn: Neukirchener Verlag, 1967).

Bamptfylde, G., 'The Similitudes of Enoch: Historical Allusions' *JSJ* 15 (1984) 9–31.

Banks, R. J., *Jesus and the Law in Synoptic Tradition* (SNTSMS 28; Cambridge: Cambridge University Press, 1975).

Barth, G., 'Das Gesetzesverständnis des Evangelisten Matthäus' *Überlie-*

ferung und Auslegung im Matthäusevangelium (eds. G. Bornkamm, G. Barth, H. J. Held; WMANT 1; Neukirchen-Vluyn: Neukirchener Verlag, 1965[4]; cf. 1960[1]) 54–154. ET: 'Matthew's Understanding of the Law' *Tradition and Interpretation in Matthew* (trans. P. Scott; London: SCM, 1963) 58–164.

Bartsch, H.-W., 'Die Passions- und Ostergeschichten bei Matthäus. Ein Beitrag zur Redaktionsgeschichte des Evangeliums' *Entmythologisierende Auslegung. Aufsätze aus den Jahren 1940 bis 1960* (TF 26; Hamburg-Bergstedt: Herbert Reich, Evangelische Verlag, 1962) 80–92. (originally in *Basileia* (FS W. Freytag; Stuttgart, 1959) 28–41).

Batey, R. A., 'Is not this the Carpenter?' *NTS* 30 (1984) 249–58.

Bauckham, R. J., 'The Eschatological Earthquake in the Apocalypse of John' *NovT* 19 (1977) 224–33.

'The Worship of Jesus in Apocalyptic Christianity' *NTS* 27 (1980f) 322–41.

Bauer, B., *Kritik der evangelischen Geschichte der Synoptiker* (3 vols.; Leipzig: O. Wigand, 1841–2).

Bauer, D. R., *The Structure of Matthew's Gospel. A Study in Literary Design* (JSNTSS 31; Sheffield: Almond Press, 1988).

Bauer, W., Arndt, W. F., Gingrich, F. W. and Danker F. W., *A Greek–English Lexicon of the New Testament and Other Early Christian Literature* (Chicago and London: University of Chicago Press, 1979[2], from Bauer's German original 1958[5]).

Baur, F. C., 'Der Ursprung und Charakter des Lukasevangelium, mit Rücksicht auf die neuesten Untersuchungen' *Theologische Jahrbücher* 5 (1846) 453–615.

Kritische Untersuchungen über die kanonischen Evangelien, ihr Verhältnis zu einander, ihren Charakter und Ursprung (Tübingen: Fues, 1847).

Das Christenthum und die christliche Kirche der drei ersten Jahrhunderte (Tübingen, 1853, 1860[2], 1863[3] (*Kirchengeschichte der drei ersten Jahrhunderte*)). Second edition cited here from Baur's *Ausgewählte Werke in Einzelausgaben* (ed. K. Scholder; Stuttgart: F. Frommann, 1966; vol. III). ET: *The Church History of the First Three Centuries* (trans A. Menzies from 1863[3]; 2 vols.; London and Edinburgh: Williams and Norgate, 1878, 1879).

Beale, G. K., *The Use of Daniel in Jewish Apocalyptic Literature and in the Revelation of St John* (Lanham/New York/London: University Press of America, 1984).

Beare, F. W., 'Review of W. R. Farmer, *The Synoptic Problem*' *JBL* 84 (1965) 295–7.

The Gospel according to Matthew. A Commentary (Oxford: Basil Blackwell, 1981).

Beavis, M. A., *Mark's Audience: The Literary and Social Setting of Mark 4. 11–12* (JSNTSS 33; Sheffield: JSOT Press, 1989).

Bellinzoni, A. J. (ed.), *The Two-Source Hypothesis: A Critical Appraisal* (Macon, GA: Mercer University Press, 1985).

Berger, K., 'Die königlichen Messiastradition des Neuen Testaments' *NTS* 20 (1973) 1–44.

Best, E., *The Temptation and the Passion: the Markan Soteriology* (SNTSMS 2; Cambridge: Cambridge University Press, 1965).
'Discipleship in Mark: Mark 8:22–10:52' *SJT* 23 (1970) 323–37.
Following Jesus: Discipleship in the Gospel of Mark (JSNTSS 4; Sheffield: JSOT Press, 1981).
Betz, H. D., 'Jesus in Nazareth. Bemerkungen zu Markus 6, 1–6' *Israel hat dennoch Gott zum Trost* (FS S. Ben-Chorin; ed. G. Müller; Trier: Paulinus, 1978) 44–60.
Bieneck, J., *Sohn Gottes als Christusbezeichnung der Synoptiker* (ATANT; Zürich: Zwingli-Verlag, 1951).
Bigg, H. C., 'The Q Debate since 1955' *Themelios* 6 (1981) 18–28.
'The Present State of the Q Hypothesis' *Vox Evangelica* 18 (1988) 63–73.
Bishop, E. F. F., 'εἰ μὴ εἶς θεός. – A Suggestion' *ExpT* 49 (1937f) 363–6.
Bittner, W., 'Gott – Menschensohn – Davidssohn: Eine Untersuchung zur Traditionsgeschichte von Daniel 7,13f' *Freiburger Zeitschrift für Philosophie* 32 (1985) 343–72.
Black, D. A., 'Some Dissenting Notes on R. Stein's *The Synoptic Problem* and Markan «Errors»' *Filologia Neotestamentaria* 1 (1988) 95–100.
Black, M., 'Messianic Doctrine in the Qumran Scrolls', *Studia Patristica* (TU 63; eds. K. Aland and F. L. Cross; Berline: Akademie, 1957) vol. I. 441–59.
An Aramaic Approach to the Gospels and Acts (Oxford: Clarendon, 1967³).
'Aramaic Barnasha and the "Son of Man"' *ExpT* 95 (1984) 200–6.
The Book of Enoch or 1 Enoch. A New English Edition with Commentary and Textual Notes (SVTP 7; Leiden: E. J. Brill, 1985).
Blackburn, B., *Theios Anēr and the Markan Miracle Traditions: A Critique of the Theios Anēr Concept as an Interpretative Background of the Miracle Traditions Used by Mark* (WUNT 2. 40; Tübingen: J. C. B. Mohr, 1991).
Blair, E. P., *Jesus in the Gospel of Matthew* (New York and Nashville: Abingdon, 1960).
Blass, F., Debrunner, A. and Funk, R. W., *A Greek Grammar of the New Testament and other Early Christian Literature* (trans. and rev. Funk from ninth–tenth German edition; Cambridge: Cambridge University Press and Chicago: University Chicago Press, 1961).
Bleek, F., *Einleitung in das Neuen Testament* (ed. J. F. Bleek (son) editions 1 & 2; W. Mangold editions 3 & 4; Berlin: Reimer, 1862, 1866², 1875³, 1886⁴). Cited from 1862 edition. ET: *An Introduction to the New Testament* (trans W Urwich; Edinburgh: T. & T. Clark, 1869–70, from 1866²).
Synoptische Erklärung der drei ersten Evangelien (2 vols.; ed. H. Holtzmann; Leipzig: Engelmann, 1862).
Blenkinsopp, J., 'The Oracle of Judah and the Messianic Entry' *JBL* 80 (1961) 55–64.
Blevins, J. L., *The Messianic Secret in Markan Research, 1901–1976* (Washington: University Press of America, 1981).
Blinzler, J., *Die Brüder und Schwestern Jesu* (SBS 21; Stuttgart: Katholisches Bibelwerk, 1967).

Boers, H., 'Jesus and the Christian Faith: New Testament Christology Since Bousset's *Kyrios Christos*' *JBL* 79 (1970) 450–6.

Boismard, M.-E., 'The Two Source Theory at an Impasse' *NTS* 26 (1979) 1–17.

'Théorie des niveaux multiples' *The Interrelations of the Gospels. A Symposium led by M.-E. Boismard – W. R. Farmer – F. Neirynck. Jerusalem 1984* (ed. D. L. Dungan; BETL 95; Leuven: Leuven University Press, 1990) 231–43.

Boobyer, G. H., *St Mark and the Transfiguration Story* (Edinburgh: T. & T. Clark, 1942).

Boring, M. E., *Sayings of the Risen Jesus: Christian Prophecy in the Synoptic Tradition* (SNTSMS 46; Cambridge: Cambridge University Press, 1982).

'The Synoptic Problem, "Minor Agreements", and the Beelzebul Pericope' *The Four Gospels 1992 Festschrift Frans Neirynck* (eds. F. van Segbroeck, C. M. Tuckett, G. Van Belle, J. Vesheyden; BETL 100; Leuven: Leuven University Press, 1992) 587–619.

Bornkamm, G., 'Die Sturmstillung im Matthäusevangelium' *Wort und Dienst. Jahrbuch der Theologischen Schule Bethel* 1 (1948) 49–54. Cited from *Überlieferung und Auslegung im Matthäusevangelium* (eds. G. Bornkamm, G. Barth, H. J. Held; WMANT 1; Neukirchen-Vluyn: Neukirchener Verlag, 1965[4]; cf. 1960[1]) 48–53. ET: 'The Stilling of the Storm in Matthew' *Tradition and Interpretation in Matthew* (London: SCM, 1963) 52–7.

'Enderwartung und Kirche im Matthäusevangelium' *The Background of the New Testament and its Eschatology* (FS C. H. Dodd; eds. W. D. Davies and D. Daube; Cambridge: Cambridge University Press, 1956). ET: 'End-Expectation and Church in Matthew', *Tradition and Interpretation in Matthew* (eds. G. Bornkamm, G. Barth, H. J. Held; London: SCM, 1963) 15–51.

'Evangelien, Synoptische' *RGG* 2 (1958[3]) 753–66.

Bousset, W., *Kyrios Christos. Geschichte des Christusglaubens von den Anfängen des Christentums bis Irenaeus* (Göttingen: Vandenhoeck and Ruprecht, © 1913, 1921[2]). ET: *Kyrios Christos: A History of the Belief in Christ from the Beginnings of Christianity to Irenaeus* (trans. J. E. Steeley; Nashville: Abingdon, 1970).

Bovon, F., *Das Evangelium nach Lukas* (EKK NT III/1 (2); Zürich: Benziger and Neukirchener, 1989).

Box, G. H., *The Ezra-Apocalypse* (London: Pitman, 1912).

'IV Ezra' *The Apocrypha and Pseudepigrapha of the Old Testament in English* (ed. R. H. Charles; Oxford: Clarendon, 1913; 2 vols.) vol. I, 542–624.

Braumann, G., 'Die Zweizahl und Verdoppelungen im Matthäusevangelium' *TZ* 24 (1968) 255–66.

Brooke, G. J., *Exegesis at Qumran: 4QFlorilegium in its Jewish Context* (JSOTSS 29; Sheffield: JSOT, 1985).

Brooks, O. S., 'Matthew xxviii 16–20 and the Design of the First Gospel' *JSNT* 10 (1981) 2–18.

Brown, P., 'Sorcery, Demons and the Rise of Christianity from Late

Antiquity into the Middle Ages' *Witchcraft: Confessions and Accusations* (ed. M Douglas; London, 1970) 17–45. Reprinted in P. Brown, *Religion and Society in the Age of St Augustine* (London and New York: Harper and Row, 1972) 119–46.

Brown, R. E., *The Gospel According to John. A New Translation with Introduction and Harmony* (AB; 2 vols.; New York: Doubleday, 1966©, 1983 reprint).

Jesus – God and Man: Modern Biblical Reflections (London: Collier Macmillan, 1967).

The Birth of the Messiah. A Commentary on the Infancy Narratives in Matthew and Luke (London: G. Chapman; New York: Doubleday, 1977).

The Death of the Messiah. From Gethsemane to the Grave. A Commentary on the Passion Narratives in the Four Gospels (ABRL; New York: Doubleday, 1994; 2 vols.).

Brown, S., '"The Secret of the Kingdom of God" (Mark 4. 11)' *JBL* 92 (1973) 60–74.

Brownlee, W. H., 'Messianic Motifs of Qumran and the New Testament' *NTS* 3 (1956f) 12–30.

Bruce, A. B., *With Open Face: or, Jesus Mirrored in Matthew, Mark, and Luke* (London: Hodder & Stoughton, 1896).

The Synoptic Gospels (The Expositor's Greek Testament Volume One) (ed. W. Robertson Nicoll; London: Hodder & Stoughton, 1897).

Bruce, F. F., 'The Oldest Greek Versions of Daniel' *OTS* 20 (1977) 22–40.

Buchanan, G. W., 'Jesus and the Upper Class' *NovT* 7 (1964f) 195–209.

Bultmann, R., *Die Geschichte der synoptischen Tradition* (Göttingen: Vandenhoeck & Ruprecht, 1921[1], 1931[2], 1958[3]). ET: *The History of the Synoptic Tradition* (trans. J. Marsh from 1958[3]; New York: Harper and Row, 1976; © 1963).

Theologie des Neuen Testaments (Tübingen: J. C. B. Mohr, 1954[2], cf. 1948[1], 1984[9]). ET: *Theology of the New Testament* (trans. K. Grobel; London: SCM, 1983 reprint of 1952–5; 2 vols.).

Burford, A., *Craftsmen in Greek and Roman Society* (London: Thames & Hudson, 1972).

Burger, C., *Jesus als Davidssohn* (FRLANT 98; Göttingen: Vandenhoeck & Ruprecht, 1970).

'Jesus Taten nach Matthäus 8 und 9' *ZTK* 70 (1973) 272–87.

Burgon, J. W., *The Traditional Text of the Holy Gospels Vindicated and Established* (ed. E. Miller; London: George Bell and Sons, 1896).

Burkett, D., 'The Nontitular Son of Man: A History and Critique' *NTS* 40 (1994) 504–21.

Burkitt, F. C., *The Gospel History and Its Transmission* (Edinburgh: T. & T. Clark, 1907[2] reprint of 1906[1]).

Burton, E. D., *Some Principles of Literary Criticism and Their Application to the Synoptic Problem* (Chicago: University Chicago Press, 1904).

A Critical and Exegetical Commentary on the Epistle to the Galatians (ICC; T. & T. Clark: Edinburgh, 1921).

Büsching, A. F., *Die vier Evangelisten mit ihren eigenen Worten zusammen-*

gesetzt vom neuen verdeutschet auch mit hinlänglichen Erklärungen versehen (Hamburg: F. C. Ritter, 1766).

Butler, B. C., *The Originality of St Matthew: A Critique of the Two-Document Hypothesis* (Cambridge: Cambridge University Press, 1951).

Byrne, B., *'Sons of God' – 'Seeds of Abraham': A Study of the Idea of the Sonship of God of All Christians in Paul against the Jewish Background* (AnBib 83; Rome: BIP, 1979).

Caird, G. B., 'Expository Problems: The Transfiguration' *ExpT* 67 (1955f) 291–4.

Caragounis, C. C., *The Son of Man. Vision and Interpretation* (WUNT 38; Tübingen: J. C. B. Mohr, 1986).

Peter and the Rock (BZNW 58; Berlin and New York: de Gruyter, 1990).

Carson, D. A., 'Christological Ambiguities in the Gospel of Matthew' *Christ the Lord. Studies in Christology* (FS D. Guthrie; ed. H. H. Rowdon; Leicester: Inter-Varsity Press, 1982) 97–114.

'Redaction Criticism: On the Legitimacy and Illegitimacy of a Literary Tool' *Scripture and Truth* (eds. D. A. Carson and J. D. Woodbridge; Grand Rapids: Zondervan, 1983) 119–42.

'Matthew' *The Expositor's Bible Commentary Vol. 8* (12 vols.; ed. F. E. Gaebelein; Grand Rapids: Zondervan, 1984).

Casey, P. M., *The Son of Man: The Interpretation and Influence of Daniel 7* (London: SPCK, 1979).

'General, Generic and Indefinite: The Use of the Term 'Son of Man' in Aramaic Sources and in the Teaching of Jesus' *JSNT* 29 (1987) 21–56.

From Jewish Prophet to Gentile God: The Origins and Development of New Testament Christology (E. Cadbury Lectures of 1985 6; Cambridge: James Clarke, 1991).

Catchpole, D. R., 'The Answer of Jesus to Caiaphas (Matt XXVI. 64)' *NTS* 17 (1970f) 213–26.

'The Synoptic Divorce Material as a Traditio-Historical Problem' *BJRL* 57 (1974) 92–127.

'Tradition History' *New Testament Interpretation: Essays on Principles and Methods* (ed. I. H. Marshall; Exeter: Paternoster, 1977) 165–80.

'The Fearful Silence of the Women at the Tomb' *JTSA* 18 (1977) 3–10.

The Quest For Q (Edinburgh: T. & T. Clark, 1993).

Cave, C. H., 'The Leper: Mark 1:40–45' *NTS* 25 (1978–9) 245–50.

Cerfaux, L., 'Le problème synoptique: À propos d'un livre récent' *NRT* 76 (1954) 494–505.

Chadwick, H., *Origen: Contra Celsum. Translated with an Introduction and Notes* (Cambridge: Cambridge University Press, 1953).

Chapman, J., *Matthew, Mark, and Luke: A Study in the Order and Interrelation of the Synoptic Gospels* (ed. J. M. T. Barton; London: Longmans, Green, 1937).

Charles, R. H., *The Book of Enoch or 1 Enoch. Translated from the editor's Ethiopic Text and edited with the introduction, notes and indexes of the first edition wholly recast, enlarged and rewritten* (Oxford: Clarendon, 1912).

Charlesworth, J. H., 'Reflections on the SNTS Pseudepigrapha Seminar at

Duke on the Testaments of the Twelve Patriarchs' *NTS* 23 (1977) 296–304.

'The Concept of the Messiah in the Pseudepigrapha' *ANRW* II. 19. 1 (1979) 188–218.

The New Testament Apocrypha and Pseudepigrapha (ATLA Bibliog. Series 17; London: ATLA & Scarecrow Press, 1987).

Charlesworth, J. H. (ed.), *The Messiah: Developments in Earliest Judaism and Christianity. The First Princeton Symposium on Judaism and Christian Origins* (Minneapolis: Fortress, 1992).

Chase, F. H., 'The Gospels in the light of Historical Criticism' *Cambridge Theological Essays: Essays on Some Theological Problems of the Day by Members of the University of Cambridge* (ed. H. B. Swete; London: Macmillan, 1905) 371–419.

Chester, A., *Divine Revelation and Divine Titles in the Pentateuchal Targumim* (TSAJ 14; Tübingen: J. C. B. Mohr (Paul Siebeck), 1986).

Chilton, B. D., 'Jesus *ben David*: Reflections on the *Davidssohnfrage*' *JSNT* 14 (1982) 88–112.

Profiles of a Rabbi. Synoptic Opportunities in Reading about Jesus (Brown Judaic Studies 177; Atlanta: Scholars, 1989).

Collins, A. Y., 'The Apocalyptic Son of Man Sayings' *The Future of Early Christianity* (FS H. Koester; ed. B. A. Pearson; Minneapolis: Fortress, 1991) 220–8.

'Establishing the Text: Mark 1:1', *Texts and Contexts: Biblical Texts in their Textual and Situational Contexts* (FS L. Hartman; eds. T. Fornberg and D. Hellholm; Oslo: Scandinavian University Press, 1995) 111–27.

Collins, J. J., 'The "Son of Man" in First Century Judaism' *NTS* 38 (1992) 448–66.

'The *Son of God* Text from Qumran' *From Jesus to John: Essays on Jesus and New Testament Christology in Honour of Marinus de Jonge* (ed. M. C. de Boer; JSNTSS 84; Sheffield: JSOT, 1993) 65–82.

'The Works of the Messiah', *Dead Sea Discoveries* 1 (1994) 98–112.

The Scepter and the Star: The Messiahs of the Dead Sea Scrolls and Other Ancient Literature (ABRL; New York: Doubleday, 1995).

Conybeare, F. C., 'The Eusebian Form of the Text Matth. 28, 19' *ZNW* 2 (1901) 275–88.

'Three Early Doctrinal Modifications of the Text of the Gospels' *Hibbert Journal* 1 (1902) 96–113.

History of New Testament Criticism (London: Watts and Co., 1910).

Conzelmann, H., *Die Mitte der Zeit: Studien zur Theologie des Lukas* (BhT 17; Tübingen: Mohr, 1954[1], cf 1977[6]). ET: *The Theology of St. Luke* (trans. G. Buswell; London: Faber, 1960; reprint Philadelphia: Fortress, 1982).

'Historie und Theologie in den synoptischen Passionsberichten' *Zur Bedeutung des Todes Jesu. Exegetische Beiträge* (ed. F. Viering; Gütersloh: Gerd Mohn, 1967[2]) 37–53. ET: 'History and Theology in the Passion Narratives of the Synoptic Gospels' *Interpretation* 24 (1970) 178–97.

Cooke, G., 'The Israelite King as Son of God' *ZAW* 73 (1961) 202–25.

Cope, O. L., *Matthew: A Scribe Trained for the Kingdom of Heaven* (CBQMS 5; Washington: CBAA, 1976).

'The Argument Revolves: The Pivotal Evidence for Markan Priority Is Reversing Itself' *New Synoptic Studies: The Cambridge Gospel Conference and Beyond* (ed. W. R. Farmer; Georgia: Mercer University Press; 1983) 143–59.

Coppens, J., 'Les logia du Fils de l'Homme dans l'évangile de Marc' *L'évangile selon Marc: Tradition et rédaction* (BETL 34; ed. M. Sabbe; Leuven: Leuven University Press, 1974) 487–528.

Corley, B. C. (ed.), *Colloquy on New Testament Studies: A Time for Reappraisal and Fresh Approaches* (Macon, GA: Mercer University Press, 1983).

Corrington, G. P., *The 'Divine Man': His Origin and Function in Hellenistic Popular Religion* (AUS VII. 17; New York/Berne/Frankfurt: Peter Lang, 1986).

Cranfield, C. E. B., *The Gospel According to Saint Mark* (CGTC; Cambridge: Cambridge University Press, 1966, 1959).

Creed, J. M., *The Gospel According to St Luke. The Greek Text with Introduction, Notes, and Indices* (London: Macmillan & Co., 1930; cited from 1942 reprint).

Cross, F. M., 'Qumran Cave 1' *JBL* 75 (1956) 121–5.

Crossan, J. D., *The Historical Jesus: The Life of a Mediterranean Jewish Peasant* (Edinburgh: T. & T. Clark, 1991).

Cullmann, O., *Die Christologie des Neuen Testaments* (Tübingen: J. C. B. Mohr, 1957). ET: *The Christology of the New Testament* (trans. S. C. Guthrie and C. A. M. Hall; London: SCM, 1963[2], 1980 reprint).

Dahl, N. A., 'Die Passionsgeschichte bei Matthäus' *NTS* 2 (1955f) 17–32. ET: 'The Passion Narrative in Matthew' *The Interpretation of Matthew* (ed. G. N. Stanton; London: SPCK, 1983) 42–55.

Dalman, G. H., *Die Worte Jesu mit Berücksichtung des nachkanonischen jüdischen Schrifttums und der aramäischen Sprache* (Leipzig: J. C. Hinrichs, 1898). ET: *The Words of Jesus Considered in Light of Post-Biblical Jewish Writings and the Aramaic Language* (trans. D. M. Kay; Edinburgh: T. & T. Clark, 1902).

Danker, F. W., ' "God With Us": Hellenistic Christological Perspectives in Matthew' *CurTM* 19 (1992) 433–9.

Daube, D., *The New Testament and Rabbinic Judaism* (Jordan Lectures, 1952; London: Athlone Press, 1956).

Davidson, S., *An Introduction to the Study of the New Testament: Critical, Exegetical, and Theological. Third Edition, Revised and Improved* (London: Kegan Paul, Trench, Trübner, 1894[3]; 2 vols.).

Davies, W. D. and Allison, D. C., Jr, *A Critical and Exegetical Commentary on the Gospel According to Saint Matthew* (ICC; vols. I and II, Edinburgh: T. & T. Clark, 1988, 1991).

Davies, W. D., *The Setting of the Sermon on the Mount* (Cambridge: Cambridge University Press, 1964).

'The Jewish Sources of Matthew's Messianism' *The Messiah: Developments in Earliest Judaism and Christianity. The First Princeton Symposium on Judaism and Christian Origins* (Minneapolis: Fortress, 1992) 494–511.

Dehandschutter, B., 'The Gospel of Thomas and the Synoptics: the Status Quaestionis' *Studia Evangelica Vol VII: Papers presented to the Fifth International Congress on Biblical Studies held at Oxford, 1973* (ed. E. A. Livingstone; TU 126; Berlin: Akademie-Verlag, 1982) 157–60.

Deissmann, G. A., *Bibelstudien. Beitrage zumeist aus den Papyri und Inschriften, zur Geschichte der Sprache, des Schrifttums und der Religion des hellenistischen Judentums und des Urchristentums* (Marburg: Elwert, 1895). ET: *Bible Studies: Contributions chiefly from Papyri and Inscriptions to the History of the Language, the Literature, and the Religion of Hellenistic Judaism and Primitive Christianity* (Edinburgh: T. & T. Clark, 1901).

Licht von Osten: Das Neue Testament und die neuentdeckten Texte der hellenistisch-römischen Welt (Tübingen: J. C. B. Mohr (Paul Siebeck), 1923, fourth edition; first German edition 1908). ET: *Light from the Ancient East: The New Testament Illustrated by Recently Discovered Texts of the Graeco-Roman World* (trans. L. R. M. Strachan; London: Hodder & Stoughton, 1927 2nd English edition, from 1923⁴ German; first ET 1910).

de Lacey, D. R., ' "One Lord" in Pauline Christology' *Christ the Lord. Studies in Christology presented to Donald Guthrie* (ed. H. H. Rowdon; Leicester: Inter-Varsity Press, 1982) 191–203.

Delling, G., 'Die Bezeichnung »Söhne Gottes« in der jüdischen Literatur der hellenistisch-römischen Zeit' *God's Christ and His People* (FS N. A. Dahl; eds. J. Jervell and W. A. Meeks; Oslo: Universitetsforlaget, 1977) 18–28.

'Johann Jakob Griesbach: seine Zeit, sine Leben, sein Werk' *TZ* 33 (1977) 81–99. ET cited here: 'Johann Jakob Griesbach: His Life, Work and Times' *J. J. Griesbach: Synoptic and text-critical studies 1776–1976* (eds. B. Orchard and T. R. W. Longstaff; SNTSMS 34; Cambridge: Cambridge University Press, 1978) 5–21.

Derrett, J. D. M., 'Law in the New Testament: The Palm Sunday Colt' *NovT* 13 (1971) 241–58.

Descamps, A., 'Rédaction et christologie dans le récit matthéen de la Passion' *L'évangile selon Matthieu. Rédaction et théologie* (ed. M. Didier; BETL 29; Gembloux: Duculot, 1972) 359–415.

'Pour une histoire du titre «Fils de Dieu». Les antécédents par rapport à Marc', *L'évangile selon Marc. Tradition et rédaction* (ed. M. Sabbe; BETL 34; Leuven: Leuven University Press, 1988²) 529–71.

Deutsch, C., *Hidden Wisdom and the Easy Yoke: Wisdom, Torah and Discipleship in Matthew 11. 25–30* (JSNTSS 18; Sheffield: JSOT Press, 1987).

Dibelius, M., *Die Formgeschichte des Evangeliums* (ed. G. Bornkamm; Tübingen: J. C. B. Mohr (Paul Siebeck), 1959³). ET: *From Tradition to Gospel* (trans. B. L. Woolf; London: Ivor Nicholson and Watson, 1934).

'The Contribution of Germany to New Testament Science' *ExpT* 41 (1929f) 535–9.

Gospel Criticism and Christology (London: Ivor Nicholson & Watson, 1935).

Donahue, J. R., 'Temple, Trial, and Royal Christology (Mark 14:53–65)', *The Passion in Mark. Studies on Mark 14–16* (ed. W. H. Kelber; Philadelpia: Fortress, 1976).

'Jesus as the Parable of God in the Gospel of Mark' *Int* 32 (1978) 369–86.

'A Neglected Factor in the Theology of Mark' *JBL* 101 (1982) 563–94.

'Recent Studies on the Origin of "Son of Man" in the Gospels' *CBQ* 48. 3 (1986) (= *A Wise and Discerning Heart* (FS J. A. Fitzmyer)) 484–98.

Donaldson, T. L., *Jesus on the Mountain. A Study in Matthean Theology* (JSNTSS 8; Sheffield: JSOT Press, 1985).

Dormeyer, D., *Die Passion Jesu als Verhaltensmodel. Literarische und theologische Analyse der Tradition- und Redaktionsgeschichte der Markuspassion* (Münster: Aschendorff, 1974).

Downing, F. G., 'Redaction Criticism: Josephus' Antiquities and the Synoptic Gospels (I) and (II)' *JSNT* 8 (1980) 46–65; 9 (1980) 29–48.

Drury, C., 'Who's in, Who's out?' *What About the New Testament?* (FS C. F. Evans; ed. M. Hooker and C. Hickling; London: SCM, 1975) 223–33.

Drury, J., *Tradition and Design in Luke's Gospel: A Study in Early Christian Historiography* (London: Darton, Longman and Todd, 1976).

Duling, D. C., 'Solomon, Exorcism, and Son of David' *HTR* 68 (1975) 235–52.

'The Therapeutic Son of David: An Element in Matthew's Christological Apologetic' *NTS* 24 (1978) 392–410.

Dungan, D. L., 'Mark – The Abridgement of Matthew and Luke' *Jesus and Man's Hope* (2 vols.; ed. D. G. Miller; Perspective; Pittsburgh Theological Seminary, 1970) I. 51–97.

'Reactionary Trends in the Gospel Producing Activity of the Early Church: Marcion, Tatian, Mark' *L'évangile selon Marc. Tradition et rédaction* (ed. M. Sabbe; BETL 34; Leuven: Leuven University Press, 1974, 1988²) 179–202.

'The Purpose and Provenance of the Gospel of Mark according to the "Two-Gospel" (Owen–Griesbach) Hypothesis' *New Synoptic Studies: The Cambridge Gospel Conference and Beyond* (ed. W. R. Farmer; Georgia: Mercer University Press, 1983) 411–40. This was slightly revised and republished as 'The Purpose and Provenance of the Gospel of Mark according to the "Two-Gospel" (Griesbach) Hypothesis' in *Colloquy on New Testament Studies: A Time for Reappraisal and Fresh Approaches* (ed. B. C. Corley; Macon, GA: Mercer University Press, 1983) 133–56.

'A Griesbachian Perspective on the Argument from Order' *Synoptic Studies: The Ampleforth Conferences of 1982 and 1983* (ed. C. M. Tuckett; JSNTSS 7; JSOT: Sheffield, 1984) 67–74.

'The Jerusalem Symposium 1984' *The Interrelations of the Gospels. A Symposium led by M.-E. Boismard – W. R. Farmer – F. Neirynck. Jerusalem 1984* (ed. D. L. Dungan; BETL 95; Leuven: Leuven University Press, 1990) IX–XXX.

Dungan, D. L. (ed.), *The Interrelations of the Gospels. A Symposium led by*

M.-E. Boismard – W. R. Farmer – F. Neirynck. *Jerusalem 1984* (BETL 95; Leuven: Leuven University Press, 1990).

Dunn, J. D. G., 'The Messianic Secret in Mark' *TynBul* 21 (1970) 92–117. An abbreviated version is published in C. M. Tuckett (ed.), *The Messianic Secret* (IRT 1; London: SPCK, 1983) 116–31.

Christology in the Making: A New Testament Inquiry into the Origins of the Doctrine of the Incarnation (London: SCM, 1980).

'Foreword to Second Edition' *Christology in the Making: A New Testament Inquiry into the Origins of the Doctrine of the Incarnation* (London: SCM, 1989²).

du Plessis, P. J., *ΤΕΛΕΙΟΣ: The Idea of Perfection in the New Testament* (Kampen: Kok, 1959).

Earl, D., 'Prologue-form in Ancient Historiography' *ANRW* I. 2 (1972) 842–56.

Ebeling, H. J., *Das Messiasgeheimnis und die Botschaft des Marcus-Evangelisten* (BZNW (uKAK) 19; Berlin: A. Töpelmann, 1939).

Edwards, J. R., The Use of ΠΡΟΣΕΡΧΕΣΘΑΙ in the Gospel of Matthew' *JBL* 106 (1987) 65–74.

'The Baptism of Jesus according to the Gospel of Mark' *JETS* 34 (1991) 43–57.

Ehrman, B. D., 'The Text of Mark in the Hands of the Orthodox' *LQ* 5 (1991) 143–56.

The Orthodox Corruption of Scripture: The Effect of Early Christological Controversies on the Text of the New Testament (New York: Oxford University Press, 1993).

Eichhorn, J. G., 'Über die drei ersten Evangelien' *Allgemeine Bibliothek der biblischen Literatur* (Leipzig: Weidmannschen, 1794) vol. V, 759–996.

Elliott, J. K., 'The Synoptic Problem and the Laws of Tradition: A Cautionary Note' *ExpT* 82 (1972) 148–52.

'An Eclectic Textual Commentary on the Greek Text of Mark's Gospel' *New Testament Textual Criticism: Its Significance for Exegesis* (FS B. M. Metzger; eds. E. J. Epp and G. D. Fee; Oxford: Clarendon, 1981) 47–60.

Elliott, N., 'The Silence of the Messiah: The Function of the "Messianic Secret" Motifs Across the Synoptics' *SBLSP* (1993) 604–22.

Ellis, P. F., *Matthew: His Mind and His Message* (Minnesota: Liturgical Press, 1974).

Enslin, M. S., *Christian Beginnings* (New York: Harper, 1938).

Evans, C. A., *Jesus and His Contemporaries: Comparative Studies* (AGJU XXV; Leiden: E. J. Brill, 1995).

'A Note on the "First-Born Son" of 4Q369' *Dead Sea Discoveries* 2 (1995) 185–201.

Evans, C. F., *Saint Luke* (TPINTC; London: SCM and Philadelphia: TPI, 1990).

Evanson, E., *The Dissonance of the four generally received Evangelists and the Evidence of their respective authenticity examined.* (Ipswich: G. Jermyn, 1792; Gloucester, 1805²).

Ewald, H., 'Ursprung und Wesen der Evangelien' *Jahrbücher der biblischen*

Wissenschaft (Göttingen) I (1848) 113–54, II (1849) 180–224, III (1851) 140–77.

Fallon, F. T. and Cameron, R., 'The Gospel of Thomas: A Forschungsbericht and Analysis' *ANRW* II. 25. 5 (1988) 4195–251.

Farmer, W. R., *The Synoptic Problem: A Critical Analysis* (New York: Macmillan, 1964).

'The Two-Document Hypothesis as a Methodological Criterion in Synoptic Research' *ATR* 48 (1966) 380–96.

'The Lachmann Fallacy' *NTS* 14 (1967f) 441–3.

'Modern Developments of Griesbach's Hypothesis' *NTS* 23 (1977) 275–95.

'The Present State of the Synoptic Problem' *PSTJ* 32 (1978) 1–7.

'The Synoptic Problem: The Inadequacies of the Generally Accepted Solution' *PSTJ* 33 (1980) 20–7.

'Introduction' *New Synoptic Studies: The Cambridge Gospel Conference and Beyond* (ed. W. R. Farmer; Macon, GA: Mercer University Press, 1983) vii–xli.

'Is Streeter's Fundamental Solution to the Synoptic Problem Still Valid?' *The New Testament Age* (FS B. Reicke; ed. W. C. Weinrichs; Macon, GA: Mercer University Press, 1984) 1. 147–64.

'Luke's Use of Matthew: A Christological Inquiry' *PSTJ* 40 (1987) 39–50.

'Source Criticism: Some Comments on the Present Situation' *USQR* 42 (1988) 49–57.

'The Two-Gospel Hypothesis: The Statement of the Hypothesis' *The Interrelations of the Gospels* (ed. D. L. Dungan; BETL 95; Leuven: Leuven University Press, 1990) 125–56.

'The Passion Prediction Passages and the Synoptic Problem: A Test Case' *NTS* 36 (1990) 558–70.

'State *Interesse* and Marcan Primacy 1870–1914' *The Four Gospels 1992 Festschrift Frans Neirynck* (eds. F. van Segbroeck, C. M. Tuckett, G. Van Belle, J. Veshegden; BETL 100; Leuven: Leuven University Press, 1992) 2477–98.

'The *Minor Agreements* of Matthew and Luke Against Mark and the Two Gospel Hypothesis: A Study of These Agreements in Their Compositional Contexts' *Minor Agreements Symposium Göttingen 1991* (ed. G. Strecker; GTA 50; Göttingen: Vandenhoeck & Ruprecht, 1993) 163–207.

Farmer, W. R. (ed.), *New Synoptic Studies: The Cambridge Gospel Conference and Beyond* (Macon, GA: Mercer University Press, 1983).

Farmer, W. R., Dungan, D. L., McNicol, A. J., Peabody, D. B. and Schuler, P. L., 'Narrative Outline of the Markan Composition According to the Two Gospel Hypothesis' *SBLSP* (1990) 212–39.

Farrer, A. M., *St Matthew and St Mark* (E. Cadbury Lectures 1953–4; London: A. & C. Black, 1954).

'On Dispensing with Q' *Studies in the Gospels. Essays in Memory of R. H. Lightfoot* (ed. D. E. Nineham; Oxford: Blackwell, 1955, 1967 reprint) 55–86.

Fee, G. D., 'Modern Text Criticism and the Synoptic Problem' *J. J. Griesbach: Synoptic and Text-Critical Studies, 1776–1976* (SNTSMS 34; eds. B. Orchard and T. R. W. Longstaff; Cambridge: Cambridge University Press, 1978) 154–69.

Fischer, K. M., 'Redaktionsgeschichtliche Bemerkungen zur Passionsgeschichte des Matthäus' *Theologische Versuche* 2 (1970) 109–38.

Fisher, L. R., '"Can this be the Son of David?"' *Jesus and the Historian* (FS E. C. Colwell; ed. F. T. Trotter; Philadelphia: Westminster, 1968) 82–97.

Fitzmyer, J. A., 'The Aramaic "Elect of God" Text from Qumran Cave 4' *CBQ* 27 (1965) 348–72.

'Anti-Semitism and the Cry of "All the People"' *Theological Studies* 26 (1965) 667–71.

The Genesis Apocryphon of Qumran Cave 1. A Commentary (Biblica et Orientalia 18; Rome: Pontifical Biblical Institute, 1966).

'Book Review: Matthew Black, *An Aramaic Approach to the Gospels and Acts*' *CBQ* 30 (1968) 417–28.

'The Priority of Mark and the "Q" Source in Luke' *Jesus and Man's Hope* (ed. D. G. Miller; 2 vols.; Perspective; Pittsburgh Theological Seminary, 1970) I. 131–70.

'The New Testament Title "Son of Man" Philologically Considered' *A Wandering Aramean: Collected Aramaic Essays* (SBLSMS 21; Missoula: Scholars Press, 1979) 143–60.

'The Semitic Background of the New Testament Kyrios-Title' *A Wandering Aramean: Collected Aramaic Essays* (SBLMS 21; Missoula: Scholars Press, 1979) 115–42.

The Gospel According to Luke. Introduction, Translation and Notes (2 vols.; AB 28 and 28A; Garden City NY: Doubleday, 1981, 1985).

'4Q246: The "Son of God" Document from Qumran' *Biblica* 74 (1993) 153–74.

'The Palestinian Background of "Son of God" as a Title for Jesus' *Texts and Contexts: Biblical Texts in their Textual and Situational Contexts* (FS L. Hartman; eds. T. Fornberg and D. Hellholm; Oslo: Scandinavian University Press, 1995) 567–77.

Fleddermann, H., '"And He Wanted to Pass by Them" (Mark 6:48c)' *CBQ* 45 (1983) 389–95.

Flusser, D., 'Two Notes on the Midrash on 2 Sam. vii' *IEJ* 9 (1959) 107–9.

Foakes-Jackson, F. J. and Lake, K. (eds), *The Beginnings of Christianity. Part One. The Acts of the Apostles* (London: Macmillan & Co., 1920–33; 5 vols., 1939 reprint).

France, R. T., 'Mark and the Teaching of Jesus' *Gospel Perspectives* 1 (Sheffield: JSOT, 1980) 101–36.

'The Formula-Quotations of Matthew 2 and the Problem of Communication' *NTS* 27 (1980f) 233–51.

'The Worship of Jesus: A Neglected Factor in Christological Debate?' *Christ the Lord. Studies in Christology presented to Donald Guthrie* (ed. H. H. Rowdon; Leicester: Inter-Varsity Press, 1982) 17–36.

Matthew: Evangelist and Teacher (Exeter: Paternoster, 1989).

Frankemölle, H., *Jahwebund und Kirche Christi* (NTAbh 10 (nF); Münster, 1984).

Fuller, R. H., *The Mission and Achievement of Jesus: An Examination of the Presuppositions of New Testament Theology* (SBT 12; London: SCM, 1954).

The Foundations of New Testament Christology (London: Lutterworth Press, 1965).

'Review Article: *The Synoptic Problem*: After Ten Years' *PSTJ* 28 (1975) 63–74. (Also includes contributions by E. P. Sanders and T. R. W. Longstaff).

'Baur versus Hilgenfeld: A Forgotten Chapter in the Debate on the Synoptic Problem' *NTS* 24 (1978) 355–70.

'The Conception/Birth of Jesus as a Christological Moment' *JSNT* 1 (1978) 37–52.

Furfey, P. H., 'Christ as *Tektōn*' *CBQ* 17 (1955) 324–35.

Gaechter, P., *Das Matthäusevangelium* (Innsbruck/Vienna/Munich: Tyrolia, 1963).

Garrett, S. R., *The Demise of the Devil: Magic and the Demonic in Luke's Writings* (Minneapolis: Fortress, 1989).

Geist, H., *Menschensohn und Gemeinde: Eine redaktionskritische Untersuchung zur Menschensohn prädikation im Matthäus-evangelium* (FB 57; Wurzburg: Echter, 1986).

Geoghegan, A. T., *The Attitude towards Labor in Early Christianity and Ancient Culture* (Washington, DC: Catholic University of America, 1945).

Gerhardsson, B., *The Testing of God's Son (Matt 4:1–11 and Par.)* (CBNT 2. 1; Lund: C. W. K. Gleerup, 1966).

'Jésus livré et abandonné d'après la Passion selon Saint Matthieu' *RB* 76 (1969) 206–27.

'Sacrificial Service and Atonement in the Gospel of Matthew' *Reconciliation and Hope* (FS L. Morris; ed. R. Banks; Exeter: Paternoster, 1974) 25–35.

The Mighty Acts of Jesus according to Matthew (Lund: C. W. K. Gleerup, 1979).

Gero, S., '"My Son the Messiah": A Note on 4 Esr 7 28–29' *ZNW* 66 (1975) 264–7.

Gibbs, J. M., 'Purpose and Pattern in Matthew's Use of the Title "Son of David"' *NTS* 10 (1964) 446–64.

Gieseler, J. K. L., *Historisch-kritischer Versuch über die Enstehung und die frühesten Schicksale der schriftlichen Evangelien* (Leipzig: W Engelmann, 1818).

Ginzberg, L., *The Legends of the Jews* (7 vols.; Philadelphia: Jewish Pub. Soc., 1913–38).

Glasswell, M. E., 'The Concealed Messiahship in the Synoptic Gospels and the Significance of this for a Study of the Life of Jesus and of the Church' (Ph.D. Durham, 1965).

Globe, A., 'Some Doctrinal Variants in Matthew 1 and Luke 2, and the Authority of the Neutral Text' *CBQ* 42 (1980) 52–72.

Glombitza, O., 'Die Titel διδάσκαλος und ἐπιστάτης für Jesus bei Lukas' *ZNW* 49 (1958) 275–8.

Glucker, J., *Antiochus and the Late Academy* (Hypomnemata 56; Göttingen: Vandenhoeck & Ruprecht, 1978).

Gnilka, J., 'Die Erwartung des messianischen Hohenpriesters von Qumran und des Neue Testaments' *RevQ* 2 (1959f) 395–426.

'Die Kirche des Matthäus und die Gemeinde von Qumran' *BZ* NF 7 (1963) 43–63.

Das Evangelium nach Markus (EKKNT 2; 2 vols.; Zürich: Benziger, 1978, 1979).

Das Matthäusevangelium (HTKNT 1; 2 vols.; Freiburg: Herder, 1986, 1988).

Gordis, R., 'The "Begotten" Messiah in the Qumran Scrolls' *VT* 7 (1957) 191–4.

Gordon, R. P., *1 and 2 Samuel. A Commentary* (Exeter: Paternoster, 1986).

Gore, C. (ed.), *Lux Mundi: A Series of Studies in the Religion of the Incarnation* (London: J. Murray, 1889).

Gore, C., *Dissertations on Subjects Connected with the Incarnation* (London: J. Murray, 1895).

The Incarnation of the Son of God (Bampton Lectures 1891; London: J. Murray, 1898).

Jesus of Nazareth (London: T. Butterworth, 1929).

Gould, E. P., *A Critical and Exegetical Commentary on the Gospel According to St Mark* (Edinburgh: T. & T. Clark, 1896).

Goulder, M. D., *Luke: A New Paradigm* (JSNTSS 20; Sheffield: JSOT Press, 1989; 2 vols.).

Grant, R. M., *Gods and the One God* (LEC 1; Philadelphia: Westminster, 1986).

Grässer, E., 'Jesus in Nazareth (Mark VI. 1–6a). Notes on the Redaction and Theology of St Mark' *NTS* 16 (1969) 1–23.

Gray, S. W., *The Least of My Brothers, Matthew 25:31–46: A History of Interpretation* (SBLDS 114; Atlanta: Scholars, 1989).

Green, F. W., *The Gospel According to Saint Matthew* (Clarendon Bible; Oxford: Clarendon, 1936).

Green, H. B., 'The Command to Baptize and Other Matthean Interpolations' *Studia Evangelica IV* (ed. F. L. Cross; TUGaL 102; Berlin: Akademie-Verlag, 1968) 60–4.

'Review of Albright and Mann, *Matthew*' *JTS* 23 (1972) 480–3.

'The Credibility of Luke's Transformation of Matthew' *Synoptic Studies: The Ampleforth Conferences of 1982 and 1983* (ed. C. M. Tuckett; JSNTSS 7; Sheffield: JSOT Press, 1984) 131–55.

'Matthew 28:19, Eusebius, and the *lex orandi*' *The Making of Orthodoxy: Essays in honour of Henry Chadwick* (ed. R. Williams; Cambridge: Cambridge University Press, 1989) 124–41.

Green, J. B., *The Death of Jesus* (WUNT 2. 33; Tübingen: J. C. B. Mohr, 1988).

Greenfield, J. C. and Stone, M. E.,'The Enochic Pentateuch and the Date of the Similitudes' *HTR* 70 (1977) 51–65.

Griesbach, J. J., *Stricturae in locum de theopneustia librorum sacrorum I–V*

(Jena, 1784–8). Reprinted in J. J. Griesbach, *Opuscula academica* (ed. J. P. Gabler; Jena: F Frommanni, 1825) II. 288–357.

Commentatio, qua Marci Evangelium totum e Matthaei et Lucae commentariis decerptum esse monstratur (Jena: J. C. G. Goepferdt, 1789, 1790). This work (with the 1794 revisions first published in Velthusen (ed.), *Commentationes theologicae*, vol. I (1794) 360–434) reprinted in J. J. Griesbach, *Opuscula academica* (ed. J. P. Gabler; Jena: F. Frommanni, 1825) II. 358–425. Also reprinted in *J. J. Griesbach: Synoptic and Text-Critical Studies 1776–1976* (SNTSMS 34; eds. B. Orchard and T. R. W. Longstaff; Cambridge: Cambridge University Press, 1978) 74–102 from which it is cited here. ET: 'Demonstration in which the entire Gospel of Mark is shown to be excerpted from the narratives of Matthew and Luke' *J. J. Griesbach: Synoptic and Text-Critical Studies 1776–1976* (SNTSMS 34; eds. B. Orchard and T. R. W. Longstaff; Cambridge: Cambridge University Press, 1978) 103–35.

Grundmann, W., *Das Evangelium nach Markus* (THKNT 2; Berlin: Evangelische Verlagsanstalt, 1959, 1980[8]).

Das Evangelium nach Matthäus (THKNT 1; Berlin: Evangelische Verlagsanstalt, 1968, 1975[4]).

Guelich, R. A., *Mark 1 – 8:26* (WBC 34a; Dallas: Word, 1989).

Gundry, R. H., *The Use of the Old Testament in St. Matthew's Gospel with special reference to the Messianic Hope* (NovTSS 18; Leiden: Brill, 1967).

Matthew. A Commentary on His Literary and Theological Art (Grand Rapids: Eerdmans, 1982).

'Matthean Foreign Bodies in Agreements of Luke with Matthew against Mark Evidence that Luke used Matthew' *The Four Gospels 1992 Festchrift Frans Neirynck* (ed. F. van Segbroeck, C. M. Tuckett, G. Van Belle, J. Vesheyden; BETL 100; Leuven: Leuven University Press, 1992) 1467–95.

Mark. A Commentary on His Apology for the Cross (Grand Rapids: Eerdmans, 1993).

Haenchen, E., *Der Weg Jesu: Eine Erklärung des Markus-Evangeliums und der kanonischen Parallelen* (Berlin: A. Töpelmann, 1966).

Hagner, D. A., *Matthew 1–13* (WBC 33A; Dallas: Word, 1993).

Hahn, F., *Das Verständnis der Mission im neuen Testament* (WMANT 13; Neukirchen-Vluyn: Neukirchener Verlag, 1963). ET: *Mission in the New Testament* (SBT 47; London: SCM, 1965).

Christologische Hoheitstitel, Ihre Geschichte im frühen Christentum (FRLANT 83; Göttingen: Vandenhoeck & Ruprecht, 1963, 1974[4]). ET: *The Titles of Jesus in Christology. Their History in Early Christianity* (trans. H. Knight and G. Ogg; London: Lutterworth, 1969).

Hawkins, J. C., *Horae Synopticae: Contributions to the Study of the Synoptic Problem* (Oxford: Clarendon, 1899, 1909[2]).

Hay, D. M., *Glory at the Right Hand: Psalm 110 in Early Christianity* (SBLMS 18; Nashville/New York: Abingdon, 1973).

Hay, L. S., 'The Son-of-God Christology in Mark' *JBR* 32 (1964) 106–14.

Head, P. M., 'Observations on Early Papyri of the Synoptic Gospels, especially on the "Scribal Habits"' *Biblica* 71. 2 (1990) 240–7.

'A Text-Critical Study of Mark 1. 1: "The Beginning of the Gospel of Jesus Christ"' *NTS* 37 (1991) 621–9.

'Tatian's Christology and its Influence on the Composition of the Diatessaron' *TynBul* 43 (1992) 121–37.

'On the Christology of the Gospel of Peter' *VC* 46 (1992) 209–24.

'Review of Wenham, *Redating Matthew, Mark, and Luke*', *Anvil* 9 (1992) 163–4.

'Christology and Textual Transmission: Reverential Alterations in the Synoptic Gospels' *NovT* 35 (1993) 105–29.

'The Foreign God and the Sudden Christ: Theology and Christology in Marcion's Gospel Redaction' *TynBul* 44 (1993) 307–21.

'Review of Linnemann, *Is There a Synoptic Problem?*' *Anvil* 10 (1993) 260–1.

'The Self-Offering and Death of Christ as a Sacrifice in the Gospels and the Acts of the Apostles' *Sacrifice in the Bible* (ed. R. T. Beckwith and M. Selman; Carlisle: Paternoster and Grand Rapids: Baker, 1995) 111–29.

'Review of Kim, *The Sources of the Synoptic Gospels*' *EvQ* 68 (1996) 242–3.

Headlam, A. C., *The Miracles of the New Testament* (London: John Murray, 1915).

The Life and Teaching of Jesus the Christ (London: John Murray, 1923).

Heil, J. P., *Jesus Walking on the Sea: Meaning and Gospel Functions of Matt 14:22–33, Mark 6:45–52 and John 6:15b-21* (AnBib 87; Rome: PBI, 1981).

Held, H. J., 'Matthäus als Interpret der Wundergeschichten' *Überlieferung und Auslegung im Matthäusevangelium* (eds. G. Bornkamm, G. Barth and H. J. Held; WMANT 1; Neukirchen-Vluyn: Neukirchener Verlag, 1965[4]; cf. 1960[1]) 155–287. ET: 'Matthew as Interpreter of the Miracle Stories' *Tradition and Interpretation in Matthew* (eds. G. Bornkamm, G. Barth and H. J. Held; London: SCM, 1963) 165–299.

Hengel, M., *Der Sohn Gottes, Die Entstehung der Christologie und die jüdisch-hellenistische Religionsgeschichte* (Tübingen: J. C. B. Mohr, 1975). ET: *The Son of God. The Origin of Christology and the History of Jewish-Hellenistic Religion* (London: SCM and Philadelphia: Fortress, 1976).

Between Jesus and Paul (London: SCM, 1983).

'Psalm 110 und die Erhöhung des Auferstandenen zur Rechten Gottes' *Anfänge der Christologie* (FS F. Hahn; eds. C. Breytenbach and H. Paulsen; Göttingen: Vandenhoeck & Ruprecht, 1991) 43–73.

Herder, J. G., 'Vom Erlöser der Menschen. Nach unsern drei ersten Evangelien' *Christliche Schriften; Zweite Sammlung* (Riga: J. F. Hartknoch, 1796). Cited from *Herders Sämmtliche Werke* (ed. B. Suphan; Berlin: Weidmannsche, 1880; 19 vols.) 139ff.

Von Gottes Sohn, der Welt Heiland, nach Johannes Evangelium. Nebst eine Regel der Zusammenstimmung unserer Evangelien aus ihrer Entstehung und Ordnung (Riga: J. F. Hartknoch, 1797). Cited from *Herders Sämmtliche Werke* (ed. B. Suphan; Berlin: Weidmannsche, 1880; 19 vols.) 380–424.

Herford, R. T., *Christianity in Talmud and Midrash* (London: Williams & Norgate, 1903).

Pirke Aboth. The Tractate 'Fathers', from the Mishnah, commonly called 'Sayings of the Fathers'. Edited with Introduction, Translation, and Commentary (New York: Jewish Institute/Bloch, 1925).

Higgins, A. J. B., 'Son of Man-*Forschung* since "The Teaching of Jesus"' *New Testament Essays* (FS T. Manson; ed. Higgins; Manchester: Manchester University Press, 1959) 119–35.

'Jewish Messianic Beliefs in Justin Martyr's *Dialogue with Trypho*' *NovT* 9 (1967) 298–305.

Hilgenfeld, A., *Das Markus-Evangelium nach seiner Composition, seiner Stellung in der Evangelien-Literatur, seinem Ursprung und Charakter* (Leipzig: Breitkopf & Härtel, 1850).

Die Evangelien, nach ihrer Entstehung und geschichtlichen Bedeutung (Leipzig: S. Hirzel, 1854).

Hill, D., *The Gospel of Matthew* (NCB; London: Marshall, Morgan & Scott, 1972; Grand Rapids: Eerdmans, 1981 reprint).

'On the Use and Meaning of Hosea VI. 6 in Matthew's Gospel' *NTS* 24 (1978) 107–19.

'Son and Servant: An Essay in Matthean Christology' *JSNT* 6 (1980) 2–16.

'The Figure of Jesus in Matthew's Story: A Response to Professor Kingsbury's Literary-Critical Probe' *JSNT* 21 (1984) 37–52.

'Matthew 27,51–53' *IBS* 7 (1985) 76–87.

Hirsch, E., *Frühgeschichte des Evangeliums* (2 vols.; Tübingen: J. C. B. Mohr, 1951²).

Hoffmann, P., *Studien zur Theologie der Logienquelle* (NTAbh nF 8; Münster: Aschendorff, 1972).

Holladay, C. H., *Theios Aner in Hellenistic Judaism: A Critique of the Use of this Category in New Testament Christology* (SBLDS 40; Missoula: Scholars, 1977).

Hollander, H. W. and Jonge, M. de, *The Testaments of the Twelve Patriarchs. A Commentary* (Studia in VTPs; Leiden: E. J. Brill, 1985).

Hollenbach, P. W., 'The Conversion of Jesus: From Jesus the Baptizer to Jesus the Healer' *ANRW* II. 25. 1 (1982) 196–219.

Holtzmann, H. J., *Die synoptischen Evangelien: Ihr Ursprung und geschichtlicher Charakter* (Leipzig: Engelmann, 1863).

Lehrbuch der historisch-kritischen Einleitung in das Neue Testament (Freiburg: Mohr, 1885, 1892³).

Die Synoptiker (HCNT 1/1; Freiburg/Tübingen: Mohr, 1889, 1892², 1901³).

Hooker, M. D., *Jesus and the Servant: The Influence of the Servant Concept of Deutero-Isaiah in the New Testament* (London: SPCK, 1959).

The Son of Man in Mark: A Study of the background of the term 'Son of Man' and its use in St Mark's Gospel (London: SPCK, 1967).

'Is the Son of Man Problem Really Insoluble?' *Text and Interpretation* (FS M. Black; eds. E. Best and R. M. Wilson; Cambridge: Cambridge University Press, 1979) 155–68.

A Commentary on the Gospel According to St Mark (BNTC; London: A. & C. Black, 1991).

'The Son of Man and the Synoptic Problem' *The Four Gospels 1992* (FS F. Neirynck; eds. F. van Segbroeck, C. M. Tuckett, G. Van Belle, J. Vesheyden; BETL 100; Leuven: Leuven University Press, 1992) 189–201.

Höpfl, H., 'Nonne hic est fabri filius?' *Biblica* 4 (1923) 41–55.

Horbury, W., 'The Messianic Associations of "The Son of Man"' *JTS* 36 (1985) 34–66.

Howard, G., 'The Tetragram and the New Testament' *JBL* 96 (1977) 63–83.

Hubbard, B. J., *The Matthean Redaction of a Primitive Apostolic Commissioning: An Exegesis of Matthew 28:16–20* (SBLDS 19; Scholars Press; Missoula, 1974).

Huggins, R. V., 'Matthean Posteriority: A Preliminary Proposal' *NovT* 34 (1992) 1–22.

Hull, J. M., *Hellenistic Magic and the Synoptic Tradition* (SBT 2. 8; London: SCM, 1974).

Hummel, R., *Die Auseinandersetzung zwischen Kirche und Judentum im Matthäusevangelium* (BVvT 33; Munich: Chr Kaiser, 1963, 1966[2]).

Hunter, A. M., *Interpreting the New Testament 1900–1950* (London: SCM, 1951, 1958 reprint).

Hurtado, L. W., 'New Testament Christology: A Critique of Bousset's Influence' *TS* 40 (1979) 306–17.

Text-Critical Methodology and the Pre-Caesarean Text: Codex W in. the Gospel of Mark (SD 43; Grand Rapids: Eerdmans, 1981).

'New Testament Christology: Retrospect and Prospect' *Semeia* 30 (1985) 15–27. (This is a revision of his 'The Study of New Testament Christology: Notes for the Agenda' *SBL Seminar Papers* (ed. K. H. Richards; Chicago: Scholars Press, 1981) 185–97.)

Ilan, T., '"Man Born of Woman . . ." (Job 14:1). The Phenomenon of Men Bearing Metronymes at the Time of Jesus' *NovT* 34 (1992) 23–45.

Isaksson, A., *Marriage and Ministry in the New Temple: A Study with Special Reference to Mt. 19. 3–12 and 1. Cor. 11. 3–16* (ASNU XXIV; Lund: C. W. K. Gleerup, 1965).

Jackson, H. L., 'The Present State of the Synoptic Problem' *Cambridge Biblical Essays: Essays on some Biblical Questions of the Day by Members of the University of Cambridge* (ed. H. B. Swete; London: Macmillan, 1909) 421–60.

Jackson, H. M., 'The Death of Jesus in Mark and the Miracle from the Cross' *NTS* 33 (1987) 16–37.

Jacobson, A. D., *The First Gospel: An Introduction to Q* (Sonoma, California: Polebridge, 1992).

Jameson, H. G., *The Origin of the Synoptic Gospels: A Revision of the Synoptic Problem* (Oxford: Blackwell, 1922).

Jellicoe, S., *The Septuagint and Modern Study* (Oxford: Clarendon, 1968).

Jeremias, J., *Neutestamentliche Theologie. 1. Die Verkündigung Jesu* (Gütersloh: Gütersloher Verlagshaus G. Mohn, 1971). ET: *New Testament Theology I: The Proclamation of Jesus* (trans. J. Bowden; London: SCM, 1971).

Johnson, E. S., 'Mark 10:46–52: Blind Bartimaeus' *CBQ* 40 (1978) 191–204.

Johnson, S. E., 'The Gospel according to Saint Matthew' *The Interpreter's Bible* (ed. G. A. Buttrick *et al.*; New York and Nashville: Abingdon, 1951; vol. VII) 231–625.

The Griesbach Hypothesis and Redaction Criticism (SBLMS 41; Atlanta, GA: Scholars Press, 1991).

Jones, J., *A Vindication of the Former Part of St Matthew's Gospel from Mr Whiston's Charge of Dislocations, or, An Attempt to prove, that our Present Greek Copies of that Gospel are in the same order wherein they were originally written by that Evangelist. In which are contained many things relating to the Harmony and History of the Four Gospels* (London: J. Osborn & W. Taylor, 1719).

Jonge, M. de, *The Testaments of the Twelve Patriarchs. A Study of their Text, Composition and Origin* (Assen: van Gorcum & Comp., 1953).

'Christian Influence in the Testaments of the Twelve Patriarchs' *NovT* 4 (1960) 182–235.

'The Use of the Word "Anointed" in the Time of Jesus' *NovT* 8 (1966) 132–46.

'The Interpretation of the Testaments of the Twelve Patriarchs in Recent Years' *Studies on the Testaments of the Twelve Patriarchs* (ed. M. de Jonge; SVTP 3; Leiden: Brill, 1975) 183–92.

'Matthew 27:51 in Early Christian Exegesis' *HTR* 79 (1986) (= *Christians Among Jews and Gentiles* (FS K. Stendahl; eds. G. Nickelsburg and G. MacRae)) 67–79.

Jonge, M. de and Woude, A. S. van der, '11Q Melchizedek and the New Testament' *NTS* 12 (1966) 301–26.

Kahle, P. E., *The Cairo Geniza* (Oxford: Basil Blackwell, 1959[2]).

Kazmierski, C. R., *Jesus, the Son of God: A Study of the Markan Tradition and its Redaction by the Evangelist* (FB 33; Würzburg: Echter, 1979, 1982).

Kealy, S. P., *Mark's Gospel: A History of its Interpretation, From the Beginning Until 1979* (New York: Paulist, 1982).

Keck, L. E., 'The Spirit and the Dove' *NTS* 17 (1970f) 41–67.

'Jesus in New Testament Christology' *Australian Biblical Review* 28 (1980) 1–20.

'Toward the Renewal of New Testament Christology' *NTS* 32 (1986) 362–77.

Kee, H. C., *Medicine, Miracle and Magic in New Testament Times* (SNTSMS 55; Cambridge: Cambridge University Press, 1986).

Keegan, T. J., 'Introductory Formulae for Matthean Discourses' *CBQ* 44 (1982) 415–30.

Keim, T., *Geschichte Jesu von Nazara in ihrer Verkettung mit dem Gesammtleben seines Volkes frei untersucht und ausführlich erzählt* (3 vols.; Zürich: Drell, Fussli & Comp., 1867). ET: *The History of Jesus of Nazara. Considered in its connection with the national life of Israel and related in detail* (6 vols.; London: Williams & Norgate, 1873–83).

Kelber, W. H., *The Oral and Written Gospel: The Hermeneutics of Speaking and Writing in the Synoptic Tradition, Mark, Paul, and Q* (Philadelphia: Fortress, 1983).

Kempthorne, R., 'The Marcan Text of Jesus' Answer to the High Priest' *NovT* 19 (1977) 198–208.

Kilpatrick, G. D., 'Some Problems in New Testament Text and Language' *Neotestamentica et Semitica* (FS M. Black; eds. E. E. Ellis and M. Wilcox; Edinburgh: T. & T. Clark, 1969) 198–208.

Kim, S., *'The 'Son of Man'' as the Son of God* (WUNT 30; Tübingen: J. C. B. Mohr, 1983).

Kingsbury, J. D., *The Parables of Jesus in Matthew 13: A Study in Redaction-Criticism* (Richmond: John Knox, 1969; London: SPCK, 1977).

'The Composition and Christology of Matt 28:16–20' *JBL* 93 (1974) 573–84.

'The Title "Son of God" in Matthew's Gospel' *BTB* 5 (1975) 3–31.

Matthew: Structure, Christology, Kingdom (Philadelphia: Fortress, 1975; London: SPCK, 1976).

'The Title "Son of David" in Matthew's Gospel' *JBL* 95 (1976) 591–602.

'Observations on the "Miracle Chapters" of Matthew 8–9' *CBQ* 40 (1978) 559–73.

'The "Divine Man" as the Key to Mark's Christology – the End of an Era' *Int* 35 (1981) 243–57.

'The Theology of St Matthew's Gospel according to the Griesbach Hypothesis' *New Synoptic Studies: The Cambridge Gospel Conference and Beyond* (ed. W. R. Farmer; Georgia: Mercer University Press; 1983) 331–61.

The Christology of Mark's Gospel (Philadelphia: Fortress, 1983).

'The Figure of Jesus in Matthew's Story: A Literary-Critical Probe' *JSNT* 21 (1984) 3–36.

Matthew as Story (Philadelphia: Fortress, 1986).

Kittel, G. and Friedrich, G. (eds.), *Theological Dictionary of the New Testament* (trans. G. Bromiley; Grand Rapids: Eerdmans, 10 vols.; 1964–74).

Klausner, J., *Jesus of Nazareth: His Life, Times, and Teaching* (trans. H. Danby; London: George Allen and Unwin, 1925).

The Messianic Idea in Israel from Its Beginning to the Completion of the Mishnah (London: George Allen & Unwin Ltd, 1956).

Klijn, A. F. J., 'The Question of the Rich Young Man in a Jewish-Christian Gospel' *NovT* 8 (1966) 149–55.

Kloppenborg, J. S., *The Formation of Q: Trajectories in Ancient Wisdom Collections* (Philadelphia: Fortress, 1987).

'The Theological Stakes in the Synoptic Problem' *The Four Gospels 1992 Festschrift Frans Neirynck* (eds. F. van Segbroeck, C. M. Tuckett, G. Van Belle, J. Vesheyden; BETL 100; Leuven: Leuven University Press, 1992) 93–120.

Klostermann, E., *Das Matthäusevangelium* (HzNT 4; Tübingen: Mohr, 1927²).

'Evangelien, Synoptische' *RGG* 2 (1928²) 422–33.

Das Markusevangelium (HzNT 3; Tübingen: Mohr, 1926², 1936³).

Knibb, M. A., *The Ethiopic Book of Enoch. A New Edition in the Light of the Aramaic Dead Sea Fragments* (2 vols.; Oxford: Clarendon, 1978). 'The Date of the Parables of Enoch: A Critical Review' *NTS* 25 (1978f) 344–57.

Knibb, M. A. and Coggins, R. J. *The First and Second Books of Esdras* (CBC; Cambridge: Cambridge University Press, 1979).

Koch, D.-A., *Die Bedeutung der Wundererzählungen für die Christologie des Markusevangelium* (Berlin: de Gruyter, 1975).

Koppe, J. B., *Marcus non epitomator Matthaei* (Helmstadii, 1782). Reprinted in D. J. Pott and G. A. Ruperti, *Sylloge commentationum theologicarum* . . . (Helmstadii: C. G. Fleckeisen; volume I, 1800) 35–69.

Köstlin, K. R., *Der Ursprung und die Komposition der synoptischen Evangelien* (Stuttgart: Mächen, 1853).

Krentz, E., 'The Extent of Matthew's Prologue' *JBL* 83 (1964) 409–14.

Kruijf, Th. de, *Der Sohn des lebendigen Gottes: Ein Beitrag zur Christologie des Matthäusevangeliums* (AnBib 14; Rome: PBI, 1962).

Kümmel, W. G., 'New Testament Research and Teaching in Present-Day Germany' *NTS* 1 (1955) 229–34.

Das neue Testament: Geschichte der Erforschung seiner Probleme (München: K. A. Freiburg, 1958). ET: *The New Testament: The History of the Investigation of its Problems* (trans. S. M. Gilmour and H. C. Kee; London: SCM, 1973).

Kuthirakkattel, S., *The Beginning of Jesus' Ministry According to Mark's Gospel (1,14–3,6) : A Redaction Critical Study* (AnBib 123; Rome: PIB, 1990).

Kynes, W. L., *A Christology of Solidarity: Jesus as the Representative of His People in Matthew* (Lanham/New York/London: University Press of America, 1991).

Lacocque, A., 'The Vision of the Eagle in 4Esdras, a Rereading of Daniel 7 in the First Century CE' *SBLSP* (1981) 237–58.

Lagrange, M. J., *Evangile selon Saint Matthieu* (Paris: Lecoffre, 1948). *Evangile selon Saint Marc* (Paris: Lecoffre, 1966).

Lampe, G. W. H. (ed.), *A Patristic Greek Lexicon* (Oxford: Clarendon Press, 1961).

Lane, W. L., *The Gospel According to Mark* (Grand Rapids: Eerdmans, 1979, 1974).

'Theios Anēr Christology and the Gospel of Mark' *New Dimensions in New Testament Study* (ed. R. Longenecker and M. C. Tenney; Grand Rapids: Zondervan, 1974) 144–61.

Lange, J., *Das Erscheinen des Auferstandenen im Evangelium nach Matthäus: Eine traditions- und redaktions- geschichtliche Untersuchung zu Mt 28, 16–20* (FzB11; Würzburg: Echter, 1973).

Langford, T. A., *In Search of Foundations: English Theology 1900–1920* (Nashville/NY: Abingdon, 1969).

Lawton, J. S., *Conflict in Christology: A Study of British and American Christology from 1889 to 1914* (London: SPCK, 1947).

Leivestad, R., 'Der Apokalyptische Menschensohn ein theologische Phantom' *ASTI* 6 (1967f) 49–105.

Lemcio, E. E., *The Past of Jesus in the Gospels* (SNTSMS 68; Cambridge: Cambridge University Press, 1991).

Léon-Dufour, X., 'Autour de la question synoptique' *RSR* 42 (1954) 549–84.

'Passion (Récits de la)' *DBSup* (ed. H. Cazelles; Paris: Librairie Letouzey et Ané, 1960) vol. VI, 1419–92.

Levey, S. H., *The Messiah: An Aramaic Interpretation. The Messianic Exegesis of the Targum* (Monographs of HUC; Jerusalem/Cincinnati/New York/Los Angeles: Hebrew Union College Press, 1974).

Liddell, H. G., Scott, R. and Jones, H. S., *A Greek–English Lexicon* (Oxford: Clarendon Press, 1985 reprint incorporating 1940⁹ and 1968 Supplement).

Lightfoot, J. B., *Saint Paul's Epistle to the Philippians. A Revised Text with Introduction, Notes, and Dissertations* (London: Macmillan, 1898 reprint of 1878⁴ (with alterations), 1868¹).

Lightfoot, R. H., *History and Interpretation in the Gospels* (Bampton Lectures 1934; London: Hodder & Stoughton, 1935).

Lincoln, A. T., 'The Promise and the Failure: Mark 16:7, 8' *JBL* 108 (1989) 283–300.

Lindars, B., *New Testament Apologetic: The Doctrinal Significance of the Old Testament Quotations* (London: SCM, 1961).

Jesus Son of Man. A Fresh Examination of the Son of Man Sayings in the Gospels in the Light of Recent Research (London: SPCK, 1983).

Lindsey, R. L., 'A Modified Two-Document Theory of the Synoptic Dependence and Interdependence' *NovT* 6 (1963) 239–63.

A Hebrew Translation of the Gospel of Mark Greek–Hebrew Diglot with English Introduction (Jerusalem: Dugith Pub., 1973).

Linnemann, E., *Studien zur Passionsgeschichte* (FRLANT 102; Göttingen: Vandenhoeck & Ruprecht, 1970).

Llewelyn, S. R., 'A Stylometric Analysis of Parallel Sections of the Synoptic Gospels' (unpublished Ph.D.; Sydney: Macquarrie University, 1991).

Lohmeyer, E., '"Und Jesus ging vorüber"' *Nieuw theologisch Tijdschrift* (Haarlem) 23 (1934) 206–24. Reprinted in *Urchristliche Mystik. Neutestamentliche Studien* (Darmstadt: Wissenschaftliche Buchgesellschaft, 1955) 59–79.

Das Evangelium des Markus (KEK 2; Göttingen: Vandenhoeck & Ruprecht, 1951, 1959, 1967).

Das Evangelium des Matthäus (KEK Sonderband; Göttingen: Vandenhoeck & Ruprecht, 1956).

Longenecker, R. N., 'The Messianic Secret in the Light of Recent Discoveries' *EvQ* 41 (1969) 207–15.

The Christology of Early Jewish Christianity (Grand Rapids: Baker, 1970).

Longstaff, T. R. W., *Evidence of Conflation in Mark? A Study in the Synoptic Problem* (SBLDS 28; Missoula: Scholars, 1977).

'At the Colloquium's conclusion' *J. J. Griesbach: Synoptic and Text-Critical Studies 1776–1976* (eds. B. Orchard and T. R. W. Longstaff; SNTSMS 34; Cambridge: Cambridge University Press, 1978) 170–5.

'Crisis and Christology: The Theology of Mark' *New Synoptic Studies: The Cambridge Gospel Conference and Beyond* (ed. W. R. Farmer; Georgia: Mercer University Press, 1983) 373–92.

Louw, J. P. and Nida, E. A., *Greek–English Lexicon of the New Testament based. on Semantic Domains* (2 vols.; New York: United Bible Societies, 1988).

Lövestam, E., 'Wunder und Symbolhandlung. Eine Studie über Matthäus 14, 28–31' *KD* 8 (1962) 124–35.

Lowe, M., 'The Demise of Arguments from Order for Markan Priority' *NovT* 24 (1982) 27–36.

Luck, U., 'Die Frage nach dem Guten. Zu Mt 19,16–30 und Parr.' *Studien zum Text und zur Ethik des Neuen Testaments. Festschrift zum 80. Geburtstag von Heinrich Greeven* (ed. W. Schrage; Berlin: de Gruyter, 1986) 282–97.

Lummis, E. W., *How Luke Was Written. (Considerations Affecting the Two-Document Theory with Special Reference to the Phenomena of Order in the Non-Marcan Matter Common to Matthew and Luke.)* (Cambridge: Cambridge University Press, 1915).

Lust, J., 'Dan 7. 13 and the Septuagint' *ETL* 54 (1978) 62–9.

Luz, U., 'Das Geheimnismotiv und die Markinische Christologie' *ZNW* 56 (1965) 9–30. ET: 'The Secrecy Motif and the Marcan Christology' *The Messianic Secret* (IRT 1; ed. C. M. Tuckett; London: SPCK, 1983) 75–96.

'Die Junger im Matthäusevangelium' *ZNW* 62 (1971) 141–71. ET: 'The Disciples in the Gospel according to Matthew' *The Interpretation of Matthew* (IRT 3; ed. G. N. Stanton; London: SPCK, 1983) 98–128.

Das Evangelium nach Matthäus (EKKNT 1; 2 vols. incomplete; Zürich: Benziger/Neukirchen: Neukirchener, 1985, 1990). ET: *Matthew 1–7* (Edinburgh: T. & T. Clark, 1990).

'The Son of Man in Matthew: Heavenly Judge or Human Christ?' *JSNT* 48 (1992) 3–21.

Lyons, J., *Semantics* (2 vols.; Cambridge: Cambridge University Press, 1977).

Language and Linguistics: An Introduction (Cambridge: Cambridge University Press, 1981).

MacDonald, J., *The Theology of the Samaritans* (London: SCM, 1964).

Maddox, R., 'The Function of the Son of Man according to the Synoptic Gospels' *NTS* 15 (1968f) 45–74.

Maisch, I., 'Die österliche Dimension des Todes Jesus. Zur Osterverkündigung in Mt 27,51–54' *Auferstehung Jesu – Auferstehung der Christen: Deutungen des Osterglaubens* (ed. L. Oberlinner; QD 105; Freiburg: Herder, 1986) 96–123.

Malbon, E. S., 'τῇ οἰκίᾳ αὐτοῦ: Mark 2. 15 in Context' *NTS* 31 (1985) 282–92.

Mann, C. S., *Mark: A New Translation with Introduction and Commentary* (AB 27; New York: Doubleday & Co., 1986).

Manson, T. W., *Studies in the Gospels and Epistles* (Manchester: Manchester University Press, 1962).

Marcus, J., *The Way of the Lord: Christological Exegesis of the Old Testament in the Gospel of Mark* (Louisville, Kentucky: Westminster/ John Knox, 1992).

Marguerat, D., *Le jugement dans l'évangile de Matthieu* (Geneva: Labor & Fides, 1981).

Marsh, H., *A Dissertation on the Origin and Composition of our Three First Canonical Gospels* (Cambridge: J. Burges (for University Press), 1801). Also published in ET of J. D. Michaelis, *Introduction to the New Testament* (London: Rivington, 1823).

Marshall, C. D., *Faith as a Theme in Mark's Narrative* (SNTSMS 64; Cambridge: Cambridge University Press, 1989).

Marshall, I. H., 'The Synoptic Son of Man Sayings in Recent Discussion' *NTS* 12 (1965f) 327–51.

'The Divine Sonship of Jesus' *Int* 21 (1967) 87–103.

'Son of God or Servant of Yahweh? – A Reconsideration of Mark 1. 11' *NTS* 15 (1968f) 326–36.

'The Son of Man in Contemporary Debate' *EvQ* 42 (1970) 67–87.

The Gospel of Luke (NIGTC; Exeter: Paternoster/Grand Rapids: Eerdmans, 1978).

'Incarnational Christology in the New Testament' *Christ the Lord* (FS D. Guthrie; ed. H. Rowdon: Leicester: Inter-Varsity Press, 1982).

'The Synoptic "Son of Man" Sayings in the Light of Linguistic Study' *To Tell the Mystery: Essays on New Testament Eschatology* (FS R. H. Gundry; eds. T. E. Schmidt and M. Silva; JSNTS 100; Sheffield: JSOT, 1994) 72–94.

Marxsen, W., *Der Evangelist Markus: Studien zur Redaktionsgechichte des Evangeliums* (FRLANT 67; Göttingen: Vandenhoeck & Ruprecht, 1956, 1959²). ET: *Mark the Evangelist: Studies on the Redaction History of the Gospel* (trans. J. Boyce, D. Juel, W. Poehlmann and R. A. Harrisville; Nashville: Abingdon Press, 1969).

Massaux, E., *Influence de l'évangile de saint Matthien sur la littérature chrétienne avant saint Irénée* (BETL 75; Louvain: Presses universitaires de Louvain, 1986; originally published. in 1950). ET: *The Influence of the Gospel of Saint Matthew on Christian Literature before Saint Irenaeus* (trans. N. J. Belval and S. Hecht; ed. A. J. Bellinzoni; New Gospel Studies 5; Macon, GA: Mercer University Press, 1990, 1990, 1993; 3 vols.).

Matera, F. J., *The Kingship of Jesus: Composition and Theology in Mark 15* (SBLDS 15; Chico, CA: Scholars Press, 1982).

Mayer, B., 'Überlieferungs- und redaktionsgeschichtliche Überlegungen zu Mk 6, 1–6a' *BZ* 22 (1978) 187–98.

McArthur, H. K., 'Son of Mary' *NovT* 15 (1973) 38–58.

McCarter, P. K., *II Samuel. A New Translation with Introduction, Notes and Commentary* (AB 9; New York: Doubleday, 1984).

McCown, C. C., 'ὁ τέκτων' *Studies in Early Christianity* (ed. S. J. Case; New York and London: Century, 1928) 173–89.

McGuckin, J. A., *The Transfiguration of Christ in Scripture and Tradition* (SBEC 9; Lewiston/Queenston: Edwin Mellen, 1986).

McNeil, B., 'The Son of Man and the Messiah: A Footnote' *NTS* 26 (1979f) 419–21.

McNeile, A. H., *The Gospel According to St Matthew: The Greek Text with Introduction, Notes, and Indices* (London: Macmillan & Co., 1915).

McNicol, A. J., 'The Two Gospel Hypothesis Under Scrutiny: A Response to C. M. Tuckett's Analysis of Recent Neo-Griesbachian Gospel Criticism' *PSTJ* 40 (1987) 5–13.

Mearns, C. L., 'Dating the Similitudes of Enoch' *NTS* 25 (1978f) 360–9.

Meier, J. P., *The Vision of Matthew: Christ, Church and Morality in the First Gospel* (New York: Paulist, 1979).

Matthew (NTMessage 3; Dublin: Veritas, 1984 reprint of 1980).

Meijboom, H. U., *Geschiedenis en critiek der Marcushypothese* (Dissertation for University of Groningen; Amsterdam: Kraay, 1866). ET: *A History and Critique of the Origin of the Marcan Hypothesis 1835–1866. A Contemporary Report Rediscovered* (ed. and trans. J. J. Kiwiet; NGS 8; Macon, GA: Mercer University Press, 1993).

Metzger, B. M. (ed.), *A Textual Commentary on the Greek New Testament* (London: UBS, 1975).

Metzger, B. M., *Manuscripts of the Greek Bible. An Introduction to Greek Palaeography* (New York and Oxford: Oxford University Press, 1981).

Meye, R. P., 'Messianic Secret and Messianic Didache in Mark's Gospel' *Oikonomia: Heilsgeschichte als Thema der Theologie* (FS O. Cullmann; ed. F. Christ; Hamburg-Bergstedt: H. Reich, 1967) 57–68.

Jesus and the Twelve: Discipleship and Revelation in Mark's Gospel (Grand Rapids: Eerdmans, 1968).

Michel, O., 'Der Abschluß des Matthäusevangeliums: Ein Beitrag zur Geschichte der Osterbotschaft' *EvT* 10 (1950,1) 16–26. ET: 'The Conclusion of Matthew's Gospel: A Contribution to the History of the Easter Message' *The Interpretation of Matthew* (IRT 3; ed. G. N. Stanton; London: SPCK, 1983) 30 41.

Michel, O. and Betz, O., 'Von Gott gezeugt', *Judentum Urchristentum Kirche* (BZNW 26; FS J. Jeremias; ed. W. Eltester; Berlin: A. Töplemann, 1960) 3–23.

Milik, J. T., *The Books of Enoch: Aramaic Fragments of Qumrān Cave 4* (NB with collaboration of M. Black; Oxford: Clarendon, 1976).

Miller, D. G. (ed.), *Jesus and Man's Hope* (2 vols.; Perspective; Pittsburgh Theological Seminary, 1970).

Miller, M. P., 'The Function of Isa 61. 1–2 in 11Q Melchizedek' *JBL* 88 (1969) 467–9.

Minear, P. S., 'The Disciples and the Crowds in the Gospel of Matthew' *Gospel Studies in Honor of Sherman Elbridge Johnson* (eds.. M. H. Shepherd and E. C. Hobbs; *ATR* Supp. Series No. 3; 1974) 28–44.

Monasterio, R. A., *Exegesis de Mateo, 27,51b–53. Para una teologia de la muerte de Jesus en el Evangelio de Mateo* (Biblica Victoriensia 4; Vitoria: ESET, 1980).

Moo, D. J., *The Old Testament in the Gospel Passion Narratives* (Sheffield: Almond Press, 1983).

Moore, G. F., *Judaism in the First Centuries of the Christian Era. The Age of the Tannaim* (3 vols.; Cambridge, MA: Harvard University Press, 1927–30).

Mora, V., *Le refus d'Israël. Matthieu 27,25* (Lectio Divina 124; Paris: Cerf, 1986).

Morgan, R., 'Non angeli sed angli: Some Anglican Reactions to Tübingen Gospel Criticism' *Festgabe für F. Lang* (eds. O. Bayer and G. -U. Wanzeck; Tübingen: Mohr, 1978) 469–511.

'Historical Criticism and Christology: England and Germany' *England and Germany. Studies in Theological Diplomacy* (ed. S. W. Sykes; StIGC 25; Frankfurt: P. D. Lang, 1982) 80–112.

Morganthaler, R., *Statistische Synopse* (Zurich and Stuttgart: Gotthelf, 1971).

Moseé, C., *The Ancient World of Work* (London: Chatto and Windus, 1969).

Motyer, S., 'The Rending of the Veil: A Markan Pentecost?' *NTS* 33 (1987) 155–7.

Moule, C. F. D., 'Neglected Features in the Problem of "the Son of Man" ' *Neues Testament und Kirche* (FS R Schnackenburg; ed. J. Gnilka; Freiburg: Herder, 1974) 413–28.

The Origin of Christology (Cambridge: Cambridge University Press, 1977).

'On Defining the Messianic Secret in Mark' *Jesus und Paulus* (FS W. G. Kümmel; eds. E. E. Ellis and E. Grässer; Göttingen: Vandenhoeck and Ruprecht, 1978, 2nd edn) 239–52.

' "The Son of Man": Some of the Facts' *NTS* 41 (1995) 277–9.

Moulton, J. H. and Milligan, G., *The Vocabulary of the Greek Testament Illustrated from the Papyri and other Non-Literary Sources* (London: Hodder & Stoughton, 1914–29[1]).

Mowery, R. L., 'Subtle Differences: The Matthean "Son of God" References' *NovT* 32 (1990) 193–200.

Müller, M., *Der Ausdruck 'Menschensohn' in den Evangelien. Voraussetzungen und Bedeutung* (Acta Theologica Danica 17; Leiden: E. J. Brill, 1984).

Myers, J. M., *I and II Esdras: Introduction, Translation and Commentary* (AB 42; New York: Doubleday, 1974).

Navone, J., 'The Dynamic of the Question in the Gospel Narrative' *Milltown Studies* 17 (1986) 75–111.

Neill, S., *The Interpretation of the New Testament 1861–1961* (London: Oxford University Press, 1964).

Neirynck, F., 'La rédaction matthéenne et la structure du premier evangile' *ETL* 43 (1967) 41–73. Reprinted in *Evangelica* (ed. F. van Segbroeck; BETL 60; Leuven: Leuven University Press, 1982) 3–36.

Hawkins's Additional Notes to his «Horae Synopticae» (Analecta Lovaniensia Biblica et Orientalia Ser. V. Fasec. 2. ; Leiden: Brill, 1970).

'Minor Agreements Matthew–Luke in the Transfiguration Story' *Orientierung an Jesus: Zur Theologie der Synoptiker* (FS J. Schmid; ed. P. Hoffmann; Freiburg: Herder, 1973) 253–66.

The Minor Agreements of Matthew and Luke Against Mark with a cumulative list (BETL 37; Leuven: Leuven University Press, 1974).

'The Apocryphal Gospels and the Gospel of Mark' *The New Testament in Early Christianity. La réception des écrits néotestamentaires dans le christianisme primitif* (ed. J.-M. Sevrin; BE TL 86; Leuven: Leuven University Press, 1989) 123–75.

'Synoptic Problem' *NJBC* (1990) 587–95.

Neusner, J., Green, W. S., and Frerichs, E. S. (eds.), *Judaisms and Their Messiahs at the Turn of the Christian Era* (Cambridge: Cambridge University Press, 1987).

New, D. S. *Old Testament Quotations in the Synoptic Gospels and the Two-Document Hypothesis* (SBL Septuagint and Cognate Studies Series 37; Atlanta: Scholars, 1993).

Neyrey, J. N., 'The Thematic Use of Isa 42. 1–4 in Matthew 12' *Biblica* 63 (1983) 457–73.

Nolan, B., *The Royal Son of God: The Christology of Matthew 1–2 in the Setting of the Gospel* (Orbis Biblicus et Orientalis 23; Göttingen: Vandenhoeck & Ruprecht, 1979).

Nolland, J., *Luke* (WBC 35a, 35b, 35c; Dallas: Word, 1989, 1993, 1993).

O'Neill, J. C., 'The Silence of Jesus' *NTS* 15 (1968f) 153–67.

Oberlinner, L., *Historische Überlieferung und christologische Aussage: Zur Frage der 'Brüder Jesu' in der Synopse* (FB 19; Stuttgart: Katholisches Bibelwerk, 1975).

Orchard, B. and Longstaff, T. R. W. (eds.), *J. J. Griesbach: Synoptic and Text-Critical Studies, 1776–1976* (SNTSMS 34; Cambridge: Cambridge University Press, 1978).

Orchard, J. B., and Riley, H., *The Order of the Synoptics: Why Three Synoptic Gospels* (Macon, GA: Mercer University Press, 1987).

Owen, H., *Observations on the Four Gospels; Tending chiefly to ascertain the Times of their Publication; and to illustrate the Form and Manner of their composition* (London: T. Payne, 1764).

Page, S. H. T., 'The Suffering Servant Between the Testaments' *NTS* 31 (1985) 481–97.

Palmer, F. R., *Semantics* (Cambridge: Cambridge University Press, 1981²).

Palmer, N. H., 'Lachmann's Argument' *NTS* 13 (1967) 368–78.

Pamment, M., 'The Son of Man in the First Gospel' *NTS* 29 (1983) 116–28.

Parker, P., *The Gospel Before Mark* (Chicago: University Chicago Press, 1953).

'The Posteriority of Mark' *New Synoptic Studies: The Cambridge Gospel Conference and Beyond* (ed. W. R. Farmer; Georgia: Mercer University Press; 1983) 67–142.

Paul, A., *L'évangile de l'enfance selon saint Matthieu* (Lire la Bible 17; Paris: Cerf, 1968).

Paulus, H. E. G., *Philologisch-kritischer und historischer Commentar über das neue Testament* (Lübeck: J. F. Bohn, 1804–5).

Peabody, D. B., 'A Pre-Markan Prophetic Sayings Tradition and the Synoptic Problem' *JBL* 97 (1978) 391–409.

'The Late Secondary Redaction of Mark's Gospel and the Griesbach Hypothesis: A Response to Helmut Koester' *Colloquy on New Testa-*

ment Studies: A Time for Reappraisal and Fresh Approaches (ed. B. C. Corley; Macon, GA: Mercer University Press, 1983) 87–132.

Mark as Composer (NGS 1; Macon, GA: Mercer University Press, 1987).

'Chapters in the History of the Linguistic Argument for Solving the Synoptic Problem: The Nineteenth Century in Context' *Jesus, the Gospels, and the Church* (FS W. R. Farmer; ed. E. P. Sanders; Macon, GA: Mercer University Press, 1987) 47–68.

Perrin, N., 'Mark XIV. 62: The End Product of a Christian Pesher Tradition?' *NTS* 12 (1965f) 150–5.

'The Son of Man in Ancient Judaism and Primitive Christianity: A Suggestion' *BR* 11 (1966) 17–26.

'The Creative Use of the Son of Man Traditions by Mark' *USQR* 23 (1967f) 357–65.

'The Son of Man in the Synoptic Tradition' *BR* 13 (1968) 3–25.

'Reflections on the Publication in English of Bousset's *Kyrios Christos*' *ExpT* 82 (1971) 340–2.

A Modern Pilgrimage in New Testament Christology (Philadelphia: Fortress, 1974).

Pesch, R., 'Der Gottesohn im matthäischen Evangelienprolog (Mt 1–2). Beobachtungen zu den Zitationssformeln der Reflexionszitate' *Biblica* 48 (1967) 395–420

Das Markusevangelium (2 vols., HTK 2, Freiburg: Herder, 1976, 1977; 1977–80[2]; 1980–[3]).

Pimentel, P., 'The "unclean spirits" of St Mark's Gospel' *ExpT* 99 (1988) 173–5.

Piper, R. A., 'In Quest of Q: The Direction of Q Studies' *The Gospel Behind the Gospels: Current Studies on Q* (ed. Piper; Supp Nov Test 75; Leiden: Brill, 1995) 1–18.

Plummer, A., *An Exegetical Commentary on the Gospel According to S. Matthew* (London: Robert Scott Roxburghe House, 1909, 1915 4th impression).

Pomykala, K. E., *The Davidic Dynasty Tradition in Early Judaism: Its History and Significance for Messianism* (SBLEJL 7; Atlanta: Scholars, 1995).

Powers, B. W., 'The Shaking of the Synoptics: A Report on the Cambridge Conference on the Synoptic Gospels, August 1979' *Reformed Theological Review* 39 (1980) 33–9.

Powley, B. G., 'The Purpose of the Messianic Secret: A Brief Survey' *ExpT* 80X (1969) 308–10.

'The "Messianic Secret" in Mark's Gospel: An Historical Survey' (Ph.D.; Glasgow, 1979).

Pryke, E. J., *Redactional Style in the Marcan Gospel: A Study of Syntax and Vocabulary as Guides to Redaction in Mark* (SNTSMS 33; Cambridge: Cambridge University Press, 1978).

Przybylski, B., 'The Role of Mt 3:13–4:11 in the Structure and Theology of the Gospel of Matthew' *BTB* 4 (1974) 222–35.

Puech, E., 'Fragment d'une apocalypse en araméen (4Q246 = pseudo-Dan[d]) et le «Royaume de Dieu»' *RB* 99 (1992) 98–131.

'Une apocalypse messianique (4Q521)', *RevQ* 15 (1992) 475–519.

'Messianism, Resurrection, and Eschatology at Qumran and in the New Testament', *The Community of the Renewed Covenant: The Notre Dame Symposium on the Dead Sea Scrolls* (eds. E. Ulrich and J. VanderKam; Indiana: University of Notre Dame, 1994) 235–56.

Quesnell, Q., *The Mind of Mark: Interpretation and Method through the Exegesis of Mark 6. 52* (AnBib 38; Rome: PBI, 1969).

Räisänen, H., *Das 'Messiasgeheimnis' im Markusevangelium: Ein redaktionskritischer Versuch* (Schriften der Finnischen Exegetischen Gesellschaft 28; Helsinki, 1976). ET incorporating new material: *The 'Messianic Secret' in Mark* (trans. C. M. Tuckett; SNTW; Edinburgh: T. & T. Clark, 1990).

Rawlinson, A. E. J., *St Mark with Introduction, Commentary and Additional Notes* (Westminster Commentaries; London: Methuen & Co., 1925, cited from 1942[5]).

Reicke, B., 'Some Reflections on Worship in the New Testament' *New Testament Essays: Studies in Memory of Thomas Walter Manson, 1893–1958* (ed. A. J. B. Higgins; Manchester University Press, 1959) 194–209.

The Roots of the Synoptic Gospels (Philadelphia: Fortress, 1986).

'From Strauss to Holtzmann and Meijboom: Synoptic Theories Advanced During the Consolidation of Germany, 1830–70' *NovT* 29 (1987) 1–21.

Reinhold, M., *History of Purple as a Status Symbol in Antiquity* (Collection Latomus 116; Brussels: Latomus Revue d'etudes Latines, 1970).

Richardson, H. N., 'Some Notes on 1QSa' *JBL* 76 (1957) 108–22.

Ridderbos, H., *The Coming of the Kingdom* (Philadelphia: Presbyterian & Reformed Pub. Co., 1962).

Riesner, R., *Jesus als Lehrer. Eine Untersuchung zum Ursprung der Evangelien-Überlieferung* (WUNT 2. 7, Tübingen: J. C. B. Mohr (Paul Siebeck), 1981).

Rigaux, B., *Temoinage de l'évangile de Matthieu* (Paris-Bruges: Desclee de Brouwer, 1967). ET: *The Testimony of St Matthew* (trans. P. J. Oligny; Chicago: Franciscan Herald, 1968).

Riley, H., *The Making of Mark: An Exploration* (Macon, GA: Mercer University Press, 1989).

Rist, J. M., *On the Independence of Matthew and Mark* (SNTSMS 32; Cambridge: Cambridge University Press, 1978).

Ritschl, A., 'Ueber den gegenwärtigen Stand der Kritik der synoptischen Evangelien' *Theologischer Jahrbücher* 10 (1851) 480–538.

Robbins, V. K., 'The Healing of Blind Bartemaeus (10:46–52) in the Marcan Theology' *JBL* 92 (1973) 224–43.

'Prefaces in Greco-Roman Biography and Luke–Acts' *SBLSP* (1978) II. 193–207.

Jesus the Teacher. A Socio-Rhetorical Interpretation of Mark (Philadelphia: Fortress, 1984).

Robertson, A. T., *A Grammar of the Greek New Testament in the Light of Historical Research* (New York: Hodder & Stoughton, 1914, 1915[2], 1919[3]).

Robinson, J. A., *The Study of the Gospels* (London: Longmans, Green, 1902, 1911[2]).

St Paul's Epistle to the Ephesians: A Revised Text and Translation with Exposition and Notes (London: MacMillan & Co., 1914, 2nd edition).

Robinson, J. A. T., *Redating the New Testament* (London: SCM, 1976).

The Priority of John (ed. J. F. Coakley; London: SCM, 1985).

Robinson, J. M., *The Problem of History in Mark* (SBT 21; London, SCM, 1957).

'On the *Gattung* of Mark (and John)' *Jesus and Man's Hope* (ed. D. G. Miller; Pittsburgh Theological Seminary, 1970; 2 vols.) I. 99–129.

Rohde, J., *Die redaktionsgeschichtliche Methode* (Hamburg: Furche-Verlag, 1966). ET (incorporating revisions and additions): *Rediscovering the Teaching of the Evangelists* (NTLib; London: SCM, 1968).

Ropes, J. H., *The Synoptic Gospels* (Cambridge, MA: Harvard University Press, 1934).

Rothfuchs, W., *Die Erfüllungszitate des Matthäus-Evangeliums: Eine biblisch-theologische Untersuchung* (BWANT V. 8 = 88; Stuttgart: Kohlhammer, 1969).

Rowland, C. C., *The Open Heaven: A Study of Apocalyptic in Judaism and Early Christianity* (London: SPCK, 1982).

Russell, D. A. and Winterbottom, M. (eds.), *Ancient Literary Criticism. The Principal Texts in New Translations* (Oxford: Clarendon, 1972).

Sanday, W., 'A Survey of the Synoptic Problem' *The Expositor* Fourth Series, vol 3, 5 Parts: 81–91, 179–94, 302–16, 345–61, 411–26.

'Gospels' *A Dictionary of the Bible* (ed. W. Smith; London: 1893[2]; 2 vols.) 1217–43.

Outlines of the Life of Christ (Edinburgh: T. & T. Clark, 1906[2]).

The Life of Christ in Recent Research (Oxford: Clarendon, 1907).

'Introductory' *Studies in the Synoptic Problem. By Members of the University of Oxford* (ed. Sanday; Oxford: Clarendon, 1911) vii–xxvii.

Sanday, W. (ed.), *Studies in the Synoptic Problem. By Members of the University of Oxford* (Oxford: Clarendon, 1911).

Sanders, E. P., 'The Argument from Order and the Relationship between Matthew and Luke' *NTS* 15 (1968f) 249–61.

The Tendencies of the Synoptic Tradition (SNTSMS 9; Cambridge: Cambridge University Press, 1969).

'The Overlaps of Mark and Q and the Synoptic Problem' *NTS* 19 (1973) 453–65.

Sanders, E. P. (ed.) *Jesus, the Gospels, and the Church* (FS W. R. Farmer; Macon, GA: Mercer University Press, 1987).

Sanders, E. P. and Davies, M., *Studying the Synoptic Gospels* (London: SCM; Philadelphia: TPI, 1989).

Sanders, J. T., *The New Testament Christological Hymns: Their Historical Religious Background* (SNTSMS 15; Cambridge: Cambridge University Press, 1971).

Sandmel, S., 'Parallelomania', *JBL* 82 (1961) 1–13.

Saunier, H., *Ueber die Quellen des Evangeliums des Marcus. Ein Beitrag zu den Untersuchungen über die Entstehung unsrer kanonischen Evangelien* (Berlin: F Dümmler, 1825).

Schaberg, J., *The Father, the Son and the Holy Spirit: The Triadic Phrase in Matthew 28:19b* (SBLDS 61; Scholars Press, 1982).

Schenk, W., *Die Sprache des Matthäus. Die Text-Konstituenten in ihren makro-und mikrostrukturellen Relationen* (Göttingen: Vandenhoeck & Ruprecht, 1987).

Schlatter, A., *Die Theologie der Apostel* (Stuttgart: Calwer, 1977[3] reprint of 1922[2]).

Der Evangelist Matthäus: Seine Sprache, sein Ziel, seine Selbständigkeit. Ein Kommentar zum ersten Evangelium (Stuttgart: Calwer, 1948[3]; 1957[4]; 1959[5]; 1963[6] quoted. from 5th edition (earlier editions: *Das Evangelium des Matthäus, ausgelegt für Bibelleser* (Stuttgart: Verlag der Vereinsbuchhandlung, 1895, 1900[2]))).

Schleiermacher, F. E. D., *Einleitung ins Neue Testament aus Schleiermacher's handschriftlichen Nachlasse und nachgeschriebenen Vorlesungen* (eds. F. Lücke and G. Wolde) *Sämmtliche Werke* (Abth 1; vol. VIII; Berlin: G. Reimer, 1845).

Das Leben Jesu. Vorlesungen an der Universität zu Berlin im Jahr 1832 (ed. K. A. Rütenik; Berlin: G. Reimer, 1864). ET: *The Life of Jesus* (ed. J. C. Verheyden; trans. S. M. Gilmour; Philadelphia: Fortress, 1975).

Schmidt, D., 'Luke's "Innocent" Jesus: A Scriptural Apologetic' *Political Issues in Luke-Acts* (eds. R. J. Cassidy and P. J. Scharper; Maryknoll: Orbis, 1983) 111–21.

Schmidt, K. L., *Der Rahmen der Geschichte Jesu: literarkritische Untersuchungen zur ältesten Jesusüberlieferung* (Berlin: Trowitzsch, 1919).

Schmithals, W., *Einleitung in die drei ersten Evangelien* (Berlin and New York: Walter de Gruyter, 1985).

Schnackenburg, R., 'Die Vollkommenheit des Christen nach den Evangelien' *Geist und Leben* 32 (1959) 420–33.

Matthäusevangelium (2 vols.; NEB; Würzburg: Echter, 1985 and 1987).

Schneider, G., 'Zur Vorgeschichte des christologischen Prädikats "Sohn Davids"' *Trierer theologische Zeitschrift* 80 (1971) 247–53.

'Die Davidssohnfrage (Mk 12, 35–37)' *Biblica* 53 (1972) 65–90.

Die Passion Jesu nach den drei älteren Evangelien (Biblische Handbibliothek XI; Munich: Kösel, 1973).

Schramm, T., *Der Markus-Stoff bei Lukas: eine literarkritische und redaktions-geschichtliche Untersuchung* (SNTSMS 14; Cambridge: Cambridge University Press, 1971).

Schulz, S., *Die Stunde der Botschaft: Einführung in die Theologie der vier Evangelisten* (Hamburg: Furche-Verlag, 1967).

Q: Die Spruchquelle der Evangelisten (Zürich: Theologischer Verlag, 1972).

Schürer, E., rev. *The History of the Jewish People in the Age of Jesus Christ (175 BC – AD 135). A New English Version* (rev. and eds.: G. and P. Vermes, F. Millar, M. Black; Edinburgh: T. & T. Clark, 3 vols. in 4; 1973, 1979, 1986, 1987).

Schürmann, H., *Das Lukasevangelium* (HTKNT III; Freiburg/Basel/Vienna: Herder, 1969).

Schwegler, A., *Das nachapostolische Zeitalter in den Hauptmomenten seiner Entwicklung* (2 vols.; Tübingen: Fues, 1846).

Schweitzer, A., *Geschichte der Leben-Jesu-Forschung* (Tübingen: J. C. B. Mohr (Paul Siebeck), 1933[5], a reprint of 1913[2]). ET: *The Quest of the Historical Jesus: A Critical Study of its Progress From Reimarus to Wrede* (trans. W. Montgomery; London: A. & C. Black, 1936[2] from 1906[1], *Von Reimarus zu Wrede*).

Schweizer, E., *Das Evangelium nach Matthäus* (Göttingen: Vandenhoeck & Ruprecht, 1973). ET: *The Good News According to Matthew* (trans. D. E. Green; London: SPCK, 1976).

'Neuere Markus-Forschung in USA' *EvT* 33 (1973) 533–7.

Scrivener, F. H. A., *A Plain Introduction to the Criticism of the New Testament for the use of Biblical students* (ed. E. Miller; 2 vols.; London: George Bell and Sons, 1894[4]).

Segbroeck, F. van, 'Jésus rejeté par sa patrie (Mt 13,54–58)' *Biblica* 49 (1968) 167–98.

Senior, D. P., 'The Death of Jesus and the Resurrection of the Holy Ones (Matthew 27:51–53)' *CBQ* 38 (1976) 312–29.

The Passion Narrative according to Matthew. A Redactional Study (BETL 39; Leuven: Leuven University Press, 1975).

The Passion of Jesus in Mark (Wilmington: M. Glazier, 1984).

'Matthew's Special Material in the Passion Story: Implications for the Evangelist's Redactional Technique and Theological Perspective' *ETL* 63 (1987) 272–94.

Sibinga, J. S., 'Matthew 14:22–33 Text and Composition' *New Testament Textual Criticism: Its Significance for Exegesis. Essays in Honour of Bruce M. Metzger* (eds. E. J. Epp and G. D. Fee; Oxford: Clarendon, 1981) 15–33.

Sieffert, F., *Ueber den Ursprung des ersten kanonishen Evangeliums: eine kritische Abhandlung* (Königsberg: J. H. Bon, 1832).

Simon, R., *Historie critique du texte du Nouveau Testament* (Rotterdam, 1689); ET: *A Critical History of the Text of the New Testament; wherein is firmly established. the Truth of those Acts on which the Foundation of Christian Religion is laid* (London: R. Taylor, 1689 (NB page numbers in Cambridge University Library volume out of order, cited here by corrected page number)).

Simons, E., *Hat der dritte Evangelist den kanonischen Matthäus benutzt?* (Bonn: C. Georgi, 1880).

Slingerland, H. D., *The Testaments of the Twelve Patriarchs. A Critical History of Research* (SBLMS 21; Missoula, MA: Scholars Press, 1977).

Smedes, L. B., *The Incarnation: Trends in Modern Anglican Thought* (Kampen: J. H. Kok, 1953).

Smith, J. Z., 'Good News Is No News: Aretalogy and Gospel' *Christianity, Judaism and other Greco-Roman Cults* (FS M. Smith; ed. J. Neusner; SJLA 12; Leiden: E. J. Brill) I. 21–38.

Smith, M., 'Comments on Taylor's Commentary on Mark' *HTR* 48 (1955) 21–64.

Jesus the Magician (New York: Harper & Row, 1978).

Snodgrass, K. R., 'Streams of Tradition emerging from Isaiah 40:1–5 and their adaptation in the New Testament' *JSNT* 8 (1980) 24–45.

Snoy, T., 'Mark 6,48: «. . . et il voulait les dépasser.» Proposition pour la solution d'une énigme' *L'évangile selon Marc: tradition et rédaction* (BETL 34; ed. M. Sabbe; Leuven: Leuven University Press and Gembloux: Duculot, 1974) 347–63.

Soards, M. L., 'The Question of a PreMarcan Passion Narrative' *The Death of the Messiah. From Gethsemane to the Grave. A Commentary on the Passion Narratives in the Four Gospels* (ABRL; New York: Doubleday, 1994; 2 vols.) vol. II, pp. 1492–524.

Soares Prabhu, G. M., *The Formula Quotations in the Infancy Narrative of Matthew* (AnBib 63; Rome: Biblical Institute Press, 1976).

Stanton, G. N., 'Matthew as a Creative Interpreter of the Sayings of Jesus' *Das Evangelium und die Evangelien* (ed. P. Stuhlmacher; Tübingen, 1983) 273–87.

'Salvation Proclaimed. X. Matthew 11. 28–30: Comfortable Words?' *ExpT* 94 (1982) 3–9.

'The Origin and Purpose of Matthew's Gospel: Matthean Scholarship from 1945 to 1980' *ANRW* II. 25. 3 (1985) 1889–951.

The Gospels and Jesus (Oxford: Oxford University Press, 1989).

'Matthew's Christology and the Parting of the Ways' *Jews and Christians: the parting of the ways AD 70 to 135* (ed. J. D. G. Dunn; WUNT 66; Tübingen: J. C. B. Mohr, 1992) 99–116.

A Gospel for a New People: Studies in Matthew (Edinburgh: T. & T. Clark, 1992).

Starcky, J., 'Un texte messianique araméen de la grotte 4 de Qumrân' *Ecole des langues orientales anciennes de l'Institut Catholique de Paris: mémorial du cinquantenaire 1914–1964* (TICP 10; Paris: Bloud & Gay, 1964) 51 66.

Stauffer, E., 'Jeschu ben Mirjam: Kontroversgeschichtliche Anmerkungen zu Mk 6:3' *Neotestamentica et Semitica: Studies in Honour of Matthew Black* (eds. E. E. Ellis and M. Wilcox; Edinburgh: T. & T. Clark, 1969) 119–28.

Stegner, W. R., 'Lucan Priority in the Feeding of the Five Thousand' *BR* 21 (1976) 19–28.

'The Priority of Luke: An Exposition of Robert Lindsey's Solution to the Synoptic Problem' *BR* 27 (1982) 26–38.

Steichele, H.-J., *Der leidende Sohn Gottes: Eine Untersuchung einiger alttestamentlicher Motive in der Christologie des Markusevangeliums* (BU 14; Regensburg: Friedrich Pustet, 1980).

Stein, R. H., 'The *Redaktionsgeschichtlich* Investigation of a Markan Seam (Mc 1,21f)' *ZNW* 61 (1970) 70–94.

'Is the Transfiguration (Mark 9:2–8) a Misplaced Resurrection Account?' *JBL* 95 (1976) 79–96.

The Synoptic Problem. An Introduction (Grand Rapids: Baker Book House, 1987).

Steinhauser, M. G., 'The Form of the Bartimaeus Narrative (Mark 10. 46–52)' *NTS* 32 (1986) 583–95.

Stendahl, K., *The School of St Matthew, and Its Use of the Old Testament* (Lund: Gleerup, 1954, 1968[2] = Philadelphia: Fortress).

'Quis et Unde? An Analysis of Mt 1–2' *Judentum, Urchristentum, Kirche* (ed. W. Eltester; Berlin: Töpelmann, 1960) 94–105. Cited from *The Interpretation of Matthew* (IRT 3; ed. G. N. Stanton; London: SPCK, 1983) 56–66.

Stoldt, H. H., *Geschichte und Kritik der Markus-hypothese* (Göttingen: Vandenhoeck & Ruprecht, 1977). ET: *History and Criticism of the Marcan Hypothesis* (trans. D. L. Niewyk; Georgia: Mercer University Press and Edinburgh: T. and T. Clark, 1981).

Stone, M. E., *Features of the Eschatology of IV Ezra* (Harv. Sem. St. 35; Atlanta Georgia: Scholars Press, 1989; reprint of 1965 Ph.D. Harvard).

A Commentary on the Book of Fourth Ezra (Hermeneia; Minneapolis: Fortress, 1990).

Stonehouse, N. B., *The Witness of Matthew and Mark to Christ* (London: Tyndale Press,1944; reprint: Grand Rapids: Baker, 1979).

Origins of the Synoptic Gospels: Some Basic Questions (Grand Rapids: Baker Book House, 1979; reprint of Eerdmans, 1963).

(Strack, H. L. and) Billerbeck, P. *Kommentar zum Neuen Testament aus Talmud und Midrasch* (Munich: C. H. Beck, 1922–8; 5 vols.).

Strack, H. L. and Stemberger, G., *Introduction to the Talmud and Midrash* (trans. M. N. A. Bockmuehl; Edinburgh: T. & T. Clark, 1991).

Strauss, D. F., *Das Leben Jesu kritisch bearbeitet* (2 vols.; Stuttgart: P. Balz, 1835, 1836); cited here (Tübingen: C. F. Osiander, 1837, 2nd edition). ET: *The Life of Jesus critically examined* (trans. from 4th edn by G. Eliot; 3 vols.; London: Chapman Brothers, 1846). Cited here from the SCM reprint of this edition: *The Life of Jesus Critically Examined* (ed. P. C. Hodgson; London: SCM, 1973).

Das Leben Jesu für das deutsche Volk bearbeitet (Leipzig: Brockhaus, 1864). ET: *A New Life of Jesus* (London: Williams & Norgate, 1865; 2 vols.).

Strecker, G., *Der Weg der Gerechtigkeit: Untersuchung zur Theologie des Matthäus* (FRLANT 82; Göttingen: Vandenhoeck & Ruprecht, 1962, 1971[3]).

Strecker, G. (ed.), *Minor Agreements Symposium Göttingen 1991* (Gottinger Theologische Arbeiten 50; Göttingen: Vandenhoeck & Ruprecht, 1993).

Streeter, B. H., 'The Historic Christ' *Foundations: A Statement of Christian Belief in Terms of Modern Thought. By Seven Oxford Men* (London: Macmillan, 1912).

The Four Gospels A Study of Origins. Treating of the Manuscript Tradition, Sources, Authorship, and Dates (London: Macmillan & Co., 1930 impression).

Stuckenbruck, L. T., ' "One like a Son of Man as the Ancient of Days" in the Old Greek Recension of Daniel 7, 13: Scribal Error or Theological Translation?' *ZNW* 86 (1995) 268–76.

Styler, G. M., 'The Priority of Mark' Excursus 4 in C. F. D. Moule, *The Birth of the New Testament* (London: A. & C. Black, 1981[3]) 285–316.

'Stages in Christology in the Synoptic Gospels' *NTS* 10 (1964) 398–409.

Suggs, M. J., *Wisdom, Christology and Law in Matthew's Gospel* (Cambridge, MA: Harvard University Press, 1970).

Suhl, A., *Die Funktion der alttestamentlichen Zitate und Anspielungen im Markusevangelium* (Gütersloh: G. Mohn, 1965).

'Der Davidssohn im Matthäusevangelium' *ZNW* 59 (1968) 67–81.

Swartley, W. M., 'The Structural Function of the Term "Way" (*Hodos*) in Mark's Gospel' *The New Way of Jesus: Essays Presented to Howard Charles* (ed. W. Klassen; Kansas: Faith & Life Press, 1980) 73–86.

Swete, H. B., *The Gospel according to St Mark. The Greek Text with Introduction, Notes, and Indices* (London and New York: Macmillan, 1920³; cf. 1902²; 1898¹).

Talman, S., 'The Concepts of *Māšîah* and Messianism in Early Judaism' *The Messiah: Developments in Earliest Judaism and Christianity* (ed. J. H. Charlesworth; Minneapolis: Fortress, 1992) 79–115.

Tannehill, R. C., 'The Disciples in Mark: the Function of a Narrative Role' *Journal of Religion* 57 (1977) 386–405.

Tatum, W. B., 'The Matthaean Infancy Stories: Their Form, Structure, and Relation to the Theology of the First Evangelist' (Ph.D., Duke University, 1966; UMI).

' "The Origin of Jesus Messiah' (Matt 1:1, 18a) : Matthew's Use of the Infancy Traditions' *JBL* 96 (1977) 523–535.

Taylor, V., *The Formation of the Gospel Tradition* (London: Macmillan & Co., 1933).

The Names of Jesus (London: MacMillan, 1953).

The Gospel According to St Mark (London: MacMillan, 1977, 1966², 1952¹).

Telford, G. B., 'Mark 1:40–45' *Int* 36 (1982) 54–8.

Theisohn, J., *Der auserwählte Richter. Untersuchungen zum traditionsgeschichtlichen Ort der Menschensohngestalt der Bilderreden des Äthiopischen Henoch* (SUNT 12; Göttingen: Vandenhoeck & Ruprecht, 1975).

Theissen, G., *Urchristliche Wundergeschichten: Ein Beitrag zur formgeschichtlichen Erforschung der synoptischen Evangelien* (Gütersloh, 1974). ET: *The Miracle Stories of the Early Christian Tradition* (Edinburgh: T. & T. Clark, 1983).

Thiselton, A. C., 'Semantics and New Testament Interpretation' *New Testament Interpretation: Essays on Principles and Methods* (ed. I. H. Marshall; Grand Rapids: Eerdmans, 1981) 75–104.

Thompson, M. M., 'The Structure of Matthew: A Survey of Recent Trends' *Studia Biblica et Theologica* 12 (1982) 195–238.

Thompson, W. G., 'Reflections on the Composition of Mt 8:1–9:34' *CBQ* 33 (1971) 365–88.

Tödt, H. E., *The Son of Man in the Synoptic Tradition* (trans. D. M. Barton from *Der Menschensohn in der synoptischen Überlieferung*, 1963²; London: SCM, 1965).

Tregelles, S. P., *An Account of the Printed Text of the Greek New Testament; with Remarks on its Revision upon Critical Principles. Together with A Collation of the critical texts of Griesbach, Scholz, Lachmann, and*

Tischendorf, with that in common use (London: S. Bagster & Sons, 1854).

Trilling, W., *Das wahre Israel: Studien zur Theologie des Matthäusevangeliums* (Erfurter Theologischen Studien 7; Leipzig: St Benno, 1959; Dritte Auflage: StANT X; Munich: Kösel, 1964, 3rd edn used here).

Tuckett, C. M., 'The Griesbach Hypothesis in the 19th Century' *JSNT* 3 (1979) 29–60.

'The Present Son of Man' *JSNT* 14 (1982) 58–81.

'Luke 4,16–30, Isaiah and Q' *Logia. Les paroles de Jésus – The Sayings of Jesus. Mémorial Joseph Coppens* (BETL 59X; ed. J. Delobel; Leuven: Leuven University Press, 1982) 343–54.

'Introduction: The Problem of the Messianic Secret' *The Messianic Secret* (ed. C. M. Tuckett; IRT 1; London: SPCK, 1983) 1–28.

The Revival of the Griesbach Hypothesis: An Analysis and Appraisal (SNTSMS 44; Cambridge: Cambridge University Press, 1983).

'Arguments from Order: Definition and Evaluation' *Synoptic Studies: The Ampleforth Conferences of 1982 and 1983* (ed. C. M. Tuckett; JSNTSS 7; JSOT: Sheffield, 1984) 197–219.

'The Two Gospel Hypothesis Under Scrutiny: A Response' *PSTJ* 40 (1987) 25–31.

'Thomas and the Synoptics' *NovT* 30 (1988) 132–57.

'The Existence of Q' *The Gospel Behind the Gospels: Current Studies on Q* (ed. R. A. Piper; Supp Nov Test 75; Leiden: Brill, 1995) 19–47.

Tuckett, C. M. (ed.), *Synoptic Studies: The Ampleforth Conferences of 1982 and 1983* (JSNTSS 7; Sheffield: JSOT Press, 1984).

Turner, C. H., 'A Textual Commentary on Mark 1' *JTS* 28 (1927) 145–58.

'Marcan Usage: Notes, Critical and Exegetical, on the Second Gospel', 'VIII. (*sic*) Auxiliary . . . verbs' *JTS* 28 (July 1927) 349–62.

Twelftree, G. H., *Christ Triumphant: Exorcism Then and Now* (London: Hodder & Stoughton, 1985).

Jesus the Exorcist: A Contribution to the Study of the Historical Jesus (WUNT 2. 54; Tübingen: J. C. B. Mohr (Paul Siebeck), 1993).

Tyson, J. B., 'The Two-Source Hypothesis: A Critical Appraisal' *The Two-Source Hypothesis: A Critical Appraisal* (ed. A. J. Bellinzoni; Macon, GA: Mercer University Press, 1985) 437–52.

Ullendorff, E. and Knibb, M. A., 'Review of Milik, *The Books of Enoch*' *BSOAS* 40 (1977) 601–2.

Urbach, E. E., *The Sages: Their Concepts and Beliefs* (2 vols.; trans. I. Abrahams; Jerusalem: Magnes Press – Hebrew University, 1979[2]).

Vaganay, L., *Le problème synoptique: une hypothèse de travail* (Tournai: Desclée, 1954).

van der Horst, P. W., 'Moses' Throne Vision in Ezekiel the Dramatist' *JJS* 34 (1983) 21–9.

Vanderkam, J. C., 'Righteous One, Messiah, Chosen One, and Son of Man in 1 Enoch 37–71' *The Messiah: Developments in Earliest Judaism and Christianity* (ed. J. H. Charlesworth; Minneapolis: Fortress, 1992) 169–91.

van der Loos, H., *The Miracles of Jesus* (NovTSS 9; Leiden: E. J. Brill, 1965).

Vanhoye, A., 'Structure et théologie des récits de la Passion dans les évangiles synoptiques' *NRT* 89 (1967) 135–63.

van Tilborg, S., *The Jewish Leaders in Matthew* (Leiden: E. J. Brill, 1972).

Van Unnik, W. C., 'Die "geöffneten Himmel" in der Offenbarungsvision des Apokryphons des Johannes' *Sparsa Collecta: The Collected Essays of W. C. Van Unnik Part Three: Patristica, Gnostica, Liturgica* (NovTSS 31; Leiden: Brill, 1983, essay original 1964) 273–284.

Vermes, G., 'The Use of נשא בר / בר נשא in Jewish Aramaic', Appendix E, M. Black, *An Aramaic Approach to the Gospels and Acts* (Oxford: Oxford University Press, 1967, 3rd edn) 310–28.

'The Present State of the "Son of Man" Debate' *JJS* 29 (1978) 123–34.

Jesus the Jew: A Historian's Reading of the Gospels (London: SCM, 1983²).

Verseput, D., *The Rejection of the Humble Messianic King. A Study of the Composition of Matthew 11–12* (European University Studies, Series XXIII; vol. 291; Frankfurt/Bern/New York: Peter Lang, 1986).

'The Role and Meaning of the "Son of God" Title in Matthew's Gospel' *NTS* 33 (1987) 532–56.

Via, D. O., *The Ethics of Mark's Gospel: In the Middle of Time* (Philadelphia: Fortress, 1985).

Vielhauer, P., 'Zu W. Anderson' *EvT* 12 (1952f) 481–4. (Response to W. Anderson, 'Die Autorität der apostolischen Zeugnisse!' *EvT* 12 (1952f) 467–81.)

'Gottesreich und Menschensohn in der Verkündigung Jesu' *Festschrift für Günther Dehn zum 75. Geburtstag am 18. April dargebracht* (ed. W. Schneemelcher; Neukirchen: Erziehungsvereins, 1957) 51–79.

'Jesus und der Menschensohn. Zur Diskussion mit Heinz Eduard Tödt und Eduard Schweizer' *ZTK* 60 (1963) 133–77.

'Ein Weg der neutestamentlichen Theologie? Prüfung der Thesen Ferdinand Hahns' *EvT* 25 (1965) 24–72.

Vögtle, A., 'Die Genealogie Mt 1, 2–16 und die matthäische Kindheitsgeschichte' *Das Evangelium und die Evangelien* (Dusseldorf: Patmos, 1971) 57–102.

Wagner, W., 'In welchem Sinne hat Jesus das Prädikat ΑΓΑΘΟΣ von sich abgewiesen?' *ZNW* 8 (1907) 143–61.

Wainwright, A. W., *The Trinity in the New Testament* (London: SPCK, 1962).

Walker, W. O., 'The Origin of the Son of Man Concept as applied to Jesus' *JBL* 91 (1972) 482–90.

'The Son of Man Question and the Synoptic Problem' *NTS* 28 (1982) 374–88.

'The Son of Man: Some Recent Developments' *CBQ* 45 (1983) 584–607.

Walker, W. O. Jr (ed.), *The Relationships Among the Gospels: An Interdisciplinary Dialogue* (San Antonio: Trinity University Press, 1978).

Walter, N., 'Zur Analyse von Mark 10:17–31' *ZNW* 53 (1962) 206–18.

Wansbrough, H., 'Mark 3,21 – Was Jesus out of His Mind?' *NTS* 18 (1972) 233–5.

Warfield, B. B., 'Jesus' Alleged Confession of Sin' *Princeton Theological*

Review 12 (1914) 177–228. Cited from *Christology and Criticism* (New York: Oxford University Press, 1929) 97–145.

Watts, R. E., 'The Influence of the Isaianic New Exodus on the Gospel of Mark' (Ph.D., Cambridge, 1990).

Webb, R. L., *John the Baptizer and Prophet: A Socio-Historical Study* (JSNTSS 62; Sheffield: JSOT, 1991).

Weeden, T. J., 'The Heresy that Necessitated Mark's Gospel' *ZNW* 59 (1968) 145–58. Cited from *The Interpretation of Mark* (IRT 7; ed. W. Telford; London: SPCK, 1985, orig. 1968) 64–79.

Mark: Traditions in Conflict (Philadelphia: Fortress, 1971).

Weiss, B., 'Zur Enstehungsgeschichte der drei synoptische Evangelien' *TSK* (1861) 29–100; 646–713.

Das Matthäus-Evangelium (KeKNT (Meyer) 1; Göttingen: Vandenhoeck & Ruprecht, 1898, 9th edn).

Die Quellen der synoptischen Überlieferung (TU 32; Leipzig: Hinrichs, 1908).

Weisse, C. H., *Die evangelische Geschichte kritisch und philosophisch bearbeitet* (Leipzig: Breitkopf & Hartel, 1838, 2 vols.).

Wellhausen, J., *Das Evangelium Marci* (Berlin: G. Reimer, 1903, 1909[2]).

Das Evangelium Matthaei übersetzt und erklärt (Berlin: G. Reimer, 1904).

Wenham, D., 'The Meaning of Mark iii. 21' *NTS* 21 (1974f) 295–300.

Wenham, J. W., 'Why do you ask me about the good? A Study of the Relation between Text and Source Criticism' *NTS* 28 (1982) 116–25.

Redating Matthew, Mark and Luke: A Fresh Assault on the Synoptic Problem (London: Hodder & Stoughton, 1991).

Wernle, P., *Die Synoptische Frage* (Freiburg: J. C. B. Mohr, 1889).

Westcott, B. F., *An Introduction to the Study of the Gospels. With Historical and Explanatory Notes* (London: Macmillan, 1860).

Wette, W. M. L. de, *Lehrbuch der historisch-kritischen Einleitung in die kanonischen Bücher des Neuen Testaments* (Zweiter Teil: *Die Einleitung in das NT enthaltend*; of *Lehrbuch der historisch-kritischen Einleitung in die Bibel Alten und Neuen Testaments*) (Berlin: G. Reimer, 1826[2] but 1st was *AT*, 1822, (1860[6] actually only second or third edn of *NT* eds. Messner and Lunemann). Cited from 1860 edition. ET: *An Historical-critical Introduction to the Canonical Books of the New Testament* (trans. F. Frothingham; Boston: Crosby, 1858 from 1848[5]).

White, H. J., 'The "Dogmatic" Variations in Matthew' *CQR* 80 (1915) 302–21.

Wilke, C. G., *Der Urevangelist oder exegetisch kritische Untersuchung über das Verwandtschaftsverhältnis der drei ersten Evangelien* (Leipzig: G. Fleischer, 1838).

Wilkens, W., 'Die Versuchung Jesu nach Matthäus' *NTS* 28 (1982) 479–89.

Winer, G. B., *A Treatise on the Grammar of New Testament Greek, regarded as a sure basis for New Testament Exegesis* (trans. W. F. Moulton; Edinburgh: T. & T. Clark, 1882[9]).

Wink, W., *John the Baptist in the Gospel Tradition* (SNTSMS 7; Cambridge: Cambridge University Press, 1968).

Winter, B. W., 'The Messiah as the Tutor: The Meaning of καθηγητής in Matthew 23:10' *TynBul* 42 (1991) 152–57.

Wise, M. O. and Tabor, J. D., 'The Messiah at Qumran' *BARev* 18. 6 (1992) 60–5.

Woods, F. H., 'The Origin and Mutual Relation of the Synoptic Gospels' *Studia Biblica et Ecclesiastica: Essays Chiefly in Biblical and Patristic Criticism* (ed. S. R. Driver, J. K. Cheyne, W. Sanday; Oxford: Clarendon, 1890, 2 vols.) II. 59–104.

Wrede, W., *Das Messiasgeheimnis in den Evangelien: Zugleich ein Beitrag zum Verständnis des Markusevangeliums* (Göttingen: Vandenhoeck & Ruprecht, 1901, 1913², 1963³). ET: *The Messianic Secret* (trans. J. C. G. Greig; Cambridge and London: James Clarke, 1971).

Wright, N. T., *The Climax of the Covenant: Christ and the Law in Pauline Theology* (Edinburgh: T. & T. Clark, 1991).

Yadin, Y., 'A Crucial Passage in the Dead Sea Scrolls. 1QSa ii. 11–17' *JBL* 77 (1959) 238–41.

'A Midrash on 2 Sam. vii and Ps. i–ii (4Q Florilegium)' *IEJ* 9 (1959) 95–8.

'A Note on Melchizedek and Qumran' *IEJ* 15 (1965) 152–4.

Zahn, T., *Einleitung in das Neue Testament* (2 vols.; Leipzig: Deichert, 1900²). ET: *Introduction to the New Testament* (3 vols.; Edinburgh: T. & T. Clark, 1909).

Das Evangelium des Matthäus (Leipzig: A. Deichert, 1903).

Zeller, E., 'Studien zur neutestamentlichen Theologie. 4. Vergleichende Uebersicht über den Wörtervorrath der sämmtlichen neutestamentlichen Schriftsteller' *Theologische Jahrbücher* 2 (1843) 443–543.

Zimmermann, H., 'Das absolute Ἐγώ εἰμι als die neutestamentliche Offenbarungsformel' *BZ* 4 (1960) 54–69, 226–76.

INDEX OF PASSAGES

II. NEW TESTAMENT

SELECT INDEX OF NAMES AND SUBJECTS